JEWISH ROOTS IN
SOUTHERN SOIL

JEWISH ROOTS IN
SOUTHERN SOIL
A NEW HISTORY

EDITED BY

MARCIE COHEN FERRIS

AND

MARK I. GREENBERG

BRANDEIS UNIVERSITY PRESS

Waltham, Massachusetts

Published by

UNIVERSITY PRESS OF NEW ENGLAND

Hanover and London

BRANDEIS UNIVERSITY PRESS
Published by
University Press of New England,
One Court Street, Lebanon, NH 03766
www.upne.com
© 2006 by Brandeis University Press
Printed in the United States of America

5 4 3 2

Library of Congress Cataloging-in-Publication Data
Jewish roots in southern soil : a new history / edited by Marcie Cohen Ferris
and Mark I. Greenberg.
p.   cm. — (Brandeis series in American Jewish history, culture, and life)
Includes bibliographical references and index.
ISBN-13: 978–1–58465–588–6 (cloth : alk. paper)
ISBN-10: 1–58465–588–7 (cloth : alk. paper)
ISBN-13: 978–1–58465–589–3 (pbk. : alk. paper)
ISBN-10: 1–58465–589–5 (pbk. : alk. paper)
1. Jews—Southern states—History.   2. Jews—Southern States—Identity.
3. Judaism—Southern States—History.   4. Southern states—Ethnic relations.
I. Ferris, Marcie Cohen.   II. Greenberg, Mark I.
F220.J5J46 2006
975'.004924—dc22   2006022009

FOR HUDDY AND JERRY, AND KATHY AND NATALIE

CONTENTS

FOREWORD

ELI N. EVANS

Years ago, I was a lecturer on a restored steamboat called the *Delta Queen* and sailed down the Mississippi River with Shelby Foote, the renowned Civil War historian. It was little known that Foote's grandfather had been a Jewish peddler, so as we mixed with the passengers who had come to visit battlefields and even synagogues, we shared a common bond that enabled us to talk a great deal over the course of the weeklong voyage. Foote's three-volume Civil War series had already been declared a "modern Iliad," so it was with some trepidation that I took a deep breath and asked him how he could spend a career writing about a subject that had been painstakingly examined in more than sixty thousand books. He smiled and replied that the Civil War had been such a profound event in the history of the South and America that "each generation has an obligation to revisit it for new insights and meaning."

This welcomed book of essays, assembled by Marcie Cohen Ferris and Mark Greenberg, is an example of the opposite phenomenon. When *The Provincials* was first published in 1973, southern Jewish history was not really a field at all. There were only a few novels and books to guide me, and a handful of interested scholars along with a group mostly of amateurs and rabbis who specialized in their own congregations, cities, and states. There were glaring omissions—such as the perspectives and history of southern Jewish women, research on the history of peddlers, oral histories of the interactions between blacks and Jews, and private memoirs or autobiographies that revealed the psyche and the soul of the immigrant generation and their children.

Much has changed over the last three decades with the growing number of Jews in the South, especially in the cities and the high-tech centers around universities; the diminishing number of Jews in small communities; the growth of Jewish studies programs at public and private universities; a greater self-confidence in community after community from the growth of Jewish institutions. Today one can find Jewish schools, newspapers, community centers, and a renewed sense of the Jewish future.

Now, a new group of scholars has taken a fresh look at the story through different lenses. They have looked back on the enormous changes in the Jewish South with a critical assessment of all that has been written, including novels, films, and plays. They bring their vigorous analysis of the data, their insights into the growing literature in the field, their watchful eyes on the forces of change in southern Jewish culture, and the acknowledged perspective of gender and race. They have focused on various subjects and themes and together have created a book that opens the Jewish South to academic and student interest. This volume will stimulate inquiry, discussion, new research, and facilitate the creation of university courses across the South and the nation.

This book contains a rich gumbo of ideas and observations and a variety of perspectives that will intrigue even the casual reader. For example, six women provide a compelling centerpiece to this volume—Hasia Diner reveals the South as seen through the eyes of the Jewish peddlers who walked its roads and settled in its towns, found Jewish women to marry, put down roots, and became the fathers who created businesses for their sons who did not want them. Emily Bingham, who spent ten years analyzing more than ten thousand letters of three generations of the Mordecai family, animated by the voluminous correspondence of its intelligent and literary women, provides a rare picture of the interior complexities and souls in turmoil of Jewish women in one North Carolina family in the early eighteenth and nineteenth centuries. Jennifer Stollman describes the work of Jewish women writers before and during the Civil War. Eliza McGraw has studied southern Jewish life and figures in literature and films, heirs to what she calls an "intense heritage." Marcie Cohen Ferris takes us on an intriguing journey into the unexplored worlds of southern Jewish foodways— foods rejected and embraced— as a window into the manner in which Jews express their dual southern and Jewish identities. Dale Rosengarten offers surprising insights into objects such as candlesticks, photographs, and heirlooms from the old country that became symbolic of a generation and of deep sentimental value, as much for the stories remembered as for the objects themselves.

Other aspects of the subject are also treated, such as the clash between practices of Judaism in Mark Greenberg's study of the Ashkenazi and Sephardic Jews of eighteenth-century Savannah. Robert Rosen writes on the southern Jews who marched off to fight in the Civil War as soldiers in the armies of the Confederacy. Eric Goldstein explores the period between 1880 and World War I when southern Jews were caught in the rise of Jim Crow laws. Clive Webb describes black-Jewish relations in the twentieth century and the aftermath of the 1954 Supreme Court decision in *Brown v. Board of Education* that he asserts was the "pinnacle in the terrorist attacks against Jewish institutions." Gary Zola examines the rise of Reform Judaism in the South and how a "Jewish ideology that spurns revivalism and evangelism . . . managed to prosper . . . in a homogeneous Protestant milieu." Finally, Stuart Rockoff and Stephen Whitfield look at the implications of the changing demographics in the South and life in the new urban South.

This book is a timely contribution in the stream of books and essays flowing out of the 350th anniversary of Jews coming to America in 1654. All over the country this has been a period of renewal, reflection, and self-examination, and of a new resolve for the most free and successful Jewish community in history. Several of the writers have drawn from their previous work and contributed their most original material. It is fresh and informative in its substance, and the writing has an uncommon frankness, at times provocative and iconoclastic in spirit. The editors clearly encouraged them, as they say in the South, "to speak their minds."

In his landmark book, *American Judaism: A History*, Professor Jonathan Sarna contrasted American Jewish history with the Jewish history of Europe. He wrote that "persecution, expulsion, tragedy and mass murder are not the central themes of American Jewish life and never have been. Instead, American Jewish history offers the opportunity to explore how Jews have flourished in a free and pluralistic society where church and state are separated and where religion is entirely voluntary."

This statement resonates deeply with me. The most profound aspect of the history of Jews in the South lies not in the cross burnings of the Ku Klux Klan, the bombings of synagogues and homes, the acts of overt antisemitism and violence. The larger story resides in the hopes of immigrants who came to the South as peddlers and stayed to raise their families, began congregations and built centers of education in the American Bible Belt, where religious affiliations were expected. As they practiced their faith in town after town across the South, they were, merely by their presence and their interaction with neighbors, serving as "teachers" who every day illustrated the power of religious pluralism in an otherwise completely Christian region of America.

Jews in the South were not insular either. It is striking to observe Jewish participation and leadership in their communities, in local organizations, on the boards of public libraries, museums, schools, orchestras, book clubs, and generally as a vital part of the civic enterprise. Many were elected to city councils and other local offices. As Stuart Rockoff points out, 146 were elected as mayors of their towns. They understood that a better community for all was a better community for Jews.

This volume is important in its willingness to reexamine the past while looking freely at the present. But if I were to suggest areas of needed exploration in the coming years, one of the most fascinating questions is the way in which Jews are shaped by the ethos of the South they live in. For example, as I think back to the 1970s, no one would have predicted that the fastest-growing Christian churches in the twenty-first century would be the Evangelical and Pentecostal faiths, already representing more than 25 percent of the Christian population in the South. Jews understand that there is a continuum among the many different fundamentalist churches that extends from tolerance for differences to religious fanaticism. We need to know more about the daily relationships between the white and black churches and their Jewish neighbors, not only what the congregants believe, but how they act and feel toward Jews. We need to understand the deeply personal human interface between races and religions.

With regard to race, how has the relationship between blacks and Jews changed since the Voter Rights Act of 1965 empowered millions of black voters in the South and enabled two progressive governors from the Deep South to be elected president of the United States? Black voters have transformed southern politics, especially moderating the atmosphere of the society and the language and tone of its public dialogue. The South changed, and so did the nature of being a southerner in a place increasingly shaped by diversity, Jews included.

In the end, the pieces in the puzzle of the South keep shifting in size, shape, and character, and each aspect of southern political and social culture affects the other. To think anew is to look into a multisurfaced glass prism with the colors and light constantly changing. Shelby Foote was right. Each generation of writers, journalists, historians, playwrights, novelists, and poets must revisit the question of what it means to be a southerner and a Jew in the South, to understand the blended identity that makes up what I have called a "unique southern Jewish consciousness." Today's scholars and artists must plunge into the intersecting influences and unravel the deeply intertwined strands of religion, race, gender, history, state-by-state variations, and economic and social history. To paraphrase Arthur Miller, they will help to discover what I have stated are the central themes of my own writing—"how Jews made of the South a home."

ACKNOWLEDGMENTS

Over the course of this project, we have benefited from the insight and support of numerous colleagues, students, family, and friends. We are especially grateful to our contributors, who shared their scholarship with us for this anthology. Students in the "Shalom Y'all" seminar at the University of North Carolina at Chapel Hill explored the history of Jews in the South and yearned for a single text—instead of photocopied articles and course packs—to satisfy their thirst for information on the subject. Their enthusiasm for southern Jewish history inspired this book. Special thanks go to Wendy Weil, agent and friend, and to Phyllis Deutsch, editor in chief at the University Press of New England, who gave our book a home.

Colleagues in American Studies and the Carolina Center for Jewish Studies at the University of North Carolina at Chapel Hill and others at the University of South Florida Tampa Library provided a vibrant intellectual environment in which we explored ideas, sought advice, and found the time and support needed to prepare this manuscript for publication. Our mentors David Colburn, Jim Horton, Pam Nadell, George Pozzetta, Samuel Proctor, Robert Singerman, John Vlach, and Bertram Wyatt-Brown shepherded us through doctoral programs and showed us by example how to be historians.

Eli Evans's seminal works on the southern Jewish experience paved the way for our book and for many others. Every scholar of the Jewish South has been touched by his writing. Both as a friend and colleague, we have an enormous debt of gratitude to Eli for having inspired a new generation to research and preserve southern Jewish history.

Many have followed in Eli Evans's footsteps. Macy Hart and his staff at the Institute of Southern Jewish Life have preserved Jewish stories and artifacts since the late 1980s. We both worked with Macy in the 1990s and learned a great deal about the history he has documented so well. The Southern Jewish Historical Society also encourages the documentation of our region's Jewish history and provides a welcoming home in which to present and publish scholarship on the subject.

Sandy Berman at the William Breman Jewish Heritage Museum; Laura Clark Brown at the Southern Historical Collection, University of North Carolina at Chapel Hill; the staff at the American Jewish Archives; Dale Rosengarten at the Jewish Heritage Collection; College of Charleston, and Robert Singerman at the

Isser and Rae Price Library of Judaica, University of Florida shared their bibliographic expertise and found illustrations to accompany the book. We are especially grateful to Jonathan Sarna and Charles Reagan Wilson for their thoughtful reading of this manuscript.

Finally, to Huddy and Jerry Cohen, Helen and Charles Greenberg, Bill Ferris, and Kathy and Natalie Greenberg we owe our deepest appreciation for their love and friendship.

JEWISH ROOTS IN SOUTHERN SOIL

INTRODUCTION
JEWISH ROOTS IN SOUTHERN SOIL

MARCIE COHEN FERRIS & MARK I. GREENBERG

For more than a century historians have wrestled with the question, why study southern Jewish history?[1] What is the southern Jewish experience? Is southern Jewish culture distinctive from Jewish culture in other regions of the country, and if so, why? Is region a significant factor in American Jewish identity? How has the cultural encounter between southern Jews and African Americans shaped the regional expression of Jewish life? What areas of the Jewish South have scholars explored, and what areas have they neglected? Just as William Faulkner's character Quentin Compson wonders about his southern identity when his Harvard roommate Shreve asks him, "Tell about the South. What's it like there. What do they do there. Why do they live there. Why do they live at all,"[2] southern Jews face similar questions about who they are, why they exist, and what makes their experience worthy of discussion.

At the founding of the Southern Jewish Historical Society in 1976, Eli Evans, author and former president of the Revson Foundation, challenged historians of the Jewish South to reach beyond facts, dates, and lists of names in their research. More than thirty years have passed since this meeting and the publication of three pivotal books on southern Jewish life: *Jews in the South*, edited by Leonard Dinnerstein and Mary Dale Palsson (1973), *The Provincials* by Eli Evans (1973), and *Turn to the South: Essays on Southern Jewry* edited by Nathan Kaganoff and Melvin Urofsky (1979).[3] Inspired by the social history of the 1960s and 1970s that turned attention to ordinary American lives and the plurality of the American experience, these groundbreaking works signaled a new interest in the Jewish South by scholars, journalists, and the public at large. Each work noted the need for new scholarship on southern Judaism and each put forth a call for research, publications, oral histories, and documentary projects.

In 1998, historian Gary Zola, director of the Jacob Rader Marcus Center of the American Jewish Archives, in the inaugural issue of *Southern Jewish History*, posed the question, "why study southern Jewish history?[4] Zola suggests that study of the Jewish South both provides American Jews with a sense of continuity and widens the field of American Jewish knowledge. The South is a "Jewishly disadvantaged region," writes Zola, and thus demonstrates the perseverance of Jewish community life in places that have few Jewish resources and small Jewish populations.[5] The survival of the southern Jewish community proves that Judaism can endure in the most ominous conditions and still prevail.[6]

Jews who live in regions of the country with larger Jewish communities—seemingly "Jewishly privileged" worlds—wonder, "Who could believe Jews actually live in the South?" They suggest, "if they were really Jewish, they wouldn't live there." Such opinions emanate from memories of a mythic South, a place rife with antisemitism and racism. Today that Old South is overshadowed by an increasingly diverse, urban South known for its technology, banking, and corporate headquarters. And in the recent past, several historic civil rights–era court cases have been resolved, including the 1964 murder of two young Jewish men and one black man in Neshoba County, Mississippi. A jury of black and white citizens in Philadelphia, Mississippi, convicted Edgar R. Killen of manslaughter in the case forty-one years after the fact.

The demography of the Jewish South has changed rapidly in the past half century. While small Jewish communities have declined because of a graying of the population, urban Jewish communities have swelled with young professionals, families, and retirees. Today southern Jews describe active synagogues, religious schools, dynamic rabbis, holiday celebrations, and a dizzying schedule of organizational activities. They speak of regional social gatherings, summer camp, and vacations that draw the dispersed southern Jewish community together. In rural southern Jewish communities, dedicated members of small congregations persevere, but realistically consider options for their futures. "We've tried to honor our forefathers, our ancestors," explains Joe Erber, whose grandfather was a charter member of the Congregation Ahavath Rayim in Greenwood, a small community in the Mississippi Delta. "We've never been perfect. We've done the best we can with what we've got."[7]

Eliza McGraw, a contributor to this volume, describes southern Jewishness as a "cultural compound rather than a simple doubling of difference." She explains that being Jewish in the South is not "merely plural (and oxymoronic)." Rather, Jews in the South have a "hybrid identity," a new identity created from the existence of more than one culture within an individual. "To avoid seeing southern Jewishness as nothing more than an opposition," writes McGraw, "it needs to be examined on its own terms and turf."[8]

Historian Mark Bauman says we must study southern Jewish history because "American Jewish history is not New York City history writ large."[9] Zola and

Bauman echo American Jewish historians Jacob Rader Marcus and Eli Evans, both of whom argue that to understand the American Jewish experience we must understand our regions, as well as our cities.[10] Evans reflects: "I had always been conditioned throughout my life to believe that we were the Jews on the periphery, that it was New York, the world of our fathers, that was the center of Jewish life in America. Jews in the South were out here on the rim where it didn't matter."[11]

The South clearly does matter, because Jews have lived in the region since the late seventeenth century. Here two of the nation's earliest and most significant Jewish congregations were founded in Savannah in 1735 and Charleston in 1749. By 1800, more Jews lived in Charleston than in New York City, a pattern that continued until the 1820s. An American Reform movement found its voice in this region by the 1830s. Despite their overall small numbers in the South—Jews still constitute less than one-half of 1 percent of the southern population—they sustained and supported their communities, providing leadership in the development of economic, educational, and cultural institutions.

For more than three hundred years, southern and Jewish ethnic and religious identity has been shaped by encounters with white and black Gentile cultures. Historian George Tindall explains that Jews and southerners—both white and black—share "outsider status," Jews because of their immigrant heritage, and southerners because of their isolation from the rest of the nation.[12]

Unlike the urban Northeast, where large numbers of Jewish immigrants settled in ghettos, Jews came south in small numbers and found themselves at the center of white and black Gentile communities where they played an important, highly visible role as merchants and traders. In these worlds it was impossible for Jews to remain untouched by the history and culture of their region. Southern white and black cultures, explains Tindall, "bubbled away side by side, with some of the ingredients spilling over from one into the other." Tindall argues that the diverse population of the colonial South merged into black and white "ethnic" groups "that had much in common, however reluctant they were to acknowledge kinship."[13] Such cultural encounter was also part of the southern Jewish experience and became the basis for constructing their distinctive expression of American Jewish life.

A BRIEF HISTORY OF THE JEWISH SOUTH

The southern Jewish experience began more than fifty years prior to the first permanent Jewish settlement in Savannah, Georgia, in the 1730s, when Jews joined exploratory expeditions from Europe to the New World in the sixteenth and seventeenth centuries. Sephardic Jews who fled the Iberian Peninsula to avoid the Inquisition sought religious tolerance as well as economic opportunity in the newly developing markets of the coastal South. Other Jews came from St. Croix, Curaçao, England, Alsace and the Rhineland, Poland, Prussia, and the Netherlands, as well as northern colonial cities like New York, Philadelphia, and Newport, Rhode Island. Many settled in Savannah, founding a congregation in 1735, and later in Charleston, South Carolina, where a congregation was established in 1749. These Jews were joined by a smaller number of Ashkenazic Jews from central and western Europe. With their own traditions brought from the Old World, Jews encountered a culture influenced by Africa, England, France, Spain, Germany, and the Caribbean. Mark I. Greenberg's essay in this volume offers one case study in early southern Jewish history, focusing attention in particular on Savannah and the difficulties Sephardic and Ashkenazic Jews faced in forming a Jewish identity and community in the New World.

Colonial Jewish families throughout the Atlantic region were connected by religion, commerce, kinship, marriage, and their Old World roots. Their ties to Jewish communities around the Atlantic were so strong that when Charleston's Jews created a board of trustees for their new cemetery in 1764, they appointed men from congregations in New York, Newport, Savannah, and Jamaica.[14] The Jewish community included merchants, auctioneers, brokers, bakers, butchers, grocers, blacksmiths, journalists, shoemakers, tailors, tobacconists, pharmacists, artists, school mistresses, and shopkeepers.

When the Revolutionary War descended upon Charleston in 1779, the women prepared for the ensuing conflict, while their husbands enlisted in a local militia that included so many members of their temple that it became known as the "Jews' Company."[15] When George Washington was elected president in 1790, Charleston had more than 200 Jews, second only to New York's Jewish population of 242. By 1820, the population had increased to 700, making Charleston the largest Jewish community in the nation.[16] A Jewish congregation founded in Richmond, Virginia, in 1789, was the fourth-largest Jewish community in the nation according to the 1790 census.[17] In response to the nation's commitment to religious toleration, Jewish congregations in Savannah, Charleston, Richmond, Philadelphia, and New York sent President Washington congratulatory letters on the occasion of his inauguration.[18]

The postwar economic depression, compounded by the disruption of Atlantic trade, forced many southern country Jewish merchants to find new markets, while others abandoned transatlantic trade for more modest activities as local shopkeepers and artisans, and still others moved to larger cities.[19] The 1820s marked the movement of American Jewish settlement into the interior of the country, as merchants followed the commercial frontier from the upper South to the lower South. By 1860, the Jewish population of New Orleans had grown to two thousand. The majority of southern Jews were now native-born, English-speaking citizens, and many were the second and third generation of their families. In her work in this volume, Emily Bingham explores the lives of the Mordecais, an iconic family of this era. Jacob Mordecai, the son of colonial immigrants, and three of his children—Rachel Mordecai Lazarus, Emma Mordecai, and Alfred Mordecai—wrestled with their regional and religious identities in the first half of the nineteenth century.

In 1825, South Carolinians Isaac Harby, Philip Benjamin (father of Judah P. Benjamin who later became secretary of war and secretary of state for the Confederacy), and ten other Jews petitioned leaders of Beth Elohim to make changes in the congregation's worship service. The Reformers argued that their goal was to fight the apathy of congregants who were "wandering gradually from the true God," but other concerns lay behind their requests.[20] A growing "sense of crisis" among whites in Charleston caused the younger generation of Jews to seek reforms.[21] The Denmark Vesey slave conspiracy of 1822 terrified Charleston's white citizens, who were already concerned because of the city's economic decline. In response, young native-born Jews turned inward and sought order in their own community through a more "rational" worship service.[22]

Reformers were also influenced by the Second Great Awakening, an era of religious revival that swept the South during this period, inspiring Christian missionaries, preachers, and churchgoers to draw nonbelievers into their fold. Concerned that apathy within the Jewish community made them vulnerable to such efforts, Reformers sought to secure the survival of Judaism in fragile times, a deed so empowering that it has been described as the "first revitalization of Judaism in America."[23] The central issue was the inability of one synagogue to meet the needs of a Jewish community that included young Jews born after the Revolution who were deeply influenced by American ideas of democracy, freedom, and religious change, themes addressed in Bingham's essay.[24] This marked a transition from the Old World model of a "synagogue-community" to the New World "community of synagogues," with the transfer of power from synagogue leadership to the congregants. Charleston Reformers advocated shorter services in both Hebrew and English, vernacular prayers, a weekly sermon, and increased decorum in congregants' style of worship.[25]

Reformers sought to balance the two poles of their identity—their white southernness and the Judaism of their ancestors. The Reformers wanted Judaism to survive and sought to adapt their religion to the southern world in which they lived. Their reforms led to a split within the congregation, and the creation of the "Reformed Society of Israelites" in 1825 marked the beginning of Reform Judaism in America.

The Reformed Society of Israelites ceased to function after 1837, as economic decline in Charleston fettered attempts to raise money for a synagogue. Reform leaders like Harby moved from Charleston to more prosperous cities in the northeast and to southern cities like Savannah, Mobile, and New Orleans.[26] In spite of the failure of the independent society, Jews continued to seek reforms from within established congregations.[27] Throughout the nineteenth century, congregations across the Jewish South substituted English for Hebrew, introduced choirs and organ services, allowed mixed seating of men and women, and encouraged the rabbi to preach sermons, as did his Protestant colleagues. Yarmulkas (skullcaps) and tallitot (prayer shawls) disappeared, and a quiet, dignified decorum was encouraged during worship. Even the architecture of the new synagogues was modeled after southern churches, de-emphasizing Jewish Old World roots in a country increasingly resentful of outsiders.[28] The classical design of Charleston's elegant Beth Elohim, dedicated in 1841, was more than a nod to the architectural fashion of the day. By embracing the classical style, including Doric columns on the outside of the synagogue and an organ on the inside, the congregants affirmed their American identity.[29]

From the 1820s to the 1870s, most Jews who came to the American South were Ashkenazic from central and western Europe, including Bavaria, Western Prussia, Posen, and Alsace.[30] The diversity of this immigration was suggested by their new synagogues that offered different rites connected to Poland, Germany, and other countries of central Europe.[31] Not everyone joined these synagogues, as there was no state pressure to affiliate with a Jewish community as there had been in Europe. Others chose not to affiliate, engaged as they were in the care of their material lives rather than their souls.[32] Settling in small towns across the region, Jewish immigrants, some single and some with families, established themselves as merchants. Jewish businessmen in Charleston and Savannah provided credit to young "drummers" as they sold their goods from town to town until they could open stores of their own.[33] By taking in German Jewish boarders during the antebellum era, middle-class Jewish women in Savannah added to the family income but also provided familiar foods, language, and a religious atmosphere for newly arrived immigrants who were separated from their families in Europe.[34] Jennifer Stollman, in her essay in this anthology, shows how a distinct nineteenth-century Jewish female literary canon gave women a public voice, helped combat antisemitism, and promoted religious practice at home.

German Jewish settlers moved to Memphis from 1830 through 1850, and they were drawn by the city's economic opportunities as the nation's largest inland cotton market. Memphis has always served as the primary distribution center for the Midsouth, a region that includes Tennessee, Arkansas, Mississippi, and Missouri.[35] German Jews were a small percentage of the European immigrants who came to Memphis in the midnineteenth century and made it the fastest growing city in the nation in the 1850s and the sixth-largest southern city by 1860.[36] German Jews organized a Hebrew Benevolent Society in Memphis in 1850 and three years later established Temple B'nai Israel, whose name was later shortened to Temple Israel.

In smaller villages outside the larger cities, Jews gathered for religious services in temporary locations like a merchant's store or a Masonic Hall. Once enough Jewish families settled in a town, a familiar pattern of Jewish community development followed: they created a *chevre kadisha*, a men's benevolent organization that took title to a cemetery and dealt with issues surrounding death and burial, and a corresponding women's society. Benevolent societies were organized to administer Jewish community philanthropy, and permanent places of worship were constructed. If Jewish numbers allowed, a *shochet* (ritual slaughterer), a *hazzan* (religious leaders), and a *mohel* (circumciser) were hired.

Still other Jewish settlers emigrated from Bavaria and southwest Germany and from Alsace-Lorraine in France to New Orleans between 1830 and 1850.[37] New Orleans and rural Louisiana felt familiar to these immigrants, who found the foods and language similar to what they had known in Europe.[38] Other Jews, like Judah P. Benjamin moved to the city from Charleston and Savannah, following the westward moving cotton frontier after the War of 1812.

By 1860, more than four million African American slaves were held in bondage on plantations and in the homes and businesses of middle-class white Southerners, including southern Jews. According to Bertram Wallace Korn, "any Jew who could afford to own slaves and had need for their services would do so. Jews wanted to acclimate themselves in every way to their environment; in both a social and psychological sense, they needed to be accepted as equal by their fellow-citizens." Korn concludes it was "a matter of financial circumstance and familial status whether they were to become slave-owners."[39] Southern "Jews accepted slavery along with other distinctively southern institutions and ideas," explains Theodore Rosengarten. "Their treatment of slaves is indistinguishable from that of Gentiles ranging from cases of kindred feeling to cold calculation of profit and loss."[40]

As the South approached secession in the fall of 1860 and the nation prepared for war, both well-established southern Jewish families and recent Jewish immigrants embraced the Confederate cause. Believing that the war was about preserving the "southern way of life," including slavery, Jews demonstrated solidarity with their white Gentile neighbors. Most southern Jews owned no more than several slaves, and thus they were relatively unaffected by threats to destroy the institution of slavery. But as peddlers, shopkeepers, and merchants who dealt daily with plantation managers and farmers who did own slaves, it was in their best interest to support the Confederate cause. Such support demonstrated southern citizenship and was particularly important to Jews, who longed to be accepted as neighbors, businessmen, and loyal citizens of the South. In his contribution to this volume, Robert Rosen explores these themes and describes Jewish men's and women's active and varied participation on behalf of the Confederate war effort.

Immigration to the South virtually stopped during the Civil War. The Jewish population of New Orleans in 1860 was between four thousand and five thousand, but it swelled during the war as rural Jews moved to the relative safety of the city.[41] Some recent Jewish immigrants left New Orleans and settled upriver in rural towns and villages similar to those they had known in Alsace-Lorraine and Bavaria. French and German Jewish families settled in communities like Natchez, Mississippi, and Donaldsonville, Louisiana, where they created a Jewish life on the Lower Mississippi. In these cities, Jewish merchants and their families were intimately connected to white creole and Cajun farmers and planters, as well as to their African American slaves.

As Hasia Diner reveals in her essay in this anthology, Jewish merchants the world over typically began their businesses as peddlers, catering to specific needs of the local population. In the South, peddlers sold merchandise to large and small landowners and to slaves in the rural countryside and small villages of Louisiana and Mississippi. Peddlers purchased their goods from wholesale suppliers in larger commercial centers like Shreveport, Baton Rouge, Natchez, Memphis, and New Orleans, where they maintained strong ties to Jewish friends, family, and businessmen.[42] These personal and financial ties proved invaluable once peddlers became store owners and needed city outlets for purchasing wholesale goods, securing credit, and establishing markets for country produce and larger staples like cotton and sugar.

In the Mississippi Delta, Jewish peddlers traveled the roads between outlying plantations, towns, and villages, where they served the scattered population of planters, sharecroppers, and laborers. Progressing from packs to horse-drawn wagons to dry goods stores, Jewish merchants established homes in the Delta, purchased land, and began to farm it. In his memoir of the Delta, *Lanterns on the Levee*, William Alexander Percy explains that "every American community has its leaven of Jews. Ours arrived shortly after the Civil War with packs on their backs, peddlers from Russia, Poland, Germany, and a few from Alsace." Percy describes how the Jewish peddlers became merchants, bankers, and plantation owners; sent their children to universities; and became involved in the arts and politics. "Why shouldn't such a people inherit the earth?" he writes, "Not surely, because of their meekness, but because of a steadier fire, a tension and tenacity that makes all other whites seem stodgy and unintellectual."[43]

After the war, the end of slavery, which undermined plantation agriculture, changed the lives of all southerners, including Jewish merchant families. At first unwilling to negotiate with black freedmen, large and small white landowners were unable to secure the necessary labor to manage their cotton crops and suffered financial reversals as a result of the transformed agricultural economy.[44] As gradual acceptance of the new order took place, black laborers, Jewish merchants, and white planters reshaped plantation society. Jewish merchants filled an important niche in this cash-poor society as a restructuring of the supply system took place during Reconstruction. Local storeowners replaced planters as the suppliers of goods to black laborers.[45] "The war, in liberating the slaves flooded the plantation South with just such individuals," writes Michael Wayne. "When old patterns of supply broke down, it was the local storekeeper who stood best prepared to deal with the material needs of the freedmen."[46]

The new storeowners were former Confederate soldiers, farmers, and even some planters, but the most successful, argues Wayne, were the "Europeans, particularly the Jews."[47] To protect themselves in advancing credit to white tenant farmers and freedmen laborers, the Jewish merchants depended on the crop lien system (a promise of the forthcoming crop) and pricing that favored cash purchases.[48] Jewish merchants who were formerly middling shopkeepers and wholesalers, became large retailers and cotton factors as they gained control over crops and marketing decisions.[49]

The first Jews arrived in Atlanta in the 1840s. Jacob Haas and Henry Levi, both Germans, were attracted to the city because of its booming economy and location at the terminus of an extensive railroad system. Haas and Levi's first concern when they arrived was to establish themselves in the retail trade. Steven Hertzberg argues that because of Atlanta's distance from a port of entry where immigrants with capital and marketable skills first landed, most Jews who came to Atlanta had already lived in another city or two where they mastered some of American culture.[50] By the time they came to Atlanta, they usually spoke English, had acquired enough money to open a business, and had connections to relatives or countrymen already in the city. As in other cities across the South, the young German males in this first wave of Jewish immigration boarded with German Jewish families already settled in Atlanta.

After the creation of a Hebrew Benevolent Society in 1860, no further attempts were made to organize the Atlanta Jewish community because of the Civil War. A sefer torah and charter for Hebrew Benevolent Congregation were finally secured, and after years of worship in a temporary location, the first permanent synagogue was erected in 1875. Jewish organizations were created— the Concordia Association in 1866, Atlanta's first German Jewish social club, the Hebrew Ladies Aid Society, and Jewish fraternal lodges in the 1870s.[51] In 1877, Rabbi Edward Benjamin Morris Browne founded the South's first regional Jewish newspaper, the *Jewish South*, which was read by southern Jews in cities and towns across the region.[52]

From 1895 to 1946, the temple was led by Rabbi David Marx, a staunch defender and practitioner of classical Reform Judaism, who disregarded the Jewish dietary laws and opposed any Zionist activity.[53] Marx removed all traces of Hebrew from his services and preferred to be addressed as "doctor," rather than rabbi. A popular speaker, Marx frequently addressed church groups and club meetings, and became a one-person public relations firm for Atlanta's Jewish community.

From the 1840s through the early 1900s, the number of Jewish bakers, butchers, grocers, and shohets in southern cities grew rapidly to serve newly arrived Jewish immigrants from central and eastern Europe. During this period new Orthodox congregations were created, such as B'rith Shalom (1855) and Beth Israel (1911) in Charleston, and Kahol Kadosh B'nai B'rith Jacob (1861) and Agudath Achim (1903) in Savannah. In 1887, observant eastern European Jews in Atlanta founded Ahavath Achim Congregation, followed by Congregation Shearith Israel in 1902. Memphis's first and largest Orthodox congregation, Baron Hirsch, was established in 1892 in a former African American church.

Polish and eastern European Jews established a modest presence in New Orleans by the 1850s. Two small Orthodox synagogues, Chevra Mikveh Israel and Congregation Tememi Derech, opened in the Carondolet Street neighborhood near the fashionable congregations of Touro and Sinai.[54] An Orthodox neighborhood developed below the 1100 block of Dryades Street, and between Melpomene and Jackson avenues.[55] These congregations served newcomers who preferred traditional forms of worship.

Eastern European Jews first came to Atlanta in the 1890s. Although their numbers were small, these intrepid newcomers found their way to the South. After their long journey to New York and Baltimore, few immigrants were willing to endure an overland journey to interior cities such as Atlanta and Memphis.[56] John Higham argues that because of these challenges, eastern European immigrants who did choose to come South were "more adventurous, independent, and acculturated than the two million who remained in the North."[57] This spirit influenced their foodways, enabling them to adapt to southern tastes and put aside rigorous adherence to the rules of *kashrut*. By the beginning of World War I, eastern European Jews were the majority of Atlanta's Jewish population.

Eastern European Jewish immigrants came to Memphis between 1905 and 1912, establishing themselves as merchants and small-business owners in "the Pinch," an area associated with the city's immigrants. They also lived in adjacent black neighborhoods where they opened small groceries and dry goods stores.[58] The attachment of black and white Memphians to family and religion blended well with the traditions of eastern European Jews, whose customers respected their piety, religious traditions, and dietary habits.

Like German Jews, eastern European immigrants arrived in the South with language and business skills. Anxious to participate in the booming postwar economy, they quickly rose from peddlers who serviced outlying farms and towns to self-employed tailors, shoemakers, and shopkeepers. Eastern European Jewish immigrants significantly influenced southern Jewry from the late nineteenth century to World War II as they reintroduced Orthodoxy into their communities.[59] Among the new immigrants there was great diversity in religious observance, ranging from strict Orthodoxy to those whose Jewish connections were solely through language, community, memories of the Old World, and food.[60]

Eastern European Jews lived and worked in white and black Gentile communities where they became merchants and traders. They lived in apartments above their small shops and worshipped at nearby synagogues. Their neighbors were African Americans and immigrants from Greece, Italy, Germany, Ireland, and China.[61] There was little social mixing between the Orthodox and Reform Jews, who were divided by country of origin, class, religious observance, and memory. The absence of a shared history between Reform Jews and Orthodox Jews in the South, especially family recollections of the Civil War, distanced eastern European Jews from German Jews.[62]

Eastern European Jews organized *landsmannschaft* (fraternal organizations) including members from their European villages.[63] Shared memories of the Old World brought them together for food and fellowship at home, in the synagogue, and in food-related businesses. Excluded from the social and political worlds of both German Jewish and Gentile communities in southern cities, eastern European Jews also organized their own socialist and Zionist organizations, which celebrated their common culture and Yiddish language.

Memphis Jews organized synagogues in the late nineteenth century in an environment of economic uncertainty and racial instability. As in post–Civil War Atlanta, thousands of working-class black and white farmers and sharecroppers were driven from the land to the city by financial depression and the dissolution of the plantation cotton economy. Desperate to establish stable situations for their families, Deep South rural exiles moved to Memphis, where their music, food traditions, and religion redefined the culture of the city.[64] This in-migration of people from the countryside gave Memphis a strong rural character that was shaped by a reverence for family and evangelical Protestantism.[65] Crowded into Memphis's downtown neighborhoods, white and black workers competed for housing and jobs at the shipping docks along the river and at the city's railroad distribution centers. They interacted in these worlds with growing numbers of Jewish shop owners, peddlers, and businessmen such as Benedict Lowenstein and Henry Seessel, two German Jewish merchants who by the 1850s were peddlers in the countryside around Memphis and later developed successful department stores and grocery stores in the city.[66]

Both German Jews and the newly arrived eastern European Jews faced growing antisemitism and nativisim in the late-nineteenth-century South. German Jews already established in southern communities believed they were as vulnerable as the new immigrants and argued that it was in the best interest of all Jews to quickly assimilate the newcomers and direct attention from their "foreignness." Tensions quickly developed between these new immigrants and the already established Jews, owing in part to significant differences in religious observance.

The majority of central and eastern European-born southern Jews became middle- and upper-class southerners, although many trace their roots back to poor peddler ancestors who worked their way up from rural sales routes to owning stores in towns and cities. Class position was secured by Jews' rapid assimilation into southern society, their entry into retail businesses and professional occupations, and their general acceptance as white by Gentile southerners. On the rare occasions when "down-and-out" Jews arrived in a southern city or in a small town where they stood out from their well-to-do coreligionists, local Jews were quick to provide financial assistance, and in some cases, to encourage them to move on.

Following the eastern European immigration, a second wave of Sephardic Jews came to the South in the first decades of the twentieth century. Jews from Turkey and the Isle of Rhodes settled in Montgomery, Alabama, and Atlanta, where they found jobs as fruit peddlers, butchers, storekeepers, grocers, tailors, hatters, and shoemakers. Like eastern European Jews before them, they settled where synagogues were established and by the 1920s built their own places of worship. The racism and antisemitism of the segregated New South also affected them.

The 1913 trial and the 1915 lynching of Leo Frank, a German Jewish Atlantan, took place just as many of the Sephardic community were settling in Atlanta. Frank had moved from Brooklyn to work with his uncle, Moses Frank.[67] Accused of murdering Mary Phagan, a young girl employed in his uncle's pencil factory in Atlanta, Frank's sentence was commuted by Georgia's Governor John Slaton in June 1915.[68] In August that same year, a vigilante mob from Marietta, Georgia, Phagan's hometown, forcibly removed Frank from the State Prison Farm and lynched him.

Throughout Frank's long trial and sentencing, the Atlanta Jewish community watched in quiet disbelief. They tried to deny that such a thing could happen to a leading member of the elite German Jewish society. Although he was associated with northern Jewish industrialists, Frank was accepted into Atlanta's Jewish society because of his family connections and marriage to Lucille Selig, daughter of an established German Jewish Atlanta family.[69] Only four years old at the time of the trial, Alene Fox Uhry remembered seeing large block headlines in the newspaper and knowing that something was wrong. Her parents and their friends never mentioned the Leo Frank case. "He was one of ours," explained Uhry. "If he could be lynched, what about us?"[70] The climate of fear in the local Jewish community deeply affected the newly arrived Sephardic Jews. They remained a tight-knit community, living in the same neighborhoods, shopping at local businesses, and cooking together.

From the 1913 Leo Frank case to the 1958 bombing of the Hebrew Benevolent Congregation or "the Temple," as it was known locally, Atlanta Jews considered themselves citizens of the New South. Henry Grady, the editor of the *Atlanta Constitution*, was the leading spokesman for this movement to restore economic prosperity in the South.[71] Grady spread the creed of the New South as he called on northern investors to seed southern economic development through his editorials and talks across the nation. With its new railroads, hotels, warehouses, factories, office buildings, and warehouses, Atlanta became the "capital" of the New South.[72] Jewish businessmen from established German families, as well as those more recently arrived from eastern Europe, were important voices for southern boosterism.

The antisemitism associated with the Leo Frank case encouraged Jews to affirm their southern citizenship through civic and economic involvement and, most important, to try to position themselves on the white side of the color line. Historian Grace Elizabeth Hale argues that the Leo Frank lynching defined southern white identity and who could belong to this group.[73] Eric Goldstein's essay in this volume explores Jews' uncertain racial status in the South and argues that they actively sought to prove their "whiteness" by conforming to prevailing racial mores more diligently than Jews in any other region of the country. Goldstein believes Jews' efforts to distance themselves socially and economically from African Americans did little to improve their status in the southern racial order during the early years of the twentieth century. The clear message to southern Jews was that their place within white Protestant society could never be assumed and that daily vigilance in one's behavior, appearance, and activities was required to affirm their racial status as white. This New South world, as Ed Ayers explains, "was an anxious place, filled with longing and re-sentment, for people had been dislodged from older bases of identity and found no new ones ready at hand."[74] No groups better understood the danger of un-certain times and the strategies necessary to secure their family's safety than Jews and African Americans in Atlanta.

Excluded from the urban social clubs and organizations of the South's elite Gentile society, German Jewish families created their own institutions where, in turn, they could define who was included in elite Jewish society. From the late 1880s to the early 1900s, as antisemitism intensified in the South and across America, German Jews formed social organizations such as the Standard Club (1905) in Atlanta.[75] Jewish participation in the Cotton Carnival, Memphis's so-cial event of the year, signaled their first access to the Gentile society previously off-limits to Jews and contrasted starkly with the exclusion of Jews form Mardi Gras, an event tied closely to bloodline rather than to business. The main dif-ference between the two events was the carnival's focus on cotton, the founda-tion of Memphis's economy. From the midnineteenth century onward, as central players in the cotton business, Jews were involved in every step of its produc-tion, from the fields to the gin to the stock exchange.

From 1931 to the late 1950s, members of Atlanta's Standard Club sponsored "Ballyhoo," an annual courtship weekend attended by college-aged sons and daughters of the Temple community. The event drew Jewish youth from the "best" families across the South, which meant those with German Jewish an-cestry. Over a long weekend, participants endured an exhausting round of break-fast dates, lunch dates, tea dance dates, early evening dates, late night dates, for-mal dances, and cocktail parties, with the goal of meeting a "nice Jewish boy or girl" who might well become a spouse. Similar courtship weekends in southern cities included Montgomery, Alabama's "Falcon," Birmingham, Alabama's "Ju-bilee," and Columbus, Georgia's "Holly Days."[76] Rhoda Abraham of Montgomery remembered hosting out-of-town girls at their home for the Falcon: "I remem-ber one year we had five girls at our house, and they arrived with trunks. This is in the summertime. I thought my aunt's maid was going to faint because she had all of those dresses to iron."[77]

Throughout the South, Jewish social service agencies, founded in the late nineteenth century and first decades of the twentieth century, joined forces in cooperative federations. Organizations such as Savannah's Jewish Educational Alliance, established in 1912, was the center of Jewish social activities for the city's three congregations. After school, children gathered at the Alliance for sports, Hebrew School, and the debating team. In addition to activities for Jewish youth, the JEA also provided classes for Savannah's eastern European Jews.[78]

Other locations for socializing were Jewish summer camps like Blue Star, in Hendersonville, North Carolina, which was patronized by families from Charleston and Savannah, and today draws Jewish campers throughout the South. Founded by the Popkin brothers of Augusta, Georgia, in 1948, Blue Star provided traditional American camping activities such as swimming, water skiing, and canoeing, but in a "Jewish setting." Except for maintenance staff and African American cooks who managed the camp's kosher kitchen, Blue Star was an all-Jewish world, a strange twist for Jewish children who were always a minority in their southern communities.[79]

By the 1950s, southern Jews, no matter their country of origin, were middle- and upper-class business people, from small store owners to department store magnates. They held public offices, such as Durham's E. J. "Mutt" Evans, who was mayor from 1951 to 1963. Jewish citizens were frequently at the center of efforts to build schools, medical institutions, and cultural venues throughout the South. The attractions of white suburbia in the urban South encouraged the exodus of Jewish business owners and their families from declining downtown neighborhoods. Jews moved to suburban neighborhoods, which offered safe, middle-class, single-family homes in Jewish neighborhoods with the hope of inclusion in white society. Many southern Jews helped found Conservative congregations during this era, reflecting a national Jewish interest in religious practices that emphasized a modernized, observant Judaism.

The 1954 Supreme Court *Brown v. Board of Education* decision ended segregation and the concept of "separate, but equal." Class distinctions within the Jewish South diminished as descendants of Sephardic and eastern European immigrants gained affluence and stature within their community. Most significant, after the Holocaust such divisions among Jews suddenly had little value. Church and synagogue bombings, protest marches, and segregated lunch counters of the civil rights era unsettled southern Jewish communities. As Clive Webb explores in this anthology, some southern Jews chose to participate in the "movement," but many more feared for their physical, social, and economic security and remained conspicuously silent or supported the status quo. Southern Jewish activists on behalf of civil rights deserve attention for their relative dearth. In 1946, Rabbi James Wax came to Temple Israel in Memphis. He encouraged his congregants to participate in interfaith councils and interfaith discussions, such as the "Panel of American Women." This organization sponsored a panel of black and white women, including a Jew, a Protestant, and a Catholic, who spoke at community gatherings to promote racial and religious tolerance.

Congregants of Memphis's Temple Israel were nervous about their rabbi's taking a stand on civil rights after the bombing of the Temple in Atlanta in 1958. Rabbi Wax supported integration not through protest marches but more quietly by working with groups like the Memphis Ministers Association. The rabbi's wife, Helen Wax, explained: "He never wanted to be, as he used to say, 'a general without an army.' He never wanted to put Temple Israel out in front by itself." [80]

Following the death of Dr. Martin Luther King Jr., killed by a sniper's bullet in Memphis, Rabbi Wax did participate in a march of black and white ministers from St. Mary's Episcopal Cathedral to Mayor Henry Loeb's office in City Hall on Friday, April 5, 1968. [81] The clergy called upon Loeb to end the racial violence and social injustice in Memphis. In an address to his congregation after King's murder, Wax said: "This city shall witness a new spirit and the memory of this great prophet of our time shall be honored. There will be the bigots and the segregationists and the so-called respectable but unrighteous people who will resist. But in the scheme of history, God's will does prevail." [82]

Outside cities such as Memphis, "country Jews" experienced the challenges of practicing Judaism in the rural South in an overwhelmingly Gentile world. For most Jews it meant adjusting religious practices to live in a society that conformed to both a southern and Protestant timetable. For Jewish merchants, this meant keeping their stores open on the Sabbath. In the 1940s and 1950s, Jewish retailers were overwhelmed with business from both white and black families that began early on Saturday morning and continued late into the evening. "This street on Saturday night when I was growing up," said Joe Erber speaking of Greenwood, Mississippi's downtown, "'till one thirty, two o'clock in the morning would be packed with people. The Mississippi Delta was an agricultural-based economy, and the field hands and the farmers all paid off on Saturdays." [83]

The isolation of Jews in the rural South required lengthy road trips to the nearest synagogue for services and religious school, to purchase Jewish food supplies, and to visit Jewish family and friends. Traveling thirty to seventy miles each week for such purposes was a common fact of life. "We grew up and my parents grew up traveling somewhere to go to Sunday school or go to temple," said Leanne Lipnick Silverblatt of Indianola, Mississippi. "You know you have to do it, and you just do it."[84]

Stuart Rockoff's contribution to this book discusses the period following World War II, when few Jewish youth returned to the rural South after they experienced outside worlds during college and the military. The mechanization of cotton picking in the 1940s displaced thousands of black laborers who left the South, hoping to find jobs and better living conditions in industrial cities like Chicago. These changes, accompanied by the decline of downtown business districts and the growth of regional discount stores like Wal-Mart, pushed third- and fourth-generation Jews out of their small mercantile businesses in the rural South and into professions located in cities both in and outside the South.

As Jewish population declined in many rural areas, once-active congregations were forced to close their doors, ending a long history of Jewish life in many southern communities. In 1989, the Museum of the Southern Jewish Experience in Jackson, Mississippi, was established to help small congregations face these challenges. Today, the museum, now known as the Institute for Southern Jewish Life, works with congregations throughout the South to preserve and document the practice, culture and legacy of Judaism in the South, and to provide long-range planning assistance to congregations facing the challenges of declining membership.

Rockoff's work suggests an evolving and changing Jewish landscape away from small rural communities and toward growing urban centers. Today there are approximately 257,000 Jews in the South (excluding Florida), who constitute 4.2 percent of the nation's Jewish population and one-half of 1 percent of the South's population. The Jewish population of the Atlanta metropolitan area is 85,900; New Orleans, 13,000 (pre-Katrina); Richmond, Virginia, 12,500; Memphis, 8,500; and Charlotte, North Carolina, 8,500.[85] In each of these cities, the number of congregations is growing.

DEFINING THE JEWISH SOUTH

Defining the South today is not a simple matter, nor is defining the diverse Jewish community that resides there. Within each subregion of the South, Jewish communities both struggle and thrive, joined by their shared regional identity, religion, and family ties. There is the lowland South and the upland South, the Appalachian South, the Mississippi River South, the interior South, the Gulf Coast South, the East Coast South, the urban South, and the rural South. For the purposes of this anthology, South Florida receives its greatest attention by essayists Stuart Rockoff and Stephen Whitfied in the book's final two chapters. Largely the product of post–World War II migration from the North and Midwest, South Florida has more in common with New Jersey and Long Island than with any southern state.[86] Each of these places is home to Jewish communities shaped by the indigenous culture, which in turn has been enriched by Jewish culture and Old World origins. Given the diversity of the eleven Confederate states that comprise the South (Alabama, Arkansas, Florida, Georgia, Louisiana, Mississippi, North Carolina, South Carolina, Tennessee, Texas, and Virginia), scholars often define the region as a cultural, not geographic, area. Southern culture bleeds into neighboring regions and is equally shaped by those regions and the movement of people. Charles Reagan Wilson and William Ferris argue that "the South is found wherever southern culture is found."[87] Given these demographic and cultural changes, a new paradigm to define the southern Jewish experience may be in order, argues Stephen Whitfield in the essay that concludes this anthology.

Scholars have long debated whether southern Jews are distinctive from Jews in other regions of the United States.[88] Some argue that they are not and suggest that southern accents, cooking styles, and participation in regional activities like hunting and fishing do not define a distinctive southern Jewish identity. Because of their role as peddlers and later as merchants, their fear of antisemitism, their economic and familial ties to Jews in the North, and their minority status, some argue that Jews rarely became true southerners. These scholars conclude that southern Jews have always shared far more with Jews in small communities in the West and in New England than with their southern white Protestant neighbors.[89]

To dismiss the impact of region on Jewish identity is to underestimate the power of place.[90] The voices of Jewish southerners, past and present, eloquently attest to the deep roots of Jews in the region and their distinctive experience as American Jews. Historian Leonard Rogoff suggests that the arrival of significant numbers of German Jews in the South in the midnineteenth century coincided with secession, the period when white southerners strongly asserted their separate regional identity. White and black southerners alike created what we recognize today as southern culture, most clearly expressed in the region's music, food, politics, religious practices, class structures, and racial attitudes.[91] Newly arrived Jews in the antebellum and Civil War–era South embraced this culture and a growing sense of southern nationalism ultimately symbolized by the Confederacy. The intersection and fluidity of Jewish and southern identities can be seen in foodways, as demonstrated in Marcie Cohen Ferris's essay, in the objects found in daily life (material culture), explored in Dale Rosengarten's contribution to this volume, and in the literature of Jewish and non-Jewish southern writers, discussed later in this book by Eliza McGraw.

Why do the phrases "Jewish southerner" and "southern Jew" raise debate among scholars within and outside the region? Because behind these questions lie larger questions: "Who is a Jew?" and "Who in American Jewry can claim themselves 'distinctive'?" As a group, this collection of essays argues that all American Jews, no matter their state and region, have two things in common. They share the common experience of their Jewish heritage, although each is strongly influenced by the places they call home. These places, whether suburbs or rural farming communities or cities, distinctively shape the Jewish experience of individual Americans as a result of their unique histories and populations. The Jewish South, like other regions of the nation, is a diverse group of people—Sephardic, Ashkenazic, and German-descended; religious and irreligious; some who keep kosher and others who do not; and some who blend religion and region, and others that carefully distinguish between the two. These voices are the ones that can best answer "Who is a Jew?" and "What does it mean to be both southern and Jewish?"

In his memoir of growing up in the Reform Jewish community of Charleston, author and publisher Louis Rubin explains: "These people were part of the South, and their response to their experience was very much in terms of the Southern community. . . . Cut off from what for their forebears had been a powerful historical and self-sufficient community tradition, in effect they replaced it with the intense heritage of their new home—which was also a minority enclave within a larger cultural and political entity."[92]

Jewish Roots in Southern Soil: A New History addresses these questions through the voices of a new generation of scholars of the Jewish South. Each of the thirteen chapters that follow reflects a response to the challenge issued by scholars of the Jewish South more than thirty years ago, who called for new studies on women and gender; black-Jewish relations; the role of race, politics and economic life, and popular and material culture; and historical analysis focused on changes wrought by industrialization and urbanization in the twentieth century. To this end, chapters 1 through 8 are organized chronologically, followed by chapters 9 through 13, which analyze broader themes in southern Jewish life. The authors address historical issues in the Jewish South from the colonial era to the present, and in every region of the South, from the low country to the Mississippi Delta.

The contributors to this volume call upon a rich array of historical sources drawn from the region's Jewish archives, including the William Breman Jewish

Heritage Museum in Atlanta; organizations such as the Southern Jewish Historical Society; and synagogues such as Beth Ahabah in Richmond, Virginia, and Ahavath Rayim in Greenwood, Mississippi. National and regional institutions consulted by scholars published in this volume include the American Jewish Archives in Cincinnati, the Southern Historical Collection at the University of North Carolina at Chapel Hill, and oral history interviews and material culture assembled by the Jewish Heritage Collection at the College of Charleston and the Institute for Southern Jewish Life in Jackson, Mississippi.

This anthology includes the voices of Jews and non-Jews, whites and African Americans, men and women, southerners and non-southerners, homemakers, storekeepers, cotton factors, planters, rabbis, doctors, cooks, caretakers, teachers, and many more. The diversity of these voices speaks to the complicated experience of Jewish southerners, who, because of their relatively smaller numbers and isolation from Jewish urban centers in the Northeast and Midwest, immersed themselves in the white Christian community that surrounded them. Southern Jews were not always heroes and leading citizens of their communities, nor were they the "ghettoized" and insular Jews often portrayed in the larger story of American Jewish history.

The study of southern Jewish life has now come of age, evidenced by these essays and other award-winning publications, increasing numbers of dissertations, films, a scholarly journal devoted to regional Jewish history, regional Jewish newspapers, Jewish historical societies, annual conferences, and Jewish museums. The recent founding of Jewish studies programs at institutions of higher education such as the College of Charleston, Duke, Emory, Tulane, University of Florida, University of Miami, University of North Carolina, University of Tennessee, University of Virginia, and Vanderbilt indicates another important sign of the health and vitality of Jewish scholarship in the American South.

Southern Jews tell you that it feels different to be Jewish and southern. Whether one is a descendent of colonial Jews in Charleston or recent retiree to Chapel Hill from Chicago, the difference is deeply felt. Until the post–World War II period, the Jewish population in most southern communities was relatively small. To identify as a Jew in a palpably Protestant region that so blurred the boundaries between public and private, you had to *want* to be Jewish. The Jewish landscape in the South is changing. Some communities in the Sunbelt are growing, but in most southern towns and cities being a Jewish southerner still requires a level of commitment and a consciousness of identity that sets this region apart from others. Jews are a Diaspora in the Deep South, and the rich culture and complex history of this unceasingly interesting southern world will continue to shape a distinctive American Jewish experience for generations to come.

NOTES

1. Historian Steven Hertzberg notes that the first studies of the Jewish South were published during the years between the founding of the American Jewish Historical Society in 1892 and World War II. These early works were "biographical in orientation, apologetic in tone," and usually written by amateur historians. Stephen Hertzberg, *Strangers within the Gate City: The Jews of Atlanta, 1845–1915* (Philadelphia: Jewish Publication Society of America, 1978), 5. Historian Leah Hagedorn observes that while there are abundant memoirs, biographies, and significant articles, no full-length history of Jewish life in the American South exists. Hagedorn identifies Charleston, South Carolina, Rabbi Barnett Abraham Elzas's *The Jews of South Carolina* (Philadelphia: J. B. Lippincott, 1905) as the beginning of the field of southern Jewish history. She describes this early scholarship as "filiopietistic," celebrating "Jewish notables and achievements," rather than focusing on the differences that set Jews apart from the dominant society. Leah E. Hagedorn, "Jews and the American South, 1858–1905," (Ph. D. diss., University of North Carolina, 1999), ix-x.

2. William Faulkner, *Absalom, Absalom!* (1936; New York: Vintage Books, 1990), 142.

3. Leonard Dinnerstein and Mary Dale Palsson, eds., *Jews in the South* (Baton Rouge: Louisiana State University Press, 1973); Eli N. Evans, *The Provincials: A Personal History of Jews in the South* (New York: Free Press, 1973); Nathan M. Kaganoff and Melvin I. Urofsky, eds., *Turn to the South: Essays on Southern Jewry* (Charlottesville: University Press of Virginia, 1979).

4. Gary P. Zola, "Why Study Southern Jewish History?" *Southern Jewish History*, 1 (1998): 1–21. The Southern Jewish Historical Society was founded in 1976 after a special conference on the history of the Jewish South sponsored by the American Jewish Historical Society. The conference also resulted in one of the first anthologies on the topic, *Turn to the South: Essays on Southern Jewry* (see note 3).

5. Zola, "Why Study Southern Jewish History?" 7.

6. Ibid.

7. Joe Erber, Greenwood, Miss., *Delta Jews*, dir. Mike DeWitt, 1999.

8. Eliza R. L. McGraw, *Two Covenants: Representations of Southern Jewishness* (Baton Rouge: Louisiana State University Press, 2005), 2.

9. Quoted in Zola, "Why Study Southern Jewish History?" 4.

10. Ibid., 1–5. Marcus says that the true story of the American Jew must emerge from the "horizontal spread of the many," and not from the "eminence of the few."

11. Eli N. Evans, "Southern Jewish History: Alive and Unfolding," in Kaganoff and Urofsky, *Turn to the South*, 160.

12. George Tindall, *Natives and Newcomers: Ethnic Southerners and Southern Ethnics* (Athens: University of Georgia Press, 1995), 23.

13. Ibid., 23–24.

14. Ibid., 50.

15. Barnett A. Elzas, *The Jews of South Carolina* (Philadelphia: J. B. Lippincott, 1905),

107. Soldiers enrolled themselves in the district in which they lived. Captain Richard Lushington's district included Charleston's King Street, the principal business street where most Jews lived and worked.

16. Ibid., 111.

17. Mark Bauman, "Jewish Tradition," in *The Companion to Southern Literature*, ed. Joseph M. Flora and Lucinda H. MacKethan (Baton Rouge: Louisiana State University Press, 2002), 387.

18. Ibid., 129.

19. Eli Faber, *A Time for Planting: The First Migration, 1654–1820* (Baltimore: Johns Hopkins University Press, 1992), 112.

20. Leon A. Jick, *The Americanization of the Synagogue, 1820–1870* (Hanover, N.H.: University Press of New England, 1976), 13; and Deborah Dash Moore, "Freedom's Fruits," in *A Portion of the People: Three Hundred Years of Southern Jewish Life*, ed. Dale Rosengarten and Theodore Rosengarten (Columbia: University of South Carolina Press, 2002), 13, 20.

21. Moore, "Freedom's Fruits," 20.

22. Ibid., 13–14.

23. Jonathan D. Sarna, "American Judaism in Historical Perspective," David W. Belin Lecture in American Jewish Affairs (Ann Arbor: Jean and Samuel Frankel Center for Judaic Studies, University of Michigan, 2003), 4.

24. Jonathan D. Sarna, *American Judaism: A History* (New Haven, Conn.: Yale University Press, 2004), 55.

25. Ibid., 57.

26. Jick, *Americanization of the Synagogue*, 13. For discussion of Charleston's economic decline, see Evans, "Preface," xvii; Theodore Rosengarten, "Introduction," 3; and Moore, "Freedom's Fruits, 11, in Rosengarten and Rosengarten, *A Portion of the People*. The economic decline after 1820 was caused primarily by a drop in prices for rice and cotton, the major cash crops of the region, and the westward movement of the cotton trade to the lower South. Harby moved to New York in 1828. See Gary P. Zola, *Isaac Harby of Charleston, 1788–1828: Jewish Reformer and Intellectual* (Tuscaloosa: University of Alabama Press, 1994), 156.

27. Moore, "Freedom's Fruits," 15.

28. Louis E. Schmier, "Jewish Religious Life," in *Encyclopedia of Southern Culture*, ed. Charles R. Wilson and William R. Ferris (Chapel Hill: University of North Carolina Press, 1989), 1,290.

29. Michael A. Meyer, *Response to Modernity: A History of the Reform Movement in Judaism* (Detroit: Wayne State University Press, 1988), 234.

30. Sarna, *American Judaism*, 64.

31. Sarna, "American Judaism in Historical Perspective," 11.

32. Sarna, *American Judaism*, 73. Sarna writes that "as many as half of America's Jews were unaffiliated at mid-century."

33. Rosengarten and Rosengarten, "The Moving Frontier," in Rosengarten and Rosengarten, *A Portion of the People*, 113.

34. Mark I. Greenberg, "Savannah's Jewish Women and the Shaping of Ethnic and Gender Identity, 1830–1900," *Georgia Historical Quarterly* 82 (Winter 1998): 758.

35. Roger Biles, *Memphis in the Great Depression* (Knoxville: University of Tennessee Press, 1986), 8.

36. Ibid., 10. Biles states that the high rate of immigration to Memphis resulted in a population that was 30 percent foreign-born in 1860. This percentage, he explains, was typical of Mississippi Valley river towns in the antebellum years.

37. Elliott Ashkenazi, *The Business of Jews in Louisiana, 1840–1875* (Tuscaloosa: University of Alabama Press, 1988), 10. Ashkenazi argues that between 1822 and 1860, New Orleans received the second-largest number of immigrants to America, after New York City.

38. Ibid., 3.

39. Bertram Wallace Korn, "Jews and Slavery in the Old South, 1789–1865," in Dinnerstein and Palsson, *Jews in the South*, 96.

40. Theodore Rosengarten, "Introduction," in Rosengarten and Rosengarten, *A Portion of the People*, 4 and 5.

41. Ashkenazi, *Business of Jews in Louisiana*, 104.

42. Ibid, 14.

43. William Alexander Percy, *Lanterns on the Levee: Recollections of a Planter's Son* (1941; Baton Rouge: Louisiana State University Press, 1973), 17.

44. Michael Wayne, *The Reshaping of Plantation Society: The Natchez District, 1860–1880* (Baton Rouge: Louisiana State University Press, 1983), 39, 60.

45. Ibid., 151.

46. Ibid., 165.

47. Ibid., 167.

48. Ibid., 172.

49. Ibid., 174.

50. Hertzberg, *Strangers within the Gate City*, 36.

51. Jane D. Leavey, ed., *Creating Community: The Jews of Atlanta, from 1845 to the Present* (Atlanta: Atlanta Jewish Federation, 1994), 31.

52. Hertzberg, *Strangers within the Gate City*, 9.

53. Leavey, *Creating Community*, 11.

54. Bobbie S. Malone, *Rabbi Max Heller: Reformer, Zionist, Southerner, 1860–1929* (Tuscaloosa: University of Alabama Press, 1997), 35.

55. Lawrence N. Powell, *Troubled Memory: Anne Levy, the Holocaust and David Duke's Louisiana* (Chapel Hill: University of North Carolina Press, 2000), 368.

56. Hertzberg, *Strangers within the Gate City*, 79.

57. Quoted in Hertzberg, *Strangers within the Gate City*, 80.

58. Selma S. Lewis, *A Biblical People in the Bible Belt: The Jewish Community of Memphis, Tennessee, 1840s–1960s* (Macon, Ga.: Mercer University Press, 1998), 83–84, 100. David Goldfield identifies the "Pinch" as a twelve-block area north of downtown and adjacent to the Mississippi River that attracted Irish, Italian, German, and eastern European immigrants. The word *Pinch* probably referred to the neighborhood's first immigrants, the Irish, who were known for their pinched faces and stomachs caused by the potato famine of the 1840s. By the 1920s, the Pinch was a predominantly Jewish neighborhood. David Goldfield, "The Pinch" in *Exploring America's Communities: In Quest of Common Ground* (Washington, D.C.: American Association of Community Colleges, 1995).

59. Lee Shai Weissbach, "East European Immigrants and the Image of Jews in the Small-Town South." *American Jewish History* 85 (September 1997): 231–62. Weissbach explains that eastern European Jews who came to the South were often sent by the Industrial Removal Office, which resettled immigrants beyond the major cities of the Atlantic seaboard. Others came because of economic opportunity and the presence of already settled family and friends. See also Mark K. Bauman, *The Southerner as American: Jewish Style* (Cincinnati: American Jewish Archive, 1996), 22.

60. Sarna, *American Judaism*, 174.

61. Rosengarten and Rosengarten, "Charleston's Uptown Jews," in Rosengarten and Rosengarten, *A Portion of the People*, 155.

62. Jenna Weissman Joselit, "Land of Promise," in ibid., 27.

63. Rosengarten and Rosengarten, "Charleston's Uptown Jews," 154.

64. Pete Daniel, *Lost Revolutions: The South in the 1950s* (Chapel Hill: University of North Carolina Press, 2000), 8–9.

65. Biles, *Memphis in the Great Depression*, 6.

66. Lewis, *Biblical People*, 15–16. Seessel's was recently purchased by another corporate grocery store chain, Schnuck's, ending Seessel's more than 140-year presence in the city as a food purveyor.

67. Leonard Dinnerstein, *The Leo Frank Case* (1966; Athens: University of Georgia Press, 1987), 5.

68. Moses Frank, Leo Frank's uncle, was the principal shareholder of the factory. Sandy Berman, archivist, William Breman Jewish Heritage Museum, e-mail to Marcie C. Ferris, August 29, 2002.

69. Dinnerstein, *Leo Frank Case*, 6. Dinnerstein explains that Frank "achieved some degree of social prominence within the Jewish community." He was elected president of the local B'nai B'rith in 1912.

70. Alene Fox Uhry, interview with Marcie C. Ferris, Atlanta, August 22, 2001, p. 15, Southern Historical Collection, University of North Carolina at Chapel Hill.

71. Edward L. Ayers, *The Promise of the New South: Life after Reconstruction* (New York: Oxford University Press, 1992), 21.

72. George B. Tindall, *The Emergence of the New South: 1913–1945* (Baton Rouge: Louisiana State University Press, 1967), 99.

73. Grace Elizabeth Hale, *Making Whiteness: The Culture of Segregation in the South, 1890–1940* (NY: Pantheon Books, 1998), 237.

74. Ayers, *Promise of the New South*, viii; and C. Vann Woodward, *Origins of the New South, 1877–1913* (1951; Baton Rouge: Louisiana State University Press, 1971), 155.

75. Hertzberg, *Strangers within the Gate City*, 118–19.

76. Carolyn Lipson-Walker, "'Shalom Y'all': The Folklore and Culture of Southern Jews" (Ph.D. diss., Indiana University, 1986), 334–36.

77. Rhoda Abraham, interview with Marcie C. Ferris, Montgomery, Ala., (November 1994), in collection of the Institute of Southern Jewish Life, Jackson, Miss.

78. Jewish Educational Alliance Scrapbook, "Season 1921–1922," Collection JA002, Savannah Jewish Archives, Georgia Historical Society, Savannah.

79. Harry Popkin, interview with Marcie C. Ferris, August 22, 2001, Atlanta, 11, in Southern Historical Collection, University of North Carolina at Chapel Hill. Harry Popkin attended Georgia Tech University in the early 1940s, where he was a both a fine athlete and a leader in "AZA," the Aleph Zadik Aleph. His work in AZA was his "first taste of Jewish social service work." Harry and his brothers Ben and Herman saw the need for a camp for Jewish children in the South. They bought property for the camp near Hendersonville, North Carolina, an area that was already patronized by southern Jews who came for vacations at "Jewish" hotels like the Osceola Lakeside Inn, which served kosher meals. They named the camp "Blue Star" because they wanted "something 'Jewish' and something 'camping.'" Blue Star also referenced the flag of the new state of Israel and its pioneer kibbutz movement. The Popkins clearly promoted a connection between their camping program for Jewish youth in the United States and the pioneer youth movement in Israel.

80. Judy G. Ringel, *Children of Israel: The Story of Temple Israel, Memphis, Tennessee: 1854–2004* (Memphis: Temple Israel Books, 2004), 73.

81. Ibid.

82. Ibid., 75.

83. Joe Erber, Greenwood, Miss., *Delta Jews*, dir. Mike DeWitt, 1999.

84. Leanne Silverblatt, Indianola, Miss., *Delta Jews*, dir. Mike DeWitt.

85. *American Jewish Year Book, 2002* (Philadelphia: American Jewish Committee, 2002), 254–55. The catastrophic hurricanes of 2005 have rewritten the histories of the Gulf South and those who call it home, including thousands of Jewish southerners. Our hearts go out to all who were displaced from their homes, with hopes for their return to these historic communities, so dear to us as historians and as friends and family.

86. South Florida's Jewish community has received its own anthology in the Brandeis

Series in American Jewish History, Culture, and Life. See Andrea Greenbaum, ed., *Jews of South Florida* (Waltham, Mass.: Brandeis University Press, 2005).

87. Wilson and Ferris, *Encyclopedia of Southern Culture*, xv.

88. The argument that Jewish southerners embrace a distinctive expression of American Jewish life is informed by the work of C. Vann Woodward, W. J. Cash, George Tindall, and David Potter, who raised the question of southern identity and whose work was followed by Bertram Wyatt-Brown, Carl Degler, Edward Ayers, Charles Wilson, Charles Joyner, and many others. Central to their premise is the belief that the South as a region was distinct from the rest of the nation because, as David Blight explains, the South was conquered and had to be reimagined and re-created. Blight contends that the South is not richer in history and memory than any other region, but more of its collective energy is devoted to making meaning of the past through historical narratives. For generations, southerners, including the descendants of Jewish immigrants, have struggled to make sense of their experience through their own family histories.

89. Bauman, *The Southerner as American*, 6, 19, 30.

90. The South has always existed as a region distinct from the rest of the nation. Geography, climate, history, and economy shaped the southern experience. Historians attribute the South's distinctiveness and its strong sense of place to the legacy of slavery, the region's slow economic recovery after the Civil War, the South's commitment to agriculture, the pervasiveness of Protestant fundamentalism, the rural character of the region, the predominance of folk culture, the mix of African American and Anglo-American cultures, and the small number of ethnic groups who settled in the region.

91. Leonard Rogoff, *Homelands: Southern Jewish Identity in Durham and Chapel Hill, North Carolina* (Tuscaloosa: University of Alabama Press, 2001), 21.

92. Louis D. Rubin Jr., *My Father's People: A Family of Southern Jews* (Baton Rouge: Louisiana State University Press, 2002), 2–3.

1

ONE RELIGION, DIFFERENT WORLDS
SEPHARDIC AND ASHKENAZIC IMMIGRANTS
IN EIGHTEENTH-CENTURY SAVANNAH

MARK I. GREENBERG

On July 11, 1733, forty-one Jews aboard the schooner *William and Sarah* landed in the fledgling Georgia colony.[1] Their harrowing five-month journey had included damage to their boat in England's Thames River and a near shipwreck off the North Carolina coast. The weary travelers joined 275 Christian inhabitants already settled on the bluffs above the Savannah River. Only five months earlier James Oglethorpe had landed with a charter from King George II and the financial support of trustees to found a refuge for England's poor. The king hoped that by cultivating the desolate lands of America, the new settlers "might not only gain a comfortable subsistence, but also strengthen his Majesty's colonies and increase the trade, navigation, and wealth of his Majesty's realms."[2]

The story of Jews' early arrival to Savannah has appeared in published sources for nearly two hundred years. Over the past three decades, several important books and many more excellent essays have significantly expanded an understanding of the topic.[3] Less well known are the enduring effects of the Spanish and Portuguese Inquisitions on Jews in America's southern colonies. Georgia's eighteenth-century Sephardic (Iberian) and Ashkenazic (Germanic) settlers came from different worlds. Centuries of history, language, liturgy, and religiosity separated the secretive and assimilated Portuguese from their persecuted but proud German coreligionists. Understanding differences and similarities in Jewish history and culture *prior* to settlement in the New World sheds additional light on the conflict and cooperation that characterized Jewish communal life in early Savannah.

The impetus for the *William and Sarah*'s journey stemmed from conditions in London's Jewish community. Faced with an influx of poor Jews from Portugal, and smaller numbers from Germany, three leaders of London's wealthy Spanish-

Portuguese congregation, Bevis Marks, had received commissions from the Georgia Trustees in early 1732 to raise funds among their coreligionists for the colonization effort. The trustees assumed that collections from London Jewry would support prospective Protestant settlers. London's Jewish elites had other ideas. They viewed the Georgia venture as an opportunity to manage their financial commitment to the poor and to alleviate the perceived threat that these newcomers posed to their social status among London Christians.[4]

The prospect of Jews in Georgia upset the Common Council of the Trustees, which never expected Jews might choose to make the colony their home. Motivated by centuries-old antipathy toward Jews and Judaism, in December 1732, the council voted to bar their entry.[5] In January 1733, it agreed "that no Jews should be sent, and the deputations given them to collect should be revoked. . . . Besides, the report of our sending Jews has prevented several from subscribing to us."[6] Oglethorpe was unaware of these decisions when the group landed at Savannah on July 11. Taken off-guard by their arrival, he sought a legal opinion in Charleston on the subject of Jewish settlement in the colony. The Charleston lawyers held that because the Georgia charter guaranteed liberty of conscience and worship to all newcomers except "papists," Jews had to be admitted. The Georgia leader followed this advice.[7]

The arrival of Jews in Savannah and Oglethorpe's decision to admit them shocked the Common Council in London. The council secretary instructed Oglethorpe in an October letter to prevent the group from taking up permanent residence. "Use your best endeavours that the said Jews may be allowed no kind of settlement with any of the grantees, the Trustees being apprehensive they will be of prejudice to the Trade and Welfare of the Colony."[8] This correspondence crossed a letter from Oglethorpe, written in August, praising the Jews' good conduct, commending especially the skill of passenger Dr. Samuel Nunes Ribeiro, who had provided valuable medical attention to sick colonists during a yellow fever outbreak. Oglethorpe informed the trustees on August 12 of a "doctor of physick who immediately undertook our people and refused to take any pay for it. He proceeded by cold baths, cooling drinks and other cooling applications."[9] Although the epidemic had killed twenty, or 10 percent, of the residents, Nunes "entirely put a stop to it, so that not one died afterwards."[10] The Common Council met, debated, and fumed throughout much of the winter that Jews had arrived without its permission. In January 1734, it reiterated demands that London's Jewish commissioners return their licenses and remove the Jewish settlers from the colony. It was too late. By December 1733, Oglethorpe had assigned plots of land to fourteen men, and the Jewish arrivals began their new lives.[11]

Despite sharing a common religion and appearing culturally similar to the

Trustees, Oglethorpe, and most other Christians, Savannah's early Jews hailed from different European countries, spoke different languages, had different historical experiences, and adhered to dissimilar religious customs and practices. Thirty-four of those onboard the *William and Sarah* were from Portugal and thus of Sephardic background.[12] Dr. Nunes served as the group's leader, and his personal story sheds light on Portuguese Jewish history and culture prior to Georgia's colonization.

Dr. Diogo Nunes Ribeiro, as he was known in Portuguese records, belonged to a respected family in the north-central province of Beira. His father served as a procurator of the Customs House, and several family members practiced medicine. Among the doctor's prominent patients were Dominicans at the Lisbon monastery and, according to his daughter's memoirs, the Portuguese Grand Inquisitor. Unbeknownst to the Christians around him, Nunes lived a secret life. He was a crypto-Jew, like his ancestors for generations before him. The Catholic Church called these people *marranos*, or pigs.[13]

Nunes' story is part of the complex but fascinating history of Jews on the Iberian Peninsula. In 1492, the Spanish crown completed a four-centuries-long reconquest of Spain from the Moors, which included forced conversions of its Jews, by compelling the remaining Jewish community to adopt Catholicism or leave the country.[14] Thousands of Jews converted publicly but practiced Judaism behind closed doors. Approximately half of the one hundred thousand people who chose exile instead of conversion fled to Portugal, but within five years Spain's intolerance had spread across its western border.[15]

In 1497, King Manoel I, seeking to marry Ferdinand and Isabella's daughter, prohibited Jewish immigration and began forced conversions in Portugal. Promising not to investigate the personal lives of these "New Christians" too closely, Manoel inadvertently fostered development of a large crypto-Jewish community. Crypto-Jews dropped most overt Jewish symbols in order to maintain secrecy. Circumcision, prayer books and shawls (*tallesim*), Torah scrolls, *mezuzahs*, several public festivals, and the ritual slaughter of animals could not be maintained under close scrutiny. For centuries, Portugal's secret Jews remained cut off from European Jewish life and thus developed religious practices based on increasingly diluted traditions and curious Jewish-Catholic hybrids passed orally from one generation to the next.[16]

Loose oversight of Portugal's New Christians lasted barely forty years. In 1536, the Inquisition spread to Portugal. For the next three centuries, it sought to root out people who had lapsed back to Judaism or, worse, those who actively encouraged others to return to their ancient faith (judaisers). In 1702, a New Christian arrested and tortured by the Inquisition denounced Nunes as a fellow judaiser. According to the man's secret testimony, Nunes "had persuaded him to declare his faith in the Law of Moses, in which they would save their souls." An August 1703 warrant for his arrest and the seizure of his property opened a floodgate of new accusations from other New Christians in the Inquisition's custody. One person claimed that Nunes had disclosed his faith to her and had "spoken of the Great Fast (Kipur) and its dispensatory value." Another stated that he had told him about the "Passover of the Hebrews which ought to be kept for 2 or 3 days beforehand." Someone else declared that the doctor came to her house on a medical call "whereat certain practices took place and they declared their faith in the Law of Moses, by keeping sabbaths, not eating pork or shell-fish."[17]

In October 1703, Inquisition officials formally charged Nunes with judaising. According to Inquisitional records, he had separated himself from the Catholic faith, rejected the Trinity and Christ as the true Messiah, and observed various Jewish practices. Nunes denied the charges and attempted to mount a defense against his many secret accusers. Working blindly to reconstruct a list of those who might have enmity toward him, he correctly identified informants with whom he previously had quarreled and attempted to explain the petty motivations for their charges.[18]

Nunes finally succumbed to mounting pressure in July 1704, confessed to twenty acts of judaising, and repented. He admitted that approximately fifteen years earlier another judaiser had convinced him to believe in the Law of Moses and, though he could not practice Jewish ceremonies faithfully, to separate himself from the Catholic faith. He also reported that his own father had urged him to return to the family's ancient faith. A month later, Nunes suffered torture on the rack because he had failed to implicate his wife as an accomplice and others with whom he had clandestinely worshipped. In a September 1704 final judgment, the Inquisitional court upheld its charges against him but offered leniency in punishment. In the presence of Portugal's Inquisitor-General, Nunes publicly renounced his heresies. He swore to keep the events of his arrest, incarceration, and trial secret, and he received the holy sacrament. On November 6, 1704, fifteen months after his original arrest, he was conditionally released from prison but confined indefinitely to Lisbon. The Inquisition had treated Nunes mercifully.[19]

In the days following his ordeal, officials forced the doctor to give testimony against his wife, her parents, and various other relatives. The scope of new denunciations troubled the Lisbon Inquisition. At the September 1705 auto da fé in which his family was punished, one victim was burned at the stake and sixty-five given lesser sentences.[20] During the eighteenth century's first two decades, the Inquisition punished some 2,126 people in Portugal for practicing Judaism. Most received penances and imprisonment, but thirty-seven were burned.[21]

Faced with ever increasing oppression, at least 1,500 impoverished Portuguese Jews contracted with British and Dutch sea captains for secret passage to England between 1700 and 1735. London's Bevis Marks Synagogue paid the way for most refugees and supported them after their arrival. Nunes helped as well. His nephew and countless others fled thanks to his generosity. Finally, sometime in late spring 1726, Nunes and seventeen family members boarded a British brigantine anchored in the Tagus River and joined a growing flood escaping persecution in Portugal for religious freedom in England. For a short time he practiced medicine among Bevis Marks's poor. Five years later, he and his extended family constituted one-third of the *William and Sarah*'s passengers. Other once-secret Portuguese Jews accounted for all but seven of the remaining forty-one settlers to Georgia in July 1733.[22]

Far less is known of the specific European origins or experiences of the non-Sephardic Jews that arrived in Savannah with Nunes.[23] Abraham Minis and family, Benjamin Sheftall and his wife Perla, and bachelor Jacob Yowel were Ashkenazim—members of the branch of European Jews, historically Yiddish-speaking, who settled in northwest Europe, initially on the banks of the Rhine.[24] Minis probably was born in England, though his family likely had migrated westward from a German state, and Benjamin Sheftall came from Frankfurt an der Oder in Prussia to London about 1730.[25]

No records detail the Sheftalls, Minises, or Yowels in central Europe, but broad strokes can paint the environment in which they and their families lived before migrating to England sometime prior to 1732. Within the German states, Jews were spread unevenly, living in clusters of several dozen to several hundred people. Ninety percent of these Jews concentrated in small towns or villages where noblemen granted the community rights of residence and physical protection in return for high taxes.[26]

For their economic survival Jews depended almost entirely on trade, yet the ability to earn a living in this sphere was subject to severe limitations. Most crafts were closed to Jews, with the exception of those associated with the Jewish community's basic needs: kosher slaughtering, baking, and making articles for worship. Because officials also prohibited Jews from owning land, earning a living in agriculture was seriously curtailed. Jews clustered in irregular or distressed trades such as secondhand clothing, pawn brokering, peddling, and money lending. Since laws ordinarily prevented Jews from keeping shops, they had to seek out customers or trade illegally from their homes.[27] In rural areas they served as dealers in agricultural products and manufactured goods by exporting produce and livestock to market, importing finished wares required by farmers, and providing needed credit. In poorer regions, city merchants were not likely to grant small-scale and risky loans to unknown debtors or to accept produce in place of cash; therefore, many smallholders depended on Jewish middlemen for the movement of crops and credit between rural and urban areas.[28]

Jewish businessmen's intermediary role in the age of mercantilism made them an indispensable element throughout the German states. Unlike Catholic religious leaders, rabbinic scholars did not denigrate commerce and the profit motive, and thus historically Jews had engaged in commercial pursuits. The weakness of an indigenous capitalist and entrepreneurial class in seventeenth- and eighteenth-century Germanic states prompted princes and government officials to encourage limited Jewish settlement in their territories and to elevate a few Jewish businessmen to positions of economic power within their courts. Here, Jews drew upon an expansive network of coreligionists across central Europe to provide horses, cattle, and other goods during times of war and to serve as sources for diamonds and precious metals to fund the lavish lifestyles and political machinations of their absolutist monarchs. Horse-trading was an exclusive and prestigious position for a Jewish trader, as every prince wanted a good stable of horses for both civilian and military use.[29]

Virulent antisemitism and Jews' commercial and credit dealings contributed to constant friction in their relationship with the Christian population, especially the peasantry. Smallholders' seasonal needs often required that they seek loans, yet the uncertainties of a good harvest called into question their ability to repay. The association of Jewish creditors with economic ruin lay just below the surface in peasant consciousness and easily erupted into violence during times of crisis.[30] Economic, social, and political dislocations caused by military conflict also threatened Jews. During the Thirty Years War (1618–48) soldiers looted homes and synagogues and killed thousands of Jews across central Europe. Bloodthirsty Cossacks swept through eastern Europe in 1648 wreaking havoc in Jewish areas. Jews flooded westward, only to kindle resentment and anger in their new German homes.[31]

In a world of religious antipathies, economic inequalities, and personal uncertainties, seventeenth-century German Jews found solace in their synagogues and other communal institutions. Unlike Portugal, where Jews practiced secretly, Jewish activities in central Europe occurred openly. The synagogue served as the center of communal life, offering a focal point for worship, study, and celebration: weddings and other joyous occasions took place in the courtyard. Moreover, characteristic dress and residential clustering in the *Judengassen* (Jews' alleys) made Jews highly visible to their Christian neighbors. The nobility supported Jewish life by sanctioning *Landjudenschaften*, corporate self-governing bodies set up to administer Jewish affairs autonomously in each region. Led by a lay board, the communal organization regulated Jews' religious, social, and economic lives. Torah study and strict adherence to ancient Jewish customs, including dietary restrictions and Sabbath and holiday observance, were the norm. Frankfurt an der Oder, Benjamin Sheftall's home, contained a prestigious center of rabbinic learning and a publisher of Jewish texts.[32]

Two distinct Jewish cultures collided in early-eighteenth-century London. Minis, Sheftall, and Yowel felt at home at the German-speaking, orthodox Great Synagogue, located in the heart of the Jewish quarter for Ashkenazim, Duke's Place.[33] Nunes and four other Sephardic families that later sailed to Savannah affiliated with the city's Bevis Marks congregation, founded by fellow crypto-Jews in the early seventeenth century. Here fathers and sons underwent ritual circumcision, and husbands and wives remarried according to Jewish law.[34] These actions reveal their desire to put secrecy behind them and to sanctify their reunion with Judaism, but they could not erase centuries of isolation. Many crypto-Jews found it hard to adapt to the Orthodox Judaism practiced in London. Life in the colonies offered a chance to start again.

In the first years following settlement in Georgia, cultural differences between the Ashkenazim and Sephardim threatened to tear Savannah Jewry asunder. Some of the dissimilarities were linguistic. Minis, Sheftall, and Yowel felt most comfortable in German or a German-Hebrew hybrid.[35] The Portuguese knew neither. The arrival of seventy-eight Lutheran refugees from Salzburg in March 1734 reveals that the Ashkenazim had more in common with their fellow Germans than fellow Jews. The Salzburgers received a welcome from Benjamin Sheftall, and either Minis or Yowell.[36] The Reverend John Martin Boltzius, leader of the Salzburgers, noted in his journal the warm reception given to his flock by the two Jews and his future plans for them: "These Jews show a great love for us, and have promised to see us at our settlement, we hope we will preach the Gospel of Jesus Christ to them with good success. They are both born in Germany and speak good German."[37]

John Wesley shared Boltzius's goal for Savannah Jews' conversion, and he recognized Jews' linguistic differences. As an emissary of the Society for the Propagation of the Gospel, Wesley was expected to convert to Anglican Christianity people belonging to other faiths. To this end, he familiarized himself with Richard Kidder's The Demonstration of the Messias: In Which the Truth of the Christian Religion is Defended, Especially against the Jews and "began learning Spanish in order to converse with my Jewish parishioners; some of whom seem nearer the mind that was in Christ than many of those who called him Lord."[38] It is unclear whether Wesley meant that Jews already attended Anglican services or simply that he sought to bring them within the fold. Either way, speaking English to the

Sephardim would not suffice. Nunes served as his Spanish teacher, friend, and confidante throughout his short time in Savannah, though no evidence exists that Wesley had any success with his missionary efforts among the group.[39]

Other Christian leaders encountered early Savannah Jews and commented on their internal divisions. In July 1735, Reverend S. Quincy reported from Savannah to his Church of England mission headquarters in London on the Sephardim's and Ashkenazim's differing levels of religiosity. The Portuguese, he believed, had professed Christianity in Portugal or the Caribbean for some time and had dispensed with many Jewish practices. In fact, two young men sometimes came to his church, and thus some people thought them Christians. Quincy could not find out their true religious beliefs—"only that their education in these Countries where they were oblig'd to appear as Christians makes them less rigid and stiff in their way." He believed that the German Jews were much stricter in their religious practices and observance of Jewish law and unlikely to convert. "Their kindness shew'd to Mr. Boltzius and the Saltzburgers [sic], was owing to the Good temper and humanity of the people, and not to any inclination to Change their religion," he opined.[40]

The Reverend Boltzius noted that some Jews referred to themselves as Spanish and Portuguese, whereas others called themselves German Jews. The latter spoke "High German" and differed from the former in their religious services and in "other matters as well." In particular, the Spanish did not adhere closely to Jewish dietary laws and religious ceremonies.[41] In another letter Boltzius wrote that the German Jews wanted to be on good terms with their fellow countrymen and had done them small favors time and again. But as far as religion was concerned, they were unwilling to abandon Judaism, the Salzburgers' efforts to proselytize notwithstanding.[42]

Differences in language and religiosity may have hindered close relations, but they did not prevent Portuguese and German factions from uniting to preserve Judaism in Savannah. Ironically, the various proselytizing efforts underfoot may have pushed the two groups together.[43] In July 1735, following nearly two years of informal worship services held in people's homes, Savannah's Ashkenazic and Sephardic settlers formally gathered to establish Congregation Mickve Israel (Hope of Israel). Reverend Boltzius reported that they continued in temporary quarters for several more years, until services moved to "an old miserable hut" on Market Square (now Ellis Square), where "men and women [sat] separated" and "a boy speaking several languages and especially good in Hebrew is their reader and is paid for his services."[44] The young congregation received a second Torah, a Hanukkah menorah, and books from London's Sephardic community. Benjamin Sheftall purchased land for a Jewish cemetery to bury his infant son according to religious custom, and Savannah's third Jewish institution, a mikvah (ritual bath) was opened for the congregation's use on April 2, 1738.[45]

Establishing a congregation, cemetery, and ritual bath proved relatively easy compared with efforts to erect a synagogue. Reverend Boltzius recorded the years of strife in his correspondence. The Jews "want to build a Synagogue, but the Spanish and German Jews cannot come to terms. I do not know the special reason for this," he wrote in February 1738. The next year he elaborated. "They have no Synagogue, which is their own fault; the one element hindering the other in this regard. The German Jews believed themselves entitled to build a Synagogue and are willing to allow the Spanish Jews to use it with them in common; the latter, however, reject any such arrangement and demand preference for themselves."[46]

Precise reasons for the strife cannot be known for certain, but cultural differences likely dominated. More permanent and thus more significant than informal gatherings in people's homes, the design and operation of a synagogue generated heated debate and intractable divisions. Ashkenazim and Sephardim follow the same basic tenets of Judaism (both view the Babylonian Talmud as their ultimate authority), but significant variations exist in matters of detail and outlook. During worship services, the Torah scrolls are raised at different times in the service, the sanctuary's seating and ark placement have different arrangements, the prayers and their melodies vary in detail, even the Hebrew is not pronounced the same.[47] Given these and other significant cultural distinctions, heated arguments and deadlock on the look and function of a synagogue erupted between factions.

Ironically, a synagogue in Savannah mattered little to the divided factions just a few years later. Despite the addition of thirty-nine Sephardic immigrants from London and the birth of some twenty Jewish children in Georgia between 1733 and 1740, Savannah's Jewish population disintegrated in 1741.[48] Threat of a Spanish invasion of Georgia from Florida during the War of Jenkins' Ear (1739–42) haunted the Portuguese Jews and precipitated the community's collapse. Reminded of their ancestors' experiences, the Sephardim worried that should Spain conquer the colony, religious persecution would spread to Georgia. Nunes, now seventy-two years old, along with his son and daughter left for Charleston in August 1740. Others soon followed or went to New York. Only the German Sheftall and Minis families remained.[49] Not until 1774 would Savannah Jewry again meet for religious services.

In the decades preceding the American Revolution, Benjamin Sheftall and Abraham Minis prospered. Although both men began in Georgia as farmers, within a short time they had become merchants. In Minis's case, frequent flooding of his land made a life in agriculture unprofitable. In 1736, he began buying beef, pork, and butter from New York to sell to Thomas Causton, the colony's keeper of public stores. During the conflict between Spain and England in 1742, he traveled to New York City to purchase supplies, which he transported to Oglethorpe's forces at Fort Frederica on St. Simons Island.[50] As early as 1752, Sheftall referred to himself as a "storekeeper," and after 1760, legal documents consistently termed him a merchant. Benjamin's son Mordecai achieved considerable success as a merchant and large landowner. By the early 1760s, he engaged in timbering, saw milling, shipping, and selling manufactured goods from the Sheftall family's store. Mordecai's half-brother Levi developed a successful tannery near the city in the 1770s.[51]

In 1750, Benjamin Sheftall joined four other men to found the St. George's (or Union) Society to further the education of orphan children. The name "Union" was adopted after the first few years to emphasize that its founders subscribed to various religions yet were united around the brotherhood of man.[52] The organization's rules commanded members to contribute two pence weekly for the support of an orphan house, to hold regular meetings, and to celebrate the group's anniversary on April 23.[53]

With the outbreak of the Revolution, the city's small Jewish population was well situated economically and socially to hold positions of leadership. Mordecai Sheftall allied himself with Savannah Whigs and served as chairman of the Savannah Parochial Committee (similar to a county committee of safety) from 1775 to 1778. Levi Sheftall and Philip Minis (Abraham's son) assisted in the same body. In 1777, Mordecai received a commission as deputy commissary general of the Continental troops in Georgia and South Carolina, as well as commissary general of the Georgia troops, positions that made him a member of the Georgia General Staff. The following year, Major General Robert Howe promoted Sheftall, removing the deputy status. Providing troops with food and supplies proved especially difficult because of a lack of public funds throughout the war. In some instances Mordecai purchased goods with his own money and extended credit to the state and federal governments. Philip Minis lent almost eleven thousand dollars to the Revolutionary forces, funds that paid salaries and provisions for troops from North Carolina and Virginia.[54]

A sermon by Presbyterian minister John J. Zubly before the Georgia Provincial Congress in July 1775 suggests reasons why Jews actively participated in the colony's struggle for independence and why Georgia conferred important leadership positions on some of them. Zubly admonished the spirit of submission that other religious leaders had preached: "As to the Jewish religion it cannot be charged with favoring despotism. The whole system of that religion is so replete with laws against injustice and oppression; and by one of its rites it proclaimed liberty throughout the land to all the inhabitants thereof."[55]

The Sheftalls' and Minises' unfailing commitment to the Revolution caused them considerable hardship during the war. Most Jews, including Philip Minis, his wife and three children, and Levi Sheftall and family, fled to safety shortly before British troops captured Savannah in December 1778. In doing so, they left homes and businesses to an uncertain fate. Mordecai Sheftall and his fifteen-year-old son Sheftall Sheftall remained behind to fight the British, and Mordecai continued his responsibilities as commissary. They were soon captured and imprisoned onboard the British prison ship *Nancy* anchored in the river, in the British-held town of Sunbury, Georgia, and later on the island of St. Johns in Antigua. Upon their release two years later, they moved to the American-held city of Philadelphia, where they established ties with local Jews. In autumn 1779, Levi Sheftall and Philip Minis agreed to serve as guides for Commander Charles-Hector (Count d') Estaing and the French fleet during his ill-fated attempt to recapture Savannah. With the fall of Charleston in May 1780, Levi was again on the move—this time to Petersburg, Virginia. Distraught over separation from his family, he accepted a British offer of amnesty, returned to Charleston, and swore loyalty to the king. Savannah's Jews endured the rest of the war scattered in Georgia, Charleston, and Philadelphia.[56]

The departure of British troops from Savannah in December 1782 enabled residents who had fled to return. Mordecai Sheftall and family came back after two years in Philadelphia. While in Pennsylvania, he had purchased the schooner *Hetty* with several associates, had it outfitted as a privateer, and captured one British ship as a prize.[57] Back in Georgia, he resumed his Savannah mercantile business and began a campaign to clear Levi of charges that he was a Tory. In August 1785, Levi regained his citizenship and recommenced business activities. Rather than return to tanning and butchering, he used slave labor to develop farmland and timberland. Both Mordecai and Levi were elected to governmental positions following independence: Levi to alderman and fire master; Mordecai to city magistrate, warden, and state legislator.[58]

By 1785, the Minis and Sheftall families were no longer alone. Sephardim settled Savannah again and reconstituted a community moribund for more than four decades. Dr. Nunes' sons Moses and Daniel were among the returnees, but most were newcomers. In 1786, the community reestablished Congregation Mickve Israel under shared leadership, and a synagogue opened in a rented house in Broughton Street Lane. Philip Minis and Levi Sheftall served as the congregation's president and trustee, respectively. David Nunes Cardozo held the treasurer's position, and Emanuel De la Motta officiated during prayers. After learning of the incorporation of both an Episcopal and Congregational church by the Georgia General Assembly in late 1789, Mordecai Sheftall recommended in August 1790 that the Jews take advantage of Georgia's religious tolerance and apply for a charter for Mickve Israel. The congregation's adjunta (governing board) authorized Sheftall to appeal to Governor Edward Telfair, who in November 1790 granted the request.[59]

The rules and regulations governing Mickve Israel, written immediately following incorporation, suggest that the Ashkenazim and Sephardim had learned the art of accommodation. First and foremost, Mickve Israel followed examples set in colonial New York, Newport, and Charleston by adopting the Sephardic mode of worship. On the matter of religious observance inside and outside the synagogue, traditional Judaism prevailed. Men and women sat in separate sections of the sanctuary during services. Those who did not keep the Sabbath were subject to denial of synagogue honors. Engaging in business on the Sabbath or holidays was forbidden. The congregation prohibited its members from marrying outside the faith, and the offspring of mixed marriages were denied a Jewish burial. Finally, the board expected seat holders to eat kosher meat exclusively. The constitution gave the adjunta power to punish transgressors. In March 1792, the synagogue president and board members summoned Isaac Pollock, a Savannah merchant, to appear before them and explain why he had opened his store on the Sabbath.[60] Three years later, in 1795, the adjunta voted to deny two men the right to interment in the Jewish cemetery until they made "such concessions as the parnass [president] and adjunta shall think proper."[61]

What factors facilitated cooperation between Savannah's German and Portuguese Jews in 1790, whereas dissension had been predominant in the 1730s? Definitive answers are elusive, but it is likely that the composition of the Sephardim in the latter period played a role. Although the Sheftall and Minis families still composed the bulk of the city's German Jews, the Portuguese-Jewish population was almost entirely different in the post-Revolutionary period. Most of the original Sephardic settlers, described by the Reverends Boltzius and S. Quincy as nonreligious and confrontational, do not appear on the roster of Mickve Israel's charter members. The dozen or so Sephardic households that purchased pews after incorporation were mostly South Carolina natives and apparently held more conciliatory views and traditional Jewish beliefs than the founding generation.

The influences of time, space, and shared experiences in America also seem to have dampened differences. Portuguese and German Jews lived far from their native lands. Neither Germany's Landjudenschaften nor Portugal's Inquisitional courts guided Jewish practice in America. Instead, a half century of face-to-face interaction, a revolution against the British, and the reality of religious freedom fostered a new American national identity.[62] Mickve Israel's membership reveals the continuity of interaction. Of the twenty Jewish household heads located in the 1830 federal census, fourteen were congregants or the children of members in 1793.[63]

Intermarriage between the two groups also played a role in lessening differences and building understanding. With relatively few Ashkenazic Jews in America in the eighteenth century, the Sheftall family married Sephardim.[64] Levi Sheftall married Sarah De la Motta, daughter of Emanuel, in 1768; and Mordecai Sheftall and Frances Hart married in Charleston.[65] As distinctions between the groups broke down and cultures fused, compromise and cooperation increased. It was possible by 1800 to regard the city's Jews as a small, relatively cohesive ethnic community.

At the turn of the nineteenth century, Temple Mickve Israel had a dozen families, though numbers increased to eighty persons thirty years later. This growth paralleled Savannah's own development. The city's population increased 50 percent, from 5,166 in 1800 to 7,776 in 1830.[66] The community's expanding size, cooperation among its members, and their increasing financial resources permitted synagogue leaders to begin planning construction of a place of worship. In March 1820, a building committee, comprising Abraham DeLyon, David Leion, Moses and Sheftall Sheftall, and Jacob De la Motta, received a grant of land from the city—a lot at the corner of Whitaker Street and Perry Lane—and within four months Savannah's first synagogue was completed.[67] On June 23, 1820, acting cantor Jacob De la Motta led a processional into the new building.

De la Motta's address to the congregation that day demonstrates the existence of a Jewish community with an increasingly shared history and identity in America: "Assembled as we are, to re-establish by commemoration, the Congregation of this remnant, or small portion of the house of Israel; your expectation of a brief sketch of our History, and particularly as connected with a primeval residence in this City, and for many years past . . . shall be realized; and may I trust, it will not be uninteresting, as it will include the well known fact, that many Jews struggled, and sacrificed their dearest interest, for the independence of this country."[68]

The Jews' long history, De la Motta insisted, had much in common with the experience of all Americans: "The dawn of the Revolution, opened to their view, new scenes; and they revolved in their minds, the condition of their forefathers, who toiled and suffered under the yoke of servitude, during the reign of Pharoh. . . . Resolving to separate from the standard of Tyranny, they united with freemen for the general good; [and] contended for the independence of the states."[69] The successful overthrow of British rule and passage of a Constitution codified religious tolerance and protected Savannah Jews' right to practice their religion: "It is here, that we are reasonably to expect the enjoyment of those rewards for our constancy and sufferings, as promised by the word of God, when he declared he would not forsake us." To merit the continuation of God's favor and ensure a completion of His promise, De la Motta called for a "rigid adherence to his commandments, and an undeviating pursuit of that path, which by his protection, leads to that external and exalted kingdom, the haven of benignity."[70]

Rhetoric aside, De la Motta's sermon conveyed an important message. Jews had found freedom from religious persecution in America, but with that liberty came considerable change. Nearly one hundred years in Savannah had transformed its Jewish population. From two factions with different national and linguistic backgrounds and religious practices, a relatively cohesive community had taken shape. If in the 1730s Savannah's German Jews appeared to have more in common with the Salzburgers than their Portuguese coreligionists, by the 1820s economic growth, kinship ties, and the Revolution increasingly had brought Jews together for worship and fellowship. Many of these Jews and their descendants would remain in Savannah throughout the antebellum period, to be joined by increasing numbers of arrivals from South Carolina, Germany, and then eastern Europe.[71] Savannah Jewry would again face considerable internal tension. Eighteenth-century conflict between the Portuguese and Germans would seem insignificant compared with the social and religious battles raging between eastern European and German Jewry in 1900 Savannah.

NOTES

An earlier version of this essay appeared as "A 'Haven of Benignity': Conflict and Cooperation Between Eighteenth-Century Savannah Jews," *Georgia Historical Quarterly* 86 (Winter 2002): 544–68. It is published here courtesy of the Georgia Historical Society.

1. According to Malcolm H. Stern's definitive essay, "New Light on the Jewish Settlement of Savannah," *American Jewish Historical Quarterly* 52 (March 1963): 176, forty-two Jews left London aboard one ship; however, Isaac Nunes Henriques' child died at sea.

2. F. D. Lee and J. L. Agnew, *Historical Record of the City of Savannah* (Savannah, Ga.: J. H. Estill, 1869), 2–3.

3. For examples of early writings by state and local and American Jewish historians, see Mark I. Greenberg, "A 'Haven of Benignity': Conflict and Cooperation between Eighteenth-Century Savannah Jews," *Georgia Historical Quarterly* 86 (Winter 2002): 544n.1, 545n.2.

4. Jacob R. Marcus, *The Colonial American Jew, 1492–1776*, 3 vols. (Detroit: Wayne State

University Press, 1970), 1:351–52; B. H. Levy, "Early History of Georgia's Jews," in *Forty Years of Diversity: Essays on Colonial Georgia*, ed. Harvey H. Jackson and Phinizy Spaulding (Athens: Univeristy Press of Georgia, 1984) 164.

5. On the enormous literature exploring the depth and breadth of European anti-semitism, see Susan Sarah Cohen, ed., *Antisemitism: An Annotated Bibliography* (New York: Garland, 1987); Bernard Glassman, *Anti-Semitic Stereotypes without Jews: Images of Jews in England, 1290–1700* (Detroit: Wayne State University Press, 1975); Gavin I. Langmuir, *History, Religion, and Antisemitism* (Berkeley: University of California Press, 1990); Lionel B. Steiman, *Paths to Genocide: Antisemitism in Western History* (New York: St. Martin's Press, 1998).

6. Quoted in John Earl Perceval, *Manuscripts of the Earl of Egmont*, 3 vols. (London: H. M. Stationary, 1920–23), 1:309, 313.

7. Robert G. McPherson, ed., *The Journal of the Earl of Egmont* (Athens: University of Georgia Press, 1962), 12; Marcus, *Colonial American Jew*, 1:356.

8. Quoted in Amos Aschbach Ettinger, *James Edward Oglethorpe* (Oxford: Clarendon, 1936), 137.

9. Oglethorpe to Trustees, August 12, 1733, in Mills Lane, ed., *General Oglethorpe's Georgia: Colonial Letters, 1733–1743*, 2 vols. (Savannah, Ga.: Beehive, 1975), 1:19–23.

10. Lee and Agnew, *Historical Record of the City of Savannah*, 8–9; R. D. Barnett, "Dr. Samuel Nunes Ribeiro and the Settlement of Georgia," in *Migration and Settlement: Papers on Anglo-American Jewish History Held in London Jointly by the Jewish Historical Society of England and the American Jewish Historical Society, July 1970*, rapporteur, Audrey Newman (London: Jewish Historical Society of England, 1971): 63–97; Perceval, *Manuscripts of the Earl of Egmont*, 1:440.

11. Ettinger, *James Edward Oglethorpe*, 137; Allen D. Candler, *The Colonial Records of the State of Georgia*, 26 vols. (Atlanta, Ga.: Franklin, 1904–16), 1:75; E. Merton Coulter and Albert B. Saye, eds., *A List of the Early Settlers of Georgia* (Athens: University of Georgia Press, 1949). It appears that the fourteen Jews who received land from Oglethorpe had purchased it. On this point, see Levy, "Early History of Georgia's Jews," 168.

12. The word *Sephardic* originates from *Sepharad*, the usual Hebrew designation for the Iberian Peninsula. Sephardic Jews descend from those who lived in Spain or Portugal before the expulsion of 1492.

13. Richard D. Barnett, "Zipra Nunes's Story," in *A Bicentennial Festschrift for Jacob Rader Marcus*, ed. Bertram Wallace Korn (New York: Ktav, 1976), 49.

14. An enormous literature exists on the Jews of Spain. See Robert Singerman, comp., *Spanish and Portuguese Jewry: A Classified Bibliography* (Westport, Conn.: Greenwood, 1993). The best recent overview is Jane S. Gerber, *The Jews of Spain: A History of the Sephardic Experience* (New York: Free Press, 1992).

15. David M. Gitlitz, *Secrecy and Deceit: The Religion of the Crypto-Jews* (Philadelphia: Jewish Publication Society, 1996), 74.

16. The most comprehensive treatment of crypto-Jewish religious practices appears in Gitlitz, *Secrecy and Deceit*. Other good sources include Norman Roth, *Conversos, Inquisition, and the Expulsion of the Jews from Spain* (Madison: University of Wisconsin, 1995); B. Netanyahu, *The Marranos of Spain from the Late 14th to the Early 16th Century*, 3rd ed. (Ithaca, N.Y.: Cornell University Press, 1999); and Michael Alpert, *Crypto-Judaism and the Spanish Inquisition* (New York: Palgrave, 2001).

17. Barnett, "Dr. Samuel Nunes Ribeiro," 66–68.

18. Ibid., 69–71.

19. Ibid., 71–72.

20. An *auto da fé* (act of faith) was a public ceremony intended to show the Church's majesty and the convicted heretic's debasement. On an announced day, people gathered in a city's principal plaza to watch accused prisoners in penitential garments hear their offenses and receive their penance. See Gitlitz, *Secrecy and Deceit*, 21.

21. Barnett, "Zipra Nunes's Story," 47–50.

22. Barnett, "Dr. Samuel Nunes Ribeiro," 77–79, 84; Richard Barnett, "Dr. Jacob de Castro Sarmento and Sephardim in Medical Practice in 18th-Century London," in *Jewish Historical Society of England: Transactions*, 36 vols. (London: Jewish Historical Society of England, 1982): 27:90, 110–11; Stern, "New Light on the Jewish Settlement of Savannah," 176–77.

23. Malcolm H. Stern, "The Sheftall Diaries: Vital Records of Savannah Jewry (1733–1808)," *American Jewish Historical Quarterly* 54 (March 1965): 246–47, offers no details on the family's life prior to arrival.

24. *Encyclopaedia Judaica*, 16 vols. (Jerusalem: Keter, 1971), 3:719.

25. John McKay Sheftall, "The Sheftalls of Savannah: Colonial Leaders and Founding Fathers of Georgia Judaism," in *Jews of the South: Selected Essays from the Southern Jewish Historical Society*, ed. Samuel Proctor and Louis Schmier, with Malcolm Stern (Macon, Ga.: Mercer University Press, 1984), 66; Kaye Kole, *The Minis Family of Georga, 1733–1992* (Savannah: Georgia Historical Society, 1992), 3; B. H. Levy, *Mordecai Sheftall: Jewish Revolutionary Patroit* (Savannah: Georgia Historical Society, 1999), 1, 3.

26. Mordecai Breuer and Michael Graetz, *German-Jewish History in Modern Times*, ed. Michael A. Meyer, 4 vols. (New York: Columbia University Press, 1996), 1:82, 191.

27. David S. Landes, "The Jewish Merchant: Typology and Stereotypology in Germany," *Leo Baeck Institute Yearbook* 19 (1974): 11–13; Breuer and Graetz, *German-Jewish History in Modern Times*, 1:27–43.

28. Monika Richarz, "Emancipation and Continuity: German Jews in the Rural Economy," in *Revolution and Evolution: 1848 in German-Jewish History*, ed. Werner E. Mosse, Arnold Pauker, and Reinhard Rürup (Tübingen: Mohr, 1981), 95–96; Werner J. Cahnman, "Village and Small-Town Jews in Germany: A Typological Study," *Leo Baeck Institute Yearbook* 19 (1974): 111.

29. Werner E. Mosse, *Jews in the German Economy: The German-Jewish Elite, 1820–1935*

(Oxford: Clarendon, 1987), 24–29; Richarz, "Emancipation and Continuity," 99; Hasia R. Diner, *A Time for Gathering: The Second Generation, 1820–1880* (Baltimore, Md.: Johns Hopkins University Press, 1992), 11. For a discussion of court Jews' roles in the German economy, see Breuer and Graetz, *German-Jewish History in Modern Times*, 1:104–26.

30. William Zvi Tannenbaum, "From Community to Citizenship: The Jews of Rural Franconia, 1801–1862" (Ph.D. diss., Stanford University, 1989), 224.

31. Breuer and Graetz, *German-Jewish History in Modern Times*, 1:97–98.

32. Ibid., 1:166–224.

33. Vivian D. Lipman, *Three Centuries of Anglo-Jewish History* (Cambridge: Jewish Historical Society of England, 1961), 54; Todd M. Endelman, *The Jews of Georgian England, 1714–1830* (Philadelphia: Jewish Publication Society of America, 1979), 47; Cecil Roth, *The Great Synagogue, London, 1690–1940* (London: E. Goldston, 1950), 144. Meticulous records kept by London's Sephardic congregation contain no references to Sheftall, Minis, or Yowell, suggesting that if they belonged to a synagogue, it was Ashkenazic.

34. "R. D. Barnett, ed., "The Circumcision Register of Isaac and Abraham de Paiba (1715–1775)," in *Bevis Marks Records*, 6 vols. (Oxford: J. Johnson, 1940–97), 4:61, 62, 71; Barnett, "Dr. Samuel Nunes Ribeiro," 79, 81–82; Stern, "New Light on the Jewish Settlement of Savannah," 175–76; Richard D. Barnett and Abraham Levy, *The Bevis Marks Synagogue* (London: Society of Heshaim, 1970), 10. A sixth Sephardic couple on the *William and Sarah* remarried in Amsterdam.

35. Benjamin Sheftall (1691–1765) and his son Levi (1739–1809) kept a diary in Juedisch-Deutsch (Yiddish) from 1733 to 1808. The original did not survive, but two English translations may be found in folder 25, box 23, Keith Reid Manuscript Collection, Hargrett Library, University of Georgia Library. For an annotated version of the two diaries, see Stern, "Sheftall Diaries: Vital Records of Savannah Jewry," 243–77.

36. Stern, "New Light on the Jewish Settlement of Savannah," 184.

37. Boltzius journal entries of March 14 and 20, 1734, quoted in Leon Hühner, "The Jews of Georgia in Colonial Times," *Publications of the American Jewish Historical Society* 10 (1902): 75–76.

38. John Wesley, *The Journal of John Wesley*, ed. Percy Livingstone Parker (Chicago: Moody Press, 1952), 43.

39. John C. English, "John Wesley and His 'Jewish Parishioners': Jewish-Christian Relationships in Savannah, Georgia, 1736–1737," *Methodist History* 36 (July 1998): 222–23.

40. Quoted in Stern, "New Light on the Jewish Settlement of Savannah," 184.

41. Letter from Boltzius dated July 3, 1739, in Hühner, "Jews of Georgia in Colonial Times," 76–77.

42. Stern, "New Light on the Jewish Settlement of Savannah," 186.

43. Ibid., 185; David T. Morgan, "Judaism in Eighteenth-Century Georgia," *Georgia Historical Quarterly* 58 (Spring 1974): 43.

44. Quoted in Levy, "Early History of Georgia's Jews," 169.

45. Saul Jacob Rubin, *Third to None: The Saga of Savannah Jewry, 1733–1983* (Savannah, Ga.: Mickve Israel Congregation, 1983), 5; Sheftall, "Sheftalls of Savannah," 68.

46. Quoted in Levy, "Early History of Georgia's Jews," 170; Stern, "New Light on the Jewish Settlement of Savannah," 185.

47. *Encyclopaedia Judaica*, 14:1,168–70.

48. Stern, "New Light on the Jewish Settlement of Savannah," 181–82. At least ten ships brought Jews from London to Savannah between 1733 and 1738, including arrivals on November 12 and December 30, 1733. Philip Minis, born July 11, 1734, is considered the first Jewish white male child conceived and born in Georgia. See Kole, *Minis Family of Georgia*, 24.

49. Stern, "New Light on the Jewish Settlement of Savannah," 193; Barnett, "Dr. Samuel Nunes Ribeiro," 87–88. Jacob Yowell had died in September 1736.

50. Kole, *Minis Family of Georgia*, 3–4; Stern, "New Light on the Jewish Settlement of Savannah," 188–89.

51. Sheftall, "Sheftalls of Georgia," 69, 71–72. Mordecai Sheftall's life is told in considerable detail in Levy, *Mordecai Sheftall*.

52. Leon Hühner, "Jews of Georgia from the Outbreak of the American Revolution to the Close of the 18th Century," *Publications of the American Jewish Historical Society* 17 (1909): 90.

53. Lee and Agnew, *Historical Record of the City of Savannah*, 19, 25, 183–85.

54. Sheftall, "Sheftalls of Georgia," 73; Kole, *Minis Family of Georgia*, 25; Levy, *Mordecai Sheftall*, 65.

55. Hühner, "Jews of Georgia from the Outbreak of the American Revolution to the Close of the 18th Century," 89.

56. Ibid., 94, 99–103; Sheftall, "Sheftalls of Georgia," 74–75; Kole, *Minis Family of Georgia*, 28.

57. For more on these activities, see Levy, *Mordecai Sheftall*, 85–88.

58. Ibid., 96–97; Sheftall, "Sheftalls of Georgia," 76–77.

59. Rubin, *Third to None*, 39; Morgan, "Judaism in Eighteenth-Century Georgia," 48; Minutes of Congregation Mickve Israel, August 29, 1790, Savannah Jewish Archives, Georgia Historical Society, Savannah.

60. Morgan, "Judaism in Eighteenth-Century Georgia," 50.

61. Rubin, *Third to None*, 47, 50, 52, 55; Jacob Rader Marcus, *American Jewry: Documents; Eighteenth Century* (Cincinnati, Ohio: Hebrew Union College Press, 1959), 179; Minutes of Congregation Mickve Israel, October 4, 1791, September 17, 1793, September 20, 1795.

62. Samuel Rezneck, *Unrecognized Patriots: The Jews in the American Revolution* (Westport, Conn.: Greenwood, 1975), 48, 60, 203–4, 221.

63. Rubin, *Third to None*, 52; Ira Rosenwaike, *On the Edge of Greatness: A Portrait of American Jewry in the Early National Period* (Cincinnati, Ohio: American Jewish Archives, 1985), 156.

64. Ira Rosenwaike estimates that as late as 1830 approximately 10 percent of Jewish households in America were German. See Rosenwaike *On the Edge of Greatness*, 39.

65. Malcolm H. Stern, comp., *First American Jewish Families: 600 Genealogies, 1654–1988*, 3rd ed. (Baltimore, Md.: Ottenheimer Publishers, 1991), 267.

66. Jacob Rader Marcus, *To Count a People: American Jewish Population Data, 1585–1984* (Lanham, Md.: University Press of America, 1990), 52–53; Rosenwaike, *On the Edge of Greatness*, 31; Department of the Interior, Census Office, *Report on the Social Statistics of Cities*, pt. 2 (Washington, D.C.: Government Printing Office, 1887), 173.

67. Rubin, *Third to None*, 63–64; Minutes of Congregation Mickve Israel, April 25, 1820.

68. Quoted in Morris Schappes, *A Documentary History of the Jews in the United States, 1654–1875* (New York: Citadel, 1950), 151.

69. Ibid., 153–54.

70. Ibid., 155.

71. On nineteenth-century Savannah Jewry, see Mark I. Greenberg, "Creating Ethnic, Class, and Southern Identity in Nineteenth-Century America: The Jews of Savannah, Georgia, 1830–1880" (Ph.D. diss., University of Florida, 1997); Greenberg, "Becoming Southern: The Jews of Savannah, Georgia, 1830–1870," *American Jewish History* 86 (March 1998): 55–75; and Greenberg, "Savannah's Jewish Women and the Shaping of Ethnic and Gender Identity, 1830–1900," *Georgia Historical Quarterly* 82 (Winter 1998): 751–74.

2

AMERICAN, JEWISH, SOUTHERN, MORDECAI
CONSTRUCTING IDENTITIES TO 1865

EMILY BINGHAM

There once was a Jewish family in the South that thought of itself as a "little band of love and duty." So countless stories might begin, but this essay takes advantage of the intimate terrain of familial relationships to examine and perhaps move beyond what one scholar has called "the dialectics of assimilation." Mordecai family members in North Carolina each confronted the task of determining what it meant to be Jewish, southern, American, and a Mordecai. And despite their vaunted closeness, responses from within the extended clan ranged from energetic orthodoxy to nonpracticing but fully identified Jewishness to intermarriage to outright apostasy. Such choices evoke stereotypes—of "good" or "bad" Jews, of loyalty, carelessness, or crass self-interest—yet this tendency to weigh and measure historical phenomena for Jewish authenticity or corruption, survival or dilution, oversimplifies and dehumanizes the narrative of Jewish history in America and the South.[1]

By looking closely at the lives of Jacob Mordecai and three of his children—Rachel Mordecai Lazarus, Emma Mordecai, and Alfred Mordecai—this essay tracks four southern Jews establishing their place in America's first century. While it has become a common refrain among students of the Jewish South that the region can claim the early nineteenth century's most populous Jewish community, a certain defensiveness clings to the study of southern Jewry.[2] Over the past decade or two a steady stream of fiction, memoirs, exhibits, scholarly books and articles, along with the revitalized Southern Jewish Historical Society and its publication, *Southern Jewish History* have added greatly to what we know about Jews in the South. Early southern Jewry has received less attention. Further research is needed to clarify the still opaque experience of pre–Civil War Jews and to provide the context for Jews who later settled in the region.[3]

Threading through the Mordecais' story is the question of how southern, or how distinctive, the South really was. Part of the answer is that regional distinctions widened over the period in which the Mordecai story unfolds. Jacob and his first wife, Judy, migrated from New York in 1787, a time when slaves were held legally throughout the nation. Without pretending any one family could fully answer what it meant either to be southern or American Jews for a given era, such questions are worth asking of this family, for the simple reason that their papers are the most extensive we have. Unlike most of their coreligionists, the Mordecais' move to a small North Carolina town far from any significant Jewish center, was a path more commonly taken by Jews after the Civil War. The Mordecais' complex interactions with the majority Christian community may also seem familiar to many later American Jews. The family relied on a myth built on bourgeois domesticity, Enlightenment rationality, religious tolerance, and inclusive American opportunity as a bulwark against endemic social slights, repeated economic reverses, challenges to Jewish tradition, and, eventually, a Civil War that upset the very meaning of patriotism.

Telling the Mordecais' stories means looking closely at religious expression, doubt, searching, assimilation. But to view the family solely in that light is to forget that each member was as bewildered concerning what it meant to be a good American in a rapidly changing nation as to what it meant to be a good Jew. Generations later, in the wake of the Holocaust, with communal survival at stake, assimilation (or resistance to it) became a litmus test for American Jews. Such concerns did not preoccupy Jacob Mordecai and his children in Warrenton, North Carolina. Bertram Korn wrote in 1964 that the antebellum generation of southern Jews concerned itself more with economic stabilization and success than religious or ethnic survival. In part because of their small numbers and the relative lack of restrictions on Jews' activity, Korn noted, "Judaism was not their whole life."[4] To see assimilation as only a shorthand for a religious conundrum is to miss the real value of telling the Mordecai story, for assimilation here is defined not as the loss of Jewish identity but as the social, political, religious, and cultural evolution that has for centuries marked the American Jewish experience.

Jacob Mordecai, Esq., was almost certainly the only participant in tiny Warrenton, North Carolina's 1808 July 4 celebration who as a child had escorted members of the Continental Congress into Philadelphia. Now in his middle years, clad in a white vest, pantaloons, and an olive-colored coat, he marched to the Warren County courthouse where a seventeen-gun salute marked the thirty-second anniversary of American independence. Jacob's parents were colonial immigrants: his father was a merchant of modest means whose much younger wife converted to Judaism. Born in 1762, Jacob had several years of schooling before taking a clerkship in Philadelphia with the merchant David Franks, who made

MORDECAI FAMILY TREE

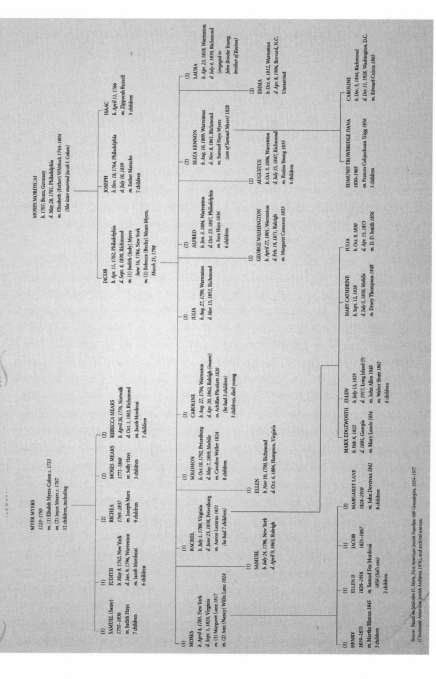

Mordecai family tree. *Genealogy chart by Jeffrey L. Ward.*

his fortune in fur and in purveying the British army during the French and Indian War. Franks maintained strong business ties with Jews, but married a Christian and raised his children in their mother's faith. Arrested and jailed on suspicion of collaborating with the British, Franks fled to England in 1780.[5]

This first job augured ill for Jacob. Then his mother, widowed during the war, remarried; her husband, Jacob I. Cohen, operated a fledgling mercantile and investment firm in Richmond, Virginia, and offered to make young Jacob a junior partner. But a shadow fell across this situation as well. Cohen, a descendent of the ancient Hebrew priestly line, broke Jewish law when he married a convert, and members of Philadelphia's synagogue were banned from participating in the union. At the age of twenty, Jacob was already tarred by his association with a British loyalist; now his mixed ancestry was a community scandal. Under such circumstances, an opportunity in distant Richmond may have looked especially appealing.[6]

One of those dismayed by Cohen's marriage was the colonial silversmith, Myer Myers. On a 1783 visit to Philadelphia from Richmond, Jacob met his hazel-eyed daughter, Judy, who shared his love of books. Upon returning to Richmond, he begged her to "endeavor my dearest girl to render mutual an affection which I have no doubt will tend to make life's tedious length with pleasure roll." It would be another year before the couple married, and then only after Jacob promised Myer Myers not to take her to any such godforsaken backwater as Virginia. This meant dissolving his partnership in Richmond, angering his stepfather, embarrassing his mother, and walking away from a solid business.[7]

After several years and no success in New York, Jacob once more turned his sights southward. The old silversmith relented, and the couple eventually settled in the village of Warrenton, North Carolina, in the state's eastern plantation district, where Jacob opened a store. They were the town's only Jews. Abiding affection for one another had carried them through difficulty and toward ease and comfort, making Judy's death in 1796 after eleven years of marriage particularly bitter. For Judy, as for countless women during this period, childbirth was a gate to the grave. But the enlightened values and family intimacy she cultivated would guide the Mordecais long after her death, Jacob's remarriage to her sister, and the birth of seven more children to join the six they had together.

In a long letter addressed to their offspring, Jacob set out the precepts his wife would have wanted them to follow in the face of their loss—as Jews, as newcomers to the South, and as Americans in a free society. This covenant, part memorial, part ethical will, became the Mordecais' road map to virtue. Religious duties received but passing acknowledgment. Shot through with Enlightenment ideals regarding reason and human progress, the letter laid out Judy's and Jacob's expectations. The Mordecais would aim for the highest levels of intellectual cultivation, family solidarity, and dedication to useful work. Theirs would be a loving family, sensitive to feelings, yet also a rational family that valued education, ideas, and books, and a liberal family that tolerated people of all faiths, embracing "virtue in whatever garb it" might appear.[8]

It was a delicate balance, always. On her deathbed, Judy asked her husband to "omit such parts" from the funeral service, which, "as from their novelty will make my Mordecai appear ridiculous." On the other hand, one of Jacob and Judy's daughters later sharply criticized her brother for his willingness to shed his Jewish affiliation in order to win the hand of a Christian. In their yearning for security, prosperity, and acceptance in a new region, the Mordecais fused middle-class domesticity, faith in reason, and religious liberalism into a set of ideas I have called "enlightened domesticity."[9]

Jacob and Judy's eldest daughter, Rachel, was eight when her mother died, old enough to absorb her precepts. Judy had strong and progressive ideas about childrearing and employed neither corporal punishment nor material rewards with her offspring.[10] Not surprisingly, Rachel set out to fill her mother's place in the family, as Jacob's intellectual partner, as a teacher of younger siblings, and as a paragon of the Mordecai standards and values.[11] As she matured, it became clear that Rachel possessed an extraordinary mind, the kind that seemed to absorb knowledge without effort, and, though she had only a brief formal education, she read widely and relentlessly cultivated learning throughout her life.[12]

Rachel was twenty—well on her way to spinsterhood—that Fourth of July in 1808 in Warrenton. The following week her father, struggling under bankruptcy, decided to open a female academy. The market for female education was expanding, and the local girls' school was in decline, but this was something no American Jew had ever attempted. While her elder brothers launched careers, Rachel had felt like a burden and often wished she could have "been a son" and helped her father by "doing something for my own support." When Jacob realized that he needed assistance and that Rachel could help him with the teaching, her wish came true.[13]

It was a heady, happy time for Rachel. Though she would not have liked anyone to say so, for the next ten years she effectively headed a successful business—the first profitable long-term business of Jacob's life. For public purposes it was vital to have a man at the helm of an educational institution, and theirs was known as "Mr. Mordecai's school." While Jacob and Rachel divided teaching duties at first, the father never achieved the daughter's confidence in the classroom. Increasingly, Jacob turned to Rachel for her opinion on school matters, and was nearly always "directed by it." It was a productive partnership that ostensibly preserved the lines of patriarchal power.[14]

Jacob's eldest daughter, Rachel Mordecai, protested the depiction of Jews in the work of the popular Anglo-Irish novelist Maria Edgeworth (1767–1849), prompting Edgeworth to pen an apology in the form of Harrington (1817). The two women remained friends, corresponding until Rachel's death in 1838. Engraving from the original painting of Edgeworth by Alonzo Chappel. By permission of the British Library, London.

The student body at Mr. Mordecai's school came overwhelmingly from Gentile families, but there were a handful of Jewish boarders whose parents were otherwise hard-pressed to find an institution where the curriculum was not infused with Christian teachings.[15] Religion could not be altogether avoided, however, and, in the school's second year, Warrenton was swept up into what textbooks blandly call the Second Great Awakening. Rachel's sister Ellen described neighbors "turning religious as fast as they can conveniently fall, without hurting, one another." The Mordecais took a dim view of such things, and occasionally attended evangelical gatherings to gawk at the assembly and critique the preaching. But this time Jacob went to revival meetings on his own and rumors began to circulate that he would convert.[16]

Jacob later wrote that during this period he was "estranged from his brethren in faith" and met the earnest invitations of friendly Christians "with a mind little trammeled by the religion" of his birth.[17] Mixed ancestry, frequent insolvency, and twenty years of geographic isolation had set Jacob and his family on the margins of the Jewish community. The Mordecais had plenty of Jewish company, however, in their somewhat haphazard religious practice, which in no way signaled a rejection of Judaism. Apostasy was something else entirely—whereas spotty observance drew criticism from certain Jewish quarters, converts were shunned.[18]

Jacob stood between two worlds. On one side were Warrenton neighbors and friends who had known Jacob for years. All were Gentiles, and for some of them religion had gained a powerful new personal meaning.[19] But on the other side was a long and ugly Old World tradition of forced conversions and violent religious persecution, endowing the conversion of a Jew with particular triumph and tarnishing Christian proselytism of any kind. While American Jews in this era experienced antisemitic discrimination in far less acute ways, the Second Great Awakening made it increasingly difficult to claim, as Rachel did, that religious affiliation "scarcely" mattered in the United States, the South, or their own village.[20]

Jacob retreated from this Rubicon, and let it be known to family and fellow Jews that he would never cross it. But it changed him, and over the next decade he rededicated himself to the faith of his birth. After twenty years in the hinterlands, Jacob found himself mourning the distance stretching between Warrenton and a Jewish community. To make up for it he began to study. Theological books requisitioned from far afield gradually filled his library. His debates with zealous Christian ministers over the divinity of Jesus were stored for family use and copied for interested fellow Jews in order that they could better answer their non-Jewish "friends" when the discussion turned to religion.[21] Jacob's curiosity about, if not flirtation with, Christianity and his subsequent public dis-avowal of its appeal to him presaged struggles to come. For her part, Rachel spent her twenties working very hard to make the school a success and to keep the family covenant. She also seized an opportunity to defend her faith, even more securely establishing her place in her father's heart.

Rachel's instructional duties did not deter her from her program of intellectual self-improvement. One of the authors she most admired was Maria Edgeworth, a bestselling Anglo-Irish novelist who also wrote extensively on pedagogy and published tales for young readers. In one of Edgeworth's novels, Rachel met a character who shocked and surprised her. Edgeworth's tale exposed moral corruption among Irish landowners squandering their wealth in London while their tenants sank helplessly into want. Moving fawningly among the story's idle rich, deftly sucking off their wealth through loans bearing exorbitant interest, was the coach maker, Mr. Mordicai. Page after page, Rachel's name and the name of her father blurred sickeningly with the image of a demon Jew. Rachel composed her letter to the novelist with care. "How can it be that [Maria Edgeworth], who on all other subjects shows such justice and liberality, should on one alone appear biased by prejudice?" Rachel implored. As an educator sensitive to the dangers of false associations, how could Edgeworth instill this "prejudice into the minds of youth!" Perhaps, Rachel suggested, religious persecution in Europe produced Shylocks and Mordicais, but "in this happy country," Rachel, sounding a note of patriotism, informed Miss Edgeworth, "where religious distinctions are scarcely known, where character and talents are all sufficient to attain advancement, we find Jews to form a respectable part of the community." In fact, Rachel knew very few Jews, but here was her family's ideal image of their nation and their own place in it.[22]

More than a year passed and Rachel heard nothing from Ireland. Then one day there was a letter, a warm letter accepting fault. "The candor and spirit of tolerance . . . you shew," Maria Edgeworth wrote, "you have right to expect from others." The following summer, Rachel's brother entered a New York bookshop and picked up Edgeworth's brand new *Harrington* (1817). Its preface credited "an extremely well-written letter . . . from a Jewish Lady, complaining of the illiberality with which the Jewish nation has been treated," with inspiring the work. *Harrington* was intended as a public apology and "reparation."[23]

No "lady" sought public renown, but word spread through the Jewish community that Rachel Mordecai was behind the literary coup for the Jewish people. One girl growing up in Philadelphia recalled that "the name of Rachel Mordecai" was "almost holy." By standing up to Edgeworth, she resembled "the martyrs and champions of old who died for the God they would not forsake."[24] Rachel, it seemed embodied the model American Jewish woman, combining piety, duty, intellect, and grace.

The exchange with Edgeworth opened a friendship that lasted the rest of Rachel's life. Other attachments and developments were more troubling. In 1817, Jacob's eldest son, a fast-rising Raleigh lawyer, intermarried, setting off emotional alarms.[25] On the other hand, the sale of the boarding school the following year and the Mordecais' removal to a farm on the outskirts of Richmond, Virginia, enabled fifty-six-year-old Jacob to regularly take part in Jewish communal life for the first time in three decades. But the comfortable country life he had sketched out soon unraveled under the duress of first-time farming (the family held over twenty slaves during this period) and the financial panic of 1819, which wiped out most of their hard-won savings. On the positive side again, Jacob's mathematically gifted son, Alfred, won a place as a cadet at the United States Military Academy at West Point, where he would honor the family by excelling in the nation's service.[26]

It disappointed Jacob when the move to Virginia did not shake loose the tie between his daughter Caroline and Achilles Plunkett, a longtime Mordecai school instructor specializing in French, art, music, and dancing. The match met vigorous opposition within the family as Plunkett, a Catholic widower with older children, could never be expected to earn enough to provide for Caroline as they thought she deserved. Jacob eventually consented to a union, fearing Caroline might otherwise take her life; but he would have nothing to do with a ceremony repugnant to his orthodox "religious principles."[27] No family members attended the small civil service in Warrenton.

Jacob's newfound focus on Jewish communal survival meant that Rachel's traditional Jewish wedding the following spring was an especially joyous occasion. Aaron Lazarus, a widowed merchant from Wilmington, North Carolina, encountered Rachel via his daughters, who had attended the academy in Warrenton. Rachel surprised herself in accepting (after first rejecting) Aaron's proposal. At thirty-three, she had long passed the typical marrying age, and "plain but solid" Aaron lacked the intellectual spark to ignite her spirit. Further, having lost her own mother and having had less than happy feelings about her father's remarriage, Rachel worried about becoming a stepmother herself. Still, Aaron was kind, pleasant, prosperous, and ultimately persuasive.[28]

Before settling into Wilmington, Rachel visited Aaron's family in Charleston, home in 1821 to the largest Jewish community in the United States. It was odd for Rachel, accustomed to being a Jew among Christians, to be surrounded by coreligionists. She entered a synagogue for the first time and celebrated Passover with the Lazarus clan, but complained of missing the chance to attend the theater owing to parties where fashion was the chief topic of conversation. Intellectual stimulation was equally rare in Wilmington. Writing home to her sister, Ellen, Rachel thanked her "for mentioning books. I hardly meet with them here." She supposed that no local household except her own could lay claim to three books "beside the prayer book and the bible [sic]."[29]

In fact, Christian prayers and Bible passages played a significant part in Rachel's world in Wilmington. With only a handful of other Jews in the town and no synagogue (the first was erected after the Civil War), Aaron took the unorthodox step in 1811 of helping prominent townsmen raise funds to fill St. James Episcopal Church's long-vacant pulpit. He purchased a pew and attended regularly, claiming he "could worship Jehovah in any temple." The family celebrated the Sabbath and high holy days in private. Neither church attendance nor domestic rituals interested Rachel; despite vigorously defending Jews to Maria Edgeworth, Rachel found religion uncompelling. In time, faith would come to matter very much, however, as Rachel underwent a shift no less significant but perhaps more difficult to explain than her father's. Family and self-improvement were her watchwords, and as a mother these imperatives weighed more heavily on her than ever.[30]

Each of Rachel Mordecai Lazarus's four pregnancies opened the emotional wound left by her mother's death after childbirth. And every additional child added immeasurably to the strain she experienced as a parent determined to instill in her offspring the behavior, ideas, and knowledge necessary to make them rational and productive citizens. Embracing theories advanced by Enlightenment philosophers who suggested that early influences could forever alter an adult's character, Rachel strove, at times obsessively, to manage every aspect of her children's experience. Teaching them within the home helped her resolve tensions between domesticity and intellect, for while confined to a private sphere, she could also view herself as a reformer aspiring toward the loftiest goals: reason and education could transform not only individuals but society at all levels.[31]

Rachel was cut off from the physical presence of family members who understood the enlightened domestic covenant she strove to fulfill. Her fears of failure were dismissed by those close to her, who saw only how blessed her children were in having "such a mother." Even when things went well (as with her first child's displays of verbal genius), Rachel resented the time and care the details of motherhood involved. "If I never have another [child] I shall account myself most happy," Rachel said when she was a mother of one.[32] More children would mean a shriveled mind, for she could not keep pace with her own improvement when so many others depended on her.

Rachel did apply considerable thought to the problem of the practice of Judaism in America. Since assuming the position of a Jewish wife, Rachel found the rituals she was responsible for increasingly frustrating. She described feeling like the psalmist who sang, "As the hart panteth after the water brooks, so panteth my soul after thee, O God," and in 1824 wrote to her father suggesting he turn his attention to "our [Orthodox] religious exercises" and "present form of prayer," deeming both in dire need of improvement.[33] Very likely, Rachel was in touch with the group who one month later divided the Charleston community and inaugurated American Reform Judaism. If so, she supplies a rare if not unique female voice for the movement; if not, Rachel independently staked out intellectual ground at the cutting edge of Jewish life.[34] Whatever the case, her opinions of Jewish religious practice met strong opposition from Jacob. Her father, who had so often been guided by his eldest daughter, dismissed her complaints out of hand and declared that traditional worship was critical to the survival of the Jewish people.[35]

Had she and Aaron lived in Charleston, they could have found a spiritual home together in the Reformed Society of Israelites. Wilmington offered no such option. Instead, Rachel felt alone, alienated, and bitter—misunderstood even within her own close family and, making matters worse, she was pregnant. Rachel delivered a baby girl, but her recovery was slow. All the while, the schism in Charleston raged with Jacob contributing from the sidelines.[36] Then Rachel was pregnant again, and this time she nearly died of fever after giving birth. Her dark night of the soul was shared with Mary Orme and Catherine DeRosset, close friends and active Christians who infused their nursing care with religious faith if not zeal. Writing to another Christian confidante, Rachel described having "walked 'through the valley of the shadow of death,' confiding in [God's] mercy for pardon of my sins and transgressions, and wholly submitting myself to his most Holy Will." She realized that her friend would want her to "say more," to embrace Christ for herself, "but of this we will not speak."[37] For a time, Rachel did speak little of it. But the baby was there, every day, bearing the name Mary Catherine. Sometimes Rachel wished she could escape Wilmington and all that had happened to her there. She and Aaron considered leaving for the North, perhaps New York.

Rachel loved her country deeply and decorated her Wilmington parlor with lithographs of the first five American presidents. But in 1831, two of Aaron Lazarus's slaves were executed for conspiracy in the aftermath of the Nat Turner Rebellion. This gruesome episode forced Rachel, Jacob, and many others to confront what it meant to be white southerners and slaveholders. With property levels at their lowest in fifty years, Aaron could not afford to liquidate his extensive warehouses and other real estate, and the idea of moving faded. Feeling trapped, Rachel lamented that it "is deplorable in the extreme" to live where "soon or late we or our descendents will become the certain victims of a band of lawless wretches." Jacob, whose lack of command had at one time been so severe that his children feared for his safety in dealings with slaves, joined prominent Richmonders in the Society for the Prevention of the Absconding and Abduction of Slaves.[38] After more than forty years' residence, the Mordecai family was, for better or worse, southern, bound to a region whose own identity and sense of distinctiveness as a slaveholding society would only intensify over the coming decades.

It was therefore a highly pleasant distraction for Rachel when Aaron, riding high in his shipping business, arranged to meet investors in New York and invited her to accompany him. She had never been further north than Virginia. Their first stop was the District of Columbia, where her younger half-brother Captain Alfred Mordecai commanded an arsenal and promised an insider's tour of the capital. Rachel considered Alfred the perfect embodiment of the Mordecai covenant. He graduated first in his class at West Point and by 1833 his talents (he became an expert in artillery, ballistics, and munitions systems) were winning him plum assignments. The recognition by non-Jews of the service he provided the nation fed the family's patriotic aspirations and confirmed the faith that Jews could attain respect and success at the highest levels. When he traveled to Europe, Rachel insisted that he present himself to Maria Edgeworth in Ireland. Rachel knew she was right about Alfred when Maria's letter came praising his "quiet manners and conversation full of sense and information, his amiable disposition and gentleman-like manly character" all of which "surpassed our expectations."[39]

At Mount Vernon they paid homage to the father of the nation, and on Capitol Hill they saw the leading spokesman for states' rights, South Carolina Senator John C. Calhoun, who had butted heads with President Andrew Jackson over his state's nullification of the tariff of 1832. Riding in a carriage one day while Aaron was busy elsewhere, Rachel questioned Alfred about his "want of religion." She said she had found new life through Jesus and urged him to seek it, too. But for her husband's objections, she was prepared to convert. Alfred was astounded. While his own attachment to Judaism was such that he had fallen in love and proposed marriage across religious lines, Alfred had no idea of the extent of his sister's spiritual investigations and never imagined her a Christian and a proselytizer. Alfred could not reconcile her appeal with her "sensible and reflecting mind," and was tempted to regard Rachel's new posture as an "abandonment of reason."[40]

Emma Mordecai (1812–1906) was Jacob's twelfth child. Although she was once engaged to a non-Jew, Emma never married. "[I]f Judaism were to be publickly [sic] professed as Christianity is, I should at once become a member of the Jewish Church," She told a family member in 1839. Her publications on Jewish affairs appeared in the first American Jewish periodical. Daguerreotype ca. 1860–70s. Courtesy of the North Carolina Office of Archives and History, Raleigh, North Carolina.

While he admitted that "want of religion" as Rachel had called it, had brought him no happiness, her announcement may, ironically, have prompted Alfred to rethink his willingness to marry outside the Jewish fold. When he announced plans to wed Sara Ann Hays, some of his siblings voiced doubt—pointing out that he was nursing a broken heart. Alfred was not deterred; of course he was well aware that the connection with an observant and respected Philadelphia Jewish family elated Jacob.[41]

Alfred's younger sister Emma experienced a more star-crossed courtship. Emma had grown up in the long shadows of her talented elder siblings, but she blossomed into a pretty and vivacious young woman. One brother observed fondly that Emma could "entertain more persons at one time than any lady" he'd ever seen. But she played a dangerous game as she negotiated her way through society. While visiting assimilated relatives in Raleigh, she reported home that for Yom Kippur she "kept her promise faithfully, eat [sic] not a mouthful and read the prayers through, repetitions and all, without interruption. But when an up-and-coming merchant won her attentions, her brother George undertook the task of mediating a situation everyone realized would raise trouble at home. His children's courting had often unnerved Jacob, but nothing vexed him more in this period than the repeated threats to the family's Jewishness. Of course, Emma knew this in 1834 when she fell in love with William Grimes.[42]

In the matter of marriage, George Mordecai complained, his sisters faced a "peculiarly disagreeable and unfortunate situation." Several of Jacob's sons intermarried, but the blows were perhaps softened by their male status and by geographical distance. As George saw it, his sisters had three choices, all wretched. Some avoided conflict by remaining spinsters; some married Jews, decent men, perhaps, but not the kind the Mordecais could truly "admire or esteem"; or else, he concluded, "they must incur the certain and lasting displeasure of their parents buy marrying out of the pale of their religion."[43]

The relative freedom of choice in marriage George wished for his sisters was part of a gradual and difficult shift away from the deference genteel families had typically expected of children in the eighteenth century. It also signaled his rating of social and intellectual congeniality over Jewish communal preservation. In cases of interfaith marriage, couples typically came to an understanding regarding their offspring's religious upbringing.[44] For Jewish-Christian couples the decision was nearly always to fold the family into Christian practice. For Jacob, it was excruciating. Having experienced his own religious revival, he increasingly measured his success and the larger fate of American Jewry by the religious identity of his children and those to whom they gave their hearts. Yet Jacob's frustration and fear manifested themselves unevenly, and his daughters caught the worst of it.

With George's support, Emma accepted Grimes's proposal. George wrote their father testifying to the suitor's good character and modest but promising "pecuniary affairs." It is not clear whether Jacob and Becky Mordecai, Judy's sister, ever responded to the letter, for hardly had it arrived before the engagement exploded in a scandal so mortifying that family correspondence was removed or destroyed—and lost to the historical record. George withdrew his support for the match and, under extreme pressure, Emma broke with her lover. While family members were relieved at the narrow escape, Emma did not see it that way. Her hopes had evaporated and in desperation she attempted suicide. Escorted home to Richmond, Emma had no choice but to accept her lot. She never married, yet found her calling in the maelstrom of religious tension that gripped the Mordecai clan in the years ahead.[45]

At the time of Emma's romantic debacle, Jacob Mordecai was secure in his role as a leading light in Richmond's Jewish community and beyond. As he entered his seventh decade he could boast little in the way of worldly success. But he had retired respectably and, though he never published his writings, Jacob had won a reputation as a font of Jewish knowledge. He was both a defender of orthodoxy against proselytizing outside the synagogue and a dedicated defender against Jewish-led reforms inside the synagogue. He was a mentor to young Jews trying to sustain traditions in the modern, and sometimes hostile, prejudiced world. He led the Richmond congregation as hazan and spoke at the dedication of Virginia's first synagogue. Over the course of two decades he compiled a commentary on each book of the New Testament, drawing attention to passages in which Christ's life did not accord with Hebrew prophecies. Jacob's "patriarchal manner" pleased Rebecca Gratz, the most prominent American Jewish woman of the day, and she applauded his efforts to, as she said, "make his own children and grandchildren well acquainted with the religion they profess."[46]

Herein lay difficulties. By 1836, three sons had intermarried, and the grandchildren from these unions were being or would be reared as Christians. Emma had come close to marrying outside the faith. Most shocking of all, his beloved Rachel had appealed to him for help resolving the quandary over religion in her life and marriage. Two years had passed since the scene in the carriage with Alfred. The situation had not changed; the strain only increased the longer she was prevented from exercising her beliefs. Aaron said that if she converted he would "separate the children from her," something fully within his legal rights but something Rachel could not bear to contemplate. Failing physical health prompted drastic measures. In 1835, she wrote to Jacob disclosing her religious views, "entreating his forgiveness, his indulgence, and his sanction to pursue the course which my feelings and convictions dictate." If only her father could understand, perhaps her husband would relent.[47]

No such rescue was forthcoming. Instead, Rachel's letter nearly undid Jacob, who demanded that she renounce Jesus Christ. Forty-seven-year-old Rachel vowed on her knees never "to adopt any faith but that of my fathers." Two years later she died after receiving baptism at her sister's home on the way to her ailing father's side. Jacob lingered a bit longer, shielded by the family from Rachel's death and apostasy.[48] Words of triumph engraved in English and in Hebrew mark Jacob Mordecai's tombstone and reflect the home he found in his faith: "God will redeem my soul from the power of the grave, for he will redeem me." Rachel's epitaph avoided the complexities of her religious journey and focused on her fulfillment of the family covenant. "Endowed with superior talents / and the most estimable virtues / She was an ornament to Society / and a blessing to her domestic circle." Yet behind the epitaphs and from beyond the grave, Jacob's and Rachel's legacies haunted those they loved and, while inspiring intense devotion, also left a Jewish family divided over its identity.[49]

The distance between father and daughter in death reflects their conflict on earth. This was a tension that came from balancing identities, the age-old tension between the adaptation and survival of Jewish tradition and the freedoms a new world offered. The processes that brought Rachel and Jacob to their respective religious commitments, however, are far too complex to fit simply into terms like orthodoxy and apostasy, and yet it is these terms by which their family members and all Jewish Americans, north and south, are at some level defined.

Meanwhile, Emma did not know what to believe. Her mother feared she was inclined to convert as her brother George and sister Ellen had in the months following Jacob's death. Certainly, the pressure was considerable from both "sides." In reflecting on her life and the role religion had played in it, twenty-seven-year-old Emma found only emptiness. "God has withdrawn His holy Spirit from me," she confided to one sister. She tried reading "pious works," both Jewish and Christian, but no voice spoke to her.[50] Then came a day when Emma announced that her inquiry was at an end. Everything "I read on either side of the question convinces me of my duty to adhere to the religion of my forefathers," she told Ellen, who had hoped and prayed for a different resolution. "My mind is made up," she continued, "and if Judaism were to be publickly [sic] professed as Christianity is, I should at once become a member of the Jewish Church."[51]

Having rounded this corner in her life, Emma seized her father's legacy and embarked on a career as an outspoken and observant Jewish woman who took a leading role in communal affairs. Well aware of Jews' often fragile ties to religious tradition and inspired by Rebecca Gratz's work in Philadelphia, Emma persuaded Richmond's hazan to open a Hebrew Sunday school. This drew the sympathy and support of Jacob's protégé, Isaac Leeser, who, in addition to his duties as hazan at Philadelphia's Mikveh Israel, published *The Occident and American Jewish Advocate* (the first national Jewish periodical) and other Jewish religious texts. Calling herself "an American Jewess," Emma published essays on Christian proselytism and the progress of American Jewry, and in 1845 Leeser brought out her *The Teachers' and Parents' Assistant; or, Thirteen Lessons Conveying to Uninformed Minds the First Ideas of God and His Attributes.* Many assumed the author of the catechism to be Rebecca Gratz herself. Such confusion likely flattered Emma, and she would have been gratified to know that Alfred's mother-in-law recommended the volume to Sara for use in bringing up their children—Jacob Mordecai's grandchildren—as faithful Jews.[52]

Alfred and Sara had six children, and their parenting fell decidedly short of the Mordecais' high moral and intellectual expectations. During a visit to Alfred's family, Emma complained that the youngsters were "slaves to their humours and their parents are slaves to them." She blamed Sara, who, aside from eight births in eleven years—two babies died young—was often unwell and suffered badly under Alfred's many professional absences. It was clear that Sara felt unappreciated by the Mordecais, and perhaps her husband did not defend her as she might have wished or expected, for the couple often did not see eye to eye, especially on religion and politics.[53]

Alfred resisted Sara's attempts to bring him closer to Judaism. With regard to religious practices within the home and the rearing of the children, Sara had a free hand. But Alfred stood apart. "My wife is of a strict Jewish family," he informed Maria Edgeworth in a letter written shortly after Rachel's death. Their children would "be instructed accordingly" until they reached the age at which they would decide for themselves what role, if any, Judaism would play in their lives. To Sara's dismay, Alfred insisted that his sons not be circumcised.[54]

Slavery, which flourished in Washington, D.C., where the couple lived for much of their early marriage, was another point of contention between Alfred and Sara, who grew up with emancipationist views. Although Alfred apparently purchased only one slave in his lifetime, he defended slavery both on moral and constitutional grounds, abhorred abolitionists, and in social relations gravitated largely toward southerners.[55] With the election of Abraham Lincoln in 1860, what it meant to be American, southern, and Jewish took on new urgency. Mordecai family members, most of them lifelong southerners and Whigs but emphatically not secessionists, generally saw the Confederacy as a "necessary" evil brought on by abolitionist machinations. In the tragic event of outright military conflict between the sections, Alfred was poised to play a pivotal role. When his brother George questioned him closely on his "position" and on what steps he would take should political compromise fail, Alfred replied that declaring one's sentiments in such sensitive matters was unbecoming to an officer of the United States Army. Such tact also made sense for a southern-born commander of an arsenal in upstate New York. Rumors circulated that the munitions whose manufacture he oversaw were destined to be wielded by Confederate rebels. In January 1861, the governor of North Carolina urged him to resign his post and prepare his native state for war. Alfred refused, pointing out that North Carolina had not even seceded. The following month, former Mississippi senator and secretary of war Jefferson Davis assumed the presidency of the newly formed Confederate States of America. He offered Alfred, whose experience made him far and away the ideal man for the post, the command of the South's Corps of Artillery. He demurred.[56]

Alfred had long regretted his inability to help his relatives financially, as his army salary barely covered his own large family's immediate needs. He now had the power to do what no other Mordecai could. At the birth of the Confederacy—

a new nation—Alfred could in one gesture render the Mordecai name glorious, a synonym for southern patriotism. In the wake of Fort Sumter's fall to South Carolina forces, enlistments began, North and South, and the spirit of mobilization overtook the Mordecai households as well. Indeed, national strife made family reconciliation possible. Ellen and Caroline, whose conversions had bruised relationships, returned to Richmond and joined their Jewish sisters and stepmother in sewing shirts, scraping lint, and winding up bandages for soldiers. They also waited impatiently for word from Alfred.[57] But Major Alfred Mordecai would not come. Having failed to obtain a transfer to a post in which he could avoid being involved in hostilities, Alfred resigned his commission. He planned to spend the war as a private citizen in Philadelphia with Sara and their younger children. "And thus," his brothers wrote bitterly, "you sink into obscurity instead of attaining the position and honors to which you are entitled."[58]

So it was that the Mordecais entered the Civil War with their southern patriotism tarnished, feeling robbed of their rightful place in the region Jacob and Judy Mordecai had adopted three-quarters of a century earlier. Since his days as a cadet, Alfred had symbolized the family's patriotism as well as their faith that their own talents and diligence would secure success and honor in America's highest places. They had applauded each commission, each promotion, and each international mission. Yet when their loyalty shifted to the Confederacy, the Mordecais were shocked to find Alfred out of step. It was a near-mortal blow to a family covenant grown threadbare through marriages, religious conflict, and, middle-class success. Their brother's choice was incomprehensible, for he seemed to forsake a crucial part of the ideal that led him to the top of his class at West Point. As a member of the professional class and national military elite, Alfred chose not to fulfill the covenant and establish, at last, a family of onetime outsiders as indisputable insiders. Instead, he acted on his own account and according to his own conscience.

Alfred concluded that other imperatives outweighed achieving the old Mordecai family dream now dressed in Confederate gray. The feelings of his immediate family ranked high in his agonizing calculations. He and Sara had six children, all of whom had grown up in Washington and points north. As the war began, their eldest son, Alfred Jr., graduated from West Point. The younger Alfred Mordecai harbored no doubts as to his loyalties and quickly enlisted in the Union Army. To assume a military position in the Confederacy would have meant fighting against his own son and dropping Sara and the other children into a world, as he told one sister, "which should be painful to them and not of their own choosing." [59] Adding to his reservations were nearly forty years of service in the U.S. Army; he well knew the South's military disadvantages, and no skill on an officer's part could make up for them. Of course, his decision made no one happy. He was criticized by family members in both sections for not aiding their respective causes, rebuked by his aged mother, and pilloried in both the Northern and Southern press as an unprincipled coward and traitor.[60]

Never had the family been more stereotypically southern than it became in 1861—and never had their southern identity created so much tension. In loyal and active service to the new nation, most of the Mordecais took up a cause that distracted from the fact that they were no longer the tightly bound "little band of love and duty," united in interests and values, of half a century before. Though robbed of the glory that Alfred's service to the South would have afforded, the Mordecais united around the Confederate cause.

In 1865, as Richmond fell, a black Union soldier stole the last horse and saddle from Emma Mordecai's household on the city's outskirts. With enormous pluck, Emma marched toward town to "see what could be done." Union officers galloped on their horses through the streets. Emancipated slaves celebrated noisily. When a volley of gunfire rang out, Emma was told that President Lincoln had landed on the banks of the James. Unwilling to share the city limits with the enemy leader, Emma turned toward home. Passing a soldier she described as "a Black ruffian," she cursed his race and Lincoln, too, as "ill bred." The man aimed his rifle at her. "You haven't got things here no longer as you *have* had them," he said. "Don't you know that? Don't you know that?"[61]

Nothing would be the same for the South, and consequently the experience of being Jewish there was forever altered. In the antebellum years, the Mordecais supported slavery *and* affiliated with the nationalistic, Whig-voting urban middle class. The war's economic devastation crippled that class of southerners. Moreover, the history of people like the Mordecais was marginalized after the conflict, as white southerners sought to regain control of a shattered social system by conjuring a mythic plantation past populated by genteel masters, happy slaves, and (occasionally) poor whites.[62] Those who made up the "Jewish South" after the war, peddlers-turned-merchants who settled in cities and scores of small towns throughout the region, were consequently cultural outsiders in ways the Mordecais were not. This generation of Jewish southerners also poured immense resources into establishing religious communities, building synagogues, and fostering social ties among Jews.[63] In this respect, the Mordecai experience with Jewish identity underscored the fragility of tradition for Jews who succeeded them.

The Mordecais also challenge the way historians of religion, including historians of Judaism and "the Jewish South," identify who "counts" as "Jewish"—or Methodist, Christian, evangelical. In the United States, it is the rare individual (and rarer family) whose faith remains utterly stable throughout his or her life. Historians easily lose track of the contentious nature of religious experiences, the contingency of spirituality or religiosity over the course of a lifetime, and how such fluidity is experienced in various historical settings.[64] The Mordecais' vivid experiences, set down on thousands of sheets of paper surviving in some cases over two centuries, describe the changing circumstances and many choices made by American Jews in the Old South. Surely such exquisite feeling and search for belonging shaped more than one "little band of love and duty" among Jewish southerners.

NOTES

Abbreviations

AJA   Jacob Rader Marcus Center, American Jewish Archives, Hebrew Union College, Cincinnati, Ohio

AM   Alfred Mordecai

AMP   Alfred Mordecai Papers, Manuscript Division, Library of Congress, Washington, D.C.

CMP   Caroline Mordecai Plunkett

DRFP   DeRosset Family Papers, Southern Historical Collection, University of North Carolina, Chapel Hill

EM   Ellen Mordecai

JM   Jacob Mordecai

JMP   Jacob Mordecai Papers, Rare Books, Manuscripts, and Special Collections Library, Duke University, Durham, N.C.

LMFP   Little-Mordecai Family Papers, North Carolina Division of Archives and History, Raleigh, N.C.

MFP   Mordecai Family Papers, Southern Historical Collection, University of North Carolina, Chapel Hill

MM   Moses Mordecai

MYFP   Myers Family Papers, Virginia Historical Society, Richmond, Va.

PMP   Pattie Mordecai Papers, North Carolina Division of Archives and History, Raleigh, N.C.

RM   Rachel Mordecai

RML   Rachel Mordecai Lazarus

SM   Samuel Mordecai

Sol   Solomon Mordecai

1. [EM], "Past Days, a Simple Story for Children," MYFP; Amos Funkenstein, "The Dialectics of Assimilation," *Jewish Social Studies* 1 (1995): 1, 4–6; also see Werner Sollors, *Be-*

yond Ethnicity: Consent and Descent in American Culture (New York: Oxford University Press, 1986).

2. In 1820, Charleston had the largest population of Jews of any U.S. city. See Jacob Rader Marcus, To Count a People: American Jewish Population Data, 1585–1984 (Lanham, Md.: University Press of America, 1990), 204, 148–49, 193.

3. Jonathan D. Sarna's American Judaism: A History (New Haven, Conn.: Yale University Press, 2004) is exceptional in that nearly one-third of the text is devoted to the years before the Civil War.

4. Bertram W. Korn, "Factors Bearing upon the Survival of Judaism in the Ante-Bellum Period," American Jewish Historical Quarterly 53 (1964): 344. There are reasons to avoid the term assimilation altogether—see Sarna, American Judaism, xix.

5. JM, "Addenda to Watson's Annals of Philadelphia: Notes by Jacob Mordecai, 1836," edited by Whitfield J. Bell Jr., Pennsylvania Magazine of History and Biography 98 (1974): 154–55; JM to Marx Edgeworth Lazarus, Aug. 25, 1828, MFP; Caroline Myers Cohen, Records of the Myers, Hays, and Mordecai Families from 1707 to 1913 (Washington, D.C., 1913), 26–27.

6. Inventory of Moses Mordecai Estate, 26 June 1781, Mordecai Family Papers, American Jewish Historical Society; Edwin Wolf II and Maxwell Whiteman, The History of the Jews of Philadelphia from Colonial Times to the Age of Jackson (Philadelphia: Jewish Publication Society of America, 1975), 126; Herbert T. Ezekiel and Gaston Lichtenstein, History of the Jews of Richmond from 1769 to 1917 (Richmond, Va.: Ezekiel, 1917), 17–18; Myron Berman, Richmond's Jewry, 1769–1976: Shabbat in Shockoe (Charlottesville: University Press of Virginia, 1979), 5–6; Jacob Rader Marcus, Early American Jewry (Philadelphia: Jewish Publication Society of America), 2:185–86.

7. JM to Judy Myers, Oct. 25, 1783, MFP; JM to SM, March 4, 1816, MFP.

8. JM to MM et al., July 20, 1796, MFP.

9. Judy quoted in JM to MM et al., July 20, 1796, MFP. Ideological developments similar to enlightened domesticity are apparent among German Jews during the eighteenth and nineteenth centuries. See, for instance, David Sorkin, The Transformation of German Jewry, 1780–1840 (New York: Oxford University Press, 1987); and Marion A. Kaplan, The Making of the Jewish Middle Class: Women, Family, and Identity in Imperial Germany (New York: Oxford University Press, 1991).

10. See Rachel's copy of JM to MM et al, July 20, 1796, MYFP. For a taste of Judy's progressive pedagogical views, see Judy Myers Mordecai to Myer Myers and Joyce Mears Myers, April 24 and Dec. 8, 1793, MFP; and JM to MM et al., July 20, 1796, MFP.

11. See for instance, SM to EM, May 6, 1815, MFP.

12. [EM], "Past Days," 82–83, MYFP.

13. RM to SM, Jan. 1, 1809, MFP; RM to SM, Oct. 15, 1805, JMP, cited in Lance J. Sussman, "Our Little World: The Early Years in Warrenton" (paper submitted to Dr. Jacob

Rader Marcus, Hebrew Union College, AJA, in Bingham's possession); RM, "Memories," MYFP; and [EM], "Past Days," 52.

14. RM to SM, July 5, 1809, MFP; Lizzie Wilson Montgomery, *Sketches of Old Warrenton, North Carolina* (Raleigh, N.C.: Edwards and Broughton, 1924), 133–41; EM to Sol, Dec. 10, 1827, JMP; EM to CMP, January 27, 1828, JMP; [EM], "Past Days," 92, 90–91. For enrollment, which varied from 70 to 110 pupils, see Penny Leigh Richards, "'A Thousand Images, Painfully Pleasing': Complicating Histories of the Mordecai School, Warrenton, North Carolina, 1809–1818," (Ph.D. diss., University of North Carolina at Chapel Hill, 1996). Such father-daughter relationships were not uncommon and are treated in Elizabeth Kowaleski-Wallace, *Their Fathers' Daughters: Hannah More, Maria Edgeworth, and Patriarchal Complicity* (New York: Oxford University Press, 1991).

15. On Bible study and school curricula, see Richards, "'A Thousand Images,'" 170–77. On Jewish students, see for instance, Sol to EM, Feb. 14, 1814, LMFP; and EM to Sol, Dec. 15, 1813, MFP.

16. On the events surrounding the Warrenton revival, see EM to SM, Sept. 7, 1810, MFP; RM to SM, July 28, 1807, JMP; RM to SM, Sept. 24, PMP; SM to RM, Oct. 3, 1810, JMP. For the impact of evangelical Christian revivals on the South in this period, see Donald G. Mathews, *Religion in the Old South* (Chicago: University of Chicago Press, 1977).

17. JM, "Introduction to the New Testament," n.d., AJA.

18. Eli Faber, *A Time for Planting: The First Migration, 1654–1820* (Baltimore, Md.: Johns Hopkins University Press, 1992), 123; Elisheva Carlebach, *Divided Souls: Converts from Judaism in Germany, 1500–1750* (New Haven, Conn.: Yale University Press, 2001), 12.

19. As the secularism of the post-Revolutionary period receded, religious belief and practice intersected for many Americans with issues of female authority, social order, and respectability. The shifting place of religion in American culture between the late eighteenth and midnineteenth centuries is outlined in Charles Beneke, "From the Many, One: The Religious Origins of American Identity," at http://are.as.wvu.edu; and Mary P. Ryan, *Cradle of the Middle Class: The Family in Oneida County, New York, 1790–1865* (New York: Cambridge University Press, 1981).

20. Carlebach, *Divided Souls*, passim; RM to ME, Aug. 7, 1815, in *The Education of the Heart: The Correspondence of Rachel Mordecai Lazarus and Maria Edgeworth*, edited by Edgar E. MacDonald (Chapel Hill: University of North Carolina Press, 1977), 6; Sarna, "The American Jewish Response to Nineteenth-Century Christian Missions," *Journal of American History* 68 (June 1981): 35–51. Further research is needed to make comparisons between the experience of assimilation and conversion in eighteenth- and nineteenth-century America and in Europe (especially England) where, as one scholar has written, religious entreaties from well-meaning Gentiles represented "a constant reminder of what the Christian community desires and requires." See Michael Ragussis, *Figures of Conversion: "The Jewish Question" and English National Identity* (Durham, N.C.: Duke University Press,

1995), 80. Alan C. Guelzo called on historians to pay closer attention to conversion and its complex intersection with individual lives in "God's Designs: The Literature of the Colonial Revivals of Religion, 1735–1760," in *New Directions in American Religious History*, edited by Harry S. Stout and D. G. Hart (New York: Oxford University Press, 1997), 147–48.

21. JM to SM, Nov. 29, 1810, MFP; SM to RM, Nov. 21, 1813, JMP; RM to EM, Jan. 30 and Mar. 20, 1814, MFP; EM to Sol, Feb. 15, 1818, JMP; RM to EM, June 22, 1823; Sol to EM, Nov. 8, 1811, MFP; SM to RM, Nov. 21, 1813, JMP; Sol to EM, Dec. 26, 1813, LMFP; SM to EM, May 28, 1814, JMP; RM to Sol, July 27, 1817, JMP; RM to SM, Apr. 24, 1814, MFP; EM to Sol, Feb. 15, 1818, JMP.

22. RM to SM, Feb. 27, 1814, PMP. On Edgeworth (1767–1849) see Marilyn Butler, *Maria Edgeworth: A Literary Biography* (Oxford: Clarendon Press, 1972). Mr. Mordicai appears in Edgeworth's *The Absentee* (1812). RM to Maria Edgeworth, Aug. 7, 1815, in *Education of the Heart*, 3–5. "Reparation," Maria Edgeworth to RM, n.d. [ca. Aug. 1816], in *Education of the Heart*, 8.

23. RM to SM, Apr. 7, 1816, MFP; RM to SM, Sept. 26, 1816, MFP; Maria Edgeworth to RM, n.d. [ca. Aug. 1816], in *Education of the Heart*, 8; Sol to SM, Sept. 17, 1817, JMP; Edgeworth, *Harrington* (1817) in *Tales and Novels of Maria Edgeworth* (London: Baldwin and Craddock, 1833), 17:v. For a discussion of *Harrington*'s details, see Emily Bingham, *Mordecai: An Early American Family* (New York: Hill and Wang, 2003), 68–69, Ragussis, *Figures of Conversion*, 77–79, and Judith W. Page, "Maria Edgeworth's *Harrington*: From Shylock to Shadowy Peddlers," *Wordsworth Circle* 32 (2001): 9–13.

24. Sara Ann Hays to RML, Sept. 12, 1833, AMP.

25. Bingham, *Mordecai*, 75–78.

26. Alfred was the third Jew to attend West Point. Jack D. Foner, "Jews and the American Military from the Colonial Era to the Eve of the Civil War," edited and introduced by Eric Foner, special supplement to the *American Jewish Archives Journal*, available at http://www.huc.edu/aja/00-3.htm.

27. JM to Achilles Plunkett, Sept. 28, 1820, MFP; Bingham, *Mordecai*, 88–90.

28. RM to Sol, Aug. 23, 1820, JMP; Bingham, *Mordecai*, 90–93.

29. For population, see note 2, above. RM to Sol, Apr. 22, 1821, JMP; RML to EM, May 4, 1823, MFP.

30. Leora Hiatt McEachern, *History of St. James Parish, 1729–1979* (Wilmington, N.C.: n.p., 1983), 70; Ida Brooks Kellam and Elizabeth Frances McKoy, *St. James Church Historical Records* (Wilmington, N.C.: n.p., 1965), 1:35–36; Tony P. Wrenn, *Wilmington, North Carolina: An Architectural and Historical Portrait* (Charlottesville, University Press of Virginia and the Junior League of Wilmington, 1984), 171; RML to EM, June 29, 1823, MFP; RML to EM, Oct. 7, 1821, JMP; RML to EM, Apr. 26, 1823, MFP. "I must be more than ever vigilant in training *myself*," Rachel wrote, now that she was responsible for new life (RML to Maria Edgeworth, July 29, 1822, in *Education of the Heart*, 30–31).

31. Bingham, *Mordecai*, 137–41 and 330–31.

32. Julia to GM, Aug. 4, 1823, LMFP; on Marx Edgeworth Lazarus's precocious speech, see Bingham, *Mordecai*, 141; RM to CMP, Nov. 11, 1822, MFP.

33. RML to JM, Oct. 10, 1824, MFP. She cited Psalms 42:1–2, King James Version. For other expressions of dissatisfaction, see RML to EM, Nov. 8, 1823, JMP; and RML to EM, Nov. 22, 1823, MFP.

34. Several of Aaron's siblings and in-laws were involved in reform in Charleston. See James William Hagy, *This Happy Land: The Jews of Colonial and Antebellum Charleston* (Tuscaloosa: University of Alabama Press, 1993), 128–60; Sarna, *American Judaism*, 58–60.

35. [JM], "Remarks on Harby's Discourse Delivered in Charleston (S.C.) on the 21st of November 1825 before the Reformed Society of Israelites on Their First Anniversary," (January 1826), typescript, Jacob Rader Marcus Center of the American Jewish Archives, 1, 7.

36. On this pregnancy and birth, see for instance, EM to Sol, July 13 and Sept. 28, 1825, JMP; on the continued religious debates, see AL and RML to JM, Dec. 25, 1826, JMP; AL and RML to JM, Jan. 8, 1827, in the collection of Richard D. Weiner, Durham, N.C.

37. Bingham, *Mordecai*, 160–61; RML to Lucy Ann Lippitt, Oct. 26, 1828, MFP.

38. RML to EM, June 18, 1826, MFP; RML to JM, Nov. 13, 1831, JMP; Moses Ashley Curtis, journal entry, Dec. 3, 1831, Moses Ashley Curtis Papers, Southern Historical Collection; Bingham, *Mordecai*, 162–63; RML to GM, Oct. 6, 1831, PMP; RM to SM, Feb. 11, 1810, PMP; Minutes of the Society for the Prevention of the Absconding and Abduction of Slaves, Richmond, Va., Nov. 30 and Dec. 9, 1833, New York Historical Society.

39. "The Life of Alfred Mordecai: As Related by Himself," edited by James A. Padgett, *North Carolina Historical Review* 22 (1945): 95; Maria Edgeworth to RML, Dec. 2, 1833, in *Education of the Heart*, 252.

40. RML to EM, Jan. 10, 1833, MFP; AM to EM, May 24, 1833, AMP. Alfred had pursued Jeannette Thruston, daughter of a federal judge in Washington, D.C., without success (Bingham, *Mordecai*, 121–22).

41. AM to EM, May 24, 1833, AMP; GM to EM, May 29 and June 6, 1836, MFP. Sara's mother was Rebecca Gratz's sister.

42. Julia to Emma, Feb. 25, 1834, MFP; Emma to EM, Sept. 24, 1833, MFP. Another beau called her "the very soul of life" (Moses Ashley Curtis journal, Jan. 14, 1831, Moses Ashley Curtis Papers, Southern Historical Collection, University of North Carolina, Chapel Hill).

43. GM to SM, Jan. 15, 1834, MFP.

44. See Anne C. Rose, *Beloved Strangers: Interfaith Families in Nineteenth-Century America* (Cambridge, Mass.: Harvard University Press, 2001).

45. GM to JM, Apr. 20, 1834, Cameron Family Papers, Southern Historical Collection, University of North Carolina, Chapel Hill; SM to GM, Apr. 26, 1834, GMP; EM to GM, Sept. 7, 1834, LMFP; Emma to EM, Oct. 1, 1834, PMP.

46. Rebecca Gratz to Maria Gist Gratz, Feb. 16, 1832, Hays Family Papers, American Jewish Historical Society, Center for Jewish History, New York. Jacob also played a critical role in the early career of Isaac Leeser, one of antebellum American Jewry's central figures—see Bingham, *Mordecai*, 110–12; and Lance J. Sussman, *Isaac Leeser and the Making of American Judaism* (Detroit: Wayne State University Press, 1995).

47. Henry Mordecai and RML to EM, July 29, 1835, MFP; RML to Catherine DeRosset, Aug. 1, 1835, DRFP; EM to Sol and CMP, July 3, 1838, MFP.

48. RM to RMM, Aug. 26, 1835, JMP; Emma journal, July 8, 1838, MFP.

49. The original inscription on Jacob's grave marker (cited above) is recorded in the Mordecai family Bible, Mordecai House, Raleigh, North Carolina. The words may be taken from Hos. 13:14. Rachel's gravestone is at Blandford Cemetery, Petersburg, Va., which lies above that city's old Episcopal church.

50. Bingham, *Mordecai*, 193–94.

51. Emma to EM, Sept. 22, 1839, MFP.

52. American Jewess [Emma Mordecai], "The Duty of Israel," *Occident and American Jewish Advocate* 2 (January 1845); and American Jewess [Emma Mordecai], "An Essay," *Occident and American Jewish Advocate* 5 (July 1847), at http://www.jewish-history.com/Occident. Richea Gratz Hays to Sara Hays Mordecai, May 16, 1845, AMP.

53. Emma to Ellen Mordecai II (1820–1916), Mar. 15, 1846, MFP; AM to SM, Feb. 12, 1846, MFP; Sara Hays Mordecai to AM, Nov. 6, 1855, AMP; SM to EM, Mar. 13, 1849, JMP.

54. AM to ME, Oct. 7, 1838, quoted in Myron Berman, *The Last of the Jews?* (Lanham, Md.: University Press of America, 1998), 91; Jacob Rader Marcus, *United States Jewry, 1776–1985* (Detroit: Wayne State University Press, 1989), 1:713 n.34. Berman suggested that after the Civil War, Alfred's interest in Judaism deepened (*Last of the Jews?* 91).

55. Wolf and Whiteman, *History of the Jews of Philadelphia*, 191, 437n.25; AM to EM, Aug. 7, 1833, AMP; Stanley L. Falk, "Divided Loyalties in 1861: The Decision of Major Alfred Mordecai," *Publications of the American Jewish Historical Society* 48 (1959): 149–50; AM to EM, Mar. 4, 1830, AMP.

56. SM to GM, Apr. 18, 1861, GMP; AM to GM, Dec. 17, 1860, GMP; AM to GM, Jan. 20, 1861, GMP; Stanley L. Falk, "Jefferson Davis and Josiah Gorgas, an Appointment of Necessity," *Journal of Southern History* 28 (1962): 84–86; AM to GM, Mar. 10, 1861, GMP; AM to Colonel H. R. Craig, Apr. 15, 1861, AMP; and Falk, "Divided Loyalties in 1861," 154.

57. Emma to Ellen Mordecai II, Apr. 26, 1861, MFP; RMM to CMP, Oct. 21, 1860, MFP.

58. GM and SM to AM, June 6, 1861, Ellen Mordecai Papers, Virginia State Archives, Library of Virginia.

59. AM to EM, June 16, 1861, AMP.

60. EM to GM, May 6, 1861, GMP; SM to GM, June 9, 1861, GMP; RMM to AM, Aug. 9, 1861 (copy), GMP; AM to EM, June 16, 1861, AMP; SM to GM, Sept. 16, 1861, GMP; "Major Alfred Mordecai," *Jewish Exponent*, Nov. 25, 1887.

61. Emma to Edward B. Cohen, Apr. 5, 1865, included in typescript copy of Emma diary, 122–29, MFP.

62. On the plantation myth, see W. J. Cash, *The Mind of the South* (New York: Alfred A. Knopf, 1941); and Paul M. Gaston, *The New South Creed: A Study in Southern Mythmaking* (New York: Alfred A. Knopf, 1970).

63. On post–Civil War southern Jews, see Eli Evans, *The Provincials: A Personal History of Jews in the South* (1973), rev. ed. (New York: Free Press, 1994); Leah Elizabeth Hagedorn, "Jews and the American South, 1858–1905" (Ph.D. diss., University of North Carolina–Chapel Hill, 1999); Gerald Sorin, *A Time for Building: The Third Migration, 1880–1920* (Baltimore: Johns Hopkins University Press, 1992), 137–38, 152–61.

64. See Emily Bingham, "'Thou Knowest Not What a Day Will Bring Forth': Intellect, Power, Conversion, and Apostasy in the Life of Rachel Mordecai Lazarus (1788–1838)," in *Religion in the American South: Protestants and Others in History and Culture*, edited by Beth Barton Schweiger and Donald G. Mathews (Chapel Hill: University of North Carolina Press, 2004), 67–98.

For Further Reading

Ashton, Dianne. *Rebecca Gratz: Women and Judaism in Antebellum America*. Detroit: Wayne State University Press, 1997.

Bingham, Emily. *Mordecai: An Early American Family*. New York: Hill and Wang, 2003.

Funkenstein, Amos. "The Dialectics of Assimilation." *Jewish Social Studies* 1 (1995): 1–14.

MacDonald, Edgar E., ed. *The Education of the Heart: The Correspondence of Rachel Mordecai Lazarus and Maria Edgeworth*. Chapel Hill: University of North Carolina Press, 1977.

Rose, Anne C. *Beloved Strangers: Interfaith Families in Nineteenth-Century America*. Cambridge, Mass.: Harvard University Press, 2001.

Sussman, Lance J. *Isaac Leeser and the Making of American Judaism*. Detroit: Wayne State University Press, 1995.

3

"THE PEN IS MIGHTIER THAN THE SWORD"
SOUTHERN JEWISH WOMEN WRITERS,
ANTISEMITISM, AND THE PROMOTION OF
DOMESTIC JUDAISM

JENNIFER A. STOLLMAN

Strive with earnest, strong endeavor
Though as well to act, to guard.
Aid the weak, the sorrowing comfort,
Loving others, love thy God!
Thus before His awful presence
Let thy great Atonement be,
Mercy's wings shall shield His splendor,
While His peace descends on thee.
—Octavia Harby Moses, "Lines for the Day of Atonement and Ten Penitential Days"

When Octavia Harby Moses wrote "Lines for the Day of Atonement and Ten Penitential Days" in 1860, she displayed not only a poetic talent, but also a central aspect of her southern identity, her Judaism.[1] She was not unique among southern Jewish women who frequently used public and private writings to express their Jewish identity and to share these thoughts with other Americans. In the past, these works were overlooked as a critical means to understand how southern Jewish women shaped their religious lives, questioned antisemitism, and promoted religiosity among fellow Jews. This chapter explores how Jewish women of the antebellum South used correspondence, composition, and poetry both to convey their opinions on national and international antisemitism and to encourage fidelity to Judaism.

The development of Jewish communities and religious conviction during a time not only of institutionalized antisemitism and proselytization, but also one of great economic, political, and social change was no easy feat for southern Jewish women. At the commencement of the antebellum era, the United

States struggled to establish its own vision of democracy and equality, while developing a healthy economy. Citizens walked a tightrope between religious tradition and Lockean reasoning. At the end of that era, the nation was engaged in its own civil war, a struggle to prevent the country from fracturing in two based on economic and social differences. American leaders espoused the philosophy that to be good citizens of the early republic, individuals must be good Christians. National observance of Christianity was tied to national success.[2] Striving for homogeneity, order, and cohesion among citizens divided by region, class, race, and gender, Revolutionary religious and lay leaders used Christianity and its associated symbols, rituals, and observance to unite the nation.[3] Christianity served as a tool for the development of nationalist consciousness.

The doctrine of Christianity embedded itself in American common law. State constitutions, laws, and local statutes invoked its importance. Laws routinely appealed to Christian beliefs, and public offices required christological oaths from all political and judicial participants.[4] Because of the prevalence of Christianity in the early Republic, Jews were viewed with some degree of suspicion. Southern Jews' rights of settlement, citizenship, suffrage, and office-holding were limited, as well as their ability to serve as witnesses and jurors and to practice law.[5] Legislation "supported secular anti-semitic rulers, parties, and policies, strongly encouraged the suppression of Jewish worship, and restricted Jews to certain living and workspaces."[6]

"Anti-Jewishness" infused itself into American culture and was a part of daily conversation, literature, religion, anti-Jewish charms, aphorisms, hymns, ballads, songs, tales, and other folklore. These familiar sources demonized Jews and Judaism and had material consequences for Jews in the South.[7] This simple, but foundational, philosophy presented problems for Jews, who did not accept Christianity or Jesus Christ as the Messiah. Jewish resistance to Christianity in the colonial and early Republic era set them apart from the rest of American society. Southern society similarly employed Christianity as a unifying philosophy for its citizens.

In addition to the anti-Jewish discourse, the religious revivals of the Second Great Awakening that swept through the South beginning in the 1790s encouraged antebellum southern Jewish women to counter charges of antisemitism. Fundamentalist Protestants espoused evangelical ideals while attempting to renew American morality, encourage missionary efforts, and institute humanitarian reform. White southern ministers, friends, neighbors, and Jews newly converted to Christianity challenged the utility as well as validity of Judaism.[8] Certain Protestant groups found the existence of Judaism in their midst dangerous. Groups like the American Society for Meliorating the Condition of the

Jews and the American Sunday School Union declared Jews "morally dead" and campaigned hard for their conversion, fearing that Judaism would ruin the nation.[9] While not as vitriolic as the Society, many southern Church sermons, published religious tracts, Sunday School primers, religious cartoons, and morality tales regularly disparaged Jews.[10] Nevertheless, there were other Christians who understood Judaism through a philo-semitic lens. They praised Jews and their religious practices as far as these related to their own Christian history and philosophy. They tended to view Jews as ancestral holders of ancient Christian traditions and thus often considered Judaism to be anachronistic. These contradictory impulses, which both praised and castigated Judaism and Jews, caused antebellum southern Jewish women through their public and private writings to creatively challenge antisemitic and philo-semitic stereotypes and events by promoting a respectable and productive image as white southerners.

Literary scholar Diane Lichtenstein concludes that a distinct nineteenth-century Jewish female literary canon existed and suggests that these women's ethnicity and religion distinguished their writing from other female writers of that time. To display their American identities, southern Jewish women called on familiar genres and themes common to American middle-class female writers. Like other nineteenth-century white women writers, Jewish women writers frequently employed the "True Woman" as a literary voice. Easily understood by popular readers, the ideology allowed southern Jewish women to express their opinions to a larger audience. To demonstrate their Jewishness, they created a literary tradition that incorporated "sacred texts, ancient wisdom, myth, and beliefs that distinguish one culture from another." Writers also employed popular Jewish literary devices, such as the "Mother in Israel," which emphasized the important role of the family in the preservation of Judaism. But their marginality was the most recognizable theme in the American Jewish woman's literary tradition.[11] This liminal position in society forced Jewish women to "negotiate among the complex fractions of selfhood: the true womanhood ideal of American middle-class Christian society, the expectations of Jewish womanhood, their identity as Americans, and as Jews."[12] Writing became a means to "explore, justify, and demonstrate the premise that dual national loyalties were possible."[13] Acutely aware of their audiences, Jewish women writers functioned "as translators of ethnicity to ignorant, and sometimes hostile, outsiders."[14]

To question antisemitism and at the same time promote tolerance of Jews and religiosity among Jews, antebellum southern Jewish women utilized two writing styles—questioner and domestic. Questioner literature confronted existing philosophies on gender, class, race, and religion. Domestic-focused writing celebrated home, family, and women's role as moral guides and protectors of the community. Though female writers of this genre accepted the ideal of women as "passive, dependent, and domestic," they recognized that these same qualities gave women important influence in their homes and communities. Pastoral and sentimental writing styles enabled female writers to assert their power and influence over others and oppose the established order.[15]

As questioners, nineteenth-century southern Jewish women writers frequently challenged "sacrosanct concepts that underlay nineteenth-century American society,"[16] especially the validity of antisemitic characterizations. Antisemitic portrayals of literary characters, international and local laws that barred Jews from full emancipation, and the rise of antisemitism in the United States and abroad troubled nineteenth-century southern Jewish women writers, who understood the potential dangers that these trends posed for the Jewish community. Through their correspondence, composition, and poetry, southern Jewish women publicly questioned and chastised those who knowingly or unknowingly promoted antisemitism.[17]

Many southern Jewish women wrote private letters to directly challenge individuals' antisemitic views. Earlier in this volume, Emily Bingham describes the experiences of Rachel Mordecai and her correspondence with famed pedagogical theorist, Maria Edgeworth. Bingham concludes that the exchanges of letters between the two women represents one American Jewish woman's attempts to counter antisemitism by employing Enlightenment rationale. She correctly asserts that Mordecai appealed to Edgeworth as an educator, pointing out that her seemingly benign depiction of antisemitic characters was not only unenlightened but stood to damage Jews' reputations. Closer examination of the twenty-six-year relationship reveals more than a simple rebuke or a discrete event. Mordecai embarked on a years'-long project to defend her religion and race, and to project a respectable Jewish image.

She first contacted Anglo-Irish author Maria Edgeworth after being offended by an antisemitic portrayal of a Jewish character in one of Edgeworth's novels. In The Absentee (1812), Edgeworth created a dishonest and unappealing coachman who happened to share the Mordecai name. Mordecai revered Edgeworth's pedagogical philosophies and was shocked by the author's unenlightened portrayal of Jews. Her outrage compelled her to write to the author and demand an explanation. After praising Edgeworth for her previous "justice and liberality," Mordecai confronted her about the versimilitude of such a character and suggested that she had been duped by antisemitic stereotypes. Mordecai asked: "Can it be believed that this race of men are by nature mean, avaricious, and unprincipled? Forbid it, mercy." She suggested that where Jews "are oppressed and made continually the subject of scorn and derision they . . . deserved censure." The

Jews in Mordecai's world did not behave like Edgeworth's unscrupulous coachman. Mordecai suggested that circumstance, not blood, led Jews and others toward evil and reasoned that anyone exposed to unintelligent and uncivilized surroundings might become unsavory. Despite their religious differences, she hoped to prove to Edgeworth that Jews lived virtuous and productive lives. Mordecai described her country, explaining that "where religious distinctions are scarcely known, where character and talents are all sufficient to attain advancement, we find the Jews to form a respectable part of the community. They are in most instances liberally educated, many following in the honourable professions of the Law, and Physick with credit and ability and associating with the best society our country affords."[18] She argued that Jews in the United States, despite their religion, pursued respectable avocations and demonstrated great skill in their labors.

Mordecai offered her family as representative of modern enlightened Jews. In response to Edgeworth's request that she reveal more about her background, she portrayed herself as a typical Jewish woman from a typical assimilated American Jewish family. Creating a portrait of Jewish productivity and respectability, Mordecai failed to mention American antisemitism and, instead, presented a sanitized picture of tolerance and acceptance of Jews. Employing sentimental language, she carefully constructed a respectable family history narrative that Edgeworth could relate to, save the fact that the family was Jewish. In providing short biographies of herself, her father, and stepmother, Mordecai described the family's commitment to female education, a subject she knew was dear to Edgeworth. Mordecai praised her stepmother, who taught her "patience, perseverance, and cheerfulness in the school of adversity." She described how she instructed her younger sister Eliza in etiquette and provided a classical education based on Edgeworthian pedagogical philosophies.[19]

Her description of a southern Jewish family mirrored domestic perfection— a hardworking patriarch who sacrificed much to provide his daughters with a solid education; a loving and strict stepmother; and a responsible, devoted daughter and sister. Mordecai's description of her father as a scholar, headmaster, and businessman appealed to Edgeworth's bourgeois sense of class. This portrait countered Edgeworth's subtle implications that Jews were clannish, unethical, and unscrupulous. Mordecai explained that despite being the only Jewish family in their town, the family had successfully assimilated and bonded with non-Jews. In characteristically American fashion, Mordecai and her friends had been trained to look upon religious variations as a matter of course—these were differences that existed in every society.[20] She politely, but effectively, countered Edgeworth's antisemitic literary clichés and suggested that the novelist rethink her Jewish characters. She believed the author had fallen victim to stereotypes and implied this was an injustice to herself and to her readers. She gently suggested that Edgeworth's description was the result of ignorance.

Mordecai received two responses to her first two letters, one from the author's father and one from the author herself. Mortified at the charges of antisemitism, Richard Lovell Edgeworth defended himself and his daughter. Much chagrined, he also apologized for the offense and assured Mordecai that his daughter would make amends in a forthcoming novel.[21] Although she had caused Maria Edgeworth to reconsider her conceptualization of Jews, Mordecai did not believe that Edgeworth had gone far enough. After reading the new novel, she was disappointed at the promised reconstruction of the Jew in what would become Edgeworth's best-selling novel, Harrington. True to her word, the author portrayed the novel's heroine, Berenice, as a virtuous and religious Jewish woman and in fact modeled her character after many of Mordecai's letters and incorporated many of Mordecai's thoughts and expressions into Berenice. Mordecai was quite satisfied with Berenice's father, but she was shocked by the novel's ending and the discovery that Berenice's mother was not Jewish—and, consequently, according to Jewish law, that neither was Berenice. Though she believed that Edgeworth did this so that the hero and heroine could be reunited at the novel's conclusion, Mordecai suggested that the plot had a detrimental effect. Making Berenice a Christian severed the novel's established links between Jewishness, respectability, and virtuousness. The ending implied that Berenice's goodness essentially existed because she was Christian. Again, she felt compelled to question Edgeworth's character portrayal and her implication that only Christians could truly be good and virtuous. Mordecai suggested that deep religious conviction, regardless of faith, determined a person's worth. In a letter to Edgeworth, she wrote: "Provided the heart is sincere in its adoration, the conduct governed by justice, benevolence, and morality, the modes of faith and forms of worship are immaterial; all equally acceptable to that Almighty Being, who looks down on all his creatures with an eye of mercy and forgiveness."[22]

Mordecai expected that a woman as intelligent as Edgeworth would be more enlightened in her opinions of people with different religious beliefs. She suggested that such a moral philosopher might examine and question her own character flaws rather than spending time judging those of others. Finally, the young woman advised Edgeworth to take a lesson from herself and all Jews, who "regard our own faith as sacred, but we respect that of others, and believe it equally capable of conducting them to the Throne of Grace."[23] Contesting antisemitism with Maria Edgeworth proved to be a lifelong endeavor for Mordecai. For more than twenty-two years, Edgeworth and Mordecai exchanged letters and discussed a wide range of topics, including Jews and Judaism. She continued to confront Edgeworth about antisemitism in her writing, and although the result was not always satisfying to Mordecai, her letters did cause Edgeworth to rethink her long-held assumptions regarding Jews.

Another example of a southern Jewish woman who used her literary skills to oppose antisemitism was Charleston native Penina Moise. She frequently published poetry in local and regional secular and Jewish newspapers in a campaign to question and, subsequently, eradicate antisemitism. In 1823, at the age of twenty-three, Moise submitted the poem "To Persecuted Foreigners" to the *Southern Patriot*. In the poem she confronts American anti-Jewish and anti-immigrant sentiment. Fiercely patriotic, Moise was dismayed that a democratic and ideologically tolerant nation like the United States could harbor xenophobic feelings. Incorporating American philosophies of liberty, union, freedom, and reason, she suggest that citizens betrayed their most deeply held American beliefs by subscribing to anti-Jewish sentiment. The first stanza proclaims:

Fly from the soil whose desolating creed,
Outraging Faith, makes human victims bleed.
Welcome! Where every Muse has reared a shrine,
The respect of wild Freedom to refine.

Moise reminds her readers that freedom of religion is a basic and prized right for all Americans. This inherent right encouraged members of different religions to emigrate to the United States, and after time, freedom would appropriately refine their customs. Moise writes, "Upon OUR Chieftain's brow no crown appear." No king's decree assigned a national religion in the United States. That choice, stresses Moise, is a personal matter, and the freedom to practice one's religion is a fundamental American right. She openly questions American hypocrisy at not extending religious freedom to all of its citizens and urges her readers to control their religious zeal:

Zeal is not blind in this our temp'rate soil;
She has no scourge to make the soul recoil,
Her darkness vanished when our stars did flash;
Her red arm, grasped by Reason, dropt the lash.[24]

Moise also addresses international antisemitism in her poetry. When she learned that the parliamentary "Jew Bill" that would extend political and economic rights to British Jews had been defeated, she expressed her anger in her poetry. "Lines on the Persecution of the Jews of Damascus," concerns the violence directed at Jews in Damascus after a Christian cleric was murdered and public opinion immediately indicted the Jews for this crime.[25] In "The Rejection of the Jew Bill by the House of Lords," Moise denounces British antisemitism. Chastising the House of Lords, Moise asks:

Why against Folly point satiric swords?
Rise scornful Muse and sing the House of Lords!
Let bigot pride your boldest stroke cleave.
·　·　·　·　·　·　·　·　·　·　·　·　·

Who could have dreamed a faggot yet would blaze,
Far more unquenchable than zealots raise,
Felled from the highest branches of a tree,
Rooted within the soil of Liberty?
Spotless are not the records of old Spain!
For Acts of Faith leave not so deep a stain,
Nor structures based on erring superstition,
As this Aristocratic Inquisition.[26]

Southern Jewish female writers used other literary forms to question existing ideas about Jews. Jewish Confederate hospital matron Phoebe Yates Pember composed a short story she hoped would ease anxieties about Jews and encourage tolerance of Judaism. Against a wave of antisemitic popular literary characters, Pember creates a moral Jewish hero. In "Miss Magdalena Peanuts," submitted to the *Atlantic Monthly*, Pember describes a young Christian girl and her terminally ill mother. Realizing her imminent death, the mother carefully considers who should take care of her daughter, Lizzie. She makes an unusual choice when she asks a Jewish druggist to adopt and rear her. Word of her decision spreads through the community. Presbyterian, Episcopal, Baptist, and Catholic clergy race to the woman's deathbed to interfere with her choice and to seek custody of the girl, thus preventing a Jew from raising a Christian child. The mother refuses their requests. Even the Jewish pharmacist is confused. He does not know the woman well and also wonders why she would want a Jew to raise her daughter. During a visit, he questions her decision. The mother cites the druggist's moral character and stresses that she feels he would allow Lizzie to make her own religious choices. Furthermore, the mother fears the religious zealotry of Christians who would prevent her daughter from exercising any free will. Pember encourages her readers to question whether religious freedom exists in the country and whether they uphold that right. The Jew in this story is humble, modest, and, above all, rational.[27] It is the Christian clergy, according to Pember's characterization, that is irrational and undermining fundamental secular American philosophies.

Domestic writers represent the second type of nineteenth-century southern female Jewish authors. Although they also used questioning as an effective strategy to encourage change, they wrote from an authoritative domestic standpoint to encourage religiosity among American Jews. As domestic writers, these women celebrated the home and women's ability to bring about moral change within their families and communities. Their pieces promoted Judaism in the context of the Second Great Awakening, emphasizing devotion to Judaism, the empowering nature of religious belief, and women's important role in preserving Jewish life. Many southern Jewish women writers challenged the growing detachment of southern Jews from Judaism.[28] They emphasized the importance of the Jewish community and the individual's responsibility to support it.

Poetry was a popular genre for southern Jewish women who addressed problems within the Jewish community. Both religious hymns and secular poetry promoted Judaism and adherence to Jewish ritual. The female poets suggested that continued fidelity to Judaism not only upheld their responsibilities as Jews but garnered the respect of non-Jews. During the Second Great Awakening, faith was an important measure of one's character. They clearly felt that faithful Jews countered images of Jews as avaricious and unscrupulous.

Penina Moise frequently used domestic literature to describe a strong American Jewish population dedicated to Jewish practice. In 1842, she was asked to compose several hymns for a new reformed Judaism hymnal.[29] The hymn book celebrated Judaism and encouraged personal and communal religious devotion. Its nine sections included hymns about consecration, the relationship between God and man, duties toward God and others, daily and festival prayers, confirmation, and school. The hymns promoted faith in Judaism in the midst of an evangelical Protestant South.

Moise assumes an authoritative maternal voice in her hymns. Her hymn "Number 40" speaks about proselytizing, antisemitism, and the need for Jewish devotion:

Resolving the path of duty to tread,
Though our fondest wish this may frustrate;
Never by temptation's voice to be led,
The sacred laws of God to violate:
Faith only nerves the soul
To this great self-control.

To live harmoniously with all mankind,
With favors our hurts to requite.

Undazzled by gold, by menace unmoved,
One sole Supreme Being to cherish;
To be firm in the faith our fathers loved
Though for this as martyrs we perish.[30]

Moise described the dangers facing Jews in secular America and advised them to fight attempts to shake Jewish faith. She encouraged feminine traits of repression, self-control, and denial, and demanded that Jews hold firmly to the faith of their forefathers. Reciting her hymns helped create a Jewish community that recognized its distinct ethnicity while strengthening Jewish resolve against conversion and antisemitism.

Charlestonian Octavia Harby Moses also wrote domestic poetry encouraging fellow southern Jews to re-engage their Judaism. Positioning herself as a spiritual and moral guide in an era of evangelical Protestantism—a "mother of Israel"—she argued that Jews must return to Judaism and traditional practices. Moses proposed that Jews would derive more satisfaction in their daily lives if they focused on religion, and by "building a house of Israel," her female readers would revive Judaism. In "Lines for the Day of Atonement and Ten Penitential Days," Moses advises:

Dost though walk abroad in daylight
Lifting up thy head in high?
. . . Dost thou scan thy brother's frailties
Seeking for each hidden sin
. . . At the thing thou hast not been?
Tremble! For thy footsteps falter
On the brink of sin's dark wave
'Whelmed beneath its surging water,
Thy vain soul shall find its grave.
But with swift and even motion,
Another year has passed around,
One more day of grace is granted,
. . . Search the chambers of thy heart,
Pluck from out its dark recesses,
Every thought where sins has part.
Learn to screen thy neighbor's feelings,
With the gentle hand of love.[31]

Moses counseled Jews to use the ten penitential days of the Jewish New Year to examine their own faults of the past year and to practice self-reflection. Using sentimental language from domestic literature, she gently criticized the Jewish community. Recognizing her perceived moral superiority as both a southern and Jewish female, readers tacitly accepted her spiritual guidance.

Other southern Jewish women did not formally publish their poetry as did Moise and Moses, but they still used composition to express their own faith in Judaism and to nourish these sentiments in fellow Jews. Composition books were frequently passed from friend to friend. Although the circle of readers was small, these private journals enabled southern Jewish women to encourage religious fidelity. One of them, Miriam Gratz Moses, preserved her thoughts in an elaborate leather-bound composition book. In one poem, the amateur poet describes the ancient Jewish historical experience, hoping to inspire her readers to become more observant:

> Faith came at first in Purity from heavn . . .
>   Upon Creation's glorious day:
> A bright effulgent spark to darkness givn
>   To light man grovling on his way.
>
> . . . This spark celestial, warm'd the man of God
>   Extreme afflictions to endure:
> Preferring Judah's bondage and the Rod
>   To Egypt's richest gifts and lore.
>
> Its light the bright prophetick vision shew'd!
>   The burning bush his eyes regard.
> And as with kindling joy his nature glow'd
>   Rejoic'd to see his sure Reward.
>
> Warm'd by its gentle beams, the drooping soul
>   On God, through Faith, alone relies!
> Through it alone, our passion, we control
>   Through it, alone man, Death Defies.[32]

Moses encouraged her fellow Jews to remember their ancestral experiences and God's benevolence toward the Israelite nation regardless of the political, economic, and social circumstances that made Judaism inconvenient. She emphasized Jews' "chosen" status and its inherent responsibilities. In the face of increased proselytization, antisemitism, and the lure of materialism, she reminded southern Jews to fulfill the covenant made between God and Israel. Modernity, she argued, did not dissipate Jewish responsibility.

Many of Moses' poems compared the marginal position of American Jewry to the experiences of Abel, Noah, and Moses, biblical figures who demonstrated their faith in an environment of intolerance and skepticism. Her poems urged readers to understand that even the greatest Jewish heroes strayed in their Jewish beliefs, but that God allowed, and even helped them to return to their faith. Through her poetry, she gently guided Jews back to Judaism.[33]

Octavia Harby Moses believed active faith in Judaism was an effective antidote to Jewish loneliness. She wrote Sabbath-related poems in which Judaism comforted her during the long absences of her husband and family, as in "To My Absent Children":

Today, the Sabbath day, I sit alone,
    Profoundest quiet falls on all I see,
Far from my side my little ones have roamed,
    And God and Nature dwell alone with me.[34]

Moses marked other significant moments in her life by invoking the value of Judaism and faith in God in her poetry. No celebration could be experienced without homage to Judaism; no trial overcome without the power of God and faith in Judaism. On the occasion of her daughter's marriage, she wrote an inscription in a Bible for her child:

When youth and grace have fled.
Clothed in religion's lovely garb, afflictions form shall give
The softened aspect angels hear, who wound us but to save,
Many and rich thy bridal gifts, but turn these pages o'er.
And thou shalt gather gems that earth can boast not in her store,
When friends are cold, and gifts are gone, their steady radiance given,
With brightened lustre still shall shine and point the way.[35]

Moses reminds her daughter that only Judaism would provide guidance, companionship, and comfort throughout her life.

Grace Seixas Nathan, a Charleston native, on the death of her grandson, wrote of Judaism in a poem to console her distraught daughter. Nathan describes a frostbitten geranium—a metaphor for the death of her grandchild on January 19, 1810. Despite her own sadness, Nathan takes great comfort in knowing that the child was with God and hopes that her daughter could find similar solace.

I had a bud so very sweet—its fragrance reached the skies.
The angels joined in holy league—and seized it as their prize.
They bore it to their realms of bliss—where it will ever bloom,
For in the bosom of their God they placed my rich perfume.[36]

Using both the questioner and domestic literary styles, nineteenth-century southern Jewish female writers created their own distinctive literary canon. Faced with slavery, fundamentalist Protestantism, intense proselytizing, and rigid gender roles and responsibilities, these authors melded traditional ideas about Jewish and American womanhood to counter antisemitism, fundamentalist assaults, and declining Jewish observance. Through their published and private poetry, compositions, and letters, antebellum southern Jewish women strengthened Jewish life in the South and promoted the acceptance of Jews at home and in their communities.

NOTES

1. Octavia Harby Moses, *A Mother's Poems: A Collection of Verses* (published by her children and grandchildren, private publisher, 1915), 30–31.

2. Laurence R. Moore, *Religious Outsiders and the Making of Americans* (New York: Oxford University Press, 1986), 201.

3. Naomi W. Cohen, *Jews in Christian America: The Pursuit of Religious Equality* (New York: Oxford University Press, 1992), 3.

4. Ibid.

5. David A. Gerber, ed. *Anti-Semitism in American History* (Urbana: University of Illinois Press, 1986), 14.

6. Frederik Cople Jaher, *A Scapegoat in the New Wilderness: The Origins and Rise of Anti-Semitism in America* (Cambridge, Mass.: Harvard University Press, 1994), 10.

7. Ibid., 3, 69.

8. Cohen, *Jews in Christian America*, 39.

9. Jaher, *A Scapegoat in the New Wilderness*, 143–47.

10. Jaher, *A Scapegoat in the New Wilderness*, 154; and Leonard Dinnerstein, *Anti-Semitism in America* (New York: Oxford University Press, 1994), 18–19.

11. Diane Lichtenstein, *Writing Their Nations: The Tradition of Nineteenth-Century American Jewish Women Writers* (Bloomington: Indiana University Press, 1992), ix, 2–7.

12. Joyce Warren, ed., *The (Other) American Traditions: Nineteenth-Century Women Writers* (Bloomington: Indiana University Press, 1992), 19.

13. Lichtenstein, *Writing Their Nations*, 8.

14. Warren, *The (Other) American Traditions*, 245–46.

15. Ibid., 7, 9.

16. Ibid., 12.

17. Mary Louise Weaks and Elizabeth Perry, eds., *Southern Women's Writing: Colonial to Contemporary* (Gainesville: University of Florida Press, 1995), 8.

18. Edgar E. MacDonald, ed., *The Education of the Heart: The Correspondence of Rachel Mordecai Lazarus and Maria Edgeworth* (Chapel Hill: University of North Carolina Press, 1977), 15.

19. Ibid., 10, 11–12.

20. Ibid., 6.

21. Ibid., 7.

22. Ibid., 16.

23. Ibid.

24. Penina Moise, *Secular and Religious Works of Penina Moise* (Charleston, S.C.: N. G. Duffy, 1911), all 177.

25. Ibid., 271.

26. Ibid., 212.

27. Phoebe Yates Levy Pember, "Miss Magdalena Peanuts," Phoebe Yates Levy Pember papers, Southern Historical Collection, University of North Carolina, Chapel Hill, folder 5.

28. Warren, *The (Other) American Traditions*, 9.

29. By the second edition, published in 1851, the hymnal contained 190 hymns composed by Penina Moise. Moise, *Secular and Religious Works*, 39.

30. Moise, *Secular and Religious Works*, 40.

31. Moses, *A Mother's Poems*, 31.

32. Miriam Gratz Moses, "Untitled," Commonplace book, 1824–28, Miriam Gratz Moses papers, Southern Historical Collection, University of North Carolina, Chapel Hill.

33. Moses, Commonplace book.

34. Moses, *A Mother's Poems*, 33.

35. Ibid., 32.

36. In Jacob Rader Marcus, *Jews in the American World: A Sourcebook* (Detroit: Wayne State University Press, 1996), 117.

4

ENTERING THE MAINSTREAM OF MODERN JEWISH HISTORY

PEDDLERS AND THE AMERICAN JEWISH SOUTH

HASIA DINER

In his epic work, *Kentucky*, Yiddish poet I. J. Schwartz puts on center stage the life of a Jewish peddler, who "came with pack on his shoulders." Composed between 1918 and 1922 and published initially in serial form in the literary journal *Zukunft*, *Kentucky* solidified a long-standing image, that of the "Jew from afar" who had made his way "into the unfamiliar / His feet sore, his heart heavy, / A pack on his back, a stick in his hand," who announced to all around him that "I carry my business on my back." Joshua the peddler sold to, interacted with, and commented on—with lyrical depth—both the black and white denizens of this southern state, which gives the poem its name. This literary work provides one more link in a chain of discourse that links the South, the Jews, and peddling.[1]

Yet by merely changing the place names and the descriptors of climate, topography, and makeup of the larger population, Joshua's experiences in Kentucky could be seen as one of the paradigmatic Jewish phenomena of the modern world. The story of the Jew as peddler in a new country, navigating new languages, new mores, and complex racial and religious dramas as he went about his businesses could literally have been located in any place in the new world of the eighteenth through the early twentieth centuries.

Emphasizing the near universality of Jewish peddling, both in terms of time and place, transforms southern Jewish history from a curiosity, notable for its divergence from the larger narrative of modern Jewish history or, more specifically, American Jewish history. Rather, it places it squarely into the overarching paradigm, one that posits a confluence between trade, migration, cultural flexibility, and adaptability, as well as the "betweenness" of Jews as they negotiated among diverse peoples.

For scholars of southern Jewish history who insist on the uniqueness of their region, paying focused attention to the experiences of peddlers as immigrants raises a serious question about their very enterprise. These migrations propelled the peddlers from the long-settled regions of central and eastern Europe to multiple frontier societies, new worlds that included the British Isles, a place with a very sparse Jewish presence before the nineteenth century, as well as North and South America, parts of Africa, and the Antipodes. The fact that so many Jews, almost universally young immigrant men looking for a way to get a start in a new land, came to the American South as peddlers has tended to blind observers' eyes to the global dimensions of this experience. Those Jews who decided to leave their homes in central and eastern Europe from the eighteenth century into the early years of the twentieth by means of peddling, and to relocate to the southern states, joined a global movement. Little distinguished them from their literal and metaphoric peers who went to multiple regions, lands, and continents and who did so as peddlers. The decisions they made as to where to go in order to sell to rural customers from packs on their backs, and then horse-drawn wagons, reflected familial networks, Jewish communal structures, the paucity of settled merchants able to provide goods to remote rural dwellers, rather than the particular lure of the southern part of the United States. As such, by looking at immigrant Jewish peddlers, the American South, long conceptualized by its own residents and by outsiders as unique, becomes like other parts of the United States and the modern world.

THE UBIQUITOUS JEWISH PEDDLER IN GLOBAL PERSPECTIVE

The ubiquity of Jewish peddling and its inextricable connection to migration awaits a full and systematic historical accounting.[2] Any conceptualizing about Jewish peddling and the differences between places and times must at present rely on anecdotal gleanings. But the vast trove of scattered evidence, usually derived from memoir, autobiography, the press, Jewish apologetic literature, and from local and regional histories—like that which defines the field of southern Jewish history—points to the historic truth. Jewish men considered migration and peddling as yoked phenomena. This recognition and the behavior stimulated by it represented a broad, deep, and profound historical reality. It could be seen as one of the important common Jewish experiences.

The literature produced by Jews in order to defend their people from attack, for example, offers a place to start thinking about peddling and its connection to migration in global and then local terms. Besides the larger and deeply pervasive antipathy toward Jews that existed throughout the Western world in the modern period, peddlers tended to raise local suspicions because they did not quite belong in any place. Likewise, because the mode by which they made a living differed so radically from the more "normal" means of the vast majority of those to whom they sold—agriculture—they emerged as targets sometimes of violence but more often of negative imagery. So, Israel Abrahams, the distinguished British scholar of the late nineteenth and early twentieth century, like many other Jewish intellectuals of his time, saw in the study of history a way to defend the Jews. In his most highly regarded book, *Jewish Life in the Middle Ages* (1896), in a chapter on "Trades and Occupations," he took on the French writer Anatole Leroy-Beaulieu, who had asserted that Jews shunned "arduous physical undertakings" because they tended to be "averse to dangerous occupations." Abrahams sought to prove that the Jewish tendency to avoid certain livelihoods grew out of sources other than a fear of hard work or cowardice in the face of danger. "The Jewish peddler," wrote Abrahams, "of recent centuries was no coward; had he lacked courage, he must have remained at home."[3]

Although writing about the Middle Ages, an era in which European Jews entered in large number into this field, Abrahams's words offer a template for thinking about Jewish peddling, Jewish migrations, and the linkages between these two global phenomena, which also left its profound mark on one very small corner of the world, the American South. Going out on the road, laden with a jumble of goods, or sometimes specializing in one particular type of ware, functioned in the modern (and indeed earlier) era as a profound, binding, and nearly universal Jewish experience. Not that all Jews peddled, but rather because so many did for some period of time, the history of Jewish peddling played a pivotal role in the shaping and functioning of nearly all Jewish communities. Particularly after the eighteenth century, peddling served as a powerful vehicle for fostering Jewish migrations out of more stable but economically declining regions to new lands, wide open for settlement and business. Peddlers, prosaic and peripatetic figures who left little in the way of paper trails, can be seen as the juggernauts of Jewish migrations. Their experiences on the road as the human engines who drove the massive Jewish population shift, which brought Jews out of central and eastern Europe into a variety of new lands, deserves historicization.

Historians, Abrahams's statement not withstanding, have largely ignored peddlers and peddling as a formative Jewish experience. References to peddlers abound; systematic and focused analysis does not. Scholars of the modern Jewish experience have produced a robust literature on Jews as industrial laborers, for example. Certainly in the realm of American Jewish history, historians have studied, referred to, and invested with great analytic significance, the clustering of Jews in the garment industry, primarily as laborers, and to a lesser degree as manufacturers. Studying Jewish workers in the needle trades has allowed historians to chart oppressive work conditions, worker militancy, class consciousness, and union organizing, and to connect the history of Jews with the dramatic and heroic narratives of labor history in a number of countries.[4]

But peddling, a field of Jewish enterprise, through which on a global scale, millions of Jews passed, has not been the focus of any systematic research and analysis. Indeed with the exception of a few articles, many of them with a decidedly southern focus, it has almost completely eluded the attention of historians.[5] This absence in the scholarship merits thinking about in and of itself inasmuch as Jewish peddling functioned as one of the longest and most consistent aspects of Jewish history in the modern period and before. In their pre- or nonmigratory lives, peddling represented perhaps "the" paradigmatic Jewish means of livelihood, with maybe money-lending as a competitor for that status. The particularly attractive narrative of Jewish immigrants in America as industrial workers and the dramatic tale of their union organizing may also provide a way to think about why southern Jewish history, one characterized so profoundly by commerce, has gotten short shrift.

To date few historians have attempted to study the Jewish small business sector in America at all, whether urban or small town, northern, southern, or western, whether stationary or itinerant. Historians concerned with the Jewish past have almost purposely eschewed deep research on commerce, particularly at the more modest end of the business spectrum. This is even more emphatically the case with the peddlers, whose presence caused so much negative local commentary and who stood at the bottom of the Jewish commercial hierarchy.[6] Yet Jews and peddling had a history much longer and deeper than that of Jews and industrial labor. Extending backward into the Middle Ages and encompassing nearly the entire world as known at the time, Jews engaged in the retail sale of wares from packs on their backs or from animal-driven carts. They sold to Jews and non-Jews. Both Jewish women and men developed their routes, forged relationships with customers, helped stimulate desire for new goods, and served as fixtures of many local economies. In some regions and towns peddlers outnumbered non-peddlers in the Jewish community, and the clustering of Jews in this one occupational group affected nearly all aspects of the Jewish experience.

Before turning to the peddling experience, its historical roots, and its connection to migration, two kinds of peddling need to be delineated. The first of these took place on city streets. Urban peddlers hawked their goods, both foodstuffs and finished products, from wheelbarrows, pushcarts, or other kinds of contraptions at times slung around their necks and on their backs. These women and men engaged in work described by historian Nancy Green as the "quintessential job of the urban poor and a particularly easy form of first employment for the newly arrived." They differed, however, from the peripatetic peddlers, the subject of this essay and the ones who left their impress on the rural South, in that, at the end of the day, they repaired to their places of residence. They lived in Jewish enclaves, participated in Jewish societies, and interacted with other Jews. The second kind of peddler embarked on relatively lengthy road trips, spent time among non-Jews, did not return home with nightfall, and faced the challenge of living away from settled Jewish communities. This held, although in somewhat different ways, for both Jewish peddlers who plied their wares in Europe and those who chose to join the exodus to a series of new world places.[7]

Numbers of Jewish peddlers in the premigration setting varied from place to place and changed over time. They also can be elusive in that the peddlers came in and out of towns and regions, and individuals peddled at some point or another in their lifetimes. But just a few samplings of efforts at counting peddlers in pre-migration Europe demonstrates the significance of peddling to Jewish history. In 1863, one writer for the French Jewish newspaper, *Univers Israelit*, looking backward to an earlier era, remarked that "during the First Empire peddling was the chief occupation of Jews. Thus according to the census of 1808, twenty of approximately twenty-six Jewish families of Fontainebleau were so engaged; in Versailles, Orleans and Nantes all the Jews were peddlers." In Wurttemberg in 1812, no fewer than 85.5 percent of the Jews made a living as "hucksters," and a study of Polish Jewry in the nineteenth century stated quite simply, "a majority of the Jewish population in Poland made their living in trade, but this principally meant peddled trade rather than retail." It may not be at all outrageous to suggest that every European Jew would have known peddlers as family members and neighbors, real presences in the ordinary course of everyday life.[8]

The reality of Jewish peddling not only affected the peddlers themselves and their families, but Jewish community life both responded to and took its form from the ubiquity of the peddlers' presence. Jewish communities in the premodern and premigration settings, for example, made certain that either individual Jews or the community as a whole provided food and lodging for Jewish peddlers. The existence of hundreds of scattered Jewish communities in relative proximity to each other also meant that these peddlers in the Germanic states, Poland, Alsace, and elsewhere on the continent, did not have to return home for the Sabbath. They could often avail themselves of Sabbath services in the towns along their route. They spent holidays away from their own families but still in the comfort of Jewish homes.

The European Jewish economy rode on the backs of peddlers, and this fact made their presence a constant feature of Jewish life and forged Jewish relationships independent of place of residence. Peddling along Jewish routes helped make the Jewish people transnational. It fostered a sense of themselves as cosmopolitans rather than as locals. Jews in one country came to be familiar with Jews from another. They learned each others' cooking styles and modes of dress as well as the details of lived life in the communities they came to. In the 1770s, as one of many possible examples, the bishop prince of Paderborn allowed Polish Jewish peddlers to come into his territory. Later, when their number grew too large, he rescinded the invitation.[9] Regardless of the fickle whims of the Paderborn official, local Jews came in contact with Polish Jews in their homes, synagogues, and other sites of Jewish community life. Among other profound implications, this reinforced the maintenance of Yiddish, a transnational Jewish language that allowed Jews to communicate with each other regardless of whether they hailed from Alsace in the west or as far east as Lithuania and the Russian lands. Peddling as such sustained the Jews' linguistic continuity at the same time that it exposed them to the many variants of Jewish practice.

Similarly, the peddlers took on, by circumstance, a political role as they served in the age before newspapers as crucial agents of information, linking Jewish communities and making possible the emergence of an integrated Jewish identity within and beyond the borders of particular nation-states. Historian Jacob Katz in his elegant, Out of the Ghetto, links the peddlers of "Ghetto Times," the title of the first chapter of the book, with the statement that no Jewish community, "even the largest, could be said to have been self-contained or self-sufficient. Business transactions brought members of different communities into touch. . . . It was a typical feature of Jewish economic activity that it could rely on business connections with Jewish communities in even far-flung cities and countries." Katz, expansive in the scope of his thinking, saw this internationalism as paradigmatic of both business and community life among these Jews and asserted that it characterized not just the highest levels of commerce but also "peddlers, even if they did not travel great distances or even go abroad."[10]

In the European setting, Jewish peddling played a crucial role in forging relationships between Jews and non-Jews. Jews not only sold to non-Jews, but they often bought agricultural goods as well as scraps, like bones and rags, which could be reused, from non-Jews, thus enabling interreligious contact. At times Jewish peddlers spent the night in Christian homes or in inns catering to various kinds of wayfarers. The Jewish peddlers, as it were, taught their Christian customers something about Judaism, and real, as opposed to mythic, Jews. In a family reminiscence of the peddling experience in the early nineteenth century in Rhenbischofsheim, a small German town, Moses Kahnmann's grandson recalled that his grandfather described how he "occasionally might find in a village inn or with a friendly peasant a pan especially marked with the sign of kashrut, for the exclusive use of Jewish guests," the majority of whom came as peddlers. Others, both in personal memoirs and in historical studies, observed that "the pedlars stayed overnight with peasant acquaintances with whom they left their own kosher crockery for repeated uses." Peasant meant non-Jew, and such respectful behaviors demonstrated the possibility of Jewish-Christian amity in an otherwise hostile environment and underscored the significance of the peddlers as historical actors.[11]

The history of Jewish life in Europe could be narrated around the history of peddling: its actual details, in terms of what peddlers sold, to whom, by what means, and for what price. Such a study would examine how Jewish peddlers interacted with, or avoided, non-Jewish peddlers, and the ways in which Jewish peddlers and settled town merchants, both Jewish and Gentile, influenced each other.[12] It would explore the impact of peddling on the Jews' inner communal lives and on the multiple ways in which peddling affected relationships between Jews and Christians as individuals and as members of distinct communities. How peddling figured into Christian polemics against the Jews, how it emerged as matters of the state as many rulers and decision makers pondered the assets or liabilities of the Jewish peddlers, and how Jews who represented their people to those with state power fretted over the peddlers' visibility and distinctiveness all represent crucial and conceptual issues with which such a history would be concerned.[13]

Peddling clearly provided the overarching economic, and, as such, political, social, and cultural framework for the lives of many, indeed most, European Jews in the time before the late eighteenth century, the period that heralded the onset of modernization, the beginnings of emancipation, and the first stirrings of the massive east to west migration that profoundly transformed Jewish life.

NEW WORLD IMMIGRATION AND PEDDLING

While Jewish peddling did not come to an end in eighteenth-century central and eastern Europe, at that point in time, another transformative factor entered into Jewish life and made peddling an even more significant force in the history of the Jews. From the eighteenth century onward, peddling provided central and eastern European Jews with an effective means by which they could not only enhance their chances of making a living, but it also gave them the opportunity to find new places to live, among those the American South. That is, peddling as a familiar occupation, as the Jews' economic métier, became caught up with and indeed facilitated the great movements of Jews out of long-established places of residence to a series of new worlds. Nearly every place that Jews went to as they left continental Europe, both central and eastern, was opened up to them through the actions of peddlers, men who took up their old-style trade but in radically new settings.

The act of leave-taking pivoted in a number of ways around the peddling phenomenon. Notably, these new world Jewish peddlers may not themselves have ever peddled before their migrations. Many came from the ranks of young men unable to find a place for themselves in the local economies of the regions where they had grown up. Migration offered them a way of establishing themselves as adults. They may have been too young to have ever peddled themselves, but when they needed to find a means of migration and a way to make a living in their new homes, they turned to what they knew. After all, they would have known in their immediate families and in their villages many peddlers whose experiences and skills they could draw on. In addition, these young Jewish emigrants abandoned precisely those places where Jewish overcompetition in the field of peddling had made it impossible for them, as young people, to get started with their lives. Finally, the young men poised to emigrate by taking up the peddlers' pack departed from towns and regions that no longer needed peddlers because new commercial realities undercut the peddlers'—and the Jews'—long-standing modes of making a living.

Instead, these young men began a process of moving outward, discovering as Jews a number of new worlds, and peddling, the old, familiar economic modus operandi of the Jews, structured that linked physical movement and the process of discovery. This new age of Jewish peddling took Jews out of continental Europe and brought them over the course of the next two and a half centuries to no fewer spots around the globe than the British Isles, the Americas—North, South, and Central—South Africa, and Australia.[14]

Generally, the less developed a region, the poorer the internal transportation networks, the fewer settled merchants present, the further the distance from one settlement to another, and the more agrarian the region, the more attractive immigrant Jewish peddlers found it. Certainly the southern region of the United States fit all of these criteria. The least urbanized part of the country for the longest time, the most agrarian, and the one with the least articulated system of roads and railroads, it attracted Jewish immigrant peddlers well into the early twentieth century. In the absence of focused case studies of Jewish peddling, let alone comparative ones, one can at least begin with the hunch that the South's persistent agrarianism, its fairly small commercial class, and its lag in indus-

Jewish peddler in the United States with his wagon and a customer. Daguerreotype by unknown photographer, nineteenth century. Courtesy Richard W. Welch, Graphic Antiquity and the Jacob Rader Marcus Center, American Jewish Archives, Cincinnati, Ohio.

trial and urban development as compared with other American regions made it a particularly attractive magnet for young Jews looking to gain a foothold in American commerce.

But nearly every other region of the United States also, at one time or another, drew in and used the services of Jewish peddlers. References to the arrival, commercial and communal activities, and subsequent careers of Jewish peddlers in every part of the nation testify to that historical reality. Nearly every issue of the journal *Western States Jewish History*, for example, contains articles that refer to the presence of Jewish peddlers west of the Mississippi River. So, too, publications surveying the Jewish history of other parts of the United States demonstrate the national nature of Jewish peddling.[15]

A few non-southern examples will have to suffice to point to the national scope of the phenomenon. Of Boston's Jews in the years 1845 to 1861, 25 percent peddled at one time or another, while among those in Easton, Pennsylvania, the concentration moved from 46 percent in 1840 to 70 percent in 1845. In Iowa, in 1850, 125 Jews made their home and 100 peddled around the state. A nonexhaustive list of places where peddlers were the first Jews to appear and then settle would include Rochester, New York; Berkshire County, Massachusetts; Sioux City, Iowa; Chicago; Chico, California; Monmouth County, New Jersey; Cincinnati; Lancaster, Pennsylvania; and Tupper Lake, New York. The list could go on for pages demonstrating the ubiquity of the phenomenon and also demonstrating the lack of a uniquely southern narrative.[16]

The South, then, was not the only region that supported such activities, although it may have continued to attract them for a longer period of time. Yet in each one of these places, and the many specific regions within them, peddlers as the first Jews (and sometimes the first white people) penetrated these unknown spaces. In various lands the activities of the peddlers cleared the ground for the eventual formation of settled Jewish communities, while in others the peddlers—and the Jewish presence—disappeared leaving few traces.

The lack of a distinctive southern story needs to be set in the context of this phenomenon as not being a uniquely North American one either. The vast transfer population of Jews from central and eastern Europe westward moved along peddling routes, and the history of Jewish peddling in each new world has a history of its own. Each one stands as worthy of analysis. Jewish peddling in South and Central America followed a particular course no doubt different from that of Jewish peddling in South Africa or Canada. Furthermore, within any one of these continents or countries local variations also made for many different histories of Jewish peddling and Jewish migration. For example, Jewish peddlers in Quebec who sold to French-speaking Catholic customers who evinced hostility toward the idea of Canada as a modern, liberal, and British-oriented nation had a particular set of experiences that diverged from those of Jewish peddlers who cast their lot in the Anglophone provinces where Protestantism predominated and most women and men embraced their connections to Great Britain and its economic and political practices. Likewise in South Africa, Jewish peddlers sold at one time or another to the Afrikaner Boers and to the British, as well as to native customers, who had been colonized by both these groups. Each constituency had a different set of reactions to the peddlers as Jews, immigrants (primarily from Lithuania), and bearers of consumer goods. Each history needs to be explored, and each stands on its own.

Young Jewish men who showed up in the American South to peddle their wares found a particular racial landscape, one in which the black-white divide created a set of social practices not replicated in New England or upstate New York, where differences of class rather than color structured political relationships that the peddlers had to know about and deal with. Further west, the presence of Indians and Mexicans as customers forced Jewish peddlers fresh from Posen or Lithuania to confront yet another set of on-the-ground realities as they sought to accomplish the goals of the migration: earn money, settle down, marry (or bring wives and children left behind in either Europe or some other large city), and get on with life.

INTERACTION WITH NON-JEWS

Yet certain characteristics have been shared by all new world Jewish peddling histories regardless of continent or country or region within. First, unlike old world peddling, the immigrant peddlers sold only to non-Jews. This perhaps obvious point had tremendous historical significance, not just for the peddlers themselves but for the development of Jewish communities in these places. The young Jewish man who decided to leave Alsace or Lithuania, two important sources of Jewish migrant-peddlers, and try his luck in the Mississippi Delta, the Pacific Northwest, as well as the Transvaal, the Australian outback, the Argentine Pampas, the Irish midlands, the mining regions of Wales, or the foothills of the Andes, had no string of Jewish enclaves to turn to when the day ended, or at times even when the sun set on Friday, or when Jewish holidays punctuated the calendar.

Rather, these peddlers spent the days of the week only among non-Jews, depending on their customers for a place to sleep and eat before setting out again on the road. Since Jewish peddlers divided up the countryside among themselves, no one encroaching upon another's territory, they lived pretty much devoid of contact with other Jews. This reality reflected the fact that the first of the peddlers, as pioneers, went to places where no Jew had been before. Those who immigrated later and entered the field took the place of the Jewish peddlers who had amassed enough savings to be able to own their shops in town. While the later peddlers sold to non-Jews who had already become acquainted with Jews, they still did not share the road or their weekday time with other Jews, and the newcomer peddlers, like their predecessors, spent days on end with no other Jews around them.

JEWISH FELLOWSHIP

This then meant that new world Jewish peddlers, unlike their counterparts in the old world, did not travel as far and organized their selling lives when they could in such a way as to be able to get back to Jewish enclaves for the Sabbath. The life histories of many of these immigrant peddlers repeatedly noted that their lives marched according to a kind of weekly rhythm: they went out on their routes on Sunday and returned by Friday to whatever existed in the way of a Jewish hub for Jewish food, fellowship, and rest. Joseph Jacob in his 1919 apologetic defense of the Jewish people, *The Jewish Contribution to Civilization*, described how in England, which in terms of Jewish migration history must be thought of as a new world, "it was customary for the Jews of the seaport towns . . . to send out their sons every Monday morning to neighboring villages as hawkers, who would return in time for the Friday night meal." These hawkers, the British word of choice for peddler, came to be known within the Jewish community as "Wochers," that is, "weekly people."[17] In Ireland, to which several thousand Lithuanian Jews immigrated after the 1880s and where nearly all the men peddled at one time or another, Jews described themselves and were described by their customers as "weekly men," the ones who showed up week after week at the farmhouse doors, ready to collect payment for previously purchased goods and to show the woman of the home some new things to buy.[18] In Mississippi, as in many southern Jewish communities, former peddlers-turned-shopkeepers provided accommodations for those still on the road, who needed a Sabbath resting place. In Natchez, the Millstein's house became the place where, "many of the peddlers who came home . . . after a week's work would gather . . . for the Sabbath."[19]

These spots of Jewish life scattered through the hinterlands, where peddlers spent their weekends and holidays, reflected the densely Jewish underpinnings to the migration and settlement. In these places peddlers ready to upgrade and settle met young Jewish women—daughters and female relatives of Jewish merchants. The outlines of congregations began to take shape as numbers grew, however minimally. Indeed, before congregations formed, peddlers fulfilled their Jewish obligations in these crossroad villages. The story of how the death of two Jewish peddlers in the area surrounding Meridian, Mississippi, compelled the few Jews living there in the 1860s to purchase land for a cemetery has been told as well about Woodville, Mississippi. It likewise could be and has been told about Australia, Ireland, South Africa, and Canada.[20]

The time off the road spent with other Jews, often fellows from familiar European places who spoke a common language, involved not just, or even primarily, Jewish activities but also socializing. In the country stores owned by former peddlers, those who relaxed were like Edward Cohen's grandfather, featured in Cohen's family memoir, who spent Saturday night in New Orleans, where "he'd rest, drink whiskey with the Alsation [sic] peddlers and play poker all night."[21]

Moise Cohen's recollection that he, a Romanian Jew, found fellowship with a pack of Alsatian Jewish peddlers points out yet another implication for Jewish history of peddling around the modern world. It provided a common experience for young Jewish men drawn from many different European homes. Bavarian, Bohemian, Lithuanian, Polish, Galician, and Prussian Jewish men peddled alongside Alsatians, Romanians, and others in numerous countries. This experience, despite its diversifying nature, actually served as a unifying force, representing a step on the road toward creating new Jewish identities based not on where people came from but where they had gone to. The histories of fathers as peddlers and peddling's impact on family life became important experiences that immigrant Jews in their many, newest diaspora homes shared with each other.

The connection between peddling and the creation of Jewish life in the hinterlands played itself out in other ways. For one, Jewish peddlers who traveled to the larger cities, characterized as they were by substantial and institutionally rich Jewish communities, stocked up on matzo at the same time that they settled with creditors and replenished their supply of wares to sell when they went back on the road. In places like New York, Baltimore, Cincinnati, and Philadelphia, Jewish peddlers loaded up with Jewish goods that they then brought back to Tennessee, Georgia, Mississippi, and the like. Perhaps even more dramatically, peddlers functioned as leaders of Jewish communities. No more intriguing example exists than that of Charles Wessolowsky, an immigrant peddler from Gollub, a town in the former Polish province of Posen, who, in the late 1870s, functioned as a kind of circuit rabbi throughout the American South, particularly in Georgia, selling wares at the same time that he buried the deceased, performed marriages of Jewish couples, and consecrated synagogues and cemeteries.[22] So too, Bernard Nordlinger, an Alsatian-born Jewish peddler who sold in the territory around Macon, Georgia, struck the small group of Jews living there as Judaically knowledgeable, and they asked him to become their rabbi.[23]

"BETWEEN-PEOPLE" IN RURAL ECONOMIES

The reality that Jewish peddlers spent most of their time, while peddling, with non-Jews forced them into a quick encounter with difference and put them nearly immediately on the path toward learning new languages, cultures, and social realities. Wherever they went and lived in these liminal situations, they functioned as "between-people." They had no choice but to develop relationships with the people to whom they sold and to whom, perhaps more important, they wanted to sell. By definition, they had to learn their potential customers' languages, literal and figurative, and had to ingratiate themselves with the women—most often the people to whom they sold—who opened the doors, looked in the baskets, and made the decision whether or not to buy the eyeglasses, pictures, picture frames, curtains, blankets, pots, pans, and other sundry goods. They had to acquire knowledge of local social and political relationships, to figure out who were the most likely customers and where they lived, what topics to avoid, and what aspirations to play upon.

Yet, simultaneously, in one place after another around the peddlers' globe, the entry of Jewish itinerant merchants into the rural region unsettled locally prevailing economic relationships. In places where class, religion, race, and national background mattered greatly, the fact that peddlers sold across those lines made them different and notable. The Jewish peddler in the rural South may have been the only individual to enter the homes of blacks and the homes of whites with the same goal in mind: selling goods to anyone willing to pay. So too, Jewish peddlers who made their way around the Cape Colony made no distinction between the homes of the English farmers and those of the Boers. In a profound sense the peddlers did not see groups but rather customers.

The disruptive role played by the peddlers in part stemmed from the fact that as outsiders they could, at times, transgress conventional boundaries of etiquette. They could, in essence, claim ignorance of local rules as they sought to expand the scope of their selling. That Jewish peddlers in the late nineteenth- and early-twentieth-century southern communities in the United States at times lodged with African American families, ate at their tables, and developed what for that time and place constituted respectful public relationships offers a case in point. Morris Wittcowsky, author of one of the best peddler life histories, asserted that he and his "brother" peddlers "were probably the first white people in the South who paid the Negro people any respect at all," and he and many others insisted on using the titles Mr. and Mrs. when addressing black customers.[24]

This should not be taken to imply that Jewish peddlers challenged prevailing social or power relationships. In many ways their status as outsiders and the particular nature of their commercial transactions helped retain the status quo. During the era of plantation slavery, Jewish peddlers carrying secondhand clothing, sewn (or, better, re-sewn) by Jewish tailors on New York's Chatham Street in the "slop shops" associated with that section of the city, sold to plantation owners for the use of their slaves.[25]

Peddlers could also break the rules because local people on farms, in mining camps, and on the fringes of cities not connected to downtown shopping districts reveled in the items the peddlers had for sale. This eager embrace of the peddler and his goods encompassed not just the poorer people and those, like African Americans in the South, who enjoyed the fewest rights available but also those who represented the political and economic elite. The Jewish peddlers fit into existing stratified relationships in large measure because they did not fit in at all and defied the boundaries of the accepted and established order. The Jewish peddlers, because they did not have a stake in the social order, could cross lines.

Certainly at times and in most places the peddlers not only offered new goods, new standards of consumption, and cosmopolitan styles, but they also invoked the ire of settled shopkeepers whom the peddlers could undersell. Local shopkeepers and farm women, by and large, shared religious, linguistic, and "ethnic" (for lack of a better term here) characteristics. These women, who had only limited dollars (or pounds or pesos) for purchasing goods, stood then between the Jewish peddlers and their non-Jewish compatriots, those storeowners who often had been drawn from the ranks of farm families and with whom they often shared family and kinship connections.

The peddler and the shopkeeper, in essence, both courted these relatively poor women, who thus gained power through their purchasing choices. The merchants of the place argued, directly and indirectly, that group loyalty demanded that the women buy from them. They pointed out that the Jewish peddler combined in one physical being foreignness, religious otherness, and an economic challenge to the local order. Yet the peddler offered credit, new goods, and direct access to those goods. Coming straight to the women's homes, showing them exactly how the curtains and the pictures would look, the peddler drew the women more intimately into the fantasies of consumption.

Jewish peddler/non-Jewish merchant competition occasionally led to anti-Jewish agitation and even violence. The presence of Jewish peddlers, at different times and in various places, played itself out in local and national politics, as the merchants and their representatives sought to limit the access of peddlers, defined directly or obliquely as "Jews" or "foreigners" to the privileges of the marketplace. That states like North Carolina passed laws requiring peddlers to show proof of citizenship before obtaining a license demonstrated one of the multiple ways in which the presence of foreign peddlers, Jews primarily, became politicized.[26] By 1891, enough Jewish peddlers had entered into the commercial life of Key West, Florida, to propel the city council to enact legislation that taxed immigrant peddlers at the rate of one thousand dollars a head.[27]

How much the three notorious episodes of Civil War anti-Jewish action, that perpetrated by General U. S. Grant on the Jews of the department of the Tennessee (Paducah, Kentucky), and the others in Talbotton and Thomasville, Georgia, grew out of the peddling experience deserves some consideration. In all three cases the belief that the Jews as merchants profited from wartime exigencies enflamed prejudice and led to calls that they be expelled. In these locales Jews had been peddlers, moving in and out of town and selling to farmers in the surrounding countryside. So they thus came in and out of community surveillance, and local people struggling with shortages of goods of all kinds imagined that the Jews, the shadowy peddlers, were not only treacherous but benefiting from the suffering of others.

The peddlers, those who lived in the South during the Civil War as well as those who lived in all the new world places throughout this long period, in one way or another disrupted local social patterns and entered into local dramas that did not concern them but which they affected. Consequently, the halls of city and county councils, court houses, state legislatures, and even national assemblies became places where the merits and demerits of Jewish peddling and Jewish migration were weighed.

On a personal level, memoirs and life histories of former Jewish peddlers, regardless of which new world they went to, described in painful detail the experiences of being spat upon, pelted with stones, and hounded by barking dogs, as locals verbally hurled anti-Jewish slurs at them. Jewish communal bodies and defense organizations at times also had to deal with the issue of the peddlers and the shadows they cast on the process of acceptance and integration.

Yet non-Jewish women, as the chief customers, continued to buy from the peddlers and, in the process, challenged the power of clergy and other local elites who implored them to shun the Jew, the peddler. Likewise, Jewish peddlers persevered with their routes, returning time and again to these locales to cultivate customers and abandoning these places only when better opportunities beckoned elsewhere or when they had amassed enough savings to open a store and relinquish life on the road. When they settled, particularly in the towns that served the rural regions around which they had peddled, they became respected members of the community, sometimes (and with much national and regional variation) winning enough trust of the local non-Jewish populace to hold public office. At minimum, most set themselves up as modestly successful storekeepers who maintained friendly enough relations with customers, non-Jewish in the main, who bought much of what they needed from, as Stella Suberman called it, "the Jew Store."[28]

Jewish peddlers functioned between various classes of people divided by color, religion, language, and class. Each new world in which they sold had its own deep cleavages and hierarchies. Jews fit no fixed category by which they could be understood, and they had to learn to negotiate these divides in order to sell their goods at the best price and ensure their own personal safety. In the American South, color mattered more than anything, and Jews as white people could take profound advantage of that reality. Perhaps the best statement available to historians describing this has come to us from the memoir of Oscar Straus, close confidant of Theodore Roosevelt, U.S. ambassador to Turkey, and the first Jew to hold a cabinet position. Straus's father, Lazarus, came to the United States in 1852 from Bavaria and began his American career as a peddler in Georgia. As the son looks back on his father's life he writes:

The itinerant merchant . . . filled a real want, and his vocation was looked upon as quite dignified. Indeed he was treated by the owners of the plantations with a spirit of equality. . . . This gave to the white visitor a status of equality that probably otherwise he would not have enjoyed to such a degree, provided only, therefore, that the peddler proved himself an honourable, upright man, who conscientiously treated his customer with fairness and made no misrepresentations regarding his wares, he was treated as an honored guest by the plantation owners, certainly a spirit of true democracy.[29]

Straus correctly emphasized the importance of the Jewish peddlers' whiteness. Being defined by law as white, and therefore able to share in all of the privileges that went hand in hand with that color, the Jewish peddler could sell to African American customers yet retain all the rights and honors that ipso facto accompanied whiteness. They could treat their black customers with respect but not fear that their own whiteness would be compromised. Their white-

Lazarus Straus and his wife, Sara, in Talbotton, Georgia, 1856. This photograph was taken four years after Lazarus arrived in the United States and two years after Sara and the children joined him in Talbotton, seat of Talbot County. In 1852, Lazarus began as a pushcart peddler, first in Oglethorpe, Georgia, and, then, Talbotton. He peddled enough dry goods and "Yankee notions" so that within two years he had saved enough to send for Sara and their children. Courtesy of the Straus Historical Society, Inc., Smithtown, New York.

ness played a not insignificant role in making it possible for immigrant Jewish peddlers to begin their American years in this lowly occupation and swiftly move out of it.

THE BRIEF ROAD FROM MIGRATORY TO SEDENTARY

This final distinction between new world peddling and the pre- or nonmigration peddling experience had tremendous historical significance. Jewish men who migrated to peddle (and peddled in order to migrate) did so for a relatively brief duration. Rather than being a life sentence, as it had been in Europe, Jewish peddlers in their destination homes used peddling as a way to leave the occupation. And because they pursued this trade for only a fairly short time, sons did not pick up their fathers' packs or sit down behind their fathers' horses. Rather peddling represented merely a stage in a Jewish immigrant man's life, one not passed on to subsequent generations. The actual biographies of countless peddlers in their migration destinations demonstrate the linear trajectory on and off the road. The preponderance of former peddlers among the ranks of shopkeepers, large and small, in the towns and cities of the destination countries further proves the temporary nature of new world peddling. One example, drawn from Atlanta, Georgia, is the Rich brothers, immigrants from Kaschau, Hungary, the first of whom came to the United States in 1859. By 1867, he owned one of the most significant emporiums of the city reborn from the ashes of the Civil War, a symbol almost of the commercial underpinnings of the New South. Like so many other Jewish peddling families, they had migrated serially, with one brother bringing over another, broadening their selling base, pooling their earnings, and settling down when they had among themselves saved enough to open a store.[30]

Some former peddlers did not just advance in the commercial hierarchy from itinerancy to modest storekeeping but shot up meteorically to the highest echelons of business. Henry Lehman arrived in Mobile, Alabama, in the 1840s and loaded up with the kinds of items that farm families craved. He spent only one year selling from the road until he settled in Montgomery and opened a store selling crockery, seeds, tools, dry goods, and the like. Living behind the store, he squirreled away his earnings and ended his career as one of Alabama's and the South's most successful cotton brokers. His experience resembled that of Oscar Straus, also a Bavarian immigrant, who took his place among the legions of young Jewish men who served the rural South. Both moved from the difficult life on the road to affluence and economic influence locally, regionally, and indeed nationally.[31]

The trajectory from unskilled but eager-to-learn peddler to respectable shopkeeper represented a social reality that soon became a powerful image in the Jews' quest for rights. Jews in the age of migration, in the many places to which they had dispersed, made a point of defending themselves from negative stereotyping by showing how transitory the peddling experience had been. Just give Jews the chance to immigrate, this line of reasoning went, and they would first provide the essential services of the peddler but soon transform themselves into settled and responsible community members. This argument, like the new world peddling phenomenon, also had a global dimension. Israel Abrahams offered his defense of the Jews and Jewish peddling at a time when Great Britain began debating what would in 1905 become the Aliens Act. In the United States, George Cohen, author of a 1924 book, *The Jews in the Making of America*, provided a similar way of thinking about peddlers, Jews, and Jewish mobility, articulated in a decidedly American tone. In this book, published as part of the the the Racial Contribution Series sponsored by the Knights of Columbus, Cohen intended, as did the other authors, to use history to dispel the anti-immigrant spirit, which had captured the nation and which had in that same year culminated in the passage of restrictive and racially based immigration legislation. Cohen argues that the Jews' contribution to America could not be understood without attention to their long history of migrations and commerce, with peddling as not a negative but rather a heroic part of that narrative:

> The result of the nomadic tendencies of the Jews' Bedouin ancestors still are potent forces in the make-up of the modern Jew. That restlessness which impels the race to seek newer realms and better climes imparts to it during the course of its vicissitudes an adaptability and a readiness that are useful in the life struggle. What is so potent a factor in mental development as travel, and Israel has been the most traveled of peoples. The tribe of the "wandering foot" to keep traveling had to develop the gift of quickness of thought, of improvisation, of ready comprehension.[32]

In Cohen's sweeping analysis then, the Jewish peddlers, despite the mundane nature of their lives, exerted a profound impact on Jewish history.

THE SOUTH IN GLOBAL PERSPECTIVE

The history of every Jewish population center in the new world—the United States, Canada, England and the rest of the British Isles, South Africa, Australia, Mexico, Argentina, and elsewhere in South and Central America—cannot be disassociated from the global history of peddling. Common themes, common processes, and common concerns linked these places and made the history of any one not all that different from the basic contours of another. These universals or commonalities connected the experience of being a Jewish peddler at the tip of the Cape of Good Hope with the experience of being a Jewish peddler in Newfoundland or at the tip of Cape Horn with that of Alaska. Yet local stories of Jewish migration and Jewish peddling also deserve to be told to enrich and complicate modern Jewish history. In each place the local pattern of attitudes toward consumption, allocation of power, and distribution of resources, along with basic religious, ethnic, and racial cleavages in the society, as well as ideas about foreigners shaped the ways in which Jewish peddlers as immigrants and Jewish immigrants as peddlers made their way.

From the vantage point of southern Jewish history, the focus on peddlers provides not only a way to talk about a large group of actors, the young Jewish immigrant men who traversed the roads of the South, but it helps to align what has been considered a distinctive and idiosyncratic history with the broad outlines of modern Jewish history. Not an insignificant other story, southern Jewish history provides a locus to see the drama of European Jewish immigration, the impact of a particular kind of commerce, and how Jews benefited because they defied the standard categories by which societies organized themselves. Through the experience of peddlers, southern Jewish history stops being an oddity or an anomaly. Rather, by putting peddlers center stage, the history of Jews in the South can stand for one of the paradigmatic modern Jewish experiences.

NOTES

An earlier version of this essay appeared as "Entering the Mainstream of Modern Jewish History: Peddlers and the American Jewish South," *Southern Jewish History* 8 (2005): 1–30. It is published here with permission from the Southern Jewish Historical Society.

1. I. J. Schwartz, *Kentucky*, trans. Gertrude Dubrovsky (Tuscaloosa: University of Alabama Press, 1990), 29–30, 32.

2. Peddling itself, a phenomenon of significance well beyond Jewish history, has received some scholarly attention. Laurence Fontaine, *History of Pedlars in Europe*, trans. Vicki Whittaker (Durham, N.C.: Duke University Press, 1996) refers only in one place to Jewish peddlers, but his book offers an important salvo in historicizing this occupation and giving it the scholarly attention it deserves. There are a few studies of Arab peddling, particularly Alixa Naff, *Becoming American: The Early Arab Immigrant Experience* (Carbondale: Southern Illinois University Press, 1985).

3. Israel Abrahams, *Jewish Life in the Middle Ages* (London: Macmillan, 1896), 231–32.

4. Nancy L. Green, ed., *Jewish Workers in the Modern Diaspora* (Berkeley: University of California Press, 1998).

5. The work of Rudolf Glanz stands out as particularly noteworthy. See, for example, his "Notes on Early Jewish Peddling in America," *Jewish Social Studies* 7 (April 1945): 199–236; also, Lee M. Friedman, "The Problems of Nineteenth-Century American Jewish Peddlers," *American Jewish Historical Quarterly* 44 (September 1954): 1–7. It is worth commenting on not only the scantiness of this body of literature but on how early it appeared in the development of American Jewish history as a scholarly field. Since the field has become more professionalized and more thoroughly part of the mainstream of American historical scholarship, no one has picked up on the work of Glanz or Friedman and pursued the subject with greater conceptual sophistication.

6. A notable exception is Elliott Ashkenazi, *The Business Jews of Louisiana, 1840–1875* (Tuscaloosa: University of Alabama Press, 1988). Derek Penslar has offered some trench-

ant observations on Jewish historians' discomfort with writing about Jews and business in *Shylock's Children: Economics and Identity in Modern Europe* (Berkeley: University of California Press, 2001).

7. Green, *Jewish Workers*, 234.

8. Quoted in Zosa Szajkowski, "Growth of the Jewish Population in France," *Jewish Social Studies* 8 (1946): 307; David S. Landes, "The Jewish Merchant: Typology and Stereotypology in Germany," *Leon Baeck Institute Yearbook* 9 (1974): 13; Anna Maria Orla-Bukowska, "Shtetl Communities: Another Image," *Polin* 8 (1994): 94.

9. Moses Shulvass, *From East to West: The Westward Migration of Jews from Eastern Europe during the Seventeenth and Eighteenth Centuries* (Detroit: Wayne State University Press, 1971), 85.

10. Jacob Katz, *Out of the Ghetto: The Social Background of Jewish Emancipation, 1770–1870* (New York: Schocken Books, 1973), 22.

11. Quoted in Walter J. Cahman, "Village and Small-Town Jews in Germany: A Typological Study," *Leo Baeck Institute Yearbook* 19 (1974): 112–14, 121; for other references, see Mordecai Kossover, "Inland Trade among Polish Jews in the 16th–17th Centuries," *YIVO Bletter* 15 (March–April 1940): 182; and one of the best sources on Alsatian Jewish peddling Daniel Stauben, *Scenes of Jewish Life in Alsace* (Malibu, Calif.: Joseph Simon/Pangloss Press, 1991), originally published in the *Revue des Deux Mondes* in the late 1850s.

12. On non-Jewish peddlers, the key work is Fontaine, *History of Pedlars in Europe*.

13. The book that comes closest to accomplishing this is Derek Penslar's *Shylock's Children*.

14. For the purposes of thinking about Jewish migration and peddling from the end of the eighteenth century onward, the Netherlands, despite being in continental Europe, functioned as a new world setting. From the beginning of the eighteenth century, German, Bohemian, and Polish Jews came to the Netherlands to hawk their goods in towns, many of which did not allow Jews to reside there. Referred to as *smous*, a somewhat pejorative term, Ashkenazi Jews invoked the ire of merchants in Leiden and a number of other cities for their ability to sell goods door-to-door at low prices. For Jewish migrant peddling in the Netherlands, see several articles in J.C.H. Blom, R. G. Fuks-Mansfled, and I. Schöffer, *The History of the Jews in the Netherlands* (Portland, Ore.: Littman Library of Jewish Civilization, 2002), 114, 117, 167, 227.

15. See, for example, Bernard Goldman, ed., *Index: Michigan Jewish History, Volumes 1–39: 1960–1999* (Detroit: Michigan Jewish Historical Society, n.d.), 24; and Alan S. Pine, Jean C. Hershenov, and Aaron H. Lefkowitz, *From Peddler to Suburbanite: The History of the Jews of Monmouth County, N.J.* (Deal Park, N.J.: Monmouth Jewish Community Council, 1981).

16. Hasia R. Diner, *A Time for Gathering: The Second Migration, 1820–1880* (Baltimore, Md.: Johns Hopkins University Press, 1992), 68.

17. Joseph Jacob, *Jewish Contributions to Civilization* (Philadelphia: Jewish Publication Society of America, 1919), 219.

18. On Jewish peddling in Ireland and the use of the term *weekly men*, see Louis Hyman, *The Jews of Ireland: From Earliest Times to the Year 1910* (London: Jewish Historical Society of England, 1972), 160–66.

19. Leo E. Turitz and Evelyn Turitz, *Jews in Early Mississippi* (Jackson: University Press of Mississippi, 1983), 26.

20. Ibid., 89; Mississippi Historical Records Survey Project, Division of Professional and Service Projects and Works Projects Administration, *Inventory of the Church and Synagogue Archives of Mississippi: Jewish Congregations and Organizations* (Jackson: Mississippi State Conference, B'nai B'rith, 1940.)

21. Edward Cohen, *The Peddler's Grandson: Growing Up Jewish in Mississippi* (Jackson, University Press of Mississippi, 1999), 50.

22. Louis Schmier, *Reflections of Southern Jewry: the Letters of Charles Wessolowsky, 1878–1879* (Macon, Ga.: Mercer University Press, 1982), 14.

23. Bernard I. Nordlinger, "About My Grandfather, Bernard Nordlinger, Confederate Soldier and Unofficial Rabbi," *The Record* (Jewish Historical Society of Greater Washington) 3 (1968): 26–27.

24. Quoted in Leonard Rogoff, *Homelands: Southern Jewish Identity in Durham and Chapel Hill, North Carolina* (Tuscaloosa: University of Alabama Press, 2001), 95; see also Louis Schmier, "For Him the 'Schwartzers' Couldn't Do Enough: A Jewish Peddler and His Black Customers Look at Each Other," in Maurianne Adams and John Bracey, eds., *Strangers and Neighbors: Relations Between Blacks and Jews in the United States* (Amherst: University of Massachusetts Press, 1999), 223–36.

25. See Diner, *A Time for Gathering*, 80.

26. Rogoff, *Homelands*, 56.

27. Rachel Heimovics and Marcia Zerivitz, *Florida Jewish Heritage Trail* (Tallahassee: Florida Department of State, 2000), 40.

28. Stella Suberman, *The Jew Store* (Chapel Hill: Algonquin Books of Chapel Hill, 1998).

29. Oscar Straus, *Under Four Administrations: From Cleveland to Taft* (Boston: Houghton Mifflin Co., 1922), 6.

30. Henry G. Baker, *Rich's of Atlanta: The Story of a Store since 1867* (Atlanta: Division of Research, School of Business Administration, University of Georgia, 1953), 6–12.

31. Roland Flade, *The Lehmans: From Rimpar to the New World, a Family History* (Würzburg, Germany: Königshausen & Neumann, 1999), 45.

32. George Cohen, *The Jews in the Making of America* (Boston: Stratford, 1924), 243–44.

5

JEWISH CONFEDERATES

ROBERT N. ROSEN

In March 1865, Samuel Yates Levy, a captain in the Confederate Army and a prisoner of war at Johnson's Island, wrote to his father J. C. Levy of Savannah, Georgia, "I long to breathe the free air of Dixie." Like the Levy family, southern Jews were an integral part of the Confederate States of America and had been breathing the free air of Dixie for more than two hundred years.

When the Civil War began, there were sizable Jewish communities in all of the major southern cities. Louisiana boasted more than five congregations. New Orleans had the seventh-largest Jewish population in the United States (Boston was sixth and Chicago eighth). In Charleston, South Carolina, home to three congregations (one Reform, one traditional, and one composed of Orthodox Polish immigrants) "Israelites occupy the most distinguished places," according to one Jewish traveler. The Jews of Savannah organized K.K. Mikve Israel in 1735, the third congregation in America, following those in New York and Newport, Rhode Island. There were Jewish communities in Richmond and Petersburg, Virginia; Atlanta, Macon, and Columbus, Georgia; Memphis and Nashville, Tennessee; and Galveston and Houston, Texas, and Jews lived in dozens of small towns throughout the South.[1]

Louisiana was emblematic of the acculturation and assimilation of Jews in the antebellum South. Judah P. Benjamin served as one of the state's U.S. senators. Lieutenant Governor Henry M. Hyams was Benjamin's cousin, having moved to Louisiana with Benjamin from Charleston in 1828. Edwin Warren Moise, also from South Carolina, served as Speaker of the Louisiana House of Representatives and was about to become a Confederate judge. According to the youthful Salomon de Rothschild of the great French banking family, "all these men have a Jewish heart and take an interest in me."[2]

In 1860, Louisiana was home to at least 8,000 Jews, and likely many more. The total number of Jews in the eleven states of the Confederacy was between 20,000 and 25,000, which means that Louisiana was home to 25 to 40 percent of southern Jewry. New Orleans in 1860 was the South's largest city by far. Its population of 168,675 dwarfed Charleston's (40,522), Richmond's (37,910), Mobile's (29,258), and Savannah's (22,292). Like the growing cities of the North and West, New Orleans beckoned to immigrants, and they came.[3]

Southern Jews accepted regional customs and institutions, and most significantly, its greatest pathology, slavery. Oscar Straus put it best when he wrote in his memoirs: "As a boy brought up in the South I never questioned the rights or wrongs of slavery. Its existence I regarded as matter of course, as most other customs or institutions." Jews adopted the "southern way of life," including its code of honor, dueling, slavery, and notions about race and states' rights. In 1862, Bernhard Felsenthal, a northern abolitionist rabbi wrote that "Israelites residing in New Orleans are man by man . . . ardently in favor of secession" and that Jewish German immigrants favored slavery precisely because many non-Jewish German immigrants opposed it. "No Jewish political figure of the Old South ever expressed reservations about the justice of slavery or the rightness of the Southern position," Rabbi Bertram Korn concluded.[4]

Nor is there any evidence that Jews supported slavery as a result of intimidation or fear of reprisals. The Talmud taught Jews that "the law of the land is the law." According to many rabbis, North and South, the Hebrew Bible allowed for slavery. "How dare you . . . denounce slaveholding as a sin?" Rabbi Morris J. Raphall of New York thundered at the abolitionists. "When you remember that Abraham, Isaac, Jacob, Job—the men with whom the Almighty conversed, with whose names he emphatically connects his own most holy name—all these men were slaveholders." Solomon Cohen wrote to his aunt, Rebecca Gratz of Philadelphia, that "God gave laws to his chosen people for the government of their slaves, and did not order them to abolish slavery."[5]

As most Jews in the South in 1861 were struggling or poor immigrants from the Germans states or eastern Europe, they owned few slaves. Jewish southerners were peddlers, store clerks, innkeepers, cigar makers, teachers, bartenders, petty merchants, tradesmen, and tailors. But they lived in a slaveholding society, and they accepted the institution as part of everyday life. Jews in southern cities and towns who did own small numbers of slaves utilized them as domestic servants or as workers in their trades, or they hired them out. "Acceptance of slavery was," Leonard Dinnerstein writes, "an aspect of southern life common to nearly all its white inhabitants." Indeed, it was common to its free black inhabitants, who owned more slaves than southern Jews. The free blacks of Charleston owned three times the number of slaves owned by Charleston Jewry.[6]

In 1840, three-fourths of all heads of families in Charleston owned at least one slave, and the incidence of slaveholding among Jews likely paralleled that of their neighbors. In Richmond, a few Jewish auctioneers sold slaves, and there was one Jewish slave dealer, Abraham Smith. Richmond's rabbis supported slavery. George Jacobs of Richmond hired a slave to work in his home, although he owned no slaves. Reverend Max Michelbacher prayed during the Civil War that God would protect his congregation from slave revolt and that the Union's "wicked" efforts to "beguile [the slaves] from the path of duty that they may way-lay their masters, to assassinate and slay the men, women, and children . . . be frustrated."[7]

Because Jews accepted southern customs and mores, southerners accepted Jews. Most southerners were tolerant of different religions. The Fundamental Constitution of Carolina written by John Locke in 1699 granted freedom of re-ligion to "Ye Heathens, Jues [sic] and other Disenters." Jefferson's celebrated act of religious freedom asserted that "no man shall be compelled to frequent or support any religious worship, place, or ministry whatever." Southern aristo-crats, influenced by the Anglican, Episcopalian, Presbyterian, Methodist, and liberal Protestant tradition, had few concerns about Jews in their midst. They found their Jewish neighbors to be law-abiding, educated, and cosmopolitan, characteristics they appreciated. Jewish peddlers, teachers, musicians, lawyers, doctors, druggists, merchants, and men of learning enhanced their quality of life. Because the South attracted few "foreigners," small numbers of white im-migrants were more readily accepted. Finally, southerners believed fervently in the God of the Old Testament and respected their Jewish neighbors' knowledge of and historic connection to the Bible. Oscar Straus recalled how his father, who was well versed in biblical literature, translated passages from the Hebrew Bible for local ministers over dinner in their home.[8]

In 1859, the traveling journalist I. J. Benjamin explained Jews' acceptance in the South by noting that white inhabitants "felt themselves united with, and closer to, other whites. . . . Since the Israelite there did not do the humbler kinds of work which the Negro did, he was quickly received among the upper classes and easily rose to high political rank. For this reason, until now, it was only the South which sent Jews to the Senate. Benjamin came from Louisiana; [David Levy] Yulee from Florida." Yulee was born Jewish, married a Gentile, and disas-sociated himself from his Jewish roots.[9]

This is not to say that there was no antisemitism in the Old South, because there was. It was a fact of life in the nineteenth century. Emma Holmes of Charleston wrote in her diary that she disliked "Sumter [S.C.] very much from the prevalence of sand and Jews, my great abhorrences." By 1862, she blamed all of her ills on the Jews. Jews came into conflict with the majority Christian so-ciety on issues such as conducting retail businesses on Sunday. And, of course, southerners often found Jewish customs strange. Maria Bryan Connell of Hancock County, Georgia, had a Jewish houseguest. "I did not at all comprehend the trouble occasioned by their notions of unclean and forbidden food until I had a daughter of Abraham under the roof. She will not eat one mouthful of the finest fresh pork or the most delicate ham," she wrote. It was not, Connell concluded, "an unimportant consideration with her. Pray let this be entre nous, for I feel as if I am in some respect violating the duties of hospitality in speaking of it."[10]

The northern states were not as hospitable to Jews as was the South prior to the Civil War. The first known Jew in Boston was "warned out" in the 1640s. Unlike colonial Charleston, where Jews flourished, Jews were not allowed to live in early colonial Boston. John Quincy Adams referred to David Yulee as the "squeaking Jew delegate from Florida" and to Representative Albert G. Marchand of Pennsylvania as a "squat little Jew-faced rotundity." When the South seceded, the *Boston Evening Transcript*, a Brahmin publication, went so far as to blame secession on southern Jews. Calling Benjamin "the disunion leader in the U.S. Senate," and Yulee ("whose name has been changed from the more appropriate one of Levy or Levi") an ultra–fire-eater, the newspaper claimed that "this peculiar race . . . having no country of their own," desired "that other nations shall be in the same unhappy condition." By 1864, the *New York Times* castigated the Democratic Party because its chairman, August Belmont, was "the agent of foreign jew bankers."[11]

Not all southern Jews supported secession. Edwin DeLeon was pro-secession, whereas his brother Camden DeLeon, an officer in the army, was clearly uncomfortable with disloyalty to his government. Many were concerned about Lincoln's election and the elevation of an avowed opponent of slavery to the presidency. Simon Baruch, a Prussian immigrant and medical student, carried a lantern in a parade to celebrate secession bearing the words, "There is a point beyond which endurance ceases to be a virtue." After Lincoln's election, Solomon Cohen of Savannah wrote: "our enemies have triumphed." Cohen worried about control of the federal government by "those who hate us and our institutions."[12]

The irony of Jewish slaveowners was not lost on northern critics of slavery. The antislavery senator Benjamin Wade of Ohio referred to Judah Benjamin as an "Israelite with Egyptian principles."[13] The *Jewish Messenger* of New York City called upon American Jewry to "rally as one man for the Union and the *Constitution*." In April 1861, the Jews of Shreveport, Louisiana, responded with a denunciation of the newspaper and its editor. "[W]e, the Hebrew congregation of Shreveport scorn and repel your advice. . . . We solemnly pledge ourselves to stand by, protect, and honor the flag, with its stars and stripes, the Union and Constitution of the Southern Confederacy, with our lives, liberty, and all that is dear to us." Max Baer, president of the congregation, asked that newspapers friendly to the southern cause publish their resolution.[14]

Jewish southerners perceived New Englanders as abolitionists who were frequently antisemitic. Theodore Parker, a leading abolitionist minister, believed Jews' intellects were "sadly pinched in those narrow foreheads," that Jews were "lecherous," and "did sometimes kill a Christian baby at the Passover." William Lloyd Garrison, editor of the Liberator, once described Judge Mordecai Manuel Noah of New York as "the miscreant Jew," a "Shylock," "the enemy of Christ and liberty," and a descendant "of the monsters who nailed Jesus to the cross." Similar sentiments came from Edmond Quincy, Lydia Maria Child, William Ellery Channing, and Senator Henry Wilson of Massachusetts, all leading abolitionists. Child thought Judaism rife with superstition, claiming that Jews "have humbugged the world." John Quincy Adams opposed slavery and derided Jews.[15]

It is little wonder that there was no great love lost between southern Jews, who were accustomed to being treated as equals, and New Englanders. Isaac Harby, the Charleston journalist and pioneer of the Reform movement in the United States, denounced "the abolitionist society and its secret branches." It came as no surprise to South Carolina Jewry to see the following statement from the Boston Journal reprinted in their local newspaper in March 1861: "The Jew, [Benjamin] Mordecai, at Charleston, who gave ten thousand dollars to the South Carolina Government, had just settled with his Northern creditors by paying fifty cents on the dollar. The ten thousand was thus a Northern donation to secession." The Charleston Daily Courier called the story "a willful, unmitigated and deliberate falsehood."[16]

The question of why southern Jews fought for the Confederacy is not difficult to answer. "We of the South," Solomon Cohen wrote Rebecca Gratz, "feel that prudence and self-defense demand that we should protect ourselves." Jewish Confederates fought for liberty and freedom, including the right to own slaves. They fought to preserve the southern racial caste system. They fought invaders of their hearth and home. Private Simon Mayer of Natchez wrote to his family: "I sympathize with the poor victims of abolition despotism."[17]

Jewish Johnny Rebs were also motivated by a sense of duty and honor, powerful emotions in Victorian America. "Victorians," James McPherson writes, "understood duty to be a binding moral obligation involving reciprocity: one had a duty to defend the flag under whose protection one had lived." Corporal Isaac Valentine, a fallen Jewish Confederate, was mortally wounded in the same battle as his comrade Gustavus Poznanski Jr. On his deathbed Valentine believed he had done his duty and died for his country.[18]

Letters, memoirs, and obituaries all reflect Jewish soldiers' chief reasons for fighting: to do their duty, to protect their homeland, to protect southern rights and liberty and, once the war began, to support their comrades in arms. Philip Rosenheim of Richmond had just returned home from marching to the Chickahominy and had "fallen into sweet slumber" when his sister Rebecca awoke him. The bells had tolled, informing his militia company to gather. "I was very weak and had a severe headache," he wrote to his family, "but still I dressed myself, buckled on my accouterments, thinking I would not shrink from my duty and would follow the company wherever it goes, as our Flag says, when duty calls tis ours to obey." "We were thoroughly imbued with the idea," Moses Ezekiel of Richmond wrote in his memoirs "that we were not fighting for the perpetuation of slavery, but for the principle of State's rights and free trade, and in the defense of our homes, which were being ruthlessly invaded."[19] Many a Jewish youth left the German fatherland to avoid military service only to enlist voluntarily in the Confederate army soon after arriving in Dixie.

Isaac Hirsch of Fredericksburg, Virginia, a soldier in the 30th Virginia, visited the battlefield at Second Manassas, where Stonewall Jackson defeated General Pope's army. "It is bad," he wrote in his diary, "that the dead Yankees could not be buried as I don't like to see any human being lay on the top of the earth and rot, but it is a fit emblem for the invader of our soil for his bones to bleach on the soil he invades, especially of a people that wish to be left alone and settle down to their own peaceful pursuits."[20]

Mothers and sisters encouraged Jewish men, like other southern men, to fight. At the start of the war, Catherine Ezekiel, Moses mother, said that "she would not own a son who would not fight for his home and country." In May 1862, Mary Chestnut wrote of her friend "Mem" Cohen's dedication to the cause in her diary: "Our soldiers, thank God, are men after our own heart, cries Miriam of the house of Aaron." Phoebe Pember recalled that the "women of the South had been openly and violently rebellious from the moment they thought their states' rights touched. . . . They were the first to rebel—the last to succumb."[21]

The social pressure to enlist was also a strong factor in many young Confederates' decision to join the army. According to Gary Gallagher, 75 to 85 percent of the Confederacy's available draft-age white population served in the military. Any young white southern male had a difficult time in 1862 and 1863 explaining why he was not in uniform. Simon Baruch, a Prussian from Schwersenz (and Bernard Baruch's father), immigrated to Camden, South Carolina, as did his younger brother Herman. When Simon enlisted, he admonished Herman to stay out of the war. But Herman joined the cavalry because, as he told Simon, "I could no longer stand it. I could no longer look into the faces of the ladies."[22]

There was also the adventure of war and the bounty paid in advance. Young

Phoebe Yates Pember was born in Charleston, South Carolina, in 1823 into a well-to-do Jewish family. Her father, Jacob Clavius Levy, was active in Beth Elohim. She married Thomas Pember, a Gentile, who died prior to the war. Mrs. Pember left her parents' home in Marietta, Georgia, in December 1862 and went to wartime Richmond, Virginia, to become the first matron of the Chimborazo Hospital. Courtesy of Robert N. Rosen.

men unhappy in their work saw a chance to escape. Lewis Leon was such a clerk. An unmarried immigrant, Leon spoke German as well as English and at age nineteen enlisted for six months in the Charlotte Grays, Company C, 1st North Carolina. (Most southerners believed the war would be over in six months.) He was issued a fine uniform. "We were all boys between the ages of eighteen and twenty-one. . . . Our trip was full of joy and pleasure, for at every station where our train stopped the ladies showered us with flowers and Godspeed."[23]

Jewish Confederates, like other immigrants and African Americans, had a special burden during the war. They had to prove that Jews could fight. One of the tenets of nineteenth-century antisemitism was that the Jews were disloyal, unpatriotic, and cowardly. The "Wandering Jew" was the symbolic image of antisemitism. This stereotype labeled Jews as ghetto dwellers from Europe, who refused to assimilate with their neighbors and had fled their homelands to avoid military service. Southern Jewish soldiers set out to disprove these calumnies.[24]

Other Jews fought to make a place in southern society for those who would come after them. Philip Whitlock wrote in his memoir that "especially when I was of the Jewish Faith I thought that if I am negligent in my duty as a citizen of this country, it would unfavorably reflect on the whole Jewish race and religion." Charles Wessolowsky said after the war that "sometimes he felt like a Jewish missionary among the Gentiles to show the way for other Jews to follow." Early-twentieth-century Jewish historians were anxious to defend the courage and bravery of the generation that preceded them. "There existed no occasion to threaten the young or, for that matter, the middle-aged, with the 'white feather,'" Ezekiel and Lichtenstein write in The History of the Jews of Richmond. "None held back or hesitated."[25]

Finally, Jewish tradition also played a part. From the Book of Esther and Jeremiah ("Seek the welfare of the city to which I have exiled you," Jer. 29:7) to rabbinical law, Judaism taught respect and obedience to the established government. Jews had always aligned themselves with monarchs and conservative regimes for self-protection from the masses. The traditional Jewish prayer for the government, dating to the sixteenth century, called upon God to bless the king and inspire him with benevolence "toward us and all Israel our brethren." As the new Confederacy was now their lawful government, Jewish tradition demanded loyalty to it.[26]

Thus, Jewish Johnny Rebs went off to war for patriotism and love of country, yearning for a fatherland they could believe in, defense of their new homeland, and demonstrating to the North that their rights could not be assailed. Equally compelling were the social pressures to enlist, the frenzy of secession and war, the desire to escape home and see the world, the lure of adventure and money, and to prove that Jews were fighters. "The Jews of the Confederacy had good reason to be loyal to their section," Rabbi Korn concludes. "Nowhere else in America—certainly not in the ante-bellum North—had Jews been accorded such an opportunity to be complete equals as in the old South."[27]

From the top of the social ladder to the bottom, southern Jews supported the Confederate cause. Former Senator Judah Benjamin, one of the South's most brilliant lawyers (President Millard Fillmore nominated him to the Supreme Court, but Benjamin declined the honor), became attorney general of the new Confederate States of America. "A Hebrew of Hebrews, for the map of the Holy City was traced all over his small, refined face," Thomas Cooper DeLeon later recalled, "the attorney-general was of the highest type of his race."[28]

There was little legal work for the new attorney general, and Benjamin rapidly became a close confidant of and political adviser to President Jefferson Davis. A wit, a gourmand, and a raconteur, Benjamin was a popular member of Richmond society. When the secretary of war resigned, Davis asked Benjamin to take his place. Unfortunately Benjamin had no military background. He did bring his well-known capacity for hard work and organization to the War Department, but his tenure was marked by notable failures in the field, for which he received (and accepted) the blame. After the disastrous fall of Roanoke Island, Virginia, in early 1862, Davis promoted Benjamin to secretary of state in "the very teeth of criticism."

Benjamin's Jewish heritage (he did not practice the Jewish religion) was a lightning rod for critics of the Davis administration. Congressman Henry S. Foote of Tennessee, a rabid antisemite, referred to Benjamin as "Judas Iscariot Benjamin" and the "Jewish puppeteer" behind the "Davis tyranny." John M. Daniel of the Richmond Examiner reacted to Benjamin's appointment as secretary of state by remarking that "the representation of the Synagogue is not diminished; it remains full." These, however, were minority opinions.[29]

Benjamin continued to serve as Davis's secretary of state. He was to the civilian government what Robert E. Lee was to the military: a loyal, stalwart, indefatigable, and uncomplaining patriot. He was the best-known Confederate official next to the president and vice-president and third in order of succession. Varina Howell Davis called Benjamin her husband's "right arm." Historians have described him as "the President's most intimate friend and counselor." Eli Evans portrayed Benjamin as Davis's alter ego.[30]

As the war dragged on, the Confederacy's options dwindled. On February 12, 1864, the Confederate Congress voted in secret session to create "bodies for the capture and destruction of the enemies' property." The Bureau of Special and Secret Service came into existence, and funding for these operations went to the State Department. Benjamin, as secretary of state, was the likely head of the bureau and chief of Confederate covert activities. Shortly thereafter, important agents of the Confederacy arrived in Montreal. "A few months later," according to Roy Z. Chamlee Jr., "John Wilkes Booth opened a bank account in the same Montreal bank used by the Rebels."[31]

Benjamin took on the most dangerous assignment Davis had given him, that of spymaster. This would be his last assignment for the Confederacy. He established spy rings and sent political propagandists to the North and to Canada. He enlisted the seductive Belle Boyd, the "Cleopatra of Secession," in the cause. He sent agents to Ireland to stem the tide of Irish volunteers entering the Union army. He planned the burning of federal medical stores in Louisville, Kentucky, and bridges in strategic locations across the occupied South. He also oversaw the suppression of treason against the Confederacy. Special commissioners who investigated and arrested those disloyal to the government reported to Benjamin. Colonel Henry J. Leovy, a close friend of Benjamin's from New Orleans, served as a military commissioner in southwest Virginia, where he searched for traitors.[32]

Benjamin, like many other Confederate leaders, believed Northerners would not support Lincoln indefinitely. Serious efforts were made to exploit the difference between eastern and western states, to increase public disaffection in the North for the war, and to raid prisoner of war camps. Provocateurs attempted to capture federal property in the far north. Confederate agents tried to disrupt the monetary system by urging people to convert paper money to gold. There was even an attempt—probably unknown to Benjamin but involving his agents—to set New York City on fire. Benjamin oversaw the most ambitious mission, a one million–dollar covert operation in Canada headed by Jacob Thompson. When the war ended, Benjamin fled Richmond with Davis and the Confederate cabinet.[33]

The common Jewish soldier in the field matched Benjamin's commitment to the Confederate cause. There were about 2,000 Jewish Confederate servicemen. Simon Wolf, a prominent Jewish lawyer published a book in 1895 containing a list of Jews who served in the Union and Confederate armies. His list reflects the preponderance of service in the infantry. Of the 1,340 men listed, 967 served in the infantry, 116 in the cavalry, 129 in the artillery, and 11 in the navy or marines. Rabbi Barnett Elzas's list of Jewish South Carolinians shows 117 in the infantry of a total of 167 men. In their study of Richmond's Jews, Ezekiel and Lichtenstein noted 70 of 100 soldiers in the infantry. Eric Brock's list of Confederate Jewish soldiers in Shreveport, Louisiana, comes to similar conclusions.[34]

There were Jewish Johnny Rebs in every aspect of the war. They were privates in infantry units all over the South and in every major campaign. They were cooks, sharpshooters, orderlies, teamsters, and foragers. They dug trenches, cut trees, guarded prisoners, and served on picket duty. Most of the historical information about Jewish Confederate soldiers is contained in the letters, diaries, reminiscences, and biographies of well-known, powerful, and older men, such as Judah Benjamin and Raphael Moses, a prominent commissary officer. There is little documentation for the average soldier.[35]

The average Confederate soldier was in his twenties, and this was undoubtedly true about Jewish Johnny Rebs. We know little about these young men except their names and units, but there is enough information about men in the ranks to make some generalizations. The majority enlisted in hometown companies with men whom they knew, often fellow Jews. They preferred serving in units with their friends and relatives. There were seven Rosenbalms in Company H of the 37th Virginia. Philip Rosenheim of the Richmond militia was proud of his service and his friends: "Charley Marx and David Mittledorfer, Julius Straus, Moses Hutzler, Sam and Herman Hirsh, Simon Sycles, Gus Thalheimer, Abr. Goldback, and a good many other Yuhudim all belonged to the same company, which I did."[36]

But unlike Irish and German immigrants, who formed ethnic companies, Jews did not form distinctively Jewish companies because they fervently desired to be seen as citizens of their state and nation, not as a separate nationality. They did not want to stand out as they had been forced to do in Europe. There were no Catholic or Lutheran units in the Confederate army, and, therefore, no Jewish units either. As a practical matter, there were few wealthy Jewish men with the military background and political influence needed to organize a company of troops. The majority of Jewish Confederates were recent young immigrants. They were followers, comrades-in-arms, not leaders.[37]

The majority of Jewish Confederates served as privates or corporals in the infantry, but there were Jews in all branches of the service and in all departments. One hundred and five Jews served in the Alabama infantry and twenty-one in the cavalry. There were almost as many Jews in the Arkansas cavalry as in the infantry. Leopold Levy and his brother Sampson served in Company G, 1st Virginia cavalry, commanded by Colonel J.E.B. Stuart. Texas had seventy-three Jewish infantry men and twenty-one Jewish cavalrymen.

Jews also served in artillery units such as the Washington Artillery of New Orleans. Texas and Alabama each had five Jewish artillerymen; Arkansas had eight. Edwin Kursheedt and Eugene Henry Levy served in the artillery. Marx Cohen and Gustavus A. Cohen served in James F. Hart's Company (Washington Artillery, South Carolina), initially a part of Hampton's Legion, as did five other Cohens from South Carolina. Perry Moses of Sumter served in a number of units, including Culpepper's Battery. In 1863, Moses was in charge of a twelve-pound Napoleon cannon and later that year wrote to his mother, Octavia Harby Moses: "I fought a battery of four guns for over an hour, giving them gun for gun."[38]

Some Jewish Johnny Rebs served in militia or home guards, which were organized for local self-defense. At the beginning of the war, many men who did not want to leave home or serve in the regular army joined the militia. As the war progressed and conscription was instituted, the home guards consisted of those too young, too old, or too infirm to serve, as well as those exempt by virtue of their occupations or political office. When Richmond, Virginia, was attacked in the summer of 1863, young Philip Rosenheim served in the local militia. In a letter to his sister and brother-in-law, Amelia and Isaac Meinnart, Philip stated, "I, as well as all the Boys rallied to the call and we stood firmly at our Flag ready to meet the foe."[39]

Jewish soldiers came from varied backgrounds. Some were recent immigrants, and some were from old families. Strong evidence of the southern Jewish immigrant's contribution to Confederate military service can be seen in Shreveport, Lousiana, in 1860. Eric J. Brock estimated that three hundred Jews lived in

The Moses brothers of South Carolina: Joshua Lazarus Moses (standing), Isaac Harby Moses (left), and Perry Moses (right). This photograph was taken at the beginning of the war. Perry is wearing his Citadel uniform. Josh Moses was killed at Fort Blakely near Mobile, Alabama. Perry Moses survived the war, was active in the Confederate Veterans, and served as commandant of his camp in Sumter, South Carolina. He died in 1916. Isaac Harby Moses served as a private in the Citadel Cadet Rangers and was known as "Lord Shaftsbury" because of his scholarly style of writing. He saw action late in the war and survived. Courtesy of Robert N. Rosen.

Shreveport at that time and that seventy-eight served in the Confederate armed forces. Almost all were recent immigrants who arrived in Louisiana in the 1850s. Most, like Marx Baer, were born in one of the German states or Alsace and Lorraine. Some were from Poland: Jack Citron, Company I, 3rd Louisiana, from Koval; and Jacob Gall, Company D, 19th Louisiana, from Meschisko. Some were from France: Marx Israel of Company 5, 3rd Regiment, European Brigade, was from Onepie near Metz.[40]

Leading Jews of Richmond, Virginia, had been members of the Richmond Light Infantry Blues for generations. The unit participated in quelling the Gabriel Prosser slave revolt in 1800 and was called into service in 1807 when the British man-of-war *Leopard* attacked the *Chesapeake* off Norfolk. When the Richmond Blues left the city for the war on April 24, 1861, fifteen of its ninety-nine members were Jewish, including Ezekiel J. ("Zeke") Levy, its fourth sergeant.

The Blues served as Company A, 46th Virginia, in West Virginia and saw combat at Roanoke Island in February 1862. "Soon a ball [bullet] came from the Yankees," the company's record states, and "one of our boys, Mr. L. Wasserman, replied." Henry Adler was mortally wounded. Isaacs, Lyon, Levi Wasserman, and Joseph Levy were captured and exchanged for Union prisoners that August. After suffering a great deal from his wounds, Adler died at the naval hospital in Portsmouth and was buried by the Blues, who turned out en masse to honor their first private killed in the war. The Blues served in Virginia and North Carolina, and also fought in the defense of Charleston, Richmond, Petersburg, and finally in Appomattox. With the Blue's captain killed and first lieutenant wounded, Lieutenant Ezekiel J. Levy became commanding officer in June 1864.[41]

There were dozens of Jewish officers in the Confederate service, including the quartermaster general of the Confederate army, Colonel Abraham Charles Myers, the great-grandson of the first rabbi of K. K. Beth Elohim in Charleston. After graduating from West Point, Myers became a career army officer and served in the Second Seminole and Mexican Wars. Fort Myers, Florida, was named in his honor by his father-in-law, General David Emanuel Twiggs. In 1861, Myers set up his offices on the southwest corner of 9th and Main Streets, near Capitol Square in Richmond. The Quartermaster Department included quartermasters in each state, paymasters and quartermasters in the field, manufacturing plants, special units such as the Tax-in-Kind Office, depot and post quartermasters, and purchasing agents posted abroad. Colonel Myers reported to the secretary of war.[42]

As the war continued, public concern, followed by anger and then outrage at the Commissary and Quartermaster Departments, plagued the Confederacy. It was understandable, if unjustified, that officers in charge of food, clothing, and

Capt. Ezekiel ("Zeke") J. Levy was a merchant in Richmond, Virginia, and the
secretary of Congregation Beth Ahabah when the war began. He was elected fourth sergeant of
the Richmond Light Infantry Blues in April 1861. Levy served most of the war as a lieutenant and
attained the rank of captain. He was in command of the Blues, Company A of the 46th Virginia,
at the Battle of the Crater at Petersburg, Virginia. Courtesy of the Jacob Rader Marcus Center,
American Jewish Archives, Cincinnati, Ohio.

supplies were blamed for the army's ills. The head commissary officer was the
scapegoat of the Confederate Congress. His nomination to full colonel and confirmation as commissary general provoked heated debate. Myers's nomination
to full colonel and confirmation as quartermaster general was immediately approved. T. C. DeLeon believed that Myers's "bureau was managed with an efficiency and vigor that could scarcely have been looked for in so new an organization." Early in the war, Myers enjoyed a good reputation as a competent and
honest department head.

It soon became clear that the war would not be short and that supplying an army of four-hundred-thousand men would be a formidable task. Prices rose as the blockade tightened and northern supply sources dwindled. States' rights played a part in the Confederacy's problems. The state government of North Carolina supplied uniforms for its troops with the understanding that the quartermaster would not purchase clothing from North Carolina factories, and thereby deplete their inventories. The southern economy could not keep pace with the army's huge appetite for supplies.

The Union victories of 1862 were a disaster for the Confederacy and especially for the quartermaster general. The loss of New Orleans, key border states, coastal areas, and the Mississippi Valley limited the areas from which supplies, manufactured goods, and raw materials could be obtained. Blockade-running was severely curtailed, interfering with the importation of European goods. By August 1862, Lee complained that his army lacked "much of the materials of war . . . [was] feeble in transportation, the animals being much reduced, and the men . . . poorly provided with clothes, and in thousands of instances . . . destitute of shoes."[43]

As the war dragged on, the Quartermaster Department came under severe criticism. The *Savannah Daily News* noted "that peculation and plunder, and misuse of authority for private purpose, have often been put before public duty and public service." The *Richmond Enquirer* complained that "quartermasters sometimes get rich. . . . Unfaithful, incompetent, or dishonest quartermasters or commissaries could plunge the country into ruin." Historian Richard Goff concludes that despite the criticism, under Myers's leadership, the Quartermaster Department was "as well organized and as efficient as circumstances would allow."[44]

Myers's friends in Congress sought to promote him to brigadier general, and in March 1863, the Congress passed a law providing that the rank and pay of the quartermaster general "shall be those of Brigadier General in the provisional army." Seventy-six members of Congress sent the president a letter recommending that Colonel Myers be promoted to general. Ironically, Jefferson Davis used the law to dismiss Myers from office. On August 7, 1863, he replaced Abraham Myers with his old friend Alexander R. Lawton.

Davis argued that the dismissal of Myers was in the interest of efficiency, and there was some basis for the charge. But Myers and Davis had feuded many years before, in the army and according to Richmond gossip, the true reason for the controversy lay between the men's wives. Marian Myers, who considered herself the social superior of Mrs. Davis, had called the president's wife "an old squaw," referring to Davis's dark complexion. Assistant Secretary of War A. T. Bledsoe passed along the insult in early 1862. "The Congress of 1863," Mary Chestnut wrote, "gave up its time to fighting the battle of Colonel Myers—Mrs. Myers."[45]

There is no evidence that antisemitism played any role in Myers's firing, despite sentiments expressed by John Beauchamp Jones, a clerk in the War Department. In his memoir, *A Rebel War Clerk's Diary* (1866) Jones called Myers the "Jew Quarter-Master General" and claimed the officer said, "let them suffer," when told of soldiers' pleas for blankets. But Sallie Putman, who had no love for the Jews, thought Myers was mistreated. Most important, Jefferson Davis not only had no prejudice against Jews but, to the contrary, maintained warm relationships with many southern Jews.[46]

Adolph Proskauer of Mobile was among the few Jewish immigrants who became a high-ranking Confederate officer. Proskauer was educated at the gymnasium in Breslau before coming to the United States. In May 1861, he enlisted for twelve months in Captain Augustus Stikes's company, the Independent Rifles, and was appointed first corporal. In Richmond, the Independent Rifles became company C, 12th Alabama Infantry. The 12th Alabama was a cosmopolitan regiment that included German, French, Irish, and Spanish soldiers, as well as young men from the mountains of north Alabama. Captain Robert Emory Park, an officer in the regiment, recalled their talent for foraging, stating that "the vast majority of them suffered very little from hunger" despite limited rations.

By December, Proskauer was promoted to sergeant. In April 1862, he was commissioned as a first lieutenant. He served in that rank for only twenty-six days before being promoted to captain in May, replacing Stikes, who became a major of the regiment. Proskauer was remembered as a handsome captain, the "best dressed man in the regiment." He participated in some of the fiercest battles of the war, such as the Siege of Yorktown in the late spring of 1862. He also helped lead the 12th Alabama at the Battle of Seven Pines, where it made a "gallant charge . . . into the very jaws of death."

Proskauer and his regiment marched north in Lee's Maryland campaign as part of Rodes's brigade. He was in combat at the Battle of South Mountain and Sharpsburg (Antietam), where he was wounded. On September 17, 1862, the single bloodiest day in the Civil War, Lee's Army of Northern Virginia faced George B. McClellan's Army of the Potomac: 4,710 men were killed; 18,440 men were wounded. Proskauer was shot in the abdomen during intense fighting along the Sunken Road, later called the "Bloody Lane." He recuperated and later returned to his company at Orange Court House, Virginia.

Proskauer was also at the Battle of Chancellorsville in May 1863, when the 12th fought as a part of Stonewall Jackson's famous flanking attack on Major

General Hooker's Union army. On the morning of May 3, Proskauer led the regiment, as Colonel Pickens assumed leadership of a portion of the brigade after the commander was wounded. Wounded in the battle, Proskauer was promoted to major by Colonel Pickens while he was in the hospital, and his promotion was later confirmed by the Confederate Congress in early 1864.

Major Proskauer returned to his command at the Battle of Gettysburg on July 1, 1863. A part of Rodes's division, the 12th suffered heavy casualties at Oak Ridge, northeast of Gettysburg. Years later, Captain Park wrote to Mrs. Proskauer: "I can see him now, in mental view, as he nobly carried himself at Gettysburg, standing coolly and calmly, with cigar in his mouth, at the head of the Twelfth Alabama, amid a perfect rain of bullets, shot and shell. He was the personification of intrepid gallantry, of imperturbable courage."

On July 4, 1863, Lee retreated from Pennsylvania. Major Proskauer and the 12th Alabama, "suffering, wet and anxious," on a dark, dreary, rainy night retreated south. During the remainder of the summer of 1863 they camped near Orange Courthouse. Fighting continued in Virginia, and in October, Proskauer led half the regiment on a mission to destroy railroad tracks near Warrenton Junction. In late December, he led the regiment to Paine's Mill to saw planks for the Orange Road. The regiment saw action again on May 8 at Spotsylvania Court House, where Proskauer was wounded once more, ending his involvement in the war.[47]

Like the officers and enlisted men in the field, southern rabbis supported the Confederate war effort. Rabbi Max Michelbacher of Beth Ahabah Synagogue in Richmond and the Confederate capital's Jewish community assisted Jewish soldiers. Michelbacher saw to the soldiers' needs, requested furloughs on their behalf for Jewish holidays and even published a "prayer of the C[onfederate] S[tates] Soldiers." Beginning with the Shema, it called upon the God of Israel to "be with me in the hot season of the contending strife; protect and bless me with health and courage to bear cheerfully the hardships of war. . . . Be unto the Army of this Confederacy, as thou wert of old, unto us, thy chosen people!"[48]

Rabbi James K. Gutheim of New Orleans was also a vocal supporter of the Confederacy. The spiritual leader of Dispersed of Judah congregation, Gutheim refused to swear allegiance to the Union when the federal army occupied the Crescent City. Along with many of his congregants, Gutheim left the city for Montgomery, Alabama, where he prayed from the pulpit, "Regard, O Father, in Thine abundant favor and benevolence, our beloved country, the Confederate States of America. May our young Republic increase in strength. . . . Behold, O God, and judge between us and our enemies, who have forced upon us this unholy and unnatural war."[49]

The revolution wrought by the Civil War—the freeing of the slaves; the collapse of the ancien régime; the death, destruction, and impoverishment of southern cities—was devastating to southern Jewry. Those most committed to the cause lost the most. Judah Benjamin left the country for Europe. Union officials tried to implicate him in Lincoln's assassination. Abraham C. Myers's career was ended. Many families lost fathers, brothers, and sons. Businesses suffered, and many were destroyed. Those Jews who had owned slaves, lost them. Reconstruction was as bitter for the Jewish community as it was for the rest of the white South. In a letter to a family member in April 1868, Henry Hyams, the former lieutenant governor of Louisiana, wrote, "As Israelites, we are passing through another captivity which relives and reenacts all the troubles so pathetically poured forth by the inspired Jeremiah." Emma Mordecai of Richmond could not abide the occupying army. "Richmond is a strange place," she confided to her diary. "Everything looks unnatural and desecrated."[50]

Like other southerners, Jewish southerners licked their wounds, rebuilt their lives, and memorialized their honored dead. The Jewish women of Richmond formed the Hebrew Ladies Memorial Association for the Confederate Dead. A circular was sent out "To the Israelites of the South" seeking funds to create a cemetery and to erect a monument to the Jewish Confederate dead. Time was of the essence. "While the world yet rings with the narrative of a brave people's struggle for independence," the circular stated, the soldiers' graves were neglected. Southern Jews could not abide this situation. They were urged to remember "the myriads of heroes who spilled their noble blood" in defense of the "glorious cause." The circular appealed to southern Jews' fear of antisemitism: "In time to come," it concluded, "when the malicious tongue of slander, ever so ready to assail Israel, shall be raised against us, then, with a feeling of mournful pride, will we point to this monument and say: *There is our reply.*"[51]

NOTES

1. Yates Levy to J. C. Levy, March 16, 1865, Phillips-Myers Papers #596, UNC; Robert N. Rosen, *The Jewish Confederates* (Columbia: University of South Carolina Press, 2000) (hereafter "Rosen"), 9–31; Eli Faber, *A Time for Planting: The First Migration, 1654–1820* (Baltimore: Johns Hopkins University Press, 1992). Important works on local southern Jewish history include Mark I. Greenberg, "Becoming Southern: The Jews of Savannah, Georgia, 1830–1870," *American Jewish History* 86, (March 1998): 1,997; Myron Berman, *Richmond's Jewry, 1769–1976: Shabbat in Shockoe* (Charlottesville: University Press of Virginia, 1979); Steven Hertzberg, *Strangers within the Gate City: The Jews of Atlanta, 1845–1915* (Philadelphia: Jewish Publication Society of America, 1978); Ruthe Winegarten and Cathy Schechter, *Deep in the Heart: The Lives and Legends of Texas Jews* (Austin: Eakin Press and Texas

Jewish Historical Society, 1990); James W. Hagy, *This Happy Land: The Jews of Colonial and Antebellum Charleston* (Tuscaloosa: University of Alabama Press, 1993); Belinda Gergel and Richard Gergel, *In Pursuit of the Tree of Life: A History of the Early Jews of Columbia, South Carolina, and the Tree of Life Congregation* (Columbia, S.C.: Tree of Life Congregation, 1996); Bertram Wallace Korn, *The Jews of Mobile, Alabama, 1763–1841* (Cincinnati: Hebrew Union College Press, 1970), and *The Early Jews of New Orleans* (Waltham, Mass.: American Jewish Historical Society, 1969); Selma S. Lewis, *A Biblical People in the Bible Belt: The Jewish Community of Memphis, Tennessee, 1840s–1960s* (Macon, Ga.: Mercer University Press, 1998); Janice O. Rothschild, *As But a Day: The First Hundred Years, 1867–1967* (Atlanta: Hebrew Benevolent Congregation, The Temple, 1967); Melvin I. Urofsky, *Commonwealth and Community: The Jewish Experience in Virginia* (Richmond: Virginia Historical Society and Jewish Community Federation of Richmond, 1997); Rabbi Newton J. Friedman, "A History of Temple Beth Israel of Macon, Georgia" (Ph.D. diss., Burton College and Seminary, 1955).

2. Rosen, 23–25; Jacob Rader Marcus, ed., *Memoirs of American Jews 1775–1865* (Philadelphia: Jewish Publication Society of America, 1955–56), 3:104

3. Rosen, 25; Richard C. Wade, *Slavery in the Cities: The South, 1820–1860* (Oxford: Oxford University Press, 1964), appendix; Elliott Ashkenazi, *The Business of Jews in Louisiana, 1840–1875* (Tuscaloosa: University of Alabama Press, 1988), 9–11.

4. Greenberg, "Becoming Southern," 57–58; Rosen, 37; Bertram W. Korn, *Jews and Negro Slavery in the Old South, 1789–1865* (Elkins Park, Pa.: Reform Congregation Keneseth Israel, 1961), 123.

5. Rosen, 37. Numerous rabbis and Jewish leaders in the North answered Rabbi Raphall's defense of slavery. The majority of northern Jews opposed slavery, and there were a number of northern Jewish abolitionists. Michael Heilprin, a Polish Jewish-American writer, was outraged by Raphall's "sacrilegious words." "Have we not had enough of the 'reproach of Egypt?' Must the stigma of Egyptian principles be fastened on the people of Israel by Israelitish lips themselves?" Bertram W. Korn, *American Jewry and the Civil War*, 2nd ed. (Philadelphia: Jewish Publication Society of America, 1957), 18–23.

6. Rosen, 382–83; Korn, *American Jewry and the Civil War*, 15–31, and *Jews and Negro Slavery*, also published a chapter entitled "Jews and Negro Slavery in the Old South, 1789–1865," in Leonard Dinnerstein and Mary Dale Palsson, eds., *Jews in the South* (Baton Rouge: Louisiana State University Press, 1973), 89–134; Hagy, *This Happy Land*, 93; Abraham Barkai, *Branching Out: German-Jewish Immigration to the United States, 1820–1914* (New York: Holman and Meier, 1994), 109–11.

7. Rosen, 16; Wade, *Slavery in the Cities*, 20; Michelbacher quoted in Korn, *Jews and Negro Slavery*, 111–13; Korn, *American Jewry and the Civil War*, 29.

8. Rosen, 15, 31–33; Howard M. Sachar, *A History of the Jews in America* (New York: Alfred A. Knopf, 1992), 26–27; Oscar S. Straus, *Under Four Administrations: From Cleveland to Taft* (Boston: Houghton Mifflin, 1922), 10.

9. Rosen, 31; I. J. Benjamin, *Three Years in America, 1859–1862*, Vol. 1, ed. Oscar Handlin, translated from German by Charles Reznikoff (Philadelphia: Jewish Publication Society of America, 1956), 76.

10. Rosen, 34; John F. Marszalek, ed., *The Diary of Miss Emma Holmes, 1861–1866* (Baton Rouge: Louisiana State University Press, 1979), 162, 209, 306; Carol Bleser, ed., *Tokens of Affection: The Letters of a Planter's Daughter in the Old South* (Athens: University of Georgia Press, 1996), 343.

11. Quotes from Rosen, 35. See also Jacob Rader Marcus, *Early American Jewry* (Philadelphia: Jewish Publication Society of America, 1951), vol. 1, chap. 5 ("it is . . . a matter of record that the New Englanders, with rare exception, had no use for Jews. The original Puritans were interested in Hebrew and in ancient Hebrews . . . but not in their descendants as long as they remained Jews").

12. Rosen, 35; Cohen quoted in Gergel and Gergel, *Tree of Life*, 33–35; *Confederate Veteran* 23, no. 8 (August 1915) 343. This is in a letter from Simon Baruch to the *Confederate Veteran*. Samuel Proctor and Louis Schmier, eds., with Malcolm Stern, *Jews of the South: Selected Essays from the Southern Jewish Historical Society* (Macon, Ga.: Mercer University Press, 1984), 37; Schmier, "Georgia History in Pictures. This 'New Canaan': The Jewish Experience in Georgia," *Georgia Historical Quarterly* 73 no. 4, pt. 2 (Winter 1989); Greenberg, "Becoming Southern"; Lewis, *A Biblical People*, 34.

13. Quoted in Eli N. Evans, *Judah P. Benjamin: The Jewish Confederate* (New York: Free Press, 1988), 96–97.

14. Rosen, 38; Baer quoted in Morris U. Schappes, *Documentary History of the Jews in the United States 1654–1875*, rev. ed. (New York: Citadel Press, 1952), 436–41.

15. Rosen, 38; Korn, *American Jewry and the Civil War*, 250n, 48; Frederic Cople Jaher, *A Scapegoat in the New Wilderness: The Origins of Anti-Semitism in America* (Cambridge: Harvard University Press, 1994), 138, 200–203, 215. John Weiss, *Life and Correspondence of Theodore Parker* (New York: D. Appleton, 1964): Theodore Parker, "Journal," March 1843, 1:214, and Parker to Dr. Francis, May 26, 1844, 1:236, "Letter to the Members of the 28th Congregational Society of Boston" (1859), 2:497, and "Some Thoughts on the Charities of Boston" (1858), 1:397, and to Rev. David Wasson, December 12, 1857, 1:395–96. See also Egal Feldman, *Dual Destinies: The Jewish Encounter with Protestant America* (Urbana: University of Illinois Press, 1990), 56–59; and *Liberator* 15 (May 20, 1842): 1; and 19 (May 18 and September 21, 1849): 77, 751.

Edmond Quincy, "A Jew and a Christian," *Liberator* 18 (August 11, 1848): 126. Quincy, a Boston Brahmin and a cousin of John Quincy Adams, wrote a novel, *Wensley: A Story without a Moral* (1854), in which the villain is a forger and cheat named Aaron Abrahams. The book is laced with every cliché of old-fashioned Boston anti-Semitism: the Jew as a liar, cheat, and coward. See also Jonathan D. Sarna, "The 'Mythical Jew' and the 'Jew Next Door' in Nineteenth-Century America," in David A. Gerber, ed., *Anti-Semitism in American*

History (Urbana: University of Illinois Press, 1986), 57–78; David A. Gerber, "Cutting Out Shylock: Elite Anti-Semitism and the Quest for Moral Order in the Mid-Nineteenth Century American Market Place," Journal of American History 69, no. 3 (December 1982): 615–37.

Lydia Maria Child, Letters from New-York (New York: Charles Francis; Boston: James Munroe, 1843), 12–13, 26–29, 31, 33–34, 217–18, 225 ("Judaism was rife with superstition, vengeance, blindness; its ceremonies "strange . . . spectral and flitting"). See also Patricia G. Holland and Milton Meltzer, eds., Guide to the Collected Correspondence of Lydia Maria Child, 1817–1880 (New York: Kraus Microform, 1980), s.v. "Jews," especially letters to Louisa Gilman Loring (September 4, 1846) and Ellis Gray Loring (March 5, 1854).

As to Henry Wilson's views, see The Congressional Globe, 36th Cong., 2d sess., February 21, 1861, 1,091; and 37th Cong., 2d sess., February 13, 1862, 789; Korn, American Jewry and the Civil War, 168; Robert Douthat Meade, Judah P. Benjamin: Confederate Statesman (London: Oxford University Press, 1943), 139; Jacob Rader Marcus, United States Jewry, 1776–1985 (Detroit: Wayne State University Press, 1989–93), 3:36.

16. Rosen, 121; Sachar, A History of the Jews in America, 73; and History of the Jews of Louisiana: Their Religious, Civic, Charitable and Patriotic Life (New Orleans: Jewish Historical Publishing Company of Louisiana, 1903), 33; Scherck to J. L. Meyer, Columbus, Ga., September 9, 1864, American Jewish Archives, Cincinnati (hereafter "AJA"); Charleston Daily Courier, March 11, 1861.

17. Rosen, 13–14, 49–54; Mayer quoted in Schmier, "Georgia History in Pictures," 820; Isaac Hermann, Memoirs of a Veteran Who Served as a Private in the 60s in the War between the States: Personal Incidents, Experiences, and Observations (Atlanta: Byrd Printing, 1911), 192–93. Letter, April 17, 1864, Simon Mayer Papers, box 1, Tulane University.

18. James M. McPherson, For Cause and Comrades: Why Men Fought in the Civil War (New York: Oxford University Press, 1988); Mel Young, Where They Lie Someone Should Say Kaddish (Lanham, Md.: University Press of America), 39.

19. Rosen, 49. Letter dated July 8, 1863, addressed to "Dear Brother Isaac and Sister Amelia" (Mr. and Mrs. Isaac Meinnart) in Richmond from Philip Rosenheim, AJA. Leo E. Turitz and Evelyn Turitz, Jews in Early Mississippi, 2nd ed. (Jackson: University Press of Mississippi, 1995), xvii. Typewritten autobiography of Sir Moses Ezekiel, 75–76, Beth Ahaba Archive (Richmond, Virginia). See also Joseph Gutman and Stanley F. Chyet, eds., Moses Jacob Ezekiel: Memoirs from the Baths of Diocletian (Detroit: Wayne State University Press, 1975); VMI Alumni Review (Spring 1973): 1; Stanley F. Chyet, "Moses Jacob Ezekiel: A Childhood in Richmond," Publications of the American Jewish Historical Society 62 (1973): 286–94.

20. Quoted in Berman, Richmond's Jewry, 194–95.

21. Rosen, 50; Typewritten autobiography of Moses Ezekiel, 75–76; C. Vann Woodward and Elisabeth Muhlenfeld, eds., The Private Mary Chestnut: The Unpublished Civil War Diaries (New York: Oxford University Press, 1984), 350; Phoebe Yates Pember, A Southern

Woman's Story: Life in Confederate Richmond, ed. Bell Irvin Wiley (Jackson, Tenn.: McCowat-Mercer Press, 1959; reprint, Wilmington, N.C.: Broadfoot Publishing, 1991), 24.

22. Rosen, 52; Gary W. Gallagher, *The Confederate War* (Cambridge, Mass.: Harvard University Press, 1997), 28; Bernard M. Baruch, *My Own Story* (New York: Henry Holt, 1957), 5.

23. Lewis Leon, *The Diary of a Tar Heel Confederate Soldier* (Charlotte: Stone Publishing, 1913), 1; Schappes, *Documentary History*, 481; J. R. Marcus, *Memoirs*, 3:197; and Schappes, *Documentary History*, 481, 707–8.

24. Jaher, *Scapegoat*, 3–4, 117–18, 135–36.

25. Philip Whitlock, MS, autobiography, Virginia Historical Society, Richmond, 92. Wessolowsky quoted in Herbert Ezekiel and Gaston Lichtenstein, *The History of the Jews of Richmond from 1769 to 1917* (Richmond, Va.: Herbert Ezekiel, 1917), 183, 16, 175.

26. Jonathan D. Sarna, "American Jewish Political Conservatism in Historical Perspective," *American Jewish History* 87 (June and September 1999): 113–22.

27. Bertram W. Korn, introduction to "The Jews of the Confederacy," *American Jewish Archives* 13, no. 1, "Civil War Centennial Southern Issue" (April 1961): 4.

28. Rosen, chap. 2; Thomas Cooper DeLeon, *Belles, Beaux, and Brains of the '60's* (New York: G. W. Dillingham, 1909), 91–93.

29. Richard S. Tedlow, "Judah Benjamin," in *"Turn to the South": Essays on Southern Jewry*, ed. Nathan M. Kaganoff and Melvin I. Urofsky (Charlottesville: University Press of Virginia, 1979), 46; Evans, *Judah P. Benjamin*, 147–49; S. I. Neiman, *Judah Benjamin: Mystery Man of the Confederacy* (Indianapolis: Bobbs-Merrill, 1963), 145–46; Meade, *Judah P. Benjamin*, 235; George C. Rable, *The Confederate Republic* (Chapel Hill: University of North Carolina Press, 1994), 130.

30. A. J. Hanna, *Flight into Oblivion* (Richmond, Va.: Johnson Publishing, 1938), 194; Louis Gruss, "Judah Philip Benjamin," *Louisiana Historical Quarterly* 19, no. 4 (October 1936): 1,046; Pierce Butler, *Judah P. Benjamin* (Philadelphia: W. G. Jacobs, 1907), 332; Robert Selph Henry, *The Story of the Confederacy* (Indianapolis: Bobbs-Merrill, 1931), 85, 87; Charles P. Roland, *The Confederacy* (Chicago: University of Chicago Press, 1960), 83, 111; Davis quoted in Evans, *Judah P. Benjamin*, xi–xxi.

31. Roy Z. Chamlee Jr., *Lincoln's Assassins: A Complete Account of Their Capture, Trial, and Punishment* (Jefferson, N.C.: McFarland, 1990), 401.

32. Meade, *Judah P. Benjamin*, 297–305; Evans, *Judah P. Benjamin*, 193; Rosen, 137. Col. Henry J. Leovy's activities are briefly described in William M. Robinson Jr., *Justice in Grey: A History of the Judicial System of the Confederate States of America* (Cambridge, Mass.: Harvard University Press, 1941), 409–11. His activities as a special commissioner are described in the Official Records IV, 4:802–15 and Kenneth W. Noe, "Red String Scare: Civil War Southwest Virginia and the Heroes of America," *North Carolina Historical Review* 69, no. 3 (July 1992): 301–22. Noe has Leovy's name as "Leory" because the Official Records made

the same mistake. On the flight of the cabinet, see Hanna, *Flight into Oblivion*. See Leovy's obituary, *Daily Picayune*, October 4, 1902, 10, col. 2; letters from Jefferson Davis to Leovy dated May 26, 1877, and November 10, 1883, Historic New Orleans Collection (Henry J. Leovy Papers, 1859–1900).

33. Meade, *Judah P. Benjamin*, 301–4; William A. Tidwell, *Come Retribution: The Confederate Secret Service and the Assassination of Lincoln* (Jackson: University Press of Mississippi, 1998), chap. 8; William A. Tidwell, *April '65: Confederate Covert Action in the American Civil War* (Kent, Ohio: Kent State University Press, 1995), 127–29.

34. Simon Wolf, *The American Jew as Patriot, Soldier, and Citizen* (Philadelphia: Levytype, 1895); Barnett A. Elzas, *The Jews of South Carolina from the Earliest Times to the Present Day* (Philadelphia: Lippincott, 1905); Ezekiel and Lichtenstein, *The History of the Jews of Richmond*; list of Shreveport Jewish Confederate soldiers compiled by Eric Brock, Rosen Papers, Jewish Heritage Collection, College of Charleston Library; Ezekiel and Lichtenstein, *History of the Jews of Richmond*, 176–88; The authors, writing in 1916, believed their list of Jewish Confederate soldiers to be "the best that has ever been printed, and it is safe to assume that no more complete or accurate one will ever be published" (176). Bell I. Wiley, *The Life of Johnny Reb: The Common Soldier of the Confederacy* (Garden City, N.Y.: Doubleday, 1971), 331.

35. Rosen, 162–63.

36. Rosen, 419.

37. Rosen, 163–65.

38. Wolf, *The American Jew*, passim; as to Cohens, see 374; Ashley Halsey Jr., "The Last Duel in the Confederacy," *Civil War Times Illustrated* 1, no. 7 (November 1962): 7; Elzas, *Jews of South Carolina*, 226; Joseph H. Crute Sr., *Units of the Confederate Army*, 2d. ed. (reprint; Gaithersburg, Md.: Olde Soldier Books, 1987), 271–72; Moses quoted in Dorothy Phelps Bultman, "The Story of a Good Life" (November 1963, Sumter, S.C.), 1, Jewish Heritage Collection, College of Charleston.

39. Ernest B. Furguson, *Ashes of Glory: Richmond at War* (New York: Alfred A. Knopf, 1996), 212. Letter dated July 8, 1863, from Philip Rosenheim to the Meinnarts, Korn file, AJA.

40. Rosen, 174–75; Eric Brock, "The Jewish Cemeteries of Shreveport, Louisiana" (Shreveport, La.: privately printed, 1995), Jewish Heritage Collection.

41. John A. Cutchins, *A Famous Command: The Richmond Light Infantry Blues* (Richmond: Garrett and Massies, 1934), passim; quote from company record in Berman, *Richmond's Jewry*, 93–97; Ezekiel and Lichtenstein, *History of the Jews of Richmond*, 129, 149–52; Darrell L. Collins, *46th Virginia Infantry* (Lynchburg, Va.: H. E. Howard, 1992), 151.

42. Rosen, 118–25. The best source on Abraham C. Myers is Richard D. Goff, *Confederate Supply* (Durham, N.C.: Duke University Press, 1969). Walter Burke Jr. has written a useful pamphlet entitled "Quartermaster: A Brief Account of the Life of Colonel Abraham Charles Myers, Quartermaster General C.S.A.," published in 1976. William C. Davis,

Breckinridge: Statesman, Soldier, Symbol (Baton Rouge: Louisiana State University Press, 1974); Davis, *Jefferson Davis: The Man and His Hour* (New York: Harper Collins, 1991); and Davis, *A Government of Our Own: The Making of the Confederacy* (New York: Free Press, 1994). Thomas Cooper DeLeon, the irrepressible author of *Belles, Beaux, and Brains of the '60s* and *Four Years in Rebel Capitals: An Inside View of Life in the Southern Confederacy, from Birth to Death* (Mobile: Gossip Printing, 1890), knew Myers personally and was well acquainted with his family, as was true of Mary Chestnut, who was also from South Carolina and knew the Jewish community through her close friendship with Miriam DeLeon Cohen. Her diary is a good source on Myers: Mary Boykin Miller Chestnut, *Mary Chestnut's Civil War*, ed. C. Vann Woodward (New Haven, Conn.: Yale University Press, 1981.

See also Karl H. Grismer, *The Story of Fort Myers: The History of the Land of the Caloosahatchee and Southwest Florida* (Fort Myers, Fla.: Southwest Florida Historical Society, 1949); Samuel Bernard Thompson, *Confederate Purchasing Operations Abroad* (Chapel Hill: University of North Carolina Press, 1935); Clement Eaton, *A History of the Southern Confederacy* (New York: Macmillan, 1954); Ellsworth Eliot Jr., *West Point in the Confederacy* (New York: G. A. Baker, 1941); Robert C. Black III, *The Railroads of the Confederacy* (Chapel Hill: University of North Carolina Press, 1952); John Beauchamp Jones, *A Rebel War Clerk's Diary at the Confederate States Capital*, 2 vols., ed. Howard Swiggett (New York: Old Hickory Bookshop, 1935).

43. Quoted in Rosen, 121.

44. Rosen, 132, 142; Goff, 59–60.

45. Eaton, *A History of the Southern Confederacy*, 138; Davis, *Jefferson Davis*, 537–38; Goff, *Confederate Supply*, 142; Chestnut, 437n.5.

46. Woodward, *Mary Chestnut*, 532; Sallie B. Putnam [A Richmond Lady], *Richmond during the War: Four Years of Personal Observation* (New York, 1867; reprint, Alexandria, Va.: Collector's Library of the Civil War, Time-Life Books, 1983), 275. Jones was a native of Baltimore. *A Rebel War Clerk's Diary*, condensed ed. ed. Earl Schenck Miers (New York: Sagamore Press, 1958), 1:186, 2:8; Berman, *Richmond's Jewry*, 187.

47. Rosen, 107–10; Joseph Proskauer, *A Segment of My Times* (New York: Farrar, Straus, 1950). Adolph Proskauer's daughter Jenny Proskauer wrote an unreliable recollection in 1948, which is at the AJA. The chief source of this material is Robert Emory Park, *Sketch of the Twelfth Alabama Infantry of Battle's Brigade, Rodes Division, Early's Corps, of the Army of Northern Virginia* (Richmond: W. E. Jones, 1906), originally printed in *Southern Historical Society Papers* 33 (January–December 1905):193–296. The details of Proskauer's military career are derived from his complied service record at the National Archives as well as the *Official Record*, where his name is misspelled "Proskaner." See ser. 1, vol. 25, pt. 1, 960 (Reports of Col. Samuel B. Pickens, 12th Alabama, May 5, 1863); ser. 1, vol. 36, pt. 1, 1083 (May 9, 1864); 1:27, 563; 1:25, 950–53 (Reports of Col. Edward A. O'Neal, May 12, 1863); 1:29, 891–92 (Reports of Maj. A Proskaner, January 22, 1864). Also see Young, *Where They*

Lie, 76, 78–79; Robert K. Krick, *Lee's Colonels: A Biographical Register of the Field Officers of the Army of Northern Virginia* (Dayton, Ohio: Morningside House, 1992), 266; Korn, *American Jewry*, 176; obituary of Adolph Proskauer, AJA (the AJA has an extensive file on Proskauer); Park, *Sketch*, 5.

48. Quoted in Rosen, 209–13.

49. Quoted in Rosen, 249, 256–57.

50. Rosen, 333–37; letter from Hyams dated April 19, 1868, to "My Dear Caroline," AJA; Mordecai quoted in Marcus, *Memoirs*, 3:341.

51. Undated clipping, George Jacobs scrapbook, AJA; Rosen, 338–40 (the circular is reproduced on p. 339). See also Korn, *American Jewry*, 110–12.

6

"NOW IS THE TIME TO SHOW YOUR TRUE COLORS"

SOUTHERN JEWS, WHITENESS, AND THE RISE OF JIM CROW

ERIC L. GOLDSTEIN

"Race prejudice is of two kinds," argued southern writer Thomas Dixon in a speech before the American Booksellers' Association in 1903. Dixon, whose racist novel *The Clansman* (1905) later inspired the film *Birth of a Nation* (1915), differentiated between the two varieties of prejudice by comparing the hatred of the Jew to that of the "negro." Hatred of the Jew, according to Dixon, was "a mean thing," which "exists simply because the Jewish race is the most persistent, powerful, commercially successful race that the world has ever produced." He argued that it was an example of unfair and petty jealousy and was not a matter of "self-preservation," as was hatred of African Americans. "Thousands of them have been assimilated by America and thousands more will be assimilated," he said of the Jews. "Millions of them may be swallowed by our Germanic race and that will not change your complexion—but you can't swallow a single nigger without changing your complexion."[1]

As one of the leading spokesmen for the racial radicalism that swept the South at the turn of the twentieth century, Dixon understood the Jews within a larger framework that sharply divided the world between blacks and whites. The centrality of the black-white divide was increasingly emphasized by whites in all regions of the United States during the Progressive Era. This view of society gave them a feeling of strength and superiority at a time when industrialization, urbanization, and the growing diversity of the American population threatened familiar social and moral boundaries. A rigid black-white dichotomy was most appealing in the South, however, where the changes brought on by modernity were particularly daunting and where there was a strong history of racial division to which disaffected whites could turn as they searched for solutions to their contemporary problems. Yet for native-born whites trying hard to see their world in terms of black and white, Jews and other immigrants—who were not only socially distinct but were often understood as different in "race"—often presented a thorny problem of categorization. To alleviate ambiguity about the status of such groups, white Americans of the period often felt the need to place them firmly on one or another side of the color line. This charge became especially important in the South, where the emerging complex of discriminatory laws known as "Jim Crow" demanded the clear physical separation of blacks and whites.

Dixon's attempt to paint the Jews as exemplary whites-in-the-making was one answer to the problem of Jewish racial status, an answer embraced by many southerners, including some of the region's most radical segregationists. But the notion that Jews were valuable members of "our race," as Dixon argued on a separate occasion, did not find unanimous support on the part of southern whites, who remained largely uncertain about this matter during the first decades of the twentieth century.[2] At times, Jews were distinguished from whites and were grouped and compared with African Americans in popular discourse. One southern writer, the North Carolina minister Arthur T. Abernethy, published an entire book arguing that "the Jew of to-day is essentially Negro in habits, physical peculiarities and tendencies."[3] In rare cases, like the lynching of Leo Frank by a white Georgia mob in 1915, Jews were not only grouped with blacks but also subjected to the violence and intimidation that was usually reserved for the region's more traditional racial outsiders. Even before Frank's lynching, journalist and political agitator Tom Watson had warned in a headline that "THE NEXT JEW WHO DOES WHAT FRANK DID IS GOING TO GET EXACTLY THE SAME THING WE GIVE TO NEGRO RAPISTS."[4] More commonly, however, Jews remained racially ill-defined within southern society, treated as probationary whites who had all the civic privileges of whiteness, but they were often excluded from social and cultural venues where their uncertain status might undermine the assertion of white racial purity and integrity.[5]

For acculturated southern Jews, most of whom had arrived in the mid-nineteenth century from central Europe or were born in the South of immigrant parents, the emerging system of Jim Crow produced a host of new and unwanted pressures. Well-established both socially and economically in the region and anxious to continue their drive for acceptance, these Jews were frequently unsettled by growing questions about their place within southern society. As a result, they increasingly tried to prove their racial credentials to their fellow white southerners. During the 1890s and the first decades of the twentieth century, acculturated Jews in the South took great pains to emphasize that they were different from African Americans and that they shared an essential identity with other whites. In making the case for their unambiguous whiteness, however, they sometimes found the unbending requirements of the region's racial culture to be in conflict with their own self-image as a historically persecuted minority group. The desire to fit in and win acceptance was often complicated by feelings of empathy for African Americans and an identification with their plight. The gap between the expectations of southern culture and the Jewish self-image was even greater in the case of the increasing number of new Jewish immigrants from eastern Europe, who were more visible than their acculturated counterparts and much less attentive to the racial etiquette of their new surroundings. Despite such oppositions, however, neither group of Jews was able to oppose or resist the basic social structures of the Jim Crow South in any direct or sustained way. The present article examines these tensions as they emerged from the rise of racial radicalism in the 1890s through the Leo Frank Case of 1913–15.

JIM CROW AND JEWISH RACIAL STATUS

Positioning themselves within the southern racial order was not a totally new challenge for southern Jews, as racial division had been a hallmark of life in the South ever since Jews first settled there during colonial times.[6] Before the 1890s, however, Jews rarely had to exert much effort to ensure their status as white. During the antebellum period, the clear distinction between slaves and free whites in the South assured Jews of the region a level of social acceptance unparalleled in any other Western society of the time.[7] Certainly, acculturating Jews during these years—mainly immigrants from central Europe—came to understand intuitively that the process of "becoming Southern" entailed the support of the region's dominant social and cultural mores, including those regarding race and slavery.[8] While few Jews in the South found reason to criticize the institution of slavery and many supported it vigorously, there was little sense, however, among southern Jews during these years that their attitudes toward African Americans reflected in any significant way on their own racial status.[9]

Even with the end of the Civil War and the collapse of the slave system, divisions between blacks and whites remained stable enough to forestall any major concerns about the place of Jews in the southern racial constellation. This remained true, in fact, even as the social profile of southern Jews began to shift in the years after the war, resulting in more liberal Jewish attitudes toward African Americans. During Reconstruction, a significant migration of northern Jews, mostly recent immigrants from central Europe, bolstered the region's Jewish population and reduced the proportion of Jews who had been thoroughly acculturated into the South's racial system. Jews also became heavily invested in the emerging business infrastructure of the New South, a role that led them to court the business of former slaves and to support the amelioration of racial tensions that might work against the growth of a new regional economy. Finally, with the removal of clear legal barriers between blacks and whites and with African Americans working toward education and self-improvement, Jews could increasingly see in the black struggle experiences that resonated with their own recent history.[10]

While Jews in the South were careful to remain within the range of acceptable positions on racial issues, these factors meant that by the 1880s, it was not unusual for them to align themselves with supporters of political rights and education for blacks. Edwin W. Moise, who served as adjutant and inspector general in South Carolina, embraced the paternalistic racial attitude of Governor Wade Hampton, who courted black voters and opposed the violence and intimidation practiced by racial radicals.[11] In Virginia, William J. Lovenstein, a legislator who became the highest-ranking Jewish officeholder in the state's history, also supported the rights of African Americans, pushing his fellow lawmakers to support health care and teacher training for blacks.[12] Educational projects for blacks also received the support of Jewish activists like Rabbi Judah Wechsler, who campaigned for a bond issue to pay for the first black school in Meridian, Mississippi, in 1888, and Samuel Ullman, who as a member of the Birmingham Board of Education, advocated improved facilities for black schooling as early as 1885.[13] The frequency with which prominent Jews took public stands in favor of black causes during the 1880s indicated just how little they worried about being accepted by their non-Jewish neighbors as part of the white majority.

This situation, however, began to change dramatically when economic and social upheaval, brought on by the depression of the early 1890s, devastated agricultural production in the region and threatened to undermine the entire social structure that guaranteed white privilege. The psychological impact of the depression severely damaged the confidence of southern whites, pushing them increasingly toward racial radicalism as a means of recouping their status.[14] In such an environment, Jews stood out not only as agents of the economic changes occurring in southern society, but as a group that did not fit neatly into the rigid definitions of black and white demanded by the emerging system of racial division. While some racial radicals like Dixon continued to see Jews as pillars of white society, and while Jews never lost their legal standing as white, the place of Jews in the white southern mainstream came increasingly into question.

In small part, Jews' uncertain standing within the emerging southern racial order was exacerbated by the stream of new immigrants arriving from eastern Europe. Because the immigrants often stood out as alien in dress and appearance, southerners distinguished them from whites, as did the *Richmond Times* in 1893, when it reported on an altercation between a "Polish Jew and a white man."[15] In a few cases, recently arrived Jews were actually confused with African Americans and suffered attacks on the part of hostile whites who caught them in situations considered inappropriate for blacks. In Pine Bluff, Arkansas, in 1912, a recently arrived eastern European immigrant narrowly escaped lynching because onlookers took him for a black man in the company of a white woman.[16]

But largely, Jewish racial identity became a problem not because of the new immigrants, who arrived in smaller numbers than in the North, but because southerners continued to perceive in all Jews—even the more acculturated Jews of central European origin—distinct social, economic, and political characteristics that could be pointed to as interfering with the maintenance of clear boundaries between blacks and whites. Jewish merchants not only dealt extensively with black customers across the South but often held a certain financial advantage over white farmers and factory workers, which was thought to undermine the preservation of white racial dominance. The relationship between Jews' economic position and southern race relations became clear in the early 1890s when populist "white caps" destroyed Jewish shops in a number of towns in Louisiana and Mississippi. The vigilantes were white farmers in debt to the merchants, who feared that the Jews were interfering with the racial balance in the area by renting land seized from white debtors to black tenants.[17] Southern Jews were shocked by the attacks but preferred not to interpret them as antisemitic outbursts. New Orleans Rabbi Max Heller, for example, wrote that the attacks did not interfere with the "perfect harmony prevailing between Jew and Gentile" in the South, where such virulent hatred was reserved for African Americans.[18]

Although southern Jews tried to preserve a feeling of calm, the continued deterioration of their social and political status began to drive home the realization that they were no longer seen as unambiguously white. By the late 1890s, Jewish political candidates in some parts of the South found it increasingly difficult to win election, just as southern politicians were calling for the political exclusion of African Americans. Jews had an exceptional record of political service in the South, with dozens serving as mayors, aldermen, state legislators, and members of Congress throughout the nineteenth century.[19] But as politics became more focused on the issues of racial separation, the electorate became increasingly skeptical of Jews, seeing them as a group whose racial standing was ambiguous. Edwin W. Moise of Charleston, once a prominent politician and supporter of black suffrage, was now vilified by racist South Carolina Governor Ben Tillman as "an outsider and a member of a despised and despicable race."[20] In Atlanta, Jewish politicians fell into disfavor partly because their orientation toward business led them to oppose the prohibition of alcohol, which was seen by many southern whites as a prerequisite for effective white governance.[21] The presumption that Jewish political views differed from those of white southerners led one candidate in the Richmond municipal elections of 1893 to single out "Jews and niggers" as political troublemakers.[22]

Perhaps most devastating to southern Jews was the rise of exclusive social clubs and resorts with anti-Jewish policies. Prominent Jews had been among the original founders of the Gentleman's Driving Club in Atlanta and the Boston and Pickwick Clubs in New Orleans, but by the turn of the century, none of these organizations accepted Jewish members.[23] In states where public facilities were segregated according to color, the exclusion of Jews from clubs and hotels seemed to question their social standing as whites. The fact that many hotels and resorts in the North excluded Jews made southern Jews anxious about the spread of such policies to their region. Fear fell over southern Jewry in 1906, for example, when Bertha Rayner Frank, sister of the U.S. senator from Maryland, traveled north to Atlantic City and was denied entry to the Blenheim-Marlborough Hotel. The Baltimore *Jewish Comment*, struck by the similarity of the new anti-Jewish measures to the racial segregation frequently practiced in Baltimore, urged community action to prevent Jews from being put on a level "with the negro as an undesirable in places offering accommodations to the general public."[24]

DEFENDING JEWISH WHITENESS IN THE SOUTH

In trying to rescue their position in southern society, acculturated southern Jews began to vehemently oppose any comparison between themselves and African Americans. Herbert T. Ezekiel, editor of Richmond's *Jewish South*, took local non-Jewish editors to task for their practice of distinguishing Jews from other whites in the newspapers when they were arrested for crimes. On one occasion, he demanded a retraction from the editor of the *Richmond Times*, which he published in his weekly magazine.[25] Sometimes the comparison in need of refutation came not from southern non-Jews but from northern Jews. After devastating attacks on African Americans by white mobs in Wilmington, North Carolina, in 1898, the Philadelphia *Jewish Exponent* published an editorial sympathetic to the black victims and likened their persecution to that experienced by

Jews. Outraged by such a comparison and fearful of its social repercussions, southern Jewish editors denounced the editorial vehemently. Frank Cohen, editor of the Atlanta *Jewish Sentiment*, simply dismissed the *Exponent's* comment as another example of the "deformed opinion" of northern Jews on the "negro question" in the South.[26] Ezekiel, however, made great efforts to refute the comparison in his publication. "Our people, though persecuted and driven from pillar to post," he wrote, "do not possess the criminal instincts of the colored race. . . . The comparison of Jews and negroes is, we had always thought, a pastime of our Christian neighbors, and one which we, of all people, should not countenance." Providing a litany of reasons why African Americans made undesirable citizens, Ezekiel affirmed that "there is nothing in common between the two races in this section, and if a comparison holds elsewhere, either the Jews or the negroes must be very different from what they are here."[27]

The need to invalidate the comparison between Jews and African Americans remained strong in the South through the early years of the twentieth century, especially as a number of American commentators fastened on the similarities between anti-black and anti-Jewish persecution following the eastern European pogroms of 1903 and 1905. When Booker T. Washington compared lynching and pogroms in a speech in St. Louis in 1906, the local Jewish paper, the *Modern View*, responded that he made a "poor parallel" between African Americans, "who by carnal crimes bring their people into disrepute," and Jews, who are feared because they are "thought to be too acquisitive and too able commercially, professionally and otherwise." The paper fortified its argument by contrasting the environments under which Africans Americans and Russian Jews lived, citing the protection of a free government, the fair-minded neighbors, and the educational opportunities enjoyed by American blacks, factors that should have militated against the "ignorance and idleness that makes for criminality in the negro." The Jews in Russia, explained the editorial, suffered under an "intolerant government, a bigoted priesthood and a chained press," yet still managed to remain "peaceful, industrious, free from crime," and tenacious in their religious beliefs and practices.[28]

In attempting to affirm their whiteness by negating the comparison between themselves and African Americans, southern Jews often capitalized on the fact that their place in southern society was ambiguous, rather than totally marginal. Because southern attitudes toward Jews, like American attitudes in general, often combined admiration for Jewish accomplishments with fears about Jewish difference, Jews viewed conformity to prevailing racial mores as a strategy that had great potential to resolve their uncertain place in the southern racial constellation. They were buoyed, for example, when Thomas Dixon condemned the black leader, Booker T. Washington, for comparing Jews and African Americans in his book, *The Future of the American Negro.*[29] The New Orleans *Jewish Ledger*, one of the most prominent Jewish papers in the South, responded enthusiastically to Dixon's defense of the Jews, labeling Washington an "impudent nigger" for his comments. The paper reprinted Dixon's comments in its own columns, even embellishing them with some of its own lines, which it attributed to him: "To compare the Jew, who occupies the highest pinnacle of human superiority and intellectual attainment, with the Negro who forms the mud at its base, is something only a Negro with more than the usual vanity and impudence of his race could attempt."[30]

Dixon was not the only spokesman for white supremacy whose statements allowed southern Jews to believe that a careful policy of racial conformity could help deflect attention away from Jewish difference and confirm their status as white. In 1903, Ben Tillman, who had become the United States senator from South Carolina, led a campaign against appointing black postmasters in small southern towns, citing the danger white women faced from the black officials and their friends who congregated in post offices or in the general stores where they were often located. Of special significance was Tillman's objection to the appointment of a black postmistress in Indianola, Mississippi, where the post office was located in Cohen's Brooklyn Bridge Store. As Tillman told the Senate, the presence of the black postmistress had encouraged black customers to take a bold attitude toward the white customers and employees, and violent riots almost erupted among the white population of Indianola when reports circulated that an "infamous proposition and insult from a negro man [was made] to a white woman, a poor Jewess who was clerking in the same store."[31] Tillman, who ten years earlier had vilified his Jewish political opponent, Edwin W. Moise, as a racial outsider, now defended a Jewish woman as a symbol of white female virtue and purity. Statements like those of Dixon and Tillman indicated to southern Jews that, if they carefully observed the rules of southern race relations and did not disturb increasingly rigid racial boundaries, they could assure their place as whites, and thus their full acceptance, in southern society.

In this respect, southern Jewry offered an interesting comparison with its northern counterpart. Between 1907 and 1913, in response to the same sort of social discrimination that made southern Jews fearful of being classed with African Americans, northern Jewish leaders, headed by the prominent New York attorney Louis Marshall, lobbied for the New York Civil Rights Act, which would outlaw discrimination in public accommodations on the basis of "race, faith, creed, and color."[32] In the South, however, many observers feared that a sustained public campaign against such exclusionary policies would do nothing more than underscore Jews' status as victims of "racial discrimination" and lend credence to the comparison between Jews and African Americans. Rabbi Max Heller expressed the fear characteristic of southern Jews that any law seeking to preserve Jewish rights by advocating an end to racial discrimination against blacks would "array against it . . . the whole force of prejudice against the negro."[33] Although he himself was a supporter of black rights, Heller's views were shaped by the realities of the southern racial situation, which told him that if Jews sought an end to discrimination, they would have to do it in a way that did not seriously challenge prevailing racial hierarchies.

Most southern Jews agreed with Heller that the preservation of Jewish social status relied on their conformity to southern racial standards. What remained uncertain throughout the early years of the twentieth century, however, was the *extent* to which Jews needed to embrace notions of white supremacy in order to relieve the public's doubt about their status. Most Jews, for example, abstained from promoting the harshest forms of southern racism, like mob violence and lynching. Although Richmond's *Jewish South* was vigorous in asserting the whiteness of Jews, it decried lynching as a subversion of law and government that not only "defies the dignity of man" but "profanes the sanctity of human life."[34] Yet there were at least some Jews who felt the need to support such practices, including Frank Cohen, the editor of the Atlanta *Jewish Sentiment.* "The white man will rule by fair means or by foul," Cohen warned after the Wilmington Race Riot of 1898. "God Almighty never created the negro the white man's equal and even an act of Congress will not change the trend of nature or swerve the white man from his determination to retain his supremacy."[35]

If outspoken Jewish proponents of lynching remained rare, more common were southern Jewish politicians who tried to counter prejudices against Jewish officeholding by supporting proposals for black disenfranchisement and by endorsing white political dominance. In Arkansas, a state where populist politicians frequently employed anti-Jewish imagery in denouncing "usurers" and "Rothschilds," Governor Jeff Davis and other leading Democrats were willing to overlook the Jewishness of Adjutant General Charles Jacobson because of his support for preserving white rule.[36] Maryland's Jewish attorney general, Isidor Rayner, made disenfranchisement a central tenet of his political credo, arguing in 1903 that the Declaration of Independence was wrong in proclaiming that all men were created equal.[37] Later, when Rayner became a United States senator, he lent his political clout to a state disenfranchisement bill championed by another Jewish politician and one of his successors in the attorney general's office, Isaac Lobe Straus. The bill restricting black voting rights became law in Maryland in 1908 and was named the "Straus Amendment" after its primary author.[38]

Despite the presence of some Jews in the ranks of assertive white suprema-cists, however, Jews in the South generally shied away from high-profile politi-cal engagement with racial issues. Instead, they tried to assert their whiteness in less charged ways that simply upheld the prevailing social and cultural dis-tinctions between blacks and whites. In New Orleans, for example, the local Jewish paper printed dialect stories lampooning blacks, and regularly reviewed blackface minstrel shows and performances of plays such as Dixon's *Clansman*, which it called a "thrilling" exposition of "the terrible struggle of the 'Recon-struction Era' and the frightful perils of entrusting the mastery of society to a helot race."[39] Atlanta Jews staged their own blackface minstrel show in 1898 under the auspices of the local Hebrew Association.[40] They also tried to em-phasize their stature in the city by claiming to have produced the first example of white womanhood in the area. By the turn of the century, local Jews often re-peated a founding myth that Caroline Haas, the daughter of one of Atlanta's earliest Jewish residents, was the "first white female child" born in the city.[41] Fi-nally, in order to assure their own continued access to white privilege, southern Jews also supported the prevailing system of segregated public accommoda-tions and neighborhoods. In Atlanta, a Jewish member of the Carnegie Library's board was among those who voted to ban African Americans from the institu-tion after W.E.B. Du Bois, a professor at Atlanta University, applied for reading privileges.[42] Similarly, when Atlanta's Hebrew Benevolent Congregation sold its edifice on the corner of Garnett and Forsythe Streets and moved into a new building, the directors stipulated that "said Temple is never to be sold, rented to, nor to be used by colored people."[43]

COUNTERVAILING FORCES

The tendency of southern Jews to uphold social and cultural distinctions be-tween blacks and whites while generally shying away from strong support of racial violence or disenfranchisement indicates that there was a point at which their desire for social acceptance began to conflict with feelings of unease about adopting the mantle of white supremacy. As assiduously as Jews tried to conform to the strictures of southern race relations, they sometimes found themselves unable to totally suppress an aversion to racism that had been conditioned by the Jewish historical experience and was now becoming more manifest as they tasted a bit of the social exclusion usually reserved for blacks. Though southern Jews were often forced by social pressure to downplay these feelings, there were distinct signs during the early twentieth century of the lingering reservations some Jews had about identifying unambiguously with the southern racial system.

On rare occasions, some acculturated Jews who had become totally alienated from the standards of white society entirely flouted conventions. Adolph Altschul, one of several German Jewish immigrant brothers who settled in Pine Bluff, Arkansas, and peddled in the surrounding countryside, fell in love with a former slave, Maggie Carson, and married her, apparently before such marriages became illegal in the South. He remained with her until his death and had several children, while his brothers cut off contact with him and identified exclusively with Pine Bluff's white population.[44] In Natchez, Mississippi, home to a prominent and well-integrated Jewish community that dated back to antebellum days, Charles Moritz broke the predominant Jewish pattern by establishing a "permanent alliance" (a kind of common-law marriage) with an African American woman, Dorcas Walker. Although Mississippi state law prevented Moritz and Walker from marrying, and although they conformed to local racial etiquette by living separately, they remained in a lifelong relationship and raised two daughters together.[45]

Much more common, however, was the way in which acculturated Jewish merchants sometimes deviated from white racial etiquette in their commercial relations with African Americans. Many Jews got their start in the southern business world by dealing with black customers and continued to court their trade even after branching out to serve a more diverse customer base. Within the confines of their own stores, southern Jewish merchants were sometimes able to form relationships with black customers and extend courtesies to them that might have appeared unseemly in the public square. Julius Levin, a prominent lumber merchant in Alexandria, Louisiana, who began his career as a country peddler, established close ties with many of his black customers and frequently made generous donations to the African American Shiloh Baptist Church of that city. When Levin died in 1910, local blacks published resolutions in his memory in the local paper as well as in their church publication, the *Louisiana Baptist*, calling him a "true friend of our race as well as to humanity."[46] Likewise, the Jewish merchants of Montgomery, Alabama, developed a strong rapport with Booker T. Washington and frequently supplied the needs of the Tuskegee Institute, which they also supported with financial contributions.[47] Occasionally, Jewish merchants went beyond discreet acts of friendship and assistance and took more public stands. Once, when Tuskegee faced the possibility of an economic boycott, Jacques Loeb, a French-born Jew who headed a large Montgomery grocery concern and was influential in local business affairs, resisted the pressure of non-Jewish merchants and continued to supply the school with necessities until other companies agreed to do likewise.[48]

If Jewish businessmen sometimes articulated feelings of friendship and empathy for African Americans in the context of the close economic relations between the two groups, Jewish clergy, acting on their understanding of Judaism as a religion that demanded social justice, also frequently spoke up for the needs of the black community. During the first two decades of the twentieth century, a small but significant circle of southern rabbis supported African American education, opposed lynching, and worked for what they termed interracial "harmony" and cooperation. As rabbis, these men formed their opinions on the issue of race under a somewhat different set of pressures and experiences than their congregants. First, because the South had no rabbinical seminary of its own, many of the Jewish clergy who served the region either came from the North or were recent arrivals from central or eastern Europe. As a result, they probably had much more immediate experiences with anti-Jewish persecution than their congregants did and therefore found themselves at greater odds with the southern treatment of African Americans. Second, because Jewish religious leaders were often accorded a certain respect in the South that individual Jews may not have always received, they enjoyed a degree of latitude among non-Jews in expressing their concern for African Americans, especially when such concern was voiced in the language of ethical obligation. As a result, rabbis such as Ephraim Frisch of Pine Bluff, Arkansas, and Bernard Ehrenreich of Montgomery, Alabama, felt free to use their role as civic leaders to solicit support for black schools such as Branch Normal College and Tuskegee Institute.[49]

Finally, because rabbis saw race relations in ethical terms, they were less willing than their congregants to suppress feelings of empathy for a people who were suffering many of the same indignities Jews had historically experienced. When Alfred G. Moses assumed leadership of the Shaarei Shomayim Congregation in Mobile, Alabama, in 1901, he immediately wrote to Booker T. Washington to express his interest in African American affairs. "As a preacher I feel morally bound to get at the truth," he explained, "and as a Rabbi, I have the opportunity of influencing the minds of the better class of Jewish people, as well as of the community at large."[50] Seymour Bottigsheim, the rabbi of Temple B'nai Israel of Natchez, Mississippi, ignored the concerns of some of his congregants and invited George Washington Carver to address his congregation from the pulpit.[51] In 1909, Rabbi Max Heller was denounced by some leading members of the New Orleans Jewish community when he criticized a local Christmas toy drive that provided only for white children.[52] Despite the opposition he encountered, however, Heller continued his critique of southern racism, going so far as to draw explicit parallels between blacks and Jews, which had become a virtual taboo in southern Jewish society. Knowing his congregants' strong aversion to such comparisons, Heller forcefully told them that "the Jew, like the negro, is slandered and abused as a 'race' . . . [and] is made to suffer, the mass, for the sins of the individual." He also argued that such similarities implied a duty toward African Americans on the part of Jews, who as "men who have been steeled in the furnace of persecution . . . ought to lend an uplifting hand to the weak fellow-man."[53]

While Heller stood virtually alone among his colleagues in making direct comparisons between African Americans and Jews, an unspoken belief in such a parallel no doubt pushed other southern rabbis to exceed non-Jewish clergy in their support of black causes. Despite southern rabbis' fairly liberal expression of empathy for African Americans, however, their activities ultimately underscored the great care Jews had to take in defining their place in the southern racial order. While rabbis argued for the education and "uplift" of African Americans and condemned virulent racism, they never challenged the basic structure of race relations in the South or advocated meaningful social equality for blacks. None argued for an end to segregation, or even for the protection of African Americans' right to vote and hold office. David Marx, the rabbi of Atlanta's Hebrew Benevolent Congregation, served on the commission appointed to restore order in the wake of that city's 1906 race riot, but the plan for "racial harmony" proposed by the group argued that the best way to improve relations between blacks and whites was to keep African Americans away from saloons and off the streets.[54] Even Max Heller strongly supported the maintenance of the southern system of segregation. Although he argued that African Americans could become gentlemen, he conceded that "social equality" did not mean "social mingling." The continued separation of the races, and especially the ban on interracial unions, he felt, was a necessity if whites were to effectively bear the burden of improving the more "backward" race. "It is to the interest of both races that interbreeding of any kind should be prevented," wrote Heller in 1904. "The benevolence of the separation will appear in our efforts to lift the younger brother as speedily as possible to our own level."[55] Thus, even the most outspoken Jewish supporters of African Americans continued to uphold the basic social distinction between blacks and whites, underscoring their need to position themselves on the white side of the racial divide.

EASTERN EUROPEAN JEWS AND WHITENESS IN THE SOUTH

While acculturated Jews in the South often struggled to square their own self-image with the demands of a racially segregated society, another group of Jews in the South—recently arrived immigrants from eastern Europe—felt much freer from pressure to conform to southern racial mores. Unlike their Americanized counterparts from central Europe, the newer immigrants, who began to appear in southern cities and in rural districts in increasing numbers by the end of the nineteenth century, remained preoccupied in the initial years after their arrival with the struggle for basic economic survival. Not having begun their drive for social acceptance in earnest, they remained largely insensitive to the social and cultural conventions of southern society and continued to see themselves primarily as Jews and not as "whites."

This lack of consciousness regarding the color line was most apparent in the business dealings of eastern European Jewish immigrants, who relied extensively on black trade as they sought to gain an economic foothold in their new surroundings. Stories of peddlers who were on intimate terms with black customers are exceedingly common. Nathan Klawansky, who peddled through the counties of southern Maryland in the 1890s, knew most of the African American residents of the region and regularly relied on them for meals and a place to stay.[56] Dave Pearlman, who began his business career as a peddler in southern Georgia, also accepted invitations to spend the night in the home of one of his black customers, although it was against local custom. It was on his regular visits there that he learned to speak English, and according to his own account, he returned from his peddling trips speaking like a "yidische schwarzter." Despite the admonition of his brother that he keep his social distance from his black customers, Pearlman persisted in his friendliness.[57] In 1909, a peddler who traveled through the South wrote to the New York Yiddish newspaper, Forverts, regarding his intentions toward a young black woman who was one of his customers. He fell in love with her, but the strict segregation laws in the region prevented them from being seen in public together.[58]

Such intimacy was also exhibited in southern towns and cities, where the trade with African Americans was largely in the hands of Jewish immigrants. In cities like Richmond, Norfolk, and Savannah, they ran groceries, pawnshops, secondhand stores, and saloons primary for black clientele.[59] In Atlanta, the area around Decatur Street, the center of the city's African American community, became the terminus for arriving eastern Europeans.[60] Baruch Charney-Vladeck, writing for Forverts in 1911, reported that the typical Jewish grocer lived in the black section of Atlanta, segregated from the white population and unaware of the importance of racial etiquette. Even though Vladeck came from New York and a Yiddish-speaking milieu, as a socialist intellectual he was more sensitive to the significance of black-Jewish proximity, and more apt to equate race and levels of "civilization," than were the Jewish grocers he described. "To make a living, the grocer must give up all of the comforts of the 'outside' civiliza-tion" and take up residence in the "old, ramshackle ruins" of the "negro neighbor-hood," he wrote. There, his children are "influenced by the half-wild and bar-baric street life of the black." The grocer "learns the black's English, and finds himself at a very low station in life.[61]

The distance of most Jewish immigrants from the social pressures of the white world also made it easier for them to see the black experience in terms comparable to the plight of Jews in eastern Europe. Although few acculturated Jews in the South would have dreamt of explicitly comparing black and Jewish suffering during these years, peddler Dave Pearlman regularly told stories of Jewish persecution in Russia to his black friends and customers, hoping the tales would ease the pain of their own difficult experiences.[62] Likewise, the Rus-sian-Jewish immigrant David Yampolsky, who witnessed the Atlanta Race Riot firsthand in 1906, decried the "dreadful, slavish, oppressed" state in which Af-rican Americans found themselves in the South, one which he argued was "worse than the condition of Jews in Tsarist Russia."[63]

As removed as eastern European Jewish immigrants in the South often were from the pressures of racial conformity, however, their relatively small numbers and the paucity of large Jewish residential enclaves in the region meant that they could not remain isolated from social and business contact with the dominant society to the same extent as their northern counterparts. Thus, it was not long before the need to assert a white identity, so pronounced among acculturated Jews in the South during these years, was exhibited by eastern European Jews in the region as well. As Jewish immigrant merchants attempted to improve their economic situation and court the business of a white clientele, they came to understand the stigma of living in the black neighborhoods and began to seek more "respectable" surroundings. After 1911, for example, the eastern European Jews of Atlanta began to leave the Decatur Street neighborhood and settle further south, away from the city's expanding African American population.[64] Similarly, the immigrant Jews of Durham, North Carolina, who had originally settled in modest shacks in Hayti, that city's black district, and in the adjoining neigh-borhood of Pine Street Bottoms, also fled to take up residence in white middle-class areas.[65]

Those who most thoroughly absorbed the racial culture of the region were the members of the younger generation, who had spent their formative years in the South and usually had the greatest contact with white southerners. One young immigrant, Abraham Bisno, discovered the advantages of whiteness while serving as an apprentice to a non-Jewish tailor whose family he lived with in Chattanooga, Tennessee. Working among non-Jews and barely able to speak

English, he found anti-black prejudice a potent means of identifying with his surroundings and began to harass a young African American girl who also worked in the shop. "Since the atmosphere was antagonistic to negroes," he later recalled, "I think I excelled more than any other member of the family in meanness and contempt."[66] As Charles Rubin recalled, Jewish youth were propelled by similar motivations in Atlanta, where "the term 'nigger' [was] used by Jewish sons of immigrant parents with the same venom and contempt as the tem 'Zhid' was used in the old country."[67] Like the central European Jews before them, eastern European Jews in the South were increasingly learning to position themselves as white within the highly segregated society around them.

JEWISH WHITENESS NORTH AND SOUTH

Southern Jews were by no means alone during the late nineteenth and early twentieth centuries in their accommodation to the racial culture of the larger, non-Jewish society in which they lived. Jews in the North, where the categories of black and white were also becoming more central during these years, and where Jewish racial status was also becoming uncertain, similarly found it necessary to assert their whiteness in making the case for their social inclusion. By 1903, Jewish leaders, such as Philadelphia physician Solomon Solis-Cohen, in some cases began to repeat the arguments of southern Jewish editors that pogroms against Jews in Russia could in no way be compared to the lynching of blacks in the United States.[68] Like their counterparts in Atlanta and New Orleans, members of Jewish clubs and societies in New York and Chicago regularly staged blackface minstrel shows.[69] On occasion, Jewish immigrant children in Harlem hurled racist epithets at blacks with the same vigor as Jewish youth did in southern neighborhoods.[70]

Yet despite the fact that northern and southern Jews sometimes experienced similar pressures regarding their approach to blacks, Jews in the north proved more ambivalent than their southern counterparts about strongly asserting their whiteness. Because northern Jews were more visible as a group than those in the South, they were more sensitive to the ways in which increasing racism against African Americans might also negatively influence the status of other minorities. As a result, they harbored greater reservations about the advance of racial violence, segregation and legal restrictions against blacks and frequently spoke out against them.[71] In addition, because they were free from the gravity that characterized the race question below the Mason-Dixon line, northern Jews more openly expressed the empathy for African Americans that stemmed from their own experiences of oppression and marginalization.[72] Although support of black philanthropies and involvement in civil rights organizations were typical only of an elite group of northern Jews in the years before World War I, Jewish participation in these activities was still significantly greater in the North than in the South.[73]

In the age of Jim Crow, then, Jews in the South conformed to prevailing racial mores much more diligently than in any other region of the country. To do otherwise would have been disastrous for their social status. On the other hand, the approach taken by southern Jews toward blacks seems to have done little to improve their standing in white society during the early years of the twentieth century. The trial of Leo Frank in 1913 for the murder of Mary Phagan and his subsequent lynching underscored Jews' vulnerable position two decades after the rise of racial radicalism. During Frank's trial, some non-Jewish Atlantans distributed small cards, urging their neighbors not to patronize Jewish shops, which read: "Now is the time to show your true colors; to show your true American blood."[74] By casting Jews out of the pale of whiteness, these southerners felt they were reinforcing, purifying, and removing the troubling ambiguity from their own racial identities. As for southern Jews, the trial and vigilante attack on Frank only made them more convinced that the key to acceptance lay in demonstrating *their* true colors as whites. Although the Frank Case was surely the most dramatic example of Jews' uncertain status within the southern racial order, it did not represent the beginning or end of their insecurity about racial identity.[75]

NOTES

Parts of this essay are drawn from chapter 3 of my book *The Price of Whiteness: Jews, Race, and American Identity* (Princeton, N.J.: Princeton University Press, 2006) and are reprinted here with the kind permission of Princeton University Press.

1. "The Negro a Menace Says Thomas Dixon," *New York Times*, June 9, 1903, 2.

2. See Dixon's comments on Jews in his "Booker T. Washington and the Negro," *Saturday Evening Post*, August 19, 1905, 2.

3. Arthur T. Abernethy, *The Jew a Negro: Being a Study of the Jewish Ancestry from an Impartial Standpoint* (Moravian Falls, N.C.: Dixie Publishing, 1910), 105. On Abernethy's career, see *Dictionary of North Carolina Biography*, ed. William S. Powell (Chapel Hill: University of North Carolina Press, 1979), 1:4.

4. Watson quoted in C. Vann Woodward, *Tom Watson: Agrarian Rebel* (New York: Oxford University Press, 1963), 443. For a similar casting of Frank as a "black beast rapist," see "The Leo Frank Case," *Watson's Magazine* 20 (January 1915): 143.

5. On the uncertain racial place of the Jew in southern society during this period, see

Leonard Rogoff, "Is the Jew White? The Racial Place of the Southern Jew," *American Jewish History* 85 (September 1997): 195–230.

6. See James W. Hagy, *This Happy Land: The Jews of Colonial and Antebellum Charleston* (Tuscaloosa: University of Alabama Press, 1993), chap. 4.

7. See Bertram Korn, "Jews and Negro Slavery in the Old South, 1789–1865," *Publications of the American Jewish Historical Society* 50 (March 1961): 200; Naomi W. Cohen, *Encounter with Emancipation: The German Jews in the United States, 1830–1914* (Philadelphia: Jewish Publication Society of America, 1984), 22.

8. See Mark Greenberg, "Becoming Southern: The Jews of Savannah, Georgia, 1830–1870," *American Jewish History* 86 (March 1998): 60–63.

9. According to historian Bertram Korn, who studied the attitudes of antebellum southern Jews toward African Americans extensively, there is little evidence to suggest "that these Jews gave conscious support to the slave system out of fear of arousing anti-Jewish prejudice." See Korn, "Jews and Negro Slavery," 199. Gary P. Zola's study, *Isaac Harby of Charleston, 1788–1828: Jewish Reformer and Intellectual* (Tuscaloosa: University of Alabama Press, 1994), 95–98, suggests that Korn may have underestimated the pressures on southern Jews. Still, one can still safely say that in an era in which slavery so firmly distinguished between southern blacks and whites, Jewish fear about being grouped with African Americans was certainly less significant than it was in the age of Jim Crow.

10. See, for example, the speech of Confederate veteran William Levy before students of a black school in Texas, in which he directly compares African American and Jewish history. William Levy, "A Jew Views Black Education: Texas—1890," *Western States Jewish Historical Quarterly* 8 (July 1976): 351–60.

11. Herbert Elzas, *The Jews of South Carolina from the Earliest Times to the Present Day* (New York: J. P. Lippincott, 1905), 250–51. On Wade Hampton, see C. Vann Woodward, *Origins of the New South, 1877–1913* (Baton Rouge: Louisiana State University Press, 1971), 79–80, 321.

12. Myron Berman, *Richmond's Jewry, 1769–1976: Shabbat in Shockoe* (Charlottesville: University Press of Virginia, 1979), 235.

13. Leo E. Turitz and Evelyn Turitz, *Jews in Early Mississippi, 1840–1900* (Jackson: University Press of Mississippi, n.d.), 100; Margaret England Armbrester, *Samuel Ullman and "Youth": The Life, the Legacy* (Tuscaloosa: University of Alabama Press, 1993), 39.

14. See Joel Williamson, *Crucible of Race: Black-White Relations in the American South since Emancipation* (New York: Oxford University Press, 1984), 113–15.

15. *Jewish South* (Richmond), September 29, 1893, 4.

16. Arnold Shankman, "Friend or Foe? Southern Blacks View the Jew, 1880–1935," in *Turn to the South: Essays on Southern Jewry*, ed. Nathan M. Kaganoff and Melvin I. Urofsky (Charlottesville: University Press of Virginia, 1979), 191n.49. For another case, see Maurice Fishberg, *The Jews: A Study of Race and Environment* (New York: Scribners, 1911), 120.

17. William F. Holmes, "Whitecapping: Anti-Semitism in the Populist Era," *American Jewish Historical Quarterly* 63 (1973–74): 244–61.

18. Heller quoted in Bobbie Malone, *Rabbi Max Heller: Reformer, Zionist, Southerner, 1860–1929* (Tuscaloosa: University of Alabama Press, 1997), 48.

19. For a partial list of southern Jewish officeholders during this period, see Raymond Arsenault, "Charles Jacobson of Arkansas: A Jewish Politician in the Land of the Razorbacks, 1891–1915," in Kaganoff and Urofsky, *Turn to the South*, 179n.6.

20. Tillman quoted in Leonora E. Berson, *The Negroes and the Jews* (New York: Random House, 1971), 28.

21. Steven Hertzberg, *Strangers within the Gate City: The Jews of Atlanta, 1845–1915* (Philadelphia: Jewish Publication Society of America, 1978), 157–58, 160–62.

22. *Jewish South*, September 8, 1893, 3. The exclusion of Jews from political office during this period seems to have been especially common in the larger urban centers. For a similar trend in New Orleans, see Malone, *Rabbi Max Heller*, 49.

23. Hertzberg, *Strangers within the Gate City*, 121, 171; Malone, *Rabbi Max Heller*, 37–38.

24. *Jewish Comment*, May 31, 1907, 122, quoted in Jeffrey Gurock, "The 1913 New York State Civil Rights Act," *AJS Review* 1 (1976): 98.

25. *Jewish South*, September 29, 1893, 4.

26. *Jewish Sentiment* (Atlanta), November 25, 1898, 1.

27. *Jewish South*, November 25, 1898, 6–7.

28. "A Poor Parallel," *Modern View* (St. Louis), May 4, 1906, 2.

29. Dixon, "Booker T. Washington and the Negro," 1–2.

30. "An Impudent Nigger," *Jewish Ledger* (New Orleans), September 22, 1905, 12.

31. Quoted in Williamson, *Crucible of Race*, 193. On Tillman, see Stephen Kantrowitz, *Ben Tillman and the Reconstruction of White Supremacy* (Chapel Hill: University of North Carolina Press, 2000).

32. Gurock, "The 1913 New York State Civil Rights Act," 96.

33. Max Heller, "Regulating the Summer Hotel," *American Israelite* (Cincinnati), May 30, 1907, 4.

34. *Jewish South*, September 22, 1893, 4.

35. *Jewish Sentiment*, October 28, 1898, 1. For similar articles, see December 31, 1897, 1; March 11, 1898, 1; April 22, 1898, n.p.; June 10, 1898, 1; June 24, 1898, 1, 6; November 4, 1898, 1; November 18, 1898, 1; November 25, 1898, 1; March 19, 1899, 4; April 30, 1899, 3; May 19, 1899, 3–4; August 11, 1899, 3; August 18, 1899, 3; November 10, 1899.

36. Arsenault, "Charles Jacobson of Arkansas," 60, 72–73.

37. *Baltimore Sun*, October 18, 1903, 14; October 22, 1903, 12.

38. *Afro-American* (Baltimore), November 7 and December 2, 1907, n.p.; Margaret Law Callcott, *The Negro in Maryland Politics, 1870–1912* (Baltimore: Johns Hopkins University Press, 1969), 124–29. Rayner had opposed a disenfranchisement measure in 1905 because

he feared it could threaten the voting rights of some white immigrants. This momentary opposition has led some Jewish historians to portray him improperly as a champion of black rights. See, for example, Joshua Bloch, "Isidor Rayner (1850–1912)," *Publications of the American Jewish Historical Society* 40 (March 1951): 291–92.

39. *Jewish Ledger*, August 10, 1906, 20; September 28, 1906, 16.

40. *Jewish Sentiment*, March 18, 1898, 13.

41. This claim was first made in print by Rabbi David Marx, "History of the Jews of Atlanta," *Reform Advocate* (Chicago), November 4, 1911. See also Janice O. Rothschild, *As But a Day* (Atlanta: Hebrew Benevolent Congregation, 1967), 33. This founding myth was so often repeated among Atlanta Jews in the period before World War II that it was memorialized in Alfred Uhry's Tony Award–winning play, *The Last Night of Ballyhoo* (New York: Theater Communications Group, 1997), 11.

42. Philip Foner, "Black-Jewish Relations in the Opening Years of the Twentieth Century," *Phylon* 36 (Winter 1975): 366.

43. Minutes of Hebrew Benevolent Congregation, October 14, 1901, 507, Cuba Archives, William Breman Jewish Heritage Museum, Atlanta.

44. Julius Lester, *Lovesong: Becoming a Jew* (New York: Arcade Publishing, 1988), 8–12.

45. Jack E. Davis, *Race against Time: Culture and Separation in Natchez since 1930* (Baton Rouge: Louisiana State University Press, 2001), 93–94.

46. "Resolution of Sympathy from Colored Citizens," *Alexandria Town Talk*, January 28, 1910, reprinted in Martin I. Hinchin, *Four Score and Eleven: A History of the Jews of Rapides Parish, 1828–1919* (Alexandria, La.: privately published, 1984), appendix, 108–9.

47. Louis R. Harlan, "Booker T. Washington's Discovery of Jews," in *Region, Race and Reconstruction: Essays in Honor of C. Vann Woodward*, ed. J. Morgan Kousser and James M. McPherson (New York: Oxford University Press, 1982), 271, 274.

48. Ibid., 274.

49. Carolyn Gray Le Master, *A Corner of the Tapestry: A History of the Jewish Experience in Arkansas, 1820s–1990s* (Tuscaloosa: University of Alabama Press, 1994), 56; Byron L. Scherwin, "Portrait of a Romantic Rebel: Bernard C. Ehrenreich (1876–1955)," in Kaganoff and Urofsky, *Turn to the South*, 8; Harold Wexler, "Rabbi Bernard C. Ehrenreich: A Northern Progressive Goes South," in *Jews of the South: Selected Essays from the Southern Jewish Historical Society*, ed. Samuel Proctor and Louis Schmier (Macon, Ga.: Mercer University Press, 1984), 56–57.

50. Alfred Geiger Moses to Booker T. Washington, October 8, 1901, in *The Booker T. Washington Papers*, ed. Louis Harlan (Urbana: University of Illinois Press, 1974), 6:236–38.

51. Turitz and Turitz, *Jews of Early Mississippi*, 17.

52. Malone, *Rabbi Max Heller*, 103–5.

53. Max Heller, "A Departure in Jewish Philanthropy," *American Israelite*, January 12, 1911, 4.

54. Rothschild, *As But a Day*, 50; Williamson, *Crucible of Race*, 221–22.

55. Max Heller, "A National Problem," *American Israelite*, March 17, 1904, 4.

56. Taped interview with Dr. Maurice Klawans, August 29, 1990, Jewish Museum of Maryland, Baltimore.

57. Louis Schmier, "'For Him the "Schwartzers" Couldn't Do Enough': A Jewish Peddler and His Black Customers Look at Each Other," *American Jewish History* 73 (September 1983): 39–55.

58. Isaac Metzker, ed., *A Bintel Brief: Sixty Years of Letters from the Lower East Side to the Jewish Daily Forward* (New York: Schocken Books, 1971), 95–97.

59. See Arnold Shankman, "Friend or Foe? Southern Blacks View the Jew, 1880–1935," in Kaganoff and Urofsky, *Turn to the South*, 109.

60. Hertzberg, *Strangers within the Gate City*, 184–88.

61. Baruch Charney-Vladek, "Vi azoy lebn di iden in di South?" ["How Do Jews Live in the South?"], *Forverts*, March 22, 1911, 5.

62. Schmier, "'For Him the "Schwartzers" Couldn't Do Enough,'" 50.

63. David Davis [Yampolsky], *In gang fun di yorn* (Tel Aviv: Farlag nay lebn, 1974), 160–61.

64. Hertzberg, *Strangers within the Gate City*, 187–88.

65. Eli Evans, *The Provincials: A Personal History of Jews in the South*, rev. ed. (New York: Free Press, 1997), 1–2, 15; Leonard Rogoff, *Homelands: Southern Jewish Identity in Durham and Chapel Hill, North Carolina* (Tuscaloosa: University of Alabama Press, 2001), 64–65, 94.

66. Abraham Bisno, *Abraham Bisno: Union Pioneer* (Madison: University of Wisconsin Press, 1967), 47.

67. Rubin quoted in Hertzberg, *Strangers within the Gate City*, 191. By the 1920s and 1930s, the Americanized children of eastern European Jews in Atlanta regularly staged blackface minstrel shows at the Jewish Progressive Club and featured black dialect humor in the club's newsletter. See *JPC Progress* 2 (March 1924), 1; (April 1924), 1; (September 1924): 1; (October 1924), 1; (November 1924), 1, 4; 14 (August 1931): 4; 16 (November 1935): 2–3. Original copies of these newsletters are located in the Jewish Progressive Club Records, Cuba Archives, William Breman Jewish Heritage Museum, Atlanta.

68. *The Public* (Chicago), August 22, 1903, 307–8.

69. *The Standard Club's First Hundred Years* (Chicago: Standard Club of Chicago, 1969), 38–40; YMHA [of New York] *Monthly Bulletin* 3 (Apr. 1902): 8; 5 (April 1904): 3; 6 (April 1905): 3; 12 (February 1911): 26; (March 1911): 14, 20; 13 (January 1912): 9; (November 1912): 18; 14 (February 1913): 17; 15 (February 1914): 39; (March 1914): 10; 17 (March–April 1916): 21; 18 (February 1917): 11; (March 1917): 2.

70. See Seth Scheiner, *Negro Mecca: A History of the Negro in New York City, 1865–1920* (New York: New York University Press, 1965), 133.

71. See, for example, *American Hebrew* (New York), September 11, 1903, 525; *Jewish Criterion* (Pittsburgh), August 20, 1915; and *Jewish Sentinel* (Chicago), March 10, 1916, 8; April 12, 1918.

72. For a fuller comparison between northern and southern Jews' approach to African Americans during this period, see Eric L. Goldstein, *The Price of Whiteness: Jews, Race, and American Identity* (Princeton, N.J.: Princeton University Press, 2006), chap. 3.

73. For a survey of this activity, see Hasia R. Diner, *In the Almost Promised Land: American Jews and Blacks, 1915–1933* (Westport, Conn.: Greenwood Press, 1977); Nancy J. Weiss, "Long Distance Runners of the Civil Rights Movement: The Contribution of Jews to the NAACP and the National Urban League in the Early Twentieth Century," in *Struggles in the Promised Land: Toward a History of Black-Jewish Relations in the United States*, ed. Jack Salzman and Cornell West (New York: Oxford University Press, 1997), 123–52.

74. Quoted in Hertzberg, *Strangers within the Gate City*, 213.

75. For the struggle of southern Jews with these issues in a later period, see Clive Webb, *Fight against Fear: Southern Jews and Black Civil Rights* (Athens: University of Georgia Press, 2001).

7

THE ASCENDANCY OF REFORM JUDAISM
IN THE AMERICAN SOUTH DURING
THE NINETEENTH CENTURY

GARY PHILLIP ZOLA

In 1789, the year that George Washington became the first president of the United States of America, there were six Jewish congregations in the new American republic. Three were located in northern cities: Newport, Rhode Island's Yeshuat Israel (1695), New York's Shearith Israel (1654), and Philadelphia's Mikveh Israel (1740). Three were located in the South: Charleston, South Carolina's Beth Elohim (1749),[1] Richmond, Virginia's Beth Shalome (1789), and Savannah, Georgia's Mickve Israel (1733). By the dawn of the twentieth century, the three southern congregations had become firmly identified with the Reform movement in Judaism. By contrast, the three northern congregations all remained loyal to the traditional rites used when the congregations were first established. This interesting phenomenon constitutes more than a mere coincidence. Why did all of the historic southern synagogues eventually choose to identify with Reform Judaism, while the oldest northern synagogues remained faithful to their original traditional practice?[2]

The ascendancy of Reform Judaism in the three historic southern congregations is directly related to a series of distinctive sociocultural conditions that arose after the Civil War and over the course of the nineteenth century that influenced the development of Jewish life in the American South throughout the last half of the nineteenth century. Specifically, sectional factors created an array of unique conditions and challenges for those who sought to perpetuate the practice and observance of Judaism. Reform Judaism's ideology and its approach to religious practice helped Jews in the American South address their distinctive regional circumstances effectively and successfully.

Over the centuries, New York's Shearith Israel, Newport's Yeshuat Israel (known today as the "Touro" Synagogue), and Philadelphia's Mikveh Israel have all maintained their fealty to traditional ritual practice. These northern congregations proudly identify with what is loosely referred to as the "Spanish and Portuguese" liturgical heritage. For the congregations established during the colonial period, the Spanish-Portuguese liturgical customs represented both the chain of tradition and the secret to Jewish survival. This religious tradition betokened the glory of Israel's spiritual heritage. The colonial Jews believed it was their duty to pray in precisely the same mode as did their forebears. To do so would guarantee Jewish survival.[3]

To this day, these three congregations preserve the traditional Spanish-Portuguese prayer service, recited in Hebrew, the men and women sit separately, and the male worshippers don *tallitot* (prayer shawls) and wear *kipot* (head coverings). To one degree or another, there are traces of the Spanish and Portuguese religious heritage in the culture of these congregations. For instance, New York's Shearith Israel and Philadelphia's Mikveh Israel faithfully preserve many of the liturgical prayer melodies that have been sung in those congregations for centuries. Many of these melodies may be traced back to the western Sephardic rite and were first brought to the New World by cantors trained in the western Sephardic traditions. All in all, these historic northern synagogues, still very much alive and active, consciously project themselves as historical artifacts that represent the preservation of traditional Judaism just as it was practiced in eighteenth-century America.[4]

In contrast to the religious traditionalism of these northern synagogues, the historic congregations of Charleston, Richmond, and Savannah long ago abandoned any vestige of their Spanish-Portuguese heritage. By the dawn of the twentieth century, the congregations in those three southern cities had become bastions of American Reform Judaism. The transitional process from tradition to reform was a protracted one, and generally speaking, the trajectory toward reform intensified during the postbellum period. By the last two decades of the nineteenth century—an epoch that is typically referred to as the beginning of the so-called classical period in American Reform Judaism—these three southern congregations had already adopted many customs and practices that would soon be emblematic of American Reform Judaism during this era.[5] One of the three, Charleston's Beth Elohim, actually played a central role in a religious controversy that led directly to the first organized effort to reform Judaism in the United States. To this day, a banner on Beth Elohim's stationery proudly proclaims: "The Birthplace of Reform Judaism in the United States."

The story of how three of the six original American Jewish congregations—all located in the American South—abandoned their traditional Spanish-Portuguese rites and embraced the rituals associated with liberal Jewish practice is both noteworthy and instructive. Despite the fact that the trip from tradition to reform took distinctive courses in Charleston, Richmond, and Savannah, respectively, the religious transformations that occurred in these three congregations were uniformly a reflexive response to a common series of sociocultural circumstances that, considered collectively, were distinctively southern. An analysis of the conditions that led these congregations to shed their Spanish-Portuguese heritage and, ultimately, to embrace Reform Judaism's classical ideology illuminates the unique character of Jewish religious life in the American South.

Charleston: The Cradle of Reform Judaism

The first organized attempt to reform Judaism in America occurred in Charleston's Kahal Kadosh Beth Elohim (KKBE). During the first half of the eighteenth century, Charlestown (the city's original name) emerged as a major crossroads for British trade on the Atlantic "highway." The aristocratic planters of the province of South Carolina produced an abundance of desirable commodities—indigo and rice, and later, cotton. It was, as one scholar noted, a quintessentially American city "with new opportunities constantly beckoning."[6]

The first Jews to settle in Charlestown emigrated from either England or English possessions in the western hemisphere, such as Barbados and the British West Indies. Although a few Jews settled in the colony as early as 1695, more Jewish immigrants began arriving in the 1740s, when the city's flourishing trade with England outpaced that of Boston, New York, or Philadelphia. Most Jewish settlers hoped to take advantage of the city's thriving port in order to earn a living; those with more ambition hoped to save up enough funds to purchase a plantation. While the majority of these pioneers remained petty tradesmen, a fortunate few did succeed financially and, in doing so, made a name for themselves during the pre-Revolutionary years.[7]

By the middle of the eighteenth century, Charleston's Jewish community had grown large enough to prompt the establishment of a congregation: Kahal Kadosh Beth Elohim. In those days, the majority of Charleston's Jewry were of Ashkenazic origin. The new synagogue nevertheless elected to use the traditional Spanish-Portuguese ritual just like all of the synagogues founded during the colonial period. Charleston's distinguished Unitarian minister, the Reverend

Samuel F. Gilman (1791–1858) had on at least one occasion observed the traditional ritual as it was practiced during Sabbath morning worship services at KKBE sometime toward the beginning of the 1820s. He described his impressions of the experience in an article he wrote some years later for the *North Atlantic Review*. Gilman noted that the Jews' traditional mode of worship in Charleston consisted of "readings and responses in a kind of chant, or recitative, enunciated frequently with great indistinctness and volubility, now sinking into a low murmur, and now rising into a kind of nervous and violent vociferation." Indeed, the ceremony certainly seemed odd to the outsider, and he expressed satisfaction when a group of Jews decided that the synagogue needed "to remedy these and other defects and improprieties."[8]

This nation's first formal crusade on behalf of reforming Judaism began as a result of widespread dissatisfaction among a portion of Charleston's Jewish community with KKBE's traditional liturgical practices. On Wednesday, November 21, 1824, nearly fifty disgruntled Jewish citizens gathered to discuss their dissatisfaction with the state of Jewish religious practice in their community. This group of religious dissenters was largely composed of a younger stratum of Charleston's Jewish community, people who were active participants in the general society. By the conclusion of this first gathering, the insurgents had developed a list of grievances, which also contained specific recommendations as to how their concerns could be meaningfully redressed. It was decided that a "memorial" (that is, a petition or letter of appeal) would be written and placed before KKBE's *adjunta* (board of directors).[9]

One of those in attendance that day (probably Abraham Moïse [1799–1869]) was asked to compose a memorial presented at "a meeting of the Convention of Israelites" for formal adoption. The convention met on Thursday, December 23, 1824, and forty-seven of those in attendance affixed their names to the document. They then instructed their newly appointed chairman, Aaron Phillips (1792?–1846/7), to deliver this document to KKBE's *adjunta*. The memorial was a brief rationale for the need to reform the practice of Judaism in Charleston, and in this sense it may be viewed as the first attempt in North America to explicate the objectives and principles of Jewish religious reformation in the United States.[10]

The petitioners attempted to enumerate their complaints together with their proposed solutions. First, they noted the fact that most members of the congregation no longer understood Hebrew. They did not suggest altering or reforming the traditional Hebrew text. However, the reformers most definitely wanted to understand the prayers they were saying. They consequently argued that "by causing the *Hasan*, or reader, to repeat in English such part of the Hebrew prayers as may be deemed necessary, it is confidently believed that the congregation generally would be more forcibly impressed with the necessity of Divine worship."

Second, the protestors noted the congregation's worship service was too long. They urged the *adjunta* to remove everything "superfluous" and retain only "the most solemn portions." Specifically, they intensely disliked the traditional practice of having members pledge monetary offerings just before the Torah reading. What kind of an impression did the custom of fund raising in the midst of the worship service give to children and strangers, they asked rhetorically. Instead of the congregation's customary fund-raising technique, the petitioners urged the *adjunta* to adopt a system of "annual subscriptions" so that this "irregular, indecorous, and highly to be censured" practice could be eliminated. A third request made by the dissenters, reflecting the degree to which the "memorialists" were familiar with the religious practices of the Christian community in Charleston, asked the *adjunta* to institute a weekly discourse in English on a chapter or verse from scripture "like all other ministers."

Lest the *adjunta* argue that the proposed changes constituted an unthinkable desecration of sacred tradition, the memorialists noted that a "reformation" of Judaism was already under way among their coreligionists in Holland, Germany, and Prussia. To demonstrate both the timeliness and legitimacy of their proposal, they inserted the text of a newspaper article from the *Frankfort Journal* that had recently been reprinted in the Charleston press. How ironic, they remarked, that a reformation of Judaism could flourish "amidst the intolerance of Europe." From this fact the Charleston reformers deduced that "no climes, not even tyranny itself, can forever fetter or control the human mind." If a reformation of Judaism could take place in the Old World, how much more so is the reforming spirit likely to affect the "free citizens of America."?[11]

The program these pioneering reformers advocated concerned itself exclusively with changes in ritual and practice. The authors and signatories were laymen, not rabbis, scholars, or ideologues. An improvement in American Jewish life would come, in their opinion, once the synagogue instituted various reforms in ritual practice. Their platform did not attempt to provide the community with a philosophy or ideology of Reform Judaism. Their goal was simple and stated explicitly in the document: this plan of action was intended to spark a revitalization of Jewish life and bring dozens of disaffected Jews back into the synagogue.[12]

On January 16, 1825, the petitioners convened once again and decided to organize formally. Such action was necessary, they explained, because "no plan could be adopted to effect the purposes, contained in [their memorial] petition, unless the Convention by whom it had been presented, became organized." After considerable debate and discussion, a constitution consisting of thirty-one articles (once again probably written by Abraham Moïse) was "unanimously" adopted on February 15, 1825. This constitution delineated the purpose, structure, and goals of a new organization, the Reform Society of Israelites (RSI). Initially, these advocates of Jewish reform did not view the RSI as a schism from KKBE or as a dissident synagogue. The constitution explicitly stated that the organization's primary purpose was to "devise ways and means, from time to time, of revising and altering such parts of our prevailing system of Worship, as are inconsistent with the present enlightened state of society, and not in accordance with the Five Books of Moses and the Prophets." This society, composed of what one historian has called "the best and most influential people in the community," had come together to strengthen and revitalize Judaism, and the group's various spokesmen repeatedly emphasized this point.[13]

The RSI's constitution laid out several practical goals it aspired to accomplish. In addition to reforming Jewish worship services, the society's constitution indicates that the members of this newly established organization dedicated themselves to a number of additional objectives: the society hoped, at some point in the near future, to educate Jewish youth and make them "fully competent to peform [sic] Divine Service, not only with ability, learning and dignity, but also according to the true spirit of Judaism." The society would sponsor an annual anniversary dinner meeting at which an orator would deliver an address relating to the group's raison d'être. In a paragraph that discloses the severe consequences the dissidents might be forced to face if their involvement in the society resulted in their being expelled from membership in the Charleston synagogue, the constitution mandated that the group would "take measures" to purchase a cemetery for "Jews generally, who may not be entitled to burial in the [cemetery] of KKBE."[14]

Apparently, for the first year and a half of its existence—from January 1825, when the adjunta first refused to act on the dissidents' request, until sometime in the middle of 1826—the society made no public attempt to portray itself as a break-off from KKBE. During this first year, the society attended to its constitutionally mandated mission, and there is no evidence that it held separate worship services or that it viewed itself as an alternative synagogue in Charleston.

A letter from Isaac Harby (probably the society's most noteworthy intellectual) to Esdaile P. Cohen (1792–1856), which has recently surfaced, reveals with certainty that at least some members of the society had begun to work on a "Book of Prayers" by the fall of 1826. Shortly thereafter the group began running advertisements in the local press announcing that it planned to erect a "new place of worship in honor of Almighty God" in Charleston. The advertisement outlined the society's ideology and solicited funds to establish a new temple. The circular also conveyed a sense of the dissident group's frustration with KKBE's unwillingness to respond to its spiritual needs. The announcement contended that the group had been striving for "nearly two years . . . to eradicate many acknowledged errors in the mode of worship presently observed in the Synagogue." Although the group carefully avoided making a specific reference to a schism or break with the synagogue, it failed to influence the direction of affairs at KKBE and had no alternative but to establish "a new Temple to the Service of the Almighty."[15]

It is difficult to know for certain what prompted the group to take this dramatic and undoubtedly provocative step. Perhaps KKBE's ritual intransigence provoked it into action, or perhaps the congregation's threat to withhold cemetery privileges to those who joined the society aggravated the situation. In any event, some form of group prayer and religious music was used during the society's second anniversary activities on Tuesday, November 21, 1826. The worship service commemorating the society's first anniversary may have been the first time it experienced a worship service created by some of its own members—perhaps making it the first instance of a self-consciously creative Jewish worship service to occur in the United States.[16]

The Reformed Society of Israelites enjoyed extraordinary success during the first few years of its existence and seems to have grown dramatically during this initial period. The group's halcyon days, such as they were, did not last long. When the RSI celebrated its third "anniversary meeting" on November 21, 1827, Isaac N. Cardozo (1792–1855), the orator for that occasion, reminded his colleagues that the reformer never had an easy row to hoe—his path was always "beset with a thousand obstacles."[17] After 1827, the Reformed Society of Israelites received very little public attention, and signs of the group's impending dissolution began to appear. In 1828, Isaac Harby (1788–1828) and David N. Carvalho (1784–1860)—two of the group's most distinguished spokesmen—left Charleston for New York and Baltimore, respectively. The RSI's inability to raise the funds needed to erect a new temple manifested itself in the society's decision to return (with interest) money collected for that purpose. By 1836, fourteen of the forty-three dissenters who affixed their names to the society's constitution in 1825 had resigned and another nine had died. The group itself never officially disbanded, but it ceased to endure as a separate entity sometime after 1838.[18]

In 1838, the movement to reform Judaism in Charleston rebounded in the wake of a catastrophe that struck KKBE. The congregation's beautiful building on Hasell Street, erected in 1794, burned to the ground. The congregation had been unexpectedly "deprived of its place of worship," and it resolved to build a new synagogue on the ruins of the old. KKBE's leaders began soliciting contributions from other congregations in the United States and around the world. The response to their appeal was bitterly disappointing, and congregational leaders quickly realized that if they hoped to rebuild their synagogue, they needed to fund the effort themselves. In order to achieve this goal, Charleston's Jewish community sought to unify itself and work collaboratively on the project. KKBE attempted to attract support and backing from those who had become alienated from the congregation—specifically, those who supported the establishment of the RSI.[19]

Evidently, some semblance of unity was achieved, and the congregation began to build its new home. In 1840, as the new structure was nearing completion, a large contingent of members (undoubtedly many of whom had been associated with the RSI) petitioned KKBE's trustees to install an organ in the new building "to assist in the vocal parts of the service." The trustees rejected the petition by arguing that KKBE was constitutionally committed to preserving the Sephardic ritual and that an organ played no role in that ritual. The organ's advocates were not easily discouraged. They appealed for a meeting of the entire congregation to decide the issue, and in the end, the congregation voted to install an organ in the new building.

Installation of an organ in KKBE's new building was just the first step on the long road that led to Beth Elohim's transformation into a Reform congregation. Beth Elohim's new spiritual leader, the Reverend Gustavus Poznanski (1805?–79) became hasan (liturgical reader) of the congregation in January 1837 and undertook a new reforming initiative. Educated in Hamburg, where he was undoubtedly exposed to the ideas of local reformers, Poznanski's first post in the United States was as ritual slaughterer for New York's Shearith Israel. When KKBE began searching for a hazzan in the mid-1830s, Poznanski applied for the post. His ministrations met with such success that he was elected "minister for life" even before the expiration of his first contract. This widespread communal embrace ended in 1840, when Poznanski sided with those who wished to have an organ installed in the new building. The congregation's traditionalists, who opposed the organ, resented the fact that the popular minister abetted the pro-organ faction.

The minister soon added insult to injury when on Passover 1843 he asserted in a sermon that second-day observances of the Holy Days should be abandoned. Those in the congregation who rejected such departures from tradition bitterly opposed his efforts to advocate for liturgical reform. For the next three years, the congregation's two factions battled in court over the organ's installation in the synagogue, and they carried the case to the chambers of the South Carolina Court of Appeals. Even though the Court of Appeals ultimately sided with the liberal faction in 1846, Poznanski himself apparently felt it was a Pyrrhic victory because the congregation had been sundered. In 1847, he resigned and expressed his hope that a new religious leader might reunify the community. The board rejected his resignation, but Poznanski was adamant.[20]

Many in the congregation found Poznanski to be an extremely popular and highly regarded religious leader, but KKBE had not yet begun to think of itself as a Reform congregation. The congregation had wanted Isaac Mayer Wise, then serving in Albany, New York, to succeed Poznanski, but Wise declined its offer. At that point KKBE selected a rabbi who did not fully support the religious trends that Poznanski inaugurated. Many of Poznanski's successors were moderate reformers or religious conservatives, some of whom, in contrast to Poznanski, had pugnacious and contrarian personalities.

KKBE's new spiritual leader, Rabbi Julius Eckman (1805–74), possessed neither Poznanski's liberal religious inclinations nor his interpersonal charm. Eckman was born in Rawicz, in the Polish region of Posen. He completed his doctoral studies at the Royal Frederick Wilhelm College and, simultaneously, earned his rabbinic title under the tutelage of a variety of traditional Jewish scholars in Berlin and neighboring Prenzlau. During this time, Eckman became active in Leopold Zunz's Verein fuer Kultur und Wissenschaft des Judentums (Society for Jewish Culture and Science of Judaism), and in this way he undoubtedly encountered many of Germany's reformers. Shortly after the failure of the liberal revolutions and the ensuing political repressions of 1848, Eckman emigrated to the United States.[21]

Eckman initially settled in Richmond, Virginia, where he became rabbi of Congregation Beth Shalome in 1849. In 1850, he came to Beth Elohim in Charleston. Despite his familiarity with contemporary scholarship, Eckman remained a loyal proponent of traditional Jewish practice. Described as having an "erratic" personality, Eckman spoke bitterly about his congregants' laxness in their religious practice. His tenure in Charleston lasted just one year.[22]

After Eckman's departure, KKBE endured a prolonged period of decline, instability, and inner conflict. The congregation's vicissitudes mirrored the terrible economic conditions that gripped the entire region. During the late 1850s, Beth Elohim had a contributing membership of fewer than forty. Shortly after the Civil War broke out, the congregation's trustees ceased meeting. The Civil War destroyed the city's economic life completely, and the Jewish community languished along with the rest of the city. When trustee meetings resumed in 1866, only eight members of the congregation were in attendance.[23]

Despite these hardships, the congregation struggled to persevere. In 1852, KKBE began advertising for Eckman's successor. A circular that appeared in the *Allgemeine Zeitung des Judenthums*, published in Leipzig, described the congregation's worship practices as well as the expectations they placed on their rabbi. This interesting advertisement indicates that despite numerous regularized ritual reforms, the congregation still adhered to the Spanish-Portuguese ritual. KKBE had long adjusted to the introduction of numerous religious reforms but would not jettison its Spanish-Portuguese heritage until the mid-1870s.[24]

The congregation was unable to establish a satisfactory and enduring relationship with its rabbinic leadership between the years 1852 and 1875. After Rabbi Eckman's departure, Dr. Moritz (Maurice) Mayer (1821–67), assumed Beth Elohim's pulpit. Like Eckman, Mayer had acquired a modern secular education in Munich, where he earned his degree in law, and emigrated in the aftermath of the failed revolutions of 1848. Before settling in Charleston in 1852, Mayer came to New York and earned his living as a teacher in Rabbi Max Lilienthal's (1815–82) parochial school, called the Educational Institute. Initially, Mayer's rabbinic performance was well received, and the congregation named him rabbi for life. This irenic relationship did not last. Like Eckman, Mayer openly criticized members of the congregation who abandoned traditional Jewish practice. By 1859, the rabbi for life had left the congregation.

The societal and economic disruptions caused by the Civil War made it impossible for Beth Elohim to maintain a stable rabbinate. After the war, the congregation's president pro tempore observed that the congregation had been so "disasterously [sic] diminished by death, and removals, and by the ravages of War, its property . . . seriously damaged, and its finances greatly reduced" that it had no alternative but to amalgamate with the city's other synagogue, Shearith Israel.[25] Shearith Israel was a traditional congregation that had split off from KKBE in 1841, when its organ was installed. The break-off congregation acquired additional members a few years later when KKBE adopted the worship reforms that the Reverend Poznanski had advocated. In postbellum Charleston, neither congregation could manage on its own.

The two congregations agreed to come together for a five-year period. They adopted a new constitution in 1866 that clarified the religious compromises to which both congregations agreed: (a) the service would be in accordance with the Spanish-Portuguese rite, but abbreviated; (b) there would be no donation offerings made for the honor of blessing the Torah reading and, moreover, no members of the congregation would be called up to bless the Torah; (c) the organ would not be used during Sabbath services, but women and men would be able to sing together in the choir (both in Hebrew and English); and (d) there would be worship services conducted on the second days of the festivals for all those who wanted them.[26]

After Poznanski, one rabbi after the next failed to win the congregation's support. With the amalgamation of two disparate religious rites, one might assume that it would have been even more difficult to find a rabbi who could satisfy both sides now living under one roof. In 1868, however, KKBE/Shearith Israel engaged the services of Reverend Joseph Hayim Mendes Chumaceiro to lead the congregation. As son of the highly regarded Aron Mendes Chumaceiro, rabbi of Amsterdam's historic Spanish-Portuguese synagogue and with impeccable Sephardic credentials, J.H.M. Chumaceiro proved the ideal candidate to lead KKBE through the final stages of a religious odyssey that culminated in a complete identification with American Reform.

Chumaceiro's tenure was longer than any of his predecessors since Poznanski. Under his leadership, the congregation observed the rituals delineated in the merger constitution of 1866. This required Chumaceiro to perform a delicate balancing act wherein he was, on the one hand, a liberal rabbi and, on the other, a representative of the traditional Spanish-Portuguese heritage. There is evidence that he navigated these dangerous shoals successfully for several years. Ironically, the very same organ that had provoked dissension in the congregation in 1841 once again—three decades later—upset KKBE's religious equilibrium.[27]

In 1872, the contract that had reunited KKBE and Shearith Israel in 1866 lapsed. Freed from the contract's strictures, Beth Elohim's board voted to reinstall the congregation's infamous organ, which had been in storage since the Civil War. The organ's return coincided with the outbreak of a series of disagreeable controversies between Reverend Chumaceiro and certain members of the board. It is not clear whether a renewed enthusiasm for reform ultimately led to Chumaceiro's resignation in 1874. Just six months before his departure, KKBE had joined the newly founded Union of American Hebrew Congregations (UAHC), a congregational association founded by Isaac Mayer Wise to establish a Hebrew theological college to educate American rabbis.[28]

When the Reverend Chumaceiro resigned his post in 1874, KKBE selected its first American-born religious leader—a twenty-one-year-old named David Levy (1854–1931). Levy was a high school teacher, born and educated in Philadelphia, who knew enough Hebrew to conduct a traditional worship service. He led KKBE during its final transition into a Reform congregation. When Levy first came to Charleston, KKBE was still referred to as "the old Portuguese Congregation in Charleston."[29] Relatively quickly, however, Levy encouraged the congregation to embrace its liberal inclinations fully. In a letter to his congregation written a few years after his arrival, Levy conveyed his assessment of the congregation's religious temperament: "It is not a question of orthodoxy or reform. The spirit of the former has long since departed from our midst here while that of the latter is but in the bud."[30]

Levy cultivated Reform Judaism at KKBE. In 1879, he compiled a prayer book that the congregation adopted: *Avodat Ha-Kodesh: Service of the Sanctuary.* Levy's contemporaries praised his English translations of the Hebrew prayers for their poetic and inspirational quality. Levy excelled in the post's pastoral duties and thus earned the respect of the entire community. According to one contemporary, his accepting and loving disposition made him "beloved with an affection that did not pass with the years." His ability to represent that congregation so effectively contributed to the congregation's overall support for his liberal approach to Jewish religious practice.[31]

Levy served KKBE for nearly two decades and in 1894 accepted an invitation to become rabbi of Congregation Mishkan Israel in New Haven, Connecticut. Levy's successor, Barnett A. Elzas (1867–1936), possessed "a scholar's instinct." Born in Germany but raised in England, Elzas studied at the University of London, where he earned his baccalaureate, and at Jews' College, where he received his rabbinical ordination. Elzas was one of a small but noteworthy number of Jews' College graduates who emigrated to the United States and dedicated themselves to establishing liberal Judaism in America. By 1896, KKBE was willing to put Levy's prayer book aside in favor of the Reform movement's newly published *Union Prayer Book.* Elzas's scholarly interests buttressed the congregation's affinity for Reform Judaism. His impressive research and numerous publications on the history of South Carolina's Jewish community served to underscore KKBE's role as a historic American congregation even though its religious practices had become increasingly modern.[32]

Rabbi Isaac E. Marcuson (1872–1952), an 1894 graduate of Hebrew Union College (HUC), succeeded Elzas, who departed in 1910. Symbolically, KKBE's decision to elect an HUC alumnus as its spiritual leader consummated the congregation's status as a southern congregation firmly committed to American Reform Judaism. By 1924, KKBE took great pride in vaunting its pedigree as the progenitor of American Reform Judaism by organizing a commemoration marking the centennial anniversary of the RSI's founding. The congregation whose *adjunta* had—a century earlier—refused to entertain a request from a group of congregants who were asking for some ritual reforms now proudly identified itself as "the Cradle of Reform Judaism."[33]

Richmond: Establishing Judaism in the Old Dominion

The history of religious reform in Richmond differs considerably from events in both Charleston and Savannah. Of the original six Jewish congregations in the United States, Richmond was the only one not located in a port city. Rapid demographic and economic development in Richmond did not begin until just before the Revolution. In 1775, when Patrick Henry uttered his immortal declaration in Richmond's St. John's Church, the city had not yet become the state capital. The community was barely more than a small town, and its economy was as ragged as the surroundings. One Richmond visitor's impressions, written in 1779, leaves a vivid impression of Richmond's underdeveloped state: "With the exception of two or three families, this little town is made up of Scotch factors, who inhabit small tenements here and there from the river to the hill. . . . One of these hardy Scots has thought proper to vacate his little dwelling on the hill and though our whole family can scarcely stand up all together in it, my father has determined to rent it as the only decent tenement on the Hill."[34]

Beth Shalome, Richmond's first Jewish congregation, was officially organized in the fall of 1789. During the Revolutionary period, only a few dozen Jewish souls lived in the community. Isaiah Isaacs (1747–1806) was frequently identified as Richmond's first recorded Jewish resident. Isaacs was a merchant, a trader, and a real estate speculator who arrived in the late 1770s. In 1784, he went into business with another Jewish merchant, Jacob I. Cohen (1744–1832), who was born in Oberdorf, Germany, and emigrated to the United States just before the Revolution. The firm they established, Cohen and Isaacs, specialized in land speculation. The two owners briefly benefited from the help of Cohen's second wife's son, Jacob Mordecai (1762–1838), who also came to work for the firm around this same time.[35]

Subsequently, more Jews began to set up businesses in Richmond. Marcus Elcan, another German Jewish immigrant, followed his good friend of Jacob Mordecai. Joseph Darmstadt was a sutler attached to a company of Hessian mercenary soldiers who came to America with the British army in 1776. As soon as he could, Darmstadt fled the Hessians and settled in Richmond, where he became a highly regarded member of the community. Isaacs, Cohen, Mordecai, Elcan, Darmstadt, and their family members constituted the core of Richmond's fledgling Jewish community, which sprang to life during the early national period.[36]

Most of Beth Shalome's founding members were Ashkenazic, including Jacob Mordecai, who came from Germany via England. The congregation nevertheless adopted the Spanish-Portuguese rite. During the first decades of its existence, Beth Shalome benefited from the leadership of several capable, prominent, and well-educated Jewish leaders, including Isaac B. Seixas (1782–1839), Gershon Mendes Seixas's nephew; Isaac Baer Kursheedt (1766–1852), Gershon Mendes Seixas's son-in-law; Jacob Mordecai; and a youthful Isaac Leeser (1806–68), the man who went on to become a leading proponent of traditional Jewish practice. Despite the dedicated efforts of these distinguished men, a growing percentage of Richmond's Jewish community—many of whom had recently emigrated from central Europe—was slowly becoming alienated from Beth Shalome's religious practices.

In 1841, several Richmond Jews who years earlier had founded a German Jewish social welfare association organized a synagogue called Beth Ahabah. Many of the charter members of this new Ashkenazic congregation had previously belonged to Beth Shalome, though others had recently arrived in Richmond from central Europe.[37] Historians have largely assumed that Richmond's growing German Jewish contingent became increasingly dissatisfied with Beth Shalome's liturgical practices and wanted a synagogue where the Ashkenazic rite was practiced. This may have been one consideration, but another factor likely was also at work.

In 1846, the new congregation resolved to pursue a new educational initiative. In a document that recorded the deliberations of its leadership, Beth Ahabah's members appear increasingly distressed about the lack of Jewish learning in the younger generation. The education of the "younger generation," they noted, had been "partially neglected," thus leaving young people disconnected from Jewish "moral and religious feelings." Moreover, the young had become worrisomely unacquainted "with the history of their ancestors and the signification of their religious ceremonies." To address this crisis, Beth Ahabah's leaders voted to engage a religious leader able to relate to young people by teaching them in English, leading meaningful services, and offering lectures [from the pulpit] on "lessons of morality to young and old."[38]

A newly formed committee sought to fulfill the board's resolution, and the Reverend Maximilian J. Michelbacher became Beth Ahabah's new spiritual leader. Michelbacher came to Richmond from Philadelphia and served initially as the congregation's reader as well as preceptor of the synagogue's school, known as "the Seminarium." Eventually, he worked exclusively as a congregational teacher and school preceptor. During his long association with Beth Ahabah (he remained in Richmond until his death in 1879), Michelbacher inaugurated a variety of ritual reforms, and he galvanized the congregation's support for the Jewish school that he directed.

In 1866, the rabbi organized a volunteer choir for the synagogue's worship services that featured male and female voices. The choir became an immediate success, and the need for a *hasan* evaporated. In 1867, the congregation installed family pews and an organ to accompany the choir. When Michelbacher stepped down from the pulpit to concentrate his efforts on the congregation's school, Beth Ahabah engaged a series of religious leaders who carried on his liberalizing initiatives. Over the next two decades, a series of liberal-minded, well-liked religious leaders—who abetted the move toward religious reform—led the congregation.[39]

The same year that Beth Ahabah installed its organ and family pews, Dr. Judah Wechsler (1833–1907), a proponent of reform who later became a founding member of the Central Conference of American Rabbis (CCAR), took over the congregation.[40] Dr. Albert Siegfried Bettelheim (1830–90) succeeded him in 1869.[41] An ordained rabbi and a trained scholar with a Ph.D., Bettelheim favored a more conservative approach to reform than his predecessor. He proved to be an effective leader, and Beth Ahabah's membership grew considerably during his tenure. Dr. Abraham Hofmann (1822–78) followed Bettelheim in 1875—the same year that the renowned reformer Isaac M. Wise spoke in Richmond to urge congregants to join the UAHC and to support the theological school (Hebrew Union College) then in its first academic year. Hofmann's sudden death in 1878 brought Dr. Abraham Harris (1836–91) to Richmond. Born in Edinburgh, Scotland, Harris was Beth Ahabah's first native English-speaking preacher. Having obtained his rabbinic training in Berlin, Harris followed in the scholarly tradition of his predecessors. His congregation appreciated his flawless English oratory, and it bolstered his stature in the community. Evidently, Beth Ahabah, whose founders were largely German immigrants, was no longer in need of a preacher who could lecture in German.

From 1869 through 1894, Beth Ahabah moved steadily from its starting point as a traditional Ashkenazic congregation toward complete identification with the rituals and liturgical practices of American Reform Judaism. When Abraham Harris died in Beth Ahabah's pulpit (like his predecessor Abraham Hofmann, he died while preaching), the congregation elected its first HUC graduate, a man who remained in Richmond for more than fifty years: Rabbi Edward N. Calisch (1865–1946). Under Calisch, Beth Ahabah promptly identified itself as a Reform congregation, and in doing so, successfully fashioned itself as a direct descendant of the old Spanish-Portuguese congregation, Beth Shalome.[42]

Seven years after Calisch's arrival in Richmond, Beth Shalome reunited with Beth Ahabah. Throughout the postbellum era, the two congregations had long maintained close and cordial relations. From the mid-1860s to the mid-1890s, as Beth Ahabah transformed steadily into a Reform congregation, Beth Shalome sustained close relations with its "daughter" congregation. When Beth Shalome's building closed for repair in 1866, its members worshipped at Beth Ahabah, where, without objection or incident, they encountered a mixed choir chanting the Hebrew prayers. Over the years, Beth Shalome invited Beth Ahabah's liberally inclined rabbis to preach to them. These encounters were well received.[43] Since Beth Shalome did not have a school of its own, parents sent their children to Beth Ahabah for instruction.

As Beth Shalome increasingly relied on the rabbi and school of its sister institutions in Richmond, the historic congregation began to stagnate. Soon after the Civil War, Beth Shalome contemplated merging with another congregation. Two visitors in 1866 reported that upon entering the synagogue one Friday evening, they discovered the reader facing the Holy Ark containing the Torah and intoning the prayer service even though every bench was empty. By 1867, the board explored the possibility of merging with Keneseth Israel Congregation, a strictly Orthodox synagogue founded in 1856 by Jewish immigrants who wanted to pray in accordance with the traditional Polish rite. This initiative proved unsuccessful. Among other concerns, Beth Shalome did not want to abandon its Sephardic pronunciation of the Hebrew prayers. The Reverend Isaac P. Mendes (1853–1904), a man of distinguished Sephardic lineage, became the minister of Beth Shalome in 1873. Less than five years later, recognizing that Beth Shalome was moribund, he left for Savannah's Mickve Israel Congregation. Mendes was Beth Shalome's last full-time rabbi.[44]

The very day that Reverend Mendes announced his resignation, Beth Shalome voted to initiate merger talks with Beth Ahabah. Beth Shalome suspended business meetings in October 1878, and, with one exception, the synagogue's board would not resume its regular meetings until 1886. In 1891, the congregation sold its building, and on November 6, 1898, the Beth Shalome board formally voted to consolidate with Beth Ahabah. The united congregation no longer bore the name Beth Shalome, but all members of Richmond's original synagogue were guaranteed membership for life in Beth Ahabah. Having now formally absorbed Beth Shalome and its history, Beth Ahabah (emphasizing that its founders had been members of Beth Shalome) began to memorialize Beth Shalome as its parent. To this day, Beth Ahabah considers itself an "offshoot" of Beth Shalome, and it traces its origins and congregational lineage back to 1789, when Richmond's first synagogue came into being.[45]

Savannah: Orthodoxy versus Reform

The beginnings of Jewish communal life in Savannah were unique. As Jacob Rader Marcus notes, "The Savannah Jewish community was the only one in all North America in the eighteenth century that sprang full blown from the brow of Jupiter." In July 1733, a London sea vessel—the William and Sarah—reached the Savannah River. The ship brought approximately forty Jews who wanted to settle in the new English colony of Georgia, then under the leadership of James Oglethorpe. Many of these Jews were Sephardim who had come to England in the early 1720s to escape renewed Inquisition terror in Portugal. They anticipated establishing a religious community in Georgia and brought a Torah scroll and circumcision tools with them on the William and Sarah. From the time of their arrival in Georgia, the Jewish colonists worshipped together, and in 1735 they resolved to establish a synagogue: "Mickva" (the original English spelling) Israel.[46]

The congregation in Savannah had an unusual evolution during the colonial period. The congregation ceased meeting in 1740 after most of the Jews left Georgia when the colony faced military conflict with the Spanish legions in Florida. The fear that the Spanish might defeat the English sent Savannah's Sephardic Jews looking for a safe haven in another colony. Although a handful of Ashkenazic Jews remained in Savannah, the community did not begin to regain its Jewish community until the early 1770s, when Mickve Israel Congregation began to resurrect itself. The vicissitudes of the American Revolution once again prompted the Jews of Savannah to evacuate. After the war ended and peace treaties were signed, Savannah's Jewish natives returned. Mickve Israel resumed its activities, and by the time Georgia's general assembly began incorporating religious communities in 1789, Mickve Israel quickly obtained its own charter.[47]

Surviving records detailing Mickve Israel's activities during the early national period provide a picture of a congregation adhering to essentially the same Spanish-Portuguese religious traditions that prevailed in all of the major colonial synagogues. Until the late 1820s, Savannah was a relatively small community, and though some of its citizens became prosperous businessmen, the city did not have a robust economy. Throughout this time the Jewish community remained small, and Savannah's synagogue remained a modest institution beset by a number of misfortunes. The congregation's first building, erected in 1820, burned to the ground in December 1829. Financial setbacks and the death of important congregational leaders resulted in the congregation's having to wait nearly a decade before construction of its second building was completed (1838). Since Mickve Israel did not enjoy the services of its own rabbi or *hasan* during this period, the building's dedication ceremony did not take place until 1841, when Isaac Leeser came down to Savannah from Philadelphia.

After 1840, Savannah began to grow demographically and economically. The Jewish community expanded proportionally during these same years. By 1848, Mickve Israel began advertising for a permanent "reader" for the congregation. Again on account of internal squabbling, the congregation was unable to agree on the election of a full-time reader until 1853, when the Reverend Jacob Rosenfeld (Isaac M. Wise's predecessor at Cincinnati's K. K. Bene Jeshurun) arrived in Savannah and became Mickve Israel's first permanent *hazzan*. The congregation's 1854 contract with Rosenfeld outlined his duties and responsibilities, including that he was "to read the prayers in the original Hebrew according to the Portuguese *Minhag* [rite], save the prayer for the government." He was also expected to deliver "English discourses" on the Sabbath and the first day of the festivals. As many in Savannah undoubtedly knew, Rosenfeld had successfully fulfilled these same ritual obligations when he served as *hazzan* of Charleston's Shearith Israel—a traditional congregation that split-off from Beth Elohim after an organ had been installed in that synagogue's new sanctuary in 1841.[48]

There is evidence that calls for a reformation of the worship service had been heard at Mickve Israel Congregation before Rosenfeld's tenure. At a party held in honor of the new *hazzan's* association with the congregation, the synagogue's president, Jacob De la Motta, raised his glass and offered a toast to Jewish tradition even as he prayed that Mickve Israel Congregation would "never be polluted by the misconstruction of innovations." De la Motta's concerns reflected disagreements among different factions of the congregation over who had authority to select a rabbi and about changes in the congregation's liturgy, including whether Mickve Israel would continue to maintain its Sephardic liturgy or switch to an Ashkenazic rite. On the heels of these tensions, calls for religious reform became increasingly common in Savannah's Mickve Israel Congregation.[49]

Reverend Rosenfeld was capable leader. He strengthened the congregation through his dedication to Jewish observance and education. He is credited with establishing Mickve Israel's first Sunday school. Even though he was amenable to delivering sermons in English and acquiesced to having female congregants sit with their husbands to listen to his homilies *after* the religious service itself had concluded, it is clear that Rosenfeld was anything but a reformer. He resisted attempts to introduce ritual reforms, and he eschewed signs of leniency in the observance of the dietary laws and ritual slaughter. When the congregation refused to grant his request for a raise in salary, Rosenfeld resigned his post. In 1862, he became the first president and spiritual leader of a split-off congregation called B'nai Berith Jacob.[50]

Throughout the remainder of the Civil War, Savannah's Jewish community functioned without a full-time reader. In 1867, the congregation elected its second full-time minister, the Reverend Raphael D. C. Lewin (1845–86). Little is known about Lewin's life. He was born in Jamaica, West Indies, and received his education in England. Lewin married Adeline Einstein in Augusta, Georgia, on July 20, 1867, the same year that Adeline's father, Abraham, was elected president of Savannah's Mickve Israel. Although Abraham Einstein may very well have helped his twenty-three-year-old son-in-law procure his first rabbinic position in America, how Lewin acquired his deep passion for Reform Judaism remains an enigma. What is certain is that Mickve Israel's new young minister played a pivotal and powerful role in transforming the congregation into a stalwart of Reform.[51]

Lewin had only just settled in Savannah when he threw down a gauntlet on behalf of Jewish reform. His dramatic actions suggest that he believed he would find strong backing from some members of Mickve Israel who evidently wanted to see the congregation's worship ritual reformed. On February 1, 1868, he delivered a remarkable sermon entitled "Orthodoxy vs. Reform." Lewin did not approach his subject impartially. He told his listeners that American Judaism was rife with division and quarreling over the Orthodoxy versus Reform controversy and that many blamed those who advocated reform for bringing disharmony to their communities. In truth it was the Orthodox and not Reformers who caused the conflict, he declared. "The very premises of the supporters of Orthodoxy are wrong. The advocates of Orthodoxy view the biblical laws and the rabbinic teachings as if they are of equal stature." The approach of the Orthodox was wrong, Lewin thundered, because a loving God would never have allowed the salvation of man to be dependent on a tradition or law that was "orally transmitted from generation to generation." He further asserted that the proponents of Orthodoxy in Savannah's synagogue "use brute force for argument, and dogmatism for logical reasoning." Orthodoxy's advocates in Mickve Israel, he said, justified their actions by insisting that they were merely preserving faithfully an inherited tradition. "We came into the world and found it so. Our parents acted so, and surely a good child should not question the wisdom of his parents. . . . All we have to do, is to follow in their footsteps and obey."

Using a remarkably militant tone, the young minister questioned the sincerity of Mickve Israel's staunch defenders of Orthodoxy: "Now, my orthodox brethren, and my orthodox sisters, who of you keep these laws, who of you know of these laws, who of you will even believe that these laws are to be found in the rabbinical writings? Ye scoff, and ye mock at them, and ignore them altogether. . . . Why force your Orthodoxy on your brethren? Why denounce them if they do not believe it? Why claim for it infallibility, when you yourselves do not act up to it? . . . Surely, the one who says: 'I know this is right, and yet I will not do it,' is much more guilty than the one who says: 'I do not believe this is right, and I cannot do it.'"[52]

Three days later, at a special meeting of the congregation, Lewin delineated the specific reforms he sought to inaugurate at Mickve Israel. First, he wanted to organize a choir with mixed voices and music for use in worship services. Second, he proposed eliminating celebration of the second day of the Jewish festivals. Third, he recommended curtailing some of the prayer service by doing away with certain customary repetitions. Lewin's suggestions were given over to a special committee of congregational leaders charged with the responsibility of considering the matter and making recommendations to the congregation as a whole, which planned to meet several days later.[53]

At the next congregational meeting, the ad hoc committee recommended the congregation adopt all of their minister's proposed reforms and explained their rationale. In the committee's opinion, true principles of Judaism devolved directly from biblical teachings and precepts and not rabbinical legislation; therefore, the Bible was the essential element to the Jewish religion. In addition, they noted that for decades there had been widespread dissatisfaction with the congregation's traditional mode of worship (the Spanish-Portuguese rite). The quality of the prayer service, they insisted, needed improvement. Finally, if the congregation adopted Lewin's recommendations, "peace and harmony would prevail." Members voted and unanimously adopted the reforms.[54]

Mickve Israel's shift did not last long. Solomon Cohen—a friend and admirer of Isaac Leeser—replaced Lewin's father-in-law as president of Mickve Israel six months later and promptly began a campaign to undo the reforms set in motion. Cohen was a pillar in the community who had earlier served as Mickve Israel's president for a decade (1856–66). He played a central role in holding the congregation's clashing factions together during the tenure of Reverend Rosenfeld. Lewin's desire to abandon tradition in favor of reform must have roused new opposition, and the reelection of Solomon Cohen demonstrated that many wanted to pull in the reins on Lewin's runaway reformation. A highly regarded member of the community, Cohen quickly gained control over the situation.[55]

By January 1869, Cohen's new board unanimously passed a resolution that affirmed the ritual changes recently approved. However, this same resolution also asserted that "synagogue worship involves no moral, or religious principle, and may be altered to suit the taste of the congregations." What was immutable, the resolution went on to assert, was the centrality of rabbinic law in Judaism. The new board had cleverly accepted the reality of Lewin's ritual reforms while concomitantly reasserting the congregation's commitment to tradition—"the ultimate restoration of Israel to the law of their Fathers" and to a belief in the coming of a personal messiah. The Cohen resolution asserted that Jewish law was "binding, and a part of the code of laws, which God in His wisdom, has established for the government of His people" regardless of whether community members obeyed them or not.[56]

In the face of this repudiation, Lewin promptly resigned. Over the coming months, the minister's supporters attempted to craft a compromise resolution that would enable Lewin to remain in the pulpit. This effort failed, and those who aligned themselves with the ideological principles articulated in Solomon Cohen's resolution maintained the upper hand. By 1870, Reverend Lewin had relocated to New York City, but his brief tenure in Savannah proved to be a decisive factor in the congregation's religious life. In the wake of his ministry, Mickve

Israel had formally and permanently reformed its religious praxis, even though the board subsequently reaffirmed its theoretical loyalty to Judaism's traditional system of beliefs.[57]

For nearly two years, Mickve Israel held services without a full-time spiritual leader. The congregation finally hired Dr. Abraham Harris, who had spent much of his early career in London, the man who later served Beth Ahabah in Richmond. Savannah was his first American pulpit, and life as a rabbi in the South must have taken some adjustment. Harris was a religious moderate, but the reforming spirit launched during Raphael Lewin's tenure took on a life of its own. The congregation now began to legislate its own reforms, and Harris chose to accommodate these requests. For example, the board informed their rabbi that they wanted certain prayers recited in English rather than in Hebrew. Harris was subsequently told to shorten the overall length of the worship service. The board even legislated decorum, insisting that the congregation rise and sit in unison.[58]

Harris and Mickve Israel parted ways in 1877. A small number of congregants had criticized Harris for leaving the city during the yellow fever epidemic, and an indignant Harris tendered his resignation. All attempts to smooth ruffled feathers came to naught, and once again Mickve Israel went searching for a new minister. Ironically, the city to which Harris soon moved, Richmond, sent Savannah its new minister, the Reverend Isaac P. Mendes.

Mendes was a firm traditionalist but, like Harris, he recognized from the beginning that Mickve Israel no longer viewed itself as a traditional synagogue. The congregation was happy with ritual reforms that by now had become customary. The community appreciated Mendes' distinguished Sephardic pedigree, his Jewish knowledge, and his noble character. They accepted the fact that he, personally, remained loyal to traditional Jewish practice, and they never coerced him to forsake his own personal practice. In turn, Mendes—like Harris before him— never berated Reform. To the contrary, Mendes considered Reform a valid approach to Jewish life in America. He respected Reform Judaism's emphasis on critical scholarship and embraced its impulse to make Jewish practice relevant and meaningful. Both Harris and Mendes collaborated respectfully with radical reformers, and they understood that for Mickve Israel there would be no turning back the clock on Reform.

Mendes assumed his duties just eight months before the official dedication in April 1878 of Mickve Israel's third building—an impressive Gothic structure with family pews and no women's gallery. Obviously, the question of mixed seating in Savannah had been settled. One year later the congregation voted to make the use of the marriage canopy at the synagogue optional, a decision that Mendes opposed. Next the congregation made the *kippah* (head covering) optional. Mendes spoke out ardently in opposition, and for a short while he forestalled the change. Yet by 1894, the wearing of the *kippah* was noncompulsory at Mickve Israel. In 1879, Mendes launched his most aggressive effort on behalf of traditional Jewish practice by asking all of his congregants to close their businesses and observe the Jewish Sabbath properly. After a year the rabbi abandoned the effort, telling his board that "this would be the last time he would request them [to do so]." A few years before Mendes' retirement, and a few years before the congregation formally joined the UAHC, it began using the *Union Prayer Book*.[59]

In 1902, Mendes' health began to fail, and it soon became clear that after a quarter century of service the aging rabbi would no longer be able to fulfill his duties. In 1903, Rabbi George Solomon, the congregation's first HUC graduate, was elected to succeed Isaac P. Mendes. The arrival of an HUC graduate, and Mickve Israel's decision to join the UAHC in 1904, symbolized the congregation's complete transition to Reform. Like Calisch in Richmond, Solomon remained in Savannah for nearly four decades and permanently associated this erstwhile Spanish-Portuguese congregation with traditions of American Reform Judaism.

THE SOUTH AND JEWISH REFORM:
DISTINCTIVE CHARACTERISTICS

Was it merely a random twist of fate that resulted in Reform Judaism taking root in the three historic congregations situated in the American South? Having briefly retraced the contours of religious transformation of the congregations in Charleston, Richmond, and Savannah, a pattern of Reform clearly emerges. The liturgical transformations in these three southern communities become case studies for the region as a whole. The debates over the direction of religious practice in these cases shed light on a very significant question: why did Reform become the dominant expression of Judaism in the American South?

In comparing the liturgical evolutions that occurred in Charleston, Richmond, and Savannah, we discover a number of commonalities. First, with the exception of Charleston, the religious odyssey that carried these three congregations from their origins as traditional Spanish-Portuguese synagogues to modern temples of American Reform Judaism began in earnest at the conclusion of the Civil War. For all three of the congregations, the main road to Reform took place over a period of fifty years, from the post–Civil War era to the dawn of the twentieth century. During the last half of the nineteenth-century, two conflicting factions arose within each community: those who advocated the adoption of ritual reforms and those who sought to preserve the status quo.

Second, all three communities began religious reformation by adopting a common set of ritual changes that reformers believed would elevate and enhance the Jewish worshipper's spiritual life: choirs with male and female voices, organs, the omission of prayer repetition, elimination of second day festival observance, introduction of family pews, inclusion of vernacular prayers (followed by a reduction in Hebrew recitation), and the introduction of English-language discourses that emphasized morality and served as an effective venue for Jewish education.[60]

Third, people who advocated ritual modification in their congregations did not initially link these changes to a denomination or organized movement. To the contrary, the reforms evolve in a very individualistic fashion within each congregation in accordance with its circumstances. Reformers promoted change as a necessary move to strengthen the congregation and to benefit Judaism's spiritual vitality on the local level. Finally, in all three case studies, dynamic and charismatic spiritual leaders played a crucial role in advocating, advancing, and validating the need for Jewish religious reform.[61]

These common features point to the fact that the widespread adoption of Reform Jewish practices in the American South was ultimately a response to the distinctive social context that typified Jewish life in that region during the last half of the nineteenth century. What were the specific social factors in the postbellum South that fostered an environment hospitable to a liberalization of Jewish religious praxis, and that led to the ascendancy of Reform Jewish practice throughout much of the American South?

Historians have noted that during the post–Civil War era Jewish life in the South changed significantly. Hostile outbursts and bigoted slurs toward Jews multiplied significantly during the war. The demise of the "peculiar institution" and the Confederacy's collapse resulted in new cultural realities for Jewish citizens in Dixie.[62] The assignment of blame for the region's defeat sparked a rise in nativism, xenophobia, and general resentment toward those perceived as unpatriotic to the "lost cause." Postbellum southern Jews, whose popular image before the war had been regularly associated with the much-admired Hebrew nation of the Bible, found themselves increasingly targeted as profiteers, interlopers, exploiters, and outsiders. Jews across the South responded reflexively to these assaults on their patriotism, and they consciously sought out ways to controvert the impression that Jews were communal aliens and outcasts.[63]

In the wake of the Civil War, southern Jews addressed these challenges to their reputation by joining fellow southerners in paying fervent homage to the Confederacy's "glorious cause." For example, Jewish communities throughout the South participated in the patriotic commemorations of Confederate Memorial Day. They also set aside special sections in community cemeteries for the burial of Jews who fought in the Confederate army. They erected war memorials that underscored Jewish patriotism and simultaneously disproved anti-Jewish rhetoric. In 1866, the Hebrew Ladies' Memorial Association distributed a circular to raise money for a monument to the Jewish Confederate dead. This circular's wording captured the sentiments that motivated southern Jews during this period: "In time to come, when our grief shall have become, in a measure, silenced, and when the malicious tongue of slander, ever so ready to assail Israel, shall be raised against us, then, with feeling of mournful pride, will we point to this monument and say: 'There is our reply.'" These efforts to actively identify themselves as loyal sons and daughters of the South made southern Jews increasingly southern and, in this sense, distinctive from their northern coreligionists.[64]

It was during this same period that southern Jews began to articulate a strong sense of regional *Jewish* identity. They referred to themselves as "southern Jews"—a community that possessed a strong sense of self and a keen notion that their southern Judaism had its own particular set of values and needs. The *Jewish South*, a newspaper that began publication in 1877, gave strong voice to this idea. An examination of its editorial columns and the many letters it published from subscribers throughout the region demonstrates that many southern Jews fiercely believed that a unique set of social conditions had produced what some labeled "Southern Israel." According to one southern Jew, the distinctiveness of Judaism in the South could be traced to the community's commitment to interfaith relations, the reverence it heaped on its rabbinic leaders, and the strong support it proffered to the southern synagogue.[65]

The community's increasing sensitivity to anti-Jewish sentiment, as well as a growing belief in the distinctiveness of Jewish life in the South, spurred the reformation of Judaism. Southern Jews instinctively realized that by reforming their religious practices they could counter the assertion that they were alien residents. Religiosity was critically important in the postbellum South, and Jews sought to express their religious commitment on their own terms. As one historian observes, "Southern Jews believed that religious practice would offset Civil War stereotypes and ensure respectability." By reforming their traditional ritual, southern Jews hoped to forestall depictions of themselves as religious outsiders. They sought to adapt their spiritual heritage to the norms of a region dominated by the values of Protestantism, fundamentalism, and a veneration of the biblical tradition. These circumstances made the organ, mixed choir, English prayer, and the abandonment of the second day of holiday observances so attractive in the southern synagogues. Religious reform provided southern Jewry with a "pathway to acceptance."[66]

The significant role that religion played in the South also mirrored the widespread emphasis on religious education in that region. In an 1863 letter to a national convention of public school educators, Jefferson Davis shared his conviction that "all true greatness rests upon virtue, and that religion is, in a people, the source and support of virtue."[67] Teaching religious values was a desideratum throughout the South. Bible lessons and prayer in public schools were normative. Scores of tracts on religious instruction and volumes of catechisms appeared. Attending Sunday school was de rigueur. Similarly, southern Jews wanted to provide their children with a comparable Jewish education. Religious education was so important that in small southern communities with no means to offer a Jewish education, some parents sent their children to Christian Sunday schools. Jews increasingly wanted their synagogues to provide similar learning opportunities for their children. Reformers' universal call for weekly discourses in English was rationalized on the grounds that these lectures would provide synagogue youth with a greater appreciation of their religious heritage.[68]

In a regional culture that esteemed religion and religious learning, the reverend, minister, pastor, or other spiritual leader played a prominent communal role.[69] Southern Jews wanted religious leaders of their own and particularly coveted those men who commanded respect from Christian clergy. A pronounced shortage of rabbis vexed Jewish communities throughout the South during this period, and the region's Jewish leadership expected the UAHC (and HUC, the college this body supported) to provide religious leadership for southern Jewry's "little flocks without any shepherds." During the first decade of the UAHC's existence, many southern Jews bitterly criticized the congregational association for failing to support a "circuit preaching" initiative that sought to provide at least a periodic rabbinic presence to the region's many small communities that had no access to rabbinic leadership. By the end of the nineteenth century, HUC had ordained a respectable number of rabbis. A growing number of the school's alumni began to occupy southern pulpits and this, too, abetted the growth of Reform Judaism throughout the region.[70]

Southern Jews valued those rabbis who knew how to represent the Jewish community in a language that Christians understood. This explains why rabbis who occupied southern pulpits customarily carried the title "Jewish minister" or "reverend." Jewish religious leaders well suited to fill this leadership role typically embraced Reform and communicated Jewish religiosity in ways non-Jews could easily comprehend. As a Mississippi Jew writing in 1878 pointed out: "the advent of a rabbi [to Canton, Mississippi]; able and wise enough to defend our creed in a manly manner, will create a new era of religious feeling among our people and give birth to a more liberal sentiment in a community where . . . an Episcopal Minister lately warned his fold to beware of all intercourse with the

cursed race." In this environment, proponents of Jewish reform found southern congregations particularly hospitable, and staunch traditionalists were frequently urged to relocate.[71]

The distinctive Jewish demographic conditions that prevailed in the South
also strengthened the hands of Reform Judaism's proponents. Most southern
Jewish communities existed in relative isolation from one another. In any given
locale, the nearest neighboring community was likely miles away. In contrast to
Jews who lived in large urban communities in other parts of the country during
the last half of the nineteenth century, southern Jews were, generally speaking,
more insulated and isolated. They had far less exposure to the eastern European
Jewish immigrants and the massive avalanche of traditional Judaism that blan-
keted the American Jewish communal landscape as a result of their arrival. The
histories of Jewish life in Charleston, Richmond, and Savannah, for example,
focus little attention on the arrival of the eastern European Jewish immigrant in
those communities. Eastern European Jews settled in these cities—just as they
did in communities throughout the South—but the dimensions of this significant wave of immigrants were comparatively much smaller in the South than
they were in other parts of the country.[72]

Furthermore, the Jews' minority status in the South was acute. During the
last half of the nineteenth century, they never constituted more than one-half of
1 percent of the region's total population. Most Jewish communities in the
South were only able to support one synagogue, and this fact made religious
flexibility a valued commodity. As a result of these demographic circumstances,
the standard requirements for traditional Jewish practice—authorized slaugh-
terers, ritual baths, religious articles—were not readily available. Southern Jewry
was also a pronounced minority that lived in close proximity to its non-Jewish
neighbors. Jews in the South were rarely able to sustain the kind of Jewish
neighborhoods that typified Jewish communal life in many northern cities during this same period of time. In this sense, southern Jews had no Jewish retreat,
no local Jewish bastion. They lived constantly within a Christian context—a
condition Reform Judaism accommodated particularly well.[73]

CONCLUSION

The last half of the nineteenth century witnessed a dramatic growth in Ameri-
can Reform Judaism throughout the United States and not just in the South.
Many congregations in northern, midwestern, and western states also adopted
Reform Jewish practice during these years. Yet by end of the first decade of the

twentieth century, Reform Judaism had become the predominate form to Jewish religious life in the American South. This occurred because Reform Judaism provided an approach to Jewish practice that was particularly well suited to meet the distinctive social, cultural, and demographic conditions that characterized Jewish life in that particular region.

It is interesting to note that the three historic congregations located in the North also debated whether or not to abandon traditional Spanish-Portuguese rituals that dated back to the congregations' origins. In 1841, the very year that Charleston's Beth Elohim and Richmond's Beth Ahabah installed their organs, the matriarch of America's Spanish-Portuguese synagogues, London's Bevis Marks, experienced a rift that resulted in the establishment of the West London Synagogue. In a supportive letter to Bevis Marks's governing board, Moses L. Moses, president of New York's Shearith Israel, wrote decisively about the future of his own congregation: "To this time we have in our congregation steered clear of the rock of innovation, the most trifling or immaterial has not been permitted in our public worship, fearful that it might afford argument for farther, and more important, alteration. What has kept us together as brethren under the influence of the Divine Presence for so long a period, but a strict and uniform adherence to our ceremonial laws and customs?" Throughout the last half of the nineteenth century, Shearith Israel encountered appeals to reform its religious practice. On occasion, those who wanted change came close to winning the day, but in the end a majority of members remained firmly convinced that "there is no occasion for any measures having in view any change in the ritual of the congregation."[74]

Many historically significant educational innovations occurred at Philadelphia's Mikveh Israel Congregation, particularly under the leadership of Isaac Leeser, who led the congregation from 1829 to 1850. Yet Leeser disclaimed any assertion that he was a reformer. To the contrary, he became the nation's best-known proponent of traditional Judaism, insisting that all his religious initiatives, including introduction of the English sermon and English translation of the Bible, were aimed at educating the community in traditional Jewish law and practice. Leeser's successor, Sabato Morais (1823–97), suggested a number of liturgical reforms for Mikveh Israel during the 1860s, though he subsequently assumed a more traditional stance. Ultimately, Philadelphia's Mikveh Israel preserved its traditional character and refused to abandon its Spanish-Portuguese rite.[75]

Newport's Yeshuat Israel Synagogue fell into a half century of dormancy when Newport's Jewish population all but disappeared, but the Jewish Synagogue Fund—bequests of Abraham and Judah Touro—preserved that congregation as a historical monument. The congregation sprang back to life in the 1880s when Newport's Jewish population began to revive. Although there have been many disputes concerning the liturgical direction of the Touro Synagogue over the years, it too has retained a fealty to its traditional origins.[76]

In contrast to traditionalism's endurance in the three northern congregations, Reform evolved and, eventually, became the dominant expression of Jewish religious life throughout the South. Some Orthodox congregations founded during the nineteenth century remained resolutely faithful to their traditionalist origins, but the vast majority of southern congregations elected Reform. This development, so characteristic of the Jewish South to the present day, may be traced back to a distinctive set of social forces that became acute after the Civil War and conjoined to promote the efflorescence of Reform Judaism throughout the South during the nineteenth century.

NOTES

1. Histories on the founding of Kahal Kadosh Beth Elohim (KKBE) differ as to whether the congregation began in 1749 or 1750. Dissension over the correctness of the dates of congregations is a familiar happenstance in American Jewish history. In this instance, the conflicting data are explained by Charles Reznikoff and Uriah Engelman, who note that the confusion is calendrical. KKBE was founded in "the autumn of 1749 [which was] the beginning of the Jewish year that was to end in 1750 of the Christian era." See Charles Reznikoff and Uriah Z. Engelman, The Jews of Charleston: A History of an American Jewish Community (Philadelphia: Jewish Publication Society, 1950), 17.

2. For more detailed information on the histories of the first six synagogues in the United States, see (on Charleston's Beth Elohim) James W. Hagy, This Happy Land: The Jews of Colonial and Antebellum Charleston (Tuscaloosa: University of Alabama Press, 1993); Reznikoff and Engelman, Jews of Charleston; (on Richmond's Beth Shalome) Myron Berman, Richmond's Jewry, 1769–1976: Shabbat in Shockoe (Charlottesville: University Press of Virginia, 1979); (on Savannah's Mickve Israel) Saul Jacob Rubin, Third to None: The Saga of Savannah Jewry (Savannah: Mickve Israel Congregation, 1983); (on New York's Shearith Israel) Marc D. Angel, Remnant of Israel: A Portrait of America's First Jewish Congregation, Shearith Israel (New York: Riverside, 2004); David and Tamar De Sola Pool, An Old Faith in the New World: Portrait of Shearith Israel Congregation, 1654–1954 (New York: Columbia University Press, 1955); (on Philadelphia's Mikveh Israel) Edwin Wolf II and Maxwell Whiteman, The History of the Jews of Philadelphia from Colonial Times to the Age of Jackson (Philadelphia: Jewish Publication Society, 1975); and (on Newport's Yeshuat Israel) Morris A. Gutstein, The Story of the Jews of Newport: Two and a Half Centuries of Judaism, 1658–1908 (New York: Bloch, 1936).

3. Jonathan D. Sarna writes: "Looming large among the values espoused by the synagogue community were tradition and deference. . . . At Shearith Israel, various prayers, including part of the prayer for the government, continued to be recited in Portuguese . . . the language of the community's founders and of the Portuguese Jewish Nations scattered

around the world. . . . Innovations were prohibited. . . . Sephardic Jews believed, as did the Catholics among whom they had so long lived, that ritual could unite those whom life had dispersed." See Jonathan D. Sarna, *American Judaism: A History* (New Haven, Conn.: Yale University Press, 2004), 13.

4. See Web sites for the three congregations: Shearith Israel, http://www.shearith-israel.org; Mikveh Israel, http://www.mikvehisrael.org; and Touro Synagogue (Yeshuat Israel), http://www.tourosynagogue.org.

5. In this essay, the term *classical Reform* is meant to refer to the period between 1885 and World War I when the many American Reform rabbis and lay leaders firmly identified themselves with the ideology of the "Pittsburgh Platform"—a declaration of Reform Judaism's guiding principles that was adopted by the Pittsburgh Rabbinical Conference of 1885. See Gary P. Zola, "The Common Places of American Reform Judaism's Conflicting Platforms," *Hebrew Union College Annual*, vol. 72 (Cincinnati: Hebrew Union College, 2001), 155–91.

6. George C. Rogers, *Charleston in the Age of the Pinckneys* (Norman: University of Oklahoma Press, 1969), 54ff.

7. On the beginnings of Jewish settlement in South Carolina, see Hagy, *This Happy Life*, chap. 1; on occupations of Jewish men and women during this period, see ibid., chaps. 7 and 8. For specific examples of pre-Revolutionary and Revolutionary Jewish settlers in South Carolina, see Jacob Rader Marcus, *Early American Jewry*, 1655–1790 (Philadelphia: Jewish Publication Society, 1955), 2:226–65, and Reznikoff and Engelman, *Jews of Charleston*, 3–16, 23–43.

8. Although most of the synagogue's service seemed indecorous to Gilman, he stressed that "the part of the liturgy, which consists in reading the portion of the laws, called the *Parasah*, is generally well read, devoutly, and emphatically." See Samuel Gilman, "Harby's Discourse on the Jewish Synagogue." *North American Review* 23 (July 18, 1826): 67–69. On Gilman, see especially Daniel Walker Howe, "A Massachusetts Yankee in Senator Calhoun's Court: Samuel Gilman in South Carolina," *New England Quarterly* 44, no. 2 (June 1971): 197–220.

9. Quote comes from L. C. Moïse, *Biography of Isaac Harby* (Columbia, S.C.: R. L. Bryan, 1931), 99. On Charleston's Jewish community during this period, see Hagy, *This Happy Land*. See also Robert Liberles, "Conflict over Reforms: The Case of Congregation Beth Elohim, Charleston, South Carolina," in *The American Synagogue: A Sanctuary Transformed*, ed. Jack Wertheimer (Cambridge: Cambridge University Press, 1989), 274–96.

10. For the text of "Memorial—A Petition to the Parent Congregation," see L. C. Moïse, *Biography of Isaac Harby*, 52–59, the source from which all quotations from the document in this paper have been drawn. Little is known about either the meeting on November 21, 1824, or the one held on December 23, 1824. Barnett A. Elzas noted that Abraham Moïse wrote the memorial. See Barnett A. Elzas, *Reformed Society of Israelites of Charleston, S.C.: History and Constitution* (New York: Bloch, 1916), 44. The decision to petition the *adjunta* for liturgical changes was probably made at the November meeting. During the

interim, the memorial was written. A minimum of forty-seven Israelites attended the January convention, although it is possible that others attended and decided not to sign the petition. See L. C. Moïse, Biography of Isaac Harby, 52, 59, and 99.

11. According to the text of the petition itself, the memorialists read about the attempts at reform in Europe in the Frankfort Journal. This remark has prompted some historians to insist that Jewish religious reform in Europe aroused interest in Charleston. See David Philipson, The Reform Movement in Judaism (New York: Macmillan, 1907, rev. 1931); L. C. Moïse, Biography of Isaac Harby, 41; Barnett A. Elzas, "Reformed Society of Israelites," in American Hebrew (lit. supp., Dec. 7, 1906); Bertram W. Korn, German-Jewish Intellectual Influences on American Jewish Life, 1824–1972 (Syracuse, N.Y.: Syracuse University, B. G. Rudolph Lecture Series, 1972). The fact that the dissenters quoted from the Frankfort Journal hardly proves that this information actually inspired them to establish their society based on the fledgling reforming trends in Europe. The motivating factors, as I argue elsewhere, were essentially domestic concerns or problems that they faced close to home. They mustered the example of European Jewish reform in their petition in order to authenticate the viability of their objectives.

12. See L. C. Moïse, Biography of Isaac Harby, 52–59.

13. Elzas, Reformed Society of Israelites, 32.

14. Jacob Rader Marcus, United States Jewry, 1776–1985 (Detroit: Wayne State University Press), 32, 38, 39, 41. The group's obvious concern with the matter of burial and cemetery privileges may likely be traced to the fact that Jews who were expelled from KKBE or who were children of a Jewish father but a non-Jewish mother were ineligible for burial in the synagogue's cemetery. The existence of private cemeteries (family plots) in Charleston was a practice that KKBE sought to outlaw in 1820. See Barnett A. Elzas, Constitution of the Hebrew Congregation of Kaal Kadosh Beth Elohim (Charleston: Barnett A. Elzas, 1904), 16 (article 24).

15. Isaac Harby to E. P. Cohen, May 5, 1826, a copy of which is in the American Jewish Archives (AJA). Esdaile P. Cohen was one of the founding members of the society, and for a short time he seems to have been one of its leaders. See L. C. Moïse, Biography of Isaac Harby, 74. James W. Hagy discovered, however, that the names of Aaron Phillips and E. P. Cohen disappeared from the list of the society's officials by October 1826. See Hagy, This Happy Land, 154. The content of Harby's letter to Cohen suggests the presence of internal dissension within the society by the middle of 1826. My thanks to Arnold Kaplan of the Jacob Rader Marcus Center of the American Jewish Archives' Ezra Consortium for donating a copy of this remarkable document to the AJA. For quotes, see Elzas, Reformed Society of Israelites, 23–24. In the late 1820s to early 1830s, a European visitor reported that there were two synagogues in Charleston. Undoubtedly, this comment refers to KKBE and the Reformed Society of Israelites, because the city's second synagogue, Congregation Shearith Israel, did not come into being until 1841, when forty members of KKBE left

because an organ was installed. See "Einige Mittheilungen neuster Reisenden über die Israeliten in Charleston in Sud-Carolina," which appeared in David Frankel's *Sulamith, eine Zeitschrift für Beförderung der Kultur und Humanität unter den Israeliten*, 2 (7th year):36. The use of the term *temple* was not an innovation by the society; the word had already been used in Europe for at least two decades. See Michael A. Meyer, *Response to Modernity: A History of the Reform Movement in Judaism* (New York: Oxford University Press, 1988), 42.

16. L. C. Moïse, *Biography of Isaac Harby*, 122. During the first years of its existence, the Reformed Society of Israelites held monthly business meetings. However, when the group began worshipping as a separate community, these monthly meetings evidently became superfluous, and it switched from monthly to quarterly meetings.

17. L. C. Moïse, *Biography of Isaac Harby*, 134–37. It was Lance J. Sussman who first noted that Cardozo's speech signaled a downturn in the group's fortunes. See Lance J. Sussman, "Isaac Harby, Leadership, and the Liturgy of the Reformed Society of Israelites," unpublished term paper (HUC-JIR, 1979), 15.

18. For the most thoroughgoing treatment of the society's collapse, see Marcus, *United States Jewry*, 631–37. See also Liberles, "Conflict over Reforms," 285–86; Meyer, *Response to Modernity*, 228–35; and Sussman, "Isaac Harby," 15–16. Malcolm Stern was the first scholar to recognize, on the basis of Abraham Moïse's handwritten annotations (which Barnett A. Elzas published in his booklet, *The Reformed Society of Israelites*), that the group retained some formal identification even after they decided in 1833 to return the funds they had raised for a new house of worship. Stern demonstrated how Moïse's annotated dating of "dead" and "resigned" members suggests strongly that the Reformed Society remained in existence until 1837. See Malcolm Stern, "The Reforming of Judaism," *American Jewish Historical Quarterly* 63, no. 2 (December 1973): 118. The fact that the Reformed Society of Israelites was still listed as one of Charleston's societies in Charleston's city directory of 1837–38 lends additional weight to Stern's contention. According to Maurice Mayer, former society members either (a) left Charleston, (b) rejoined KKBE, (c) dropped away from Judaism altogether, or (d) dropped away from Judaism for a time, only to join KKBE at some later date. See Maurice Mayer, "Geschichte des religiösen Umschwunges unter den Israeliten Nordamerikas," *Sinai* 1 (1856): 173.

19. Regarding the reintegration of some members of the Reformed Society of Israelites into KKBE and the subsequent establishment of Charleston's Shearith Israel congregation, see Reznikoff and Engelman, *Jews of Charleston*, 136–37. See also "Report of the Law Suit Regarding the Mode of Services to Be Used at Kaal Kadosh Beth Elohim, May 25, 1843," Records of K. K. Beth Elohim, Ms. coll. 525, box 1, folder 7, AJA. See also Hagy, *This Happy Land*, chap. 9.

20. Barnett A. Elzas, *The Organ in the Synagogue: An Interesting Chapter in the History of Reform Judaism in America* (Charleston, S.C., 1903?); Marcus, *United States Jewry*, 635–36; and Allan Tarshish, "The Charleston Organ Case," *American Jewish Historical Quarterly* 54

(1965): 411–49. That the Reform faction was in control of KKBE by 1841 and still work-ing to bring about the society's agenda is clearly demonstrated by correspondence that survives between Abraham Moïse and Isaac Leeser. See Abraham Moïse to Isaac Leeser, August 12, 1841, in L. C. Moïse, *Biography of Isaac Harby*, 83–89. Finally, it is fascinating to note that in old age Moïse modified his views on reform. Among the annotations he left in his personal copy of the 1830 prayer book, he wrote: "Time has fully satisfied me that any attempt to reform the principles of religion is always dangerous and often destruc-tive of the very end we have in [mind?]: and that it would be safe in [the?] difficulty of re-form to adhere strictly to the whole Bible and to use the wisdom of the Rabbis as a means of assisting those who cannot comprehend the word of God." See photocopy of Abra-ham Moïse's 1830 prayer book (in AJA), 7.

21. On Eckman, see Joshua Stampfer, *Pioneer Rabbi of the West: The Life and Times of Julius Eckman* (Portland, Ore.: J. Stampfer, 1988). While studying in Berlin, Eckman came under the influence of Leopold Zunz (1794–1886), scholar, historian, and pioneer of Wis-senschaft des Judentums (the "science of Judaism"), which advocated the use of modern research methods in the study of Jewish life and literature. Unlike Poznanski, who was not an ordained rabbi, Eckman was a learned scholar and an impressive rabbinic author-ity. Although his congregants were impressed by his erudition, Eckman's "bedside" man-ner left something to be desired. See Reznikoff and Engelman, *Jews of Charleston*, 138–39.

22. On Eckman's brief sojourn in Richmond, see Herbert T. Ezekiel and Gaston Lich-tenstein, *The History of the Jews of Richmond from 1769 to 1917* (Richmond, Va.: Herbert T. Ezekiel, 1917), 244.

23. Reznikoff and Engelman, *Jews of Charleston*, 157–63.

24. In this advertisement, the congregation noted that organ music would accompany the service. A choir sang Psalms in Hebrew and English, and the Torah was read through on a triennial cycle, though the haftarah and some other Hebrew portions of the service were customarily omitted. The second days of festivals were not observed. Although at this point a sermon in English was expected, the advertisement goes on to add that He-brew portions of the prayer service were to be read "according to grammatical rules, or be chaunted in the manner of the Portuguese Jews." Ibid., 163–64.

25. Ibid.

26. Ibid.

27. Ibid., 166.

28. Chumaceiro took pride in the fact that he had developed an excellent rapport with Charleston's Polish Orthodox congregation, Berith Shalom. When Berith Shalom laid a cornerstone for its new synagogue in 1874, Chumaceiro was asked to speak. He proudly informed his board that he was regularly invited to participate in circumcision cere-monies of Berith Shalom members and that the Orthodox congregation always extended "honor and respect" to him. See Reznikoff and Engelman, *Jews of Charleston*, 208. For in-

formation on the conflict that erupted between Chumaceiro and KKBE's board, see ibid., 255–57. Volume 1 of the *Union of American Hebrew Congregations Proceedings* (Cincinnati: Bloch, 1879) notes that Beth Elohim had been a member since December 14, 1873 (p. 47). It is true that some congregations belonging to the UAHC in 1875 retained their traditional religious practice. Nevertheless, the congregational union and the college it sponsored were unquestionably under the liberalizing influence of Isaac M. Wise.

29. See Isaac E. Marcuson's necrology on "David Levy" in *Central Conference of American Rabbis Yearbook* 41 (1931): 241.

30. Reznikoff and Engelman, *Jews of Charleston*, 168.

31. David Levy, *Avodat Ha-Kodesh: Service of the Sanctuary for the Sabbath and Festivals Arranged for the Use of Congregation Beth Elohim, Charleston, S.C.* (New York: M. Thalmessinger, 1879). On Levy, see Marcuson, "David Levy" (necrology), 241–42.

32. Levy radically revised the prayer book he compiled for Beth Elohim and published it for his congregation in New Haven under the name *Service of the Sanctuary* (New Haven, Conn.: S. Z. Field, 1908). The absence of Hebrew in the title is telling. The prayer book Levy published for Beth Elohim opens as a Hebrew text (pages turn from left to right), and the services contain a great deal of the traditional Hebrew text. Two decades later the revised version opens like an English volume, contains mostly English renditions of the prayers, and is ornamented by a handful of Hebrew sentences. The *Union Prayer Book* first appeared in 1894. For more on Levy, see Jonathan D. Sarna, "Innovation and Consolidation: Phases in the History of Temple Mishkan Israel," *Jews in New Haven* 3 (1981): 103ff.

33. Reznikoff and Engelman, *Jews of Charleston*, 203–4.

34. Ezekiel and Lichtenstein, *History of the Jews of Richmond*, 14.

35. On Jacob Mordecai's brief association with Cohen and Isaacs, see Emily Bigham, *Mordecai: An Early American Family* (New York: Hill and Wang, 2003), 11–13.

36. Ezekiel and Lichtenstein, *History of the Jews of Richmond*, 13–31.

37. Beth Ahabah was an outgrowth of a social welfare association that was founded by Richmond's German Jews in 1839. The association's Hebrew name was "Chebrah Ahabat Yisrael," and in English "the Association of the Love of Israel." According to Ezekiel and Lichtenstein, the founders of this association initially continued to pray at Beth Shalome. See ibid., 258.

38. Ibid., 259–60.

39. Abraham Hofmann, who delivered his sermons in "classical German," was remembered by contemporaries as a "man of loveable character, sincere, earnest, charitable and kind." Bettelheim, too, was memorialized as a man possessing a "commanding presence, a sympathetic voice, and a splendid vocabulary . . . who made friends everywhere." Albert Siegfried Bettelheim was reputedly a "fine German scholar" with a "splendid vocabulary." See Adolf Guttmacher, *A History of the Baltimore Hebrew Congregation, 1830–1905* (Baltimore: Lord Baltimore Press, 1905), 68–70.

40. After his time in Richmond, Wechsler served liberal pulpits in Chattanooga, Tennessee, and New Haven, Connecticut. He ended his career at Indianapolis Hebrew Congregation, a founding member of the UAHC. Wechsler was a founding member of the Central Conference of American Rabbis in 1889. See *Central Conference of American Rabbis Yearbook* 18 (1908): 26.

41. Bettelheim earned his doctorate at the University of Prague in 1860 and then emigrated to the United States and assumed a pulpit in Philadelphia in the early 1860s. Isaac Leeser invited Bettelheim to join the faculty of Maimonides College in 1867. Unfortunately, Maimonides closed shortly after Leeser's death in 1868, and Bettelheim accepted Beth Ahabah's offer to become the congregation's rabbi. Rebekah Kohut was Bettelheim's daughter. See Rebekah Bettelheim Kohut, *My Portion: An Autobiography* (New York: T. Seltzer, 1925).

42. Calisch became one of the most influential rabbinic figures in Richmond's history. He served the community for nearly fifty-five years, from 1891 until his death in 1946. See Myron Berman, "Edward Nathan Calisch and the Debate over Zionism in Richmond, Virginia," in *American Jewish Historical Quarterly* 62, no. 3 (1973): 295–305; and Berman, *Richmond's Jewry*.

43. Ezekiel and Lichtenstein, *History of the Jews of Richmond*, 248, 252.

44. The Mendeses were one of the prominent Jewish families that left Spain after the expulsion of 1492. Segments of the family emigrated from Spain to Portugal, and later descendants settled in Holland, England, and America. Isaac P. Mendes was related to the distinguished Sephardic ministers from New York, Drs. Henry Pereira Mendes and Frederick de Sola Mendes. See Rubin, *Third to None*, 190–226.

45. See "Our History" on Beth Ahabah's Web site: http://www.bethahabah.org/our-history.htm.

46. Rubin, *Third to None*, 1–5.

47. Ibid., 16–40.

48. Ibid., 113–14. Rosenfeld was elected by the congregation on November 5, 1852, but he did not assume his post until the middle of 1853.

49. Ibid., 115. See also Mark I. Greenberg, "Creating Ethnic, Class, and Southern Identity in Nineteenth-Century America: The Jews of Savannah, Georgia, 1830–1880" (Ph.D. diss., University of Florida, 1997), 177–218.

50. Ibid., 194–97. On Rosenfeld and the establishment of B'nai Berith Jacob, see Rubin, *Third to None*, 146–48.

51. There is some confusion about the "D. C." in Lewin's name. The initials frequently stand for DeCordova, but they alternatively represent the name de Castro and DaCosta. See Rubin, *Third to None*, 138–59; and *New York Times*, Raphael DaCosta Lewin, obituary, June 28, 1886, 5.

52. Raphael D. C. Lewin, "Orthodoxy vs. Reform" (Savannah: R. J. Durse Printer, 1868), 7–10.

53. Rubin, *Third to None*, 139–40.

54. Ibid., 141.

55. On Cohen, see Greenberg, "Creating Ethnic, Class, and Southern Identity," 204–7. See also Rubin, *Third to None*, 144–46.

56. Rubin, *Third to None*, 143.

57. Lewin's career in New York merits further research. In 1870, he published a remarkable discourse titled, *What Is Judaism? Or, A Few Words to the Jews* (New York: D. Appleton, 1870). In this fascinating explication of his own perspective on Judaism, Lewin proudly identifies himself as a complete Reformer—not a moderate—and presents a religious perspective that is fascinatingly similar to that which will characterize the renowned Pittsburgh Platform of 1885. Lewin's ideas about the importance of retaining some Hebrew usage in the context of vernacular worship are also noteworthy. He also edited an important journal titled the *New Era* which promised to "advance mankind in true religious knowledge and to unite all God's children in a common bond of brotherhood." See Jonathan D. Sarna, *American Judaism*, 124. Lewin was also associated, either as a student or teacher, with the Eclectic Collegiate Institute in New York. He served as the spiritual leader of Temple Israel in Brooklyn, for which he edited a little-known Reform prayer book, *The American-Jewish Ritual* (New York: L. H. Frank, 1870). Toward the end of his life, he edited the *Jewish Advocate*. See *New York Times*, Raphael DaCosta Lewin, obituary. On his professional career in New York, see *New York Times*, June 4, 1870; March 4, 1878; September 19, 1878; and August 13, 1883. See also Rubin, *Third to None*, 144–45.

58. Rubin, *Third to None*, 161.

59. Ibid., 200–204. On Mendes' tenure, see also Greenberg, "Creating Ethnic, Class, and Southern Identity," 212–18.

60. These reforms follow a pattern that was identified by Jerome Grollman, "The Emergence of Reform Judaism in the United States" *American Jewish Archives* 2 (1950): 3–14.

61. With regard to the individualized sequence of ritual reforms, see ibid., 10.

62. The term *peculiar institution* was used originally by southerners themselves. See Kenneth M. Stampp, *The Peculiar Institution: Slavery in the Ante-Bellum South* (New York: Vintage Books, 1989), 3.

63. The term *lost cause* first appeared after the Civil War in the writings of various apologists who sought to justify the moral rectitude of the defeated South. For example, one writer, E. A. Pollard, wrote of the Confederacy as a tragic "lost cause" and the last bastion of honorable aristocracy in a materialistic world. See E. A. Pollard, *The Lost Cause: A New Southern History of the War of the Confederates* (New York: E. B. Treat, 1867). On the impact of the "lost cause" on American Judaism, see Sarna, *American Judaism*, 123.

64. Sarna, *American Judaism*, 123. For quote, see Robert N. Rosen, *The Jewish Confederates* (Columbia: University of South Carolina Press, 2000), 338–39.

65. On the *Jewish South* and the rise of southern Jewish sectionalism—particularly in

regard to the work of the Union of American Hebrew Congregations, see Leah E. Hagedorn, "The Southern Jewish Ethos: Jews, Gentiles and Interfaith Relations in the American South, 1877–1917" (M.A. thesis, University of North Carolina at Chapel Hill, 1988),
88–109. For quotes, see 103 and 89.

66. Hagedorn's doctoral dissertation sheds a great deal of light on shifting social
conditions that southern Jewry faced after the Civil War. See Leah E. Hagedorn, "Jews
and the American South, 1858–1905" (Ph.D. diss., University of North Carolina at
Chapel Hill, 1999), especially 203, 100–102. See also Abraham J. Peck, "That Other 'Peculiar Institution': Jews and Judaism in the Nineteenth-Century South," *Modern Judaism*
7, no. 1 (February 1987): 99–114.

67. See Convention of Teachers of the Confederate States, *Proceedings of the Convention
of Teachers of the Confederate States, Assembled at Columbia, South Carolina, April 28th, 1863* (Macon,
Ga.: Burke, Boykin, 1863), 18.

68. Education was a top priority for southern rabbis. See Gary P. Zola, "Southern Rabbis and the Emergence of a National Association of Rabbis," *American Jewish History* 85,
no. 4 (December 1997): 353–72. See also Hagedorn, "Jews and the American South," 110.

69. See Ted Ownby, *Subduing Satan: Religion, Recreation, and Manhood in the Rural South*,
1865–1920 (Chapel Hill: University of North Carolina Press, 1990).

70. Hagedorn, "The Southern Jewish Ethos," 93 and passim.

71. Hagedorn, "Jews and the American South," 140.

72. From 1877 to 1905, Charleston's Jewish population grew from approximately
seven hundred to only eight hundred citizens. During this same period, millions of eastern European Jewish immigrants swelled the Jewish population in cities such as New
York, Philadelphia, Chicago, and Detroit. The same situation prevailed in Richmond, Savannah and, indeed, throughout the deep South. See Reznikoff and Engleman, *Jews of
Charleston*, 179. See also Berman, *Richmond's Jewry*, 261–63; and Rubin, *Third to None*, 218–20.

73. Hagedorn, "Jews and the American South," 110–15.

74. Quoted in Pool, *Old Faith in the New World*, 99.

75. Moshe Davis, *The Emergence of Conservative Judaism: The Historical School in Nineteenth-
Century America* (Philadelpha: Jewish Publication Society, 1965), 163–65. In contrast to
Mikveh Israel, Philadelphia's Rodeph Shalom Congregation moved incrementally toward Reform during the nineteenth century, and Congregation Keneseth Israel, founded
in 1847, became a Reform congregation in 1855.

76. On Newport's Touro Synagogue, see Theodore Lewis, "History of Touro Synagogue," *Bulletin of the Newport Historical Society* 48, no. 159 (Summer 1975): 281–320; and
Dan Vogel, "A Source of Inspiration," *American History* 31, no. 1 (March–April 1996).

8

A TANGLED WEB
BLACK-JEWISH RELATIONS IN THE
TWENTIETH-CENTURY SOUTH

CLIVE WEBB

As he assessed the civil rights victories of the 1960s, Martin Luther King Jr. enthusiastically acknowledged the contribution of Jewish activists. Some, such as the sixteen rabbis who joined the Southern Christian Leadership Conference campaign in St. Augustine, Florida, had suffered arrest and abuse by segregationist authorities. Others, most notably Michael Schwerner and Andrew Goodman, murdered by police officers during the Mississippi Freedom Summer, had made the ultimate sacrifice. Some of those Jewish activists who swelled the ranks of the civil rights movement were motivated by religious impulses, others by secular humanism. What all of them shared was that they were northern reformers who had ventured from outside the South to fight for social justice. King had an altogether different set of words to assess those Jews who actually lived within the Jim Crow South. "I think we all have to admit," he observed, "that there are Jews in the South who have not been anything like our allies in the civil rights struggle and have gone out of the way to consort with the perpetrators of the status quo."[1]

During the early decades of the twentieth century, many blacks did not perceive Jews as a religious and ethnic minority distinct from the larger white population. When African Americans did recognize Jews as being different, it was seldom to their advantage. Since their conversion to the religion of their slave masters during the antebellum era, southern blacks assessed Jews through the lens of Protestant Christianity. Although this led to an acknowledgment that the ancient Israelites of the Old Testament were God's Chosen People, it also meant blaming Jews for murdering the Savior, Jesus Christ. When social anthropologist Hortense Powdermaker began her fieldwork in Mississippi in the early 1930s, black academics Charles S. Johnson and E. Franklin Frazier advised her not to reveal her Jewish identity to the local African American community because they considered her people to be "Christ killers."[2]

The most common relationship between southern Jews and blacks was a commercial one. Jewish merchants earned a reputation among African Americans for being more willing than other white businessmen to offer both credit and basic courtesy to black customers. Social intercourse between the two peoples was nonetheless impossible. Jews understood that such a blatant transgression of the color line would lead to serious retribution by the white community. Black activist James Weldon Johnson captured the dilemma of one Jewish retailer in Atlanta who attempted to forge a fragile link across the racial divide. "Long traditions and business instincts told him when in Rome to act as Roman," Johnson observed. "Altogether his position was a delicate one, and I gave him credit for the skill he displayed in maintaining it."[3]

As Johnson implied, the desire of southern Jews to gain social acceptance from white Gentiles mitigated their sympathy toward African Americans. This is most clearly illustrated by the ethnic tensions between blacks and Jews created by the Leo Frank case. On April 29, 1913, Leo Frank, a Jewish factory manager in Atlanta, was arrested for the murder of one of his employees, a teenage girl named Mary Phagan. The principal prosecution witness was Jim Conley, a black janitor at the factory who claimed he helped carry the body of the dead girl to the coal cellar where it was later discovered by the police. Although Frank was found guilty, the defense did secure the intervention of Georgia Governor John Slaton, who commuted his sentence to life imprisonment. The actions of Governor Slaton stirred public indignation. Two months after he had been transferred to the state prison farm, Frank was seized by a lynch mob and hanged from a tree near Phagan's birthplace in Marietta.[4]

The Frank case demonstrates how the relationship between two relatively powerless minorities was mediated through their mutual reliance on the dominant white Gentile majority. It was once believed that the case instilled in Jews an understanding of their common victim status with African Americans. This, it was argued, led Jewish leaders to promote a political alliance with blacks in order to protect both peoples from racial and ethnic prejudice. Such an assessment does not stand up to close scrutiny. The case burned, rather than built, bridges between African Americans and Jews. Frank's lawyers attempted to implicate Conley for the murder by pandering to popular stereotypes of the black rapist. Attorney Luther Rosser berated the prosecution for presenting Conley as a reliable witness, having him washed, shaved, and smartly dressed, when he was, in truth, "a dirty, filthy, black, drunken, lying nigger." This strategy was intended to elicit the sympathy of the jury since the "whiteness" of the defendant increased in proportion to the "blackness" of his accuser. The black press interpreted the racial tactics of the defense team as an assault on the reputation of all African American males and closed ranks around Conley while launching a retaliatory offensive against Frank. The *Savannah Tribune* dismissed the efforts of Governor Slaton to commute Frank's sentence, commenting that he would "have a hard time convincing the people of Georgia as to the innocence" of the condemned man.[5]

The case intimidated even the more racially liberal Jews from publicly promoting reform of the southern caste system. That Frank could be convicted by a court and lynched by a mob on the testimony of an African American underlined the marginal claims of southern Jews who hoped their white racial identity afforded them social privilege and protection. The ghost of Leo Frank continued to haunt the collective consciousness of southern Jews for more than a half century. Fear of further antisemitism conditioned them to publicly embrace the social and political values of the white Gentile establishment. As Leonard Dinnerstein observed, "The fear of anti-Semitism is pervasive among Jews in the twentieth-century South. This sets the tone for a good deal of Jewish behavior in the region."[6]

How then do we explain the expectations of African American leaders that southern Jews should enlist in the civil rights movement? Two factors are of particular importance. First, the involvement of northern Jews in the nascent struggle against southern apartheid during the early decades of the twentieth century identified all Jews with progressive racial politics. The early leadership of the National Association for the Advancement of Colored People (NAACP) included a number of northern Jews, including the brothers Arthur and Joel Spingarn. Samuel Leibowitz and Joseph Brodsky, the lawyers who defended the Scottsboro boys, nine black youths accused of raping two white women in the early 1930s, were also Jewish. Southern Jews attempted to dissociate themselves from these radicals. When Rabbi Benjamin Goldstein-Lowell of Montgomery, Alabama, attended a rally in support of the Scottsboro defendants, his synagogue's board of trustees forced him to resign.[7] Nonetheless, in the minds of some African Americans the association of Jews with racial liberalism had been made.

Second, the Holocaust strengthened black perceptions of Jews as a people with a shared history of suffering. During World War II, African American leaders drew explicit parallels between the racial repression of the Jim Crow South and the genocidal persecution of Jews in Nazi-occupied Europe. The victimization of the two peoples compelled their mutual support. In 1938, the NAACP chapter in Mobile, Alabama, lobbied a Jewish department store owner to open restrooms for African American customers. When the store owner declined, local NAACP leader J. L. LeFlore accused him not only of offending blacks, but also of betraying his Jewish heritage. "We are bewildered," he wrote, "that a member of one oppressed group, because of favorable geographic and other conditions, would be unsympathetic and recalcitrant in regard to the rights of another persecuted minority."[8]

As the civil rights movement gathered political momentum in the years that followed the war, African American leaders anticipated that southern Jews would ally themselves with the struggle. On May 17, 1954, the United States Supreme Court issued its decision in Brown v. Board of Education that segregation in public schools was unconstitutional. As civil rights activists strained to secure the practical implementation of the decision, they expressed bitter disappointment in the failure of southern Jews to stand with them. King was not alone among black leaders in expressing a profound sense of betrayal at the failure of southern Jews to support the integrationist cause. In the words of Bayard Rustin, "the Jews in the South are playing no creative role in the struggle." More forcefully, Reverend Fred Shuttlesworth, president of the Alabama Christian Movement for Human Rights, insisted that the historical experience of persecution compelled Jews to intervene in the fight against southern racism. "From its deep historical past, so rich and so titanic in its contribution to history and civilization, the Jews should know what persecution means. Why do you not speak up?"[9]

Although many southern Jews were sympathetic toward the black struggle for racial equality, political circumstances constrained their actions. Jews occupied a marginal status within southern white society. Their acceptance as whites was entirely conditional on their continued compliance with the prevailing social order. In particular, this meant compliance with the subordination of the black race. Although privately many Jews opposed segregation, white Gentiles interpreted their public silence as an uncritical endorsement of Jim Crow apartheid. Despite the expressions of disappointment by black leaders, there were nonetheless a small number of southern Jews willing to risk their personal safety in support of a cause that transcended their parochial self-interest.

SOUTHERN JEWS AT THE DAWN OF THE DESEGREGATION CRISIS

By the time of the Supreme Court decision, Jews had carved a comfortable niche in southern society. Jews were still a tiny minority of the southern population: of the 40 million people who lived in the region in 1950, only 265,000 were Jewish. Particularly through their role in the retail trade, Jews nonetheless exerted an influence disproportionate to their numbers. The store names on the downtown streets of many southern communities attested to the success of Jews in assuming an economically integral, while still socially peripheral, role in the region. As sociologist Alfred Hero Jr. observed, "Jews throughout the South have been on the average much better off, better educated, more concentrated in elevated society and occupational groups . . . than Gentiles."[10]

This process of acculturation was achieved through considerable compromise. Southern Jews remained profoundly insecure about their personal security. White Southerners tolerated, even welcomed, Jews' presence, but only as long as they publicly conformed to the cultural mores of the region. The continued survival of southern Jews was therefore dependent on their ability to blur the cultural differences between themselves and the white Gentile majority. Jews did not interact with the indigenous culture of the region, so much as imitate it.

The most potent expression of this assimilationist attitude was the uncritical public acceptance of racial segregation. Although privately many southern Jews welcomed the Supreme Court decision, publicly they dared not articulate their support for fear of disturbing the delicate balance of their relationship with the white Gentile power structure. According to an opinion poll conducted in 1959, southern Jews were more enthusiastic about desegregation than were white Gentiles. Yet, so successfully had Jews concealed their convictions, that only 15 percent of Gentiles believed them to be in favor of racial reform; 67 percent simply did not know how Jews felt.[11] As the desegregation crisis would demonstrate, southern Jews had good reason to be afraid.

THE RISE OF SOUTHERN ANTISEMITISM

Throughout history, Jews have been scapegoated as the perpetrators of tumultuous social upheaval. The civil rights era was no exception. Since the colonial era, Jews and Gentiles had lived in relatively peaceful coexistence in the South. Nonetheless, antisemitism continued to stir just below the surface of daily life, ready in moments of crisis to break loose. This latent prejudice toward Jews explains the outbursts of antisemitism that occurred in times of social and economic dislocation, such as the Civil War, the agricultural depression of the late nineteenth century, and the transition from a rural to an urban and industrialized economy. In each of these instances, Jews were blamed for the problems that beset the southern people.

The desegregation crisis was the catalyst for the most dramatic outbreak of antisemitism in southern history. As political leaders mobilized a movement of massive resistance in reaction to the Supreme Court decision, so they created a sense of crisis throughout the region. Besieged and paranoid white southerners began to question the loyalties of anyone who did not stand steadfast alongside them in the struggle against desegregation. The erosion of the middle ground in southern politics left white racial moderates isolated and exposed to attack from segregationists. In the words of Pamela Tyler, those southern whites who dared to speak out in support of racial reform were considered "first inconvenient, then controversial, then dangerous."[12]

The culturally alien status of Jews made them a particular target of the segregationist backlash. The ideological defense of Jim Crow rested in part on the assumption that African Americans accepted their subordinate status in the racial hierarchy. However, this could not account for the current social revolt of southern blacks. Segregationists looked for an external influence that had incited otherwise content African Americans into rebellion. That external influence, in the opinion particularly of more militant segregationists, was "communist Jews" who conspired to encourage miscegenation as a means of destroying the social fabric and democratic order of the southern states. As one hate sheet distributed during the Little Rock school crisis proclaimed, "Mr. Jew does not have the guts to do his own fighting, but through sly and insidious agitation, is trying to stir up the gullible Negro to do the dirty work for him."[13]

According to one estimate, the distribution of antisemitic material in the South increased by 400 percent in the five years that followed the Supreme Court decision. The political dangers were more pronounced in certain parts of the South than others. Jews were especially vulnerable in the small towns of deep southern states such as Mississippi and Alabama, where they lacked security in numbers and where massive white resistance was most militant. Yet even in the more cosmopolitan cities of the South, such as New Orleans and Atlanta, Jews were confronted with outbursts of antisemitic rhetoric, death threats, and dynamite attacks.

It is only in this context of extreme danger that the consequent actions, or inaction, of southern Jews can be understood. Their standard of living, their social status, and their influence in civic affairs relied on relationships with a white Gentile majority sworn to the preservation of racial segregation. It is therefore no surprise that as a community southern Jews suffered a debilitating sense of fear throughout the desegregation crisis. When Morton Gaba, executive director of the Norfolk Community Relations Council, tried to raise the issue of racial integration, the response was blunt: "What," he was asked, "does this have to do with the Jewish community?"[14]

Organized legal resistance to the Supreme Court decision was embodied in the white citizens' councils. The first council was founded in the Mississippi Delta in July 1954. Its influence spread with particular force through the Deep South, reaching a membership estimated at three hundred thousand. Members were drawn primarily from the ranks of the middle class, who promoted the respectability of their cause by moderating the rhetoric of racial extremism and disavowing violent opposition to the law. Instead, they appealed to issues of high political principle by framing their protests against the *Brown* decision within the strict doctrine of states' rights.[15]

Despite this attempt to distance themselves from the racial demagoguery of white extremists, the citizens' councils were a harshly repressive political force. The more liberal elements of the community, which often included Jews, found themselves coerced and cajoled into joining the councils. In Montgomery, Alabama, for instance, the council "began a door-to-door membership drive threatening to publish the names of all those who refused to join." Some southern Jews, especially those isolated in small towns, found the membership fee a small price to pay compared with the threat of personal and financial reprisals. As Roy Wilkins, executive secretary of the National Association for the Advancement of Colored People, asserted: "Some have joined the Negro's opposition for safety's sake—and perhaps understandably so. What can a lone Jew, or a dozen Jews, do in a small Southern town against overwhelming white supremacy sentiment?"[16]

While the white citizens' councils created a public image of political moderation, other segregationist organizations took a more explicitly antisemitic stance. According to the Anti-Defamation League, there were as many as forty antisemitic groups operating in the South during the desegregation crisis. These organizations seized on the social dislocation created by the Supreme Court decision to accuse Jews of plotting to destroy the racial purity of the white race. By definition, extremist groups respected the traditional political process only so long as it responded to their aims. When it failed to do so, they searched for other, more dangerous, alternatives. The attempted bombing of Temple Beth-El in Charlotte, North Carolina, on November 11, 1957, marked the beginning of a series of terrorist attacks against southern synagogues. Four months later, on February 11, 1958, a valise containing thirty sticks of dynamite was discovered outside the wall of Temple Emanuel, in the neighboring city of Gastonia. Once again it was only a faulty fuse that saved the synagogue.

The terrorists did not give up. On March 16, 1958, they scored their first success, striking not once, but twice. The calm of night was shattered at 2:30 in the morning when an explosion tore through the school annex of Miami's Orthodox Congregation Beth El. Before the dust had time to settle, reports came in of a second bombing, this time at the Jewish Community Center in Nashville. The explosion, which occurred shortly after 8:00 P.M., smashed windows and front doors, and brought the ceiling in the reception hall crashing down. A month later, the bombers attacked again. Dynamite planted outside the Conservative

Beth-El synagogue in Birmingham on April 28, 1958, failed to explode when the fuse burnt out inches from the detonating caps. Just over twenty-four hours later, in Jacksonville, Florida, the Jewish Community Center survived a similar bomb attack. On the morning of October 12, 1958, an explosion ripped through the Reform temple in Atlanta.

There was no obvious pattern to the synagogue attacks. The terrorists targeted Jewish communities at random. While cities such as Birmingham and Atlanta served as the main battlegrounds for the civil rights struggle, others, such as Gastonia, seemingly had little or no bearing on the issue. With the exception of Atlanta, none of the congregations targeted by the terrorists contained any members who had played a conspicuous role in the integration issue. The indiscriminate nature of the attacks was a powerful warning to southern Jews that not even a strategy of political silence could safeguard them from racist fanatics. This approach assumed that segregationists would cease their persecution when they no longer perceived Jews as a political threat. Further, it held that segregationist policy was based on rational political calculation, rather than on irrational prejudice. What Jews were, or were not, saying about integration was largely irrelevant. Although Orthodox Jews in particular had refrained from any public association with the civil rights movement, this had not ensured the security of Congregation Beth El in Miami. Antisemites were not interested in denominational differences between Jews. All were treated with the same hatred.

The violently repressive political climate of the southern states silenced dissenting voices. Although all white racial moderates came under suspicion, Jews were especially vulnerable because of their status as ethnic outsiders. The smallness of their numbers intensified their sense of powerlessness. For southern Jews to take the political initiative in publicly opposing segregation would simply have provided political ammunition to the antisemites who already accused them of secretly masterminding the civil rights movement. The resultant backlash would have further retarded the already glacial pace of racial reform. Only when moderate voices emerged from within the white Gentile community, deflecting the antisemitic accusations of some segregationists, could Jews take a more proactive position on the race issue.

TENSIONS BETWEEN NORTHERN AND SOUTHERN JEWS

Public endorsement of the Supreme Court decision by national Jewish organizations made the personal security of southern Jews all the more precarious.

The Anti-Defamation League, the American Jewish Congress, and the American Jewish Committee all issued emphatic statements of support for state compliance with the ruling. Southern Jews were thrown into turmoil by the actions of the national defense agencies, fearing that they would inflame antisemitic extremists. Over the next several years, internecine fighting threatened to tear organized Jewry in two. Recriminations and resignations ruled the day. Thousands of southern Jews cancelled their memberships in national Jewish defense organizations and withdrew their financial support. The dilemma created for southern Jews is illustrated in an editorial written by James J. Kilpatrick of the *Richmond News Leader* in July 1958. In response to a report that the Anti-Defamation League was distributing civil rights literature in Virginia, Kilpatrick warned local Jews that the organization "is identifying all Jewry with the advocacy of compulsory integration." Local Jewish leaders immediately apologized, insisting that they were not, nor ever had been, interested in the race issue.[17]

Realizing that mutiny was rife within the ranks, all three of the Jewish defense agencies dispatched national and southern regional representatives to restore order. These officials could not calm the fears of their southern members. Social activist Albert Vorspan recalled one particularly heated discussion with Montgomery's Jewish leaders, which took place behind the locked door of a downtown hotel room. Having hoped he might convince his audience that the national Jewish organizations were taking the high moral ground in supporting integration, Vorspan was horrified to hear himself and other New York Jews described as being "worse than Adolph Hitler," because of the way they "stirred up anti-Semitism." In May 1957, the Montgomery Jewish Federation proceeded to cancel its annual financial donation to the American Jewish Committee in protest of its continued public support of integration. The federation issued a statement that read: "The white community in the South is generally opposed to desegregation. The Jewish community in the South is a part of the white community in the South."[18]

Sectional tensions within the Jewish community became even more acute in the early 1960s, when northern Jews started to travel south in support of direct action campaigns against segregation. Southern Jews had hoped that segregationists would interpret their silence on the race issue as acquiescence with the status quo. That tactic was compromised by the influx of northern Jewish activists, whose presence in the southern states confirmed claims that the civil rights movement was a Jewish conspiracy. The concerns of southern Jews were not without some legitimacy. Many of the northern activists made little or no attempt to meet with local Jewish leaders. Moreover, most of the activists remained in the region only for the duration of direct action campaigns. Having returned to the security of their northern homes, the local Jewish community faced the antisemitic backlash stirred by the activists.

Fear for their personal safety led southern Jews to publicly dissociate themselves from northern activists. The reaction of local Jews to the murder of three voter registration workers during the Mississippi Freedom Summer of 1964 is a case in point. On June 21, the three activists—Michael Schwerner and Andrew Goodman, who were both northern Jews, together with James Chaney, a black Mississippian—set out to investigate a church bombing in Neshoba County. They never returned. Six weeks later, following a massive FBI manhunt, their bodies were dragged from an earthen dam. A posse that included members of the police murdered the three men. It would take more than four decades for a Neshoba County court to convict white supremacist Edgar Ray Killen for the manslaughter of the three civil rights workers. Local Jewish leaders had at the time attempted to persuade Schwerner to leave Mississippi because of the antisemitic prejudice his presence threatened to provoke. Following his murder, local Jews became all the more frightened for their own security. Their determination not to be associated with the Freedom Summer translated into a callous public disregard for the deaths of the civil rights workers. "Sure, I felt sorry for those boys," asserted one Jewish merchant. "But nobody asked them to come down here and meddle with our way of life."[19]

JEWISH SEGREGATIONISTS

The response of southern Jews to the desegregation crisis cannot always be attributed to a fear of political reprisal. Political pressure did cause some Jews to make public expressions of support for the massive resistance movement. As one small-town Jew observed of his decision to join the white citizens' council, "This is my home and I want to stay here. I gave them my money and now maybe they'll forget it. I didn't feel I could stay here and not join."[20] Whereas this individual offered an explanation of his actions, others did not. In the absence of explanations, can we infer inner attitudes on the basis of external behavior? It follows that those who choose to stay silent on controversial issues do not provide public rationalization for their decision. In many cases, southern Jews remained silent on the race issue because they were scared of the political repercussions. In other instances, silence was an articulation of their conformity with the southern racial order.

Many older families who could trace their southern roots back several generations were so acculturated to the racial dynamics of the region as to be indistinguishable from other whites. In their own minds, these men and women were less Jews living in the South than they were southerners who also happened to be Jewish. Their support for segregation was not a pretense to appease white Gentiles but an expression of personal conviction. The racial attitudes of these older, more assimilated, Jews contrasted with the more liberal sensibilities of a younger generation, many of whom were recent migrants to the region. Over time they had developed a sense of belonging to, and a shared heritage with, the communities in which they settled. The civil rights movement was therefore as much a threat to their established way of life as it was to any other white southerner. As the journalist Hodding Carter observed, "One reason the [white citizens'] Councils do not move against the Jewish citizens of Mississippi is that in many cases they do, in truth, share the Council's views."[21]

A small number of southern Jews took conspicuously public stands in opposition to desegregation. Solomon Blatt of South Carolina issued an impassioned attack on racial integration from the floor of the state legislature. Photographs picture him stabbing his finger and waving his fist at colleagues, tears swelling in his eyes as he exclaimed, "Do you want some 16-year-old so-and-so holding the hand of your little granddaughter in the classroom?"[22] Sol Tepper of Selma, Alabama, acted as official spokesperson of notorious sheriff Jim Clark. Tepper was a member of the sheriff's posse responsible for "Bloody Sunday," a brutal assault in March 1965 on civil rights activists campaigning for black voter registration. Charles Bloch of Macon, Georgia, was an influential member of the segregationist Federation for Constitutional Government. As a lawyer, he also defended the county unit rule that effectively disenfranchised the African American population in Georgia.[23]

Although these men were not typical of southern Jews, it is important to acknowledge their existence and the fact that none of them saw any contradiction between their support of white supremacy and their own status as members of a vulnerable ethnic minority. "I'm proud of the fact that I'm a Jew," asserted Solomon Blatt, "I proclaim it to the whole world."[24] Not even when confronted by the terrorist assaults on southern synagogues were these segregationists willing to recognize that Jews and African Americans shared a common status as victims of the same oppressor. Charles Bloch refused to reconsider his support for the massive resistance movement despite an attack on a synagogue in Gadsden, Alabama, in which two members of the congregation were shot and wounded. In a letter to his political associates, Bloch insisted that the incident should not "be confused in the minds of the American people with the so-called issue of negro voting in the South." Bloch failed to appreciate that the same southern politicians that he supported created the political climate in which Jews became susceptible to terrorist attack. The defiant opposition of these politicians to the Supreme Court decision fostered an atmosphere of lawlessness in which racial terrorism flourished.[25]

At the other end of the political spectrum were a small number of southern Jews who overcame fears for their personal safety and publicly championed the cause of racial integration. Two specific elements of the Jewish community stand out for their open support of racial reform: Jewish women and the rabbinate. Jewish women performed a particularly important role in the desegregation of public schools. In Little Rock, they were among the leaders of the Women's Emergency Committee to Open Our Schools (WEC). The same was true of the New Orleans campaign group Save Our Schools. So conspicuous were Jewish women in these organizations that they were actually forced to conceal their involvement for fear of provoking an anti-semitic backlash. A letter sent to one of the members of the WEC alludes to the widespread suspicion that Jews were a fifth column within the ranks of white southern society. "Surely you are not an all white gentile!!" screeched the author. "For goodness sake, mind your own business and let the white parents try to prevent the Jews and negroes from pushing this disgraceful thing on the white people!!" Although many worked tirelessly to promote racial integration, Jewish women were forced to relinquish public roles of leadership in the civil rights struggle. As Irene Samuel of the WEC asserted, "We didn't want people to say, 'Oh, the Jews run this and the Jews run that.'"[26]

Why were so many southern Jewish women willing to support school desegregation while their husbands remained silent? Their husbands, many of whom were wealthy and prominent businessmen, dared not take a risk offending segregationist opinion for fear of retaliatory economic boycotts. By contrast, Jewish women enjoyed a degree of economic latitude that allowed them greater freedom of expression than their husbands. Because they did not own places of public business they did not run the same risk of direct attack from outraged segregationists.

It is important not to romanticize southern Jewish women's contribution to school desegregation. Principled support of racial integration motivated some women, whereas others shared the more pragmatic attitude of many southern moderates. When politicians attempted to circumvent the Supreme Court decision by closing public schools, as was the case with Arkansas Governor Orval

Faubus in Little Rock, a number of concerned white parents established protest organizations for the preservation of the education system. These parents realized that token desegregation of the schools was the price that had to be paid to ensure stability and the future progress of their communities.[27]

The most principled stand in support of racial integration by southern Jews came from the rabbinate. The majority of rabbis who participated in the integration struggle were from the ranks of Reform Judaism. The prophetic mission to combat social injustice impelled Reform Jews. Orthodox and Conservative Jews, in contrast, prioritized the preservation of the faith and traditions of their own people. Although sympathetic toward the black struggle, they largely refrained from any active support. As Orthodox rabbi Isadore Goodman of Memphis argued, Jews only "become more vulnerable when they dissipate their strength in other movements."[28]

Southern rabbis feared that the confrontational tactics of the civil rights movement would only impede racial progress by stirring greater resentment among embattled white southerners. The rabbis instead favored the tactics of moral suasion, hoping through the power of their public addresses to convince whites of the righteousness of racial integration. The rabbis provided the "quiet voices" of reason that counteracted the emotional extremism of the massive resistance movement.[29] Despite their caution, they were ultimately drawn into explicit acts of support for desegregation. By word and deed, rabbis across the region took individual and collective stands. Rabbi Ira Sanders of Little Rock testified before the Arkansas state legislature in opposition to a school law intended to circumvent the Supreme Court decision. Julian Feibelman of New Orleans was one of the principal leaders of the integrationist organization Save Our Schools. Emmet Frank of Alexandria chose the holiest night of the Jewish year, the eve of the Day of Atonement, to denounce the "Godlessness" of Virginia Senator Harry Byrd, the architect of the massive resistance movement. Perry Nussbaum came to the assistance of Freedom Riders imprisoned at the notorious Parchman State Penitentiary in Mississippi. Every Thursday throughout the summer of 1961 Nussbaum conducted interracial services for the beleaguered prisoners.

Anti-semitic extremists exploited the racial crisis to launch a campaign of hatred and terror against the Jewish community. No individual within that community was a more immediately identifiable target than the rabbi. Many suffered serious recrimination as a result of their civil rights activism. Both Ira Sanders and Julian Feibelman received numerous death threats. One anonymous letter written in reaction to Emmet Frank's attack on Harry Byrd read, "Why don't you, your nigger loving Jews, and your synagogue get out of Virginia or keep your big mouth shut."[30]

No rabbi suffered more than Perry Nussbaum. Around 10:30 on the evening of September 18, 1967, an explosion tore through Temple Beth Israel in Jackson, Mississippi. The force of the bomb was so strong that it woke residents several streets away. Eight weeks later, the terrorists struck a second time. The Nussbaums had already retired to bed on the evening of November 21 when a car slowly pulled up to the pavement outside their house. The driver walked across the lawn and deposited a small box under the outside air conditioning unit. No sooner had the car driven off into the night than the bomb blast brought the bedroom ceilings crashing down on the unsuspecting sleepers. Although he survived this vicious attack on his life, Nussbaum was never the same.[31]

These rabbis' experiences are also significant because they expose the deep fissures in the southern Jewish community that the desegregation crisis created. Some of the sternest criticism that the rabbis faced came from their own congregations. The public stand taken by rabbis in support of desegregation threatened to erode the already precarious security of southern Jews. Panicked congregations tried to constrain their rabbis' actions. These tensions between lay people and religious leaders raise the issue of who was the truly representative voice of southern Jews during the civil rights struggle. It is by no means certain which story is the more significant: the rabbis who spoke up in support of desegregation or the congregations who attempted to silence them.

The fate of Seymour Atlas in Montgomery is a telling example of how congregations tried to gag their outspoken rabbis. Atlas appeared on both television and radio in support of the Montgomery bus boycott. The rabbi found himself summoned before his board of trustees, who demanded that he publicly retract his support. At his next sermon an unrepentant Atlas delivered a defiant prayer for black protesters. Ostracized by his outraged congregation, Atlas was obliged to tender his resignation.[32]

The importance of southern rabbis should not be exaggerated: in the drama of the desegregation crisis they were but supporting players. While some rabbis risked their lives in lonely support of civil rights, others remained willfully silent. Perhaps conscious of the fate that befell Seymour Atlas, Eugene Blachschleger of Temple Beth-Or publicly dissociated himself from the Montgomery bus boycott. "If Martin Luther King passed me on the street," Blachschleger once remarked to another rabbi, "I would not recognize him. We have never spoken to each other."[33] Despite the fears that paralyzed spiritual leaders such as Blachschleger, southern rabbis were among the most active of the white southern clergymen that tried to create a climate of tolerance and understanding in their local communities. Theirs were often the lone voices of reason among the religious leadership of the white South.

During the desegregation crisis, southern Jews were torn between two contradictory instincts. A historical experience of persecution sensitized Jews to the plight of other oppressed minorities. Southern Jews were therefore more supportive of desegregation than most of the white community. At the same time, it is precisely because of that experience of persecution that Jews have striven to adapt to the laws and customs of their adopted homelands as an act of self-protection. While a small but conspicuous minority of southern Jews risked their personal and professional security in support of desegregation, fear of antisemitic reprisals forced most into uneasy neutrality. Even though their silence remained conditional, it nevertheless communicated a tacit support for racial segregation that strengthened resistance to the Supreme Court decision.

It should also be recognized that some southern Jews resisted racial reform out of a sincere conviction in white supremacism. The assimilationist impulse is a characteristic of Jews throughout the diaspora. The almost total acculturation of many southern Jews is nonetheless striking. At the same time, the strategy of southern Jews to attain social acceptance is consistent with that of other non-black minorities in the region. During the nineteenth and twentieth centuries, the Irish in Georgia and Louisiana, the Chinese of the Mississippi Delta, and the Mexicans of south Texas all attempted to claim the social, economic, and political privileges of whiteness by physically and psychologically distancing themselves from African Americans. In a racial order based on the simple binary of white supremacism and black inferiority, immigrants to the South, including Jews, made the obvious choice to secure their own social acceptance.[34]

NOTES

1. Martin Luther King Jr. to Rabbi Jacob M. Rothschild, September 28, 1967, box 8, folder 1, Jacob M. Rothschild Papers, 1933–85, Robert W. Woodruff Library, Emory University, Atlanta, Georgia.

2. Hortense Powdermaker, *Stranger and Friend: The Way of an Anthropologist* (London: Secker and Warburg, 1967), 145.

3. James Weldon Johnson, *The Autobiography of an Ex-Colored Man* (New York: Alfred A. Knopf, 1927), 158.

4. The best narratives of the trial and lynching are Leonard Dinnerstein, *The Leo Frank Case* (New York: Columbia University Press, 1968); and Steve Oney, *And the Dead Shall Rise: The Murder of Mary Phagan and the Lynching of Leo Frank* (New York: Vintage Books, 2000).

5. Nancy MacLean, "The Leo Frank Case Reconsidered: Gender and Sexual Politics in

the Making of Reactionary Populism," *Journal of American History* 78 (1991): 924; Harry Golden, *A Little Girl Is Dead* (London: Cassell, 1966), 182–83; *Savannah Tribune*, August 30, 1913. The ethnic conflict between African Americans and Jews created by the Frank case is the subject of Jeffrey Melnick, *Black-Jewish Relations on Trial: Leo Frank and Jim Conley in the New South* (Jackson: University Press of Mississippi, 2000).

6. Leonard Dinnerstein, "A Neglected Aspect of Southern Jewish History," in *Uneasy at Home: Antisemitism and the American Jewish Experience* (New York: Columbia University Press, 1987), 78.

7. Herman Pollack, "A Forgotten Fighter for Justice: Ben Goldstein-Lowell," *Jewish Currents* 30 (June 1976): 14–18. The definitive study of the case is Dan T. Carter, *Scottsboro: A Tragedy of the American South* (Baton Rouge: Louisiana State University Press, 1969).

8. J. L. LeFlore to Berney L. Strauss, October 12, 1938, Papers of the National Association for the Advancement of Colored People, part 12: selected branch files, 1913–39, series A: The South, reel 4, group 1; series G: Mobile, Alabama, branch.

9. Bayard Rustin, "The Civil Rights Struggle," *Jewish Social Studies* 27 (January 1965): 35; Shuttlesworth quoted in *National Jewish Post and Opinion*, May 17, 1957.

10. Alfred O. Hero Jr., *The Southerner and World Affairs* (Baton Rouge: Louisiana State University Press, 1965), 477.

11. Seth Forman, "The Unbearable Whiteness of Being Jewish: Desegregation in the South and the Crisis of Jewish Liberalism," *American Jewish History* 85 (1997): 131.

12. Pamela Tyler, *Silk Stockings and Ballot Boxes: Women and Politics in New Orleans, 1920–1963* (Athens: University of Georgia Press, 1996), 210. For more on the white southern reaction to the *Brown* decision, the best overview is still Numan Bartley, *The Rise of Massive Resistance: Race and Politics in the South during the 1950's* (Baton Rouge: Louisiana State University Press, 1969).

13. Al Misegadis, "Jews, Integration, Segregation," box 48, folder 30, Jim Johnson Collection, Arkansas History Commission, Little Rock.

14. Morton J. Gaba, "Segregation and a Southern Jewish Community," *Jewish Frontier* 21 (October 1954): 12.

15. For further information on the councils, see Neil R. McMillen, *The Citizens' Council: Organized Resistance to the Second Reconstruction, 1954–64* (Urbana: University of Illinois Press, 1971).

16. "Southern Jews," *The Crisis* 63 (December 1956): 603; Joshua A. Fishman, "Southern City," *Midstream* 8 (Summer 1961): 45; David Halberstam, "The White Citizens' Councils," *Commentary* 22 (October 1956): 301; Roy Wilkins, "Jewish-Negro Relations: An Evaluation," *American Judaism* 12 (Spring 1963): 4–5.

17. *Southern Israelite*, September 26, 1958; *Southern Jewish Weekly*, September 26, 1958; Oscar Cohen to Roy Wilkins, July 24, 1958, Papers of the National Association for the Advancement of Colored People, part 21, reel 13: 00363-00364; Murray Friedman, "One

Episode in Southern Jewry's Response to Desegregation: An Historical Memoir," *American Jewish Archives* 33 (November 1981): 172–81.

18. Al Vorspan, "Birmingham Revisited," *Conservative Judaism* (Fall 1993): 60; Mayer Newfield to Arthur J. Levin, January 5, 1961, Mayer Newfield Papers, 1950–73, Department of Archives and Manuscripts, Linn-Henley Research Library, Birmingham, Alabama.

19. Quoted in Eli N. Evans, *The Provincials: A Personal History of Jews in the South* (New York: Atheneum, 1973), 326. The full story of the murder of three civil rights workers has been told numerous times; the finest account is Seth Cagin and Philip Dray, *We Are Not Afraid: The Story of Goodman, Schwerner, and Chaney and the Civil Rights Campaign for Mississippi* (New York: Macmillan, 1988). Information on the conviction of Killen from BBC News, http://news.bbc.co.uk/1/hi/world/americas/4117816.stm, accessed June 22, 2005.

20. Quoted in Halberstam, "White Citizens' Councils," 301.

21. Hodding Carter III, *The South Strikes Back* (Garden City, N.Y.: Doubleday, 1959).

22. Undated article, *Greenville News*, 1966 Scrapbook, Solomon Blatt Papers, Modern Political Collections, South Carolina Library, University of South Carolina, Columbia.

23. Further analysis of Blatt can be found in Timothy D. Renick, "Solomon Blatt: An Examination into the Conservative Racial Views of a Jewish Politician in the Deep South, 1937–1986 (M.A. thesis, University of South Carolina, 1989). Tepper discusses his segregationist politics in Howell Raines, ed., *My Soul Is Rested: Movement Days in the Deep South Remembered* (New York: G. P. Putnam's Sons, 1977). Bloch is profiled in Clive Webb, "Charles Bloch, Jewish White Supremacist," *Georgia Historical Quarterly* 83 (Summer 1999): 267–92.

24. Quoted in Renick, "Solomon Blatt," 14.

25. Quoted in Webb, "Charles Bloch," 284–86.

26. "Samples of anonymous letters received by Mrs. Brewer," box 1, folder 1, Women's Emergency Committee Papers, 1958–63, Arkansas History Commission; Irene Samuel, interview with author, June 9, 1994.

27. The practical realism that prompted white moderates to publicly support school desegregation is discussed in Bartley, *Rise of Massive Resistance*, 320–39.

28. *National Jewish Post and Opinion*, December 19, 1958.

29. Mark K. Bauman and Berkley Kalin, eds., *The Quiet Voices: Southern Rabbis and Black Civil Rights, 1880s to 1990s* (Tuscaloosa: University of Alabama Press, 1997).

30. "A real Virginian" to Emmet Frank, October 1, 1958, Emmet A. Frank, newspaper clippings, letters, etc., from anti- and pro-segregationists commenting on Rabbi Frank's sermon on the desegregation issue, Alexandria, Virginia, September 23, 1958, American Jewish Archives Small Collections, Cincinnati, Ohio.

31. Jack Nelson, *Terror in the Night: The Klan's Campaign against the Jews* (New York: Simon and Schuster, 1993).

32. Harry L. Golden, "A Rabbi in Montgomery, 'He Could No Longer Serve': May

1957," in Clayborne Carson, David Garrow, Bill Kovach, and Carol Polsgrove, eds., *Reporting Civil Rights*, 2 vols. (New York: Library of America, 2003), 1:368–72.

33. Blachschleger quoted in Charles Mantinband to Harry Golden, December 19, 1963, Charles Mantinband Papers, American Jewish Archives.

34. David T. Gleeson, *The Irish in the South, 1815–1877* (Chapel Hill: University of North Carolina Press, 2001); James W. Loewen, *The Mississippi Chinese: Between Black and White* (Cambridge, Mass.: Harvard University Press, 1971); Neil Foley, "Partly Colored or Other White: Mexican Americans and Their Problem with the Color Line," in Stephanie Cole and Alison M. Parker, eds., *Beyond Black & White: Race, Ethnicity, and Gender in the U.S. South and Southwest* (College Station: Texas A&M University Press, 2004), 123–44.

9

AN "INTENSE HERITAGE" SOUTHERN JEWISHNESS IN LITERATURE AND FILM

ELIZA R. L. MCGRAW

Southern Jewish stories clamor to be told in many ways, from memoir and drama to novels and film. At the start of the twentieth century, literary representations of southern Jews were scattered and minor. But as the century progressed, the proliferation and depth of representations proved that southern Jewishness is its own identity, not merely a quirky subset of southernness or Jewishness. This identity emerges in southern literature as both Jewish and non-Jewish writers explore the broad relevance of Jewishness within the life of the South.

These stories vary depending on how their tellers, as writers or filmmakers, portray the situations of southern Jews. Salient differences exist, for example, between autobiographical narratives by southern Jews and portrayals of them in other works. In southern Jewish memoirs, writers explore questions of self within a community. Often represented as somehow unlike both their northern coreligionists and their southern neighbors, southern Jewish people use both the outsider's power to observe and comment and the insider's knowledge of their region.

Southern Jewish memoir has proliferated in the past decade. Leta Weiss Marks's *Time's Tapestry* (1997), Helen Jacobus Apte's *Heart of a Wife* (1998), Stella Suberman's *The Jew Store* (1998), Edward Cohen's *The Peddler's Grandson* (1999), and Louis Rubin's *My Father's People* (2002) narrate different strains of southern Jewish experience. Although these books vary in the eras covered, their publication at the close of the twentieth century marks a pivotal moment in southern Jewish literature.

Marks's memoir centers on her prominent New Orleans family. Her father designed buildings for Huey Long, and her Dreyfous relatives fought for civil rights in the early days of the struggle. *Time's Tapestry* is primarily concerned with family remembrances, but it also reflects on being Jewish in the South: "Since we were southerners, our culture and our beliefs reflected a long history of living in the South. We . . . feasted on raw oysters or river shrimp on special occasions, and never heard of bagels and lox. . . . I remember being told Jewish girls did not wear gold crosses, but I was not told why."[1] Any parent can identify with the urge to protect a child from feeling different: not explaining why she could not wear a cross seemed like the kinder thing to do. Marks's memoir announces that the time has come to do the opposite, simply by describing her southern Jewish experience.

Apte's book also contains more personal memory than societal reflection, but nevertheless provides insight into the life of a southern Jewish woman in the early years of the century. Her book is really the diary that her grandson, Marcus Rosenbaum, found years after her death and later edited for publication. In her writing, Apte appears comfortable with her identity as Jewish and southern, even if she does not scrutinize the concept of embodying both. "Not lost is the ancient pride of race that makes a Jew raise his head nobly," she writes.[2] Later, she hears children singing the southern anthem "Dixie," and wonders "if they felt true patriotism. . . . My heart thrilled to their fresh young voices and the ever new song."[3] Both southernness and Jewishness give her joy, and she writes as a spokeswoman for each group, a patriot of each identity.

Stella Suberman's *The Jew Store* spends much more time than Apte's pondering the question of what it means to be both Jewish and southern, and ultimately deems it impossible. Suberman describes events that happened to her family even before she was born, a method she terms "family memoir." She recounts life in a Tennessee Jewish storekeeper's family, featuring characters such as Miss Brookie, the kindly Gentile neighbor, and her own sister, who falls in love with a local non-Jewish boy. Partially because of this relationship, the family eventually moves back to the North, afraid that their children will never find Jewish spouses if they remain in the South.[4]

With *My Father's People*, Louis Rubin tells the story of his family, who would never consider the move that the Subermans made. The Rubin family adored and romanticized their hometown of Charleston, South Carolina. Rubin writes, "The Old South, with its aristocratic ideal and its martial bearing, was Uncle Harry's Eldorado."[5] Rubin speculates on why his relatives became so entrenched in their communities and careers: Since they were "cut off from what for their forebears had been a powerful historical and self-sufficient community tradition, in effect they replaced it with the intense heritage of their new home— which was also a minority enclave within a larger cultural and political entity."[6] Rubin uses the idea of an "intense heritage" to describe southernness. But the concept embraces southernness and Jewishness simultaneously, drawing parallels between the two situations that demonstrate how being southern suits Jewish people.

This synchronizing process is not always easy. *The Peddler's Grandson*, Edward Cohen's memoir of growing up in midcentury Mississippi, shows the perplexing side of southern Jewish identity. "One can hardly hail from two more losing causes than the South and Judaism," he writes. "Both my cultures have long, tragic pasts, and not one jot of it has been forgotten. If my Jewishness and my southernness meant that I would not have a home, no resting spot, I would at least have a singular view of the shore."[7] Cohen finds the common ground between southernness and Jewishness, but also sees how the two identities merge. His "singular view" demonstrates the cohesion of southern Jewishness itself.

Although they are not memoirs in the same way that the recollections of Marks, Apte, Suberman, Rubin, and Cohen are, some of the works of David Cohn, Lillian Hellman, Eli Evans, and other writings by Louis Rubin use autobiography to explore Cohen's "singular view" granted by southern Jewishness. Through first-person essays and books that recall personal experience and reflect on their backgrounds, these authors question their identity and create their southern Jewishness.

David Cohn was born in 1894 to Polish immigrant parents who ran a clothing store in downtown Greenville, Mississippi. He planned to study law, then to write, but financial pressures forced him into business before he could turn to a literary life. Eventually his articles appeared in magazines, including the *Atlantic Monthly* and the *Saturday Review*. His book about the Mississippi Delta of his childhood, *God Shakes Creation* (1935), was later subsumed into and enhanced in *Where I Was Born and Raised* (1948). More memoirs remained in an archive until they were edited and published posthumously under the title *The Mississippi Delta and the World* in 1995.

Cohn writes with an almost anthropological detachment about southern Jews, balancing his distant observations with discussion of the ways of the South. "The Jews, by legend both intellectual and shrewd, seem in this soft climate to have lost both these qualities," he writes. "They are distinguished neither by learning nor by riches. The national frenzy for uniformity is at work here as elsewhere in the United States."[8] Although disparaging, Cohn also entrenches Jews as southerners with his sweeping claim of assimilation. In the Delta, he writes, Jewish people are just like everyone else.

Cohn envisions this sameness as beneficial to southerners. He writes in the *Atlantic* that his relatives emigrated to become cotton planters in the Mississippi Delta, and his parents soon followed: "There they met with unaffected kindness in an atmosphere hostile to bigotry."[9] This might seem like an overly rosy picture of the pre–civil rights era South, but Cohn defends it, describing his town's graveyards to further explain this loving environment: "For as long as I can remember, the Roman Catholic Church, the First Baptist Church, and the Synagogue have stood within a stone's throw of one another. Over them all was the benison of God and the grateful shade, in summer, of leafy oaks and magnolias. Living, their communicants got on well together. Dead, they were buried in adjoining grounds where weeping willows flow and mockingbirds make mimic song."[10] Using religious differences as shorthand for the South's heterogeneous population, Cohn protects his beloved hometown, which, like any idealized southern place, lies in the shade of a magnolia.

His portrayal of the South as a place without prejudice is somewhat unique, but Cohn is not alone in his insistence on the southern landscape as an important touchstone. Playwright and essayist Lillian Hellman also sees southern topography as a focal point of her identity. She writes: "There's nothing like the look of Southern land, or there's no way for me to get over thinking so. It's home for me still."[11] Even when she discusses southern literature, the land becomes a powerful symbol. "[William Faulkner's] Popeye is the South I knew, full of vines and elephant ear leaves, heavy with swamp air, home and frightening land."[12] Her South is a real place, rather than a sketchily defined literary space.

Hellman's idea of her own Jewishness is somewhat less distinct. As a child, she puts a dime in the poor box of the Baptist church, which Sophronia, her African American nanny, duly reports to her father. "Why don't you give it to the Synagogue?" he asks. " 'Maybe we never told you that's where you belong.' I said I couldn't do that because there was no synagogue for Negroes and my father said that was perfectly true, he'd never thought about that before."[13] While the father considers his daughter's act an attempt to forgo Jewishness, she sees it as simply trying to perform a good deed for her beloved Sophronia. Eventually, her father accepts her action. His comment demonstrates that he considers the family Jewish, even without going to synagogue. The question of how to situate themselves nags both parent and child as they find their way in the Jewish South.

Setting these intricate questions more clearly in a literary context, Louis Rubin's 1967 essay, "The Experience of Difference: Southerners and Jews," maintains a common ground between southerners and Jews. Rubin identifies himself as "one who is both a Southerner and a Jew, which is to say . . . one with a foot in each camp."[14] He positions the groups together because both understand the "experience of racial and cultural 'difference' [which] would appear to be closely involved with the directions that American writing seems to take."[15]

Eli Evans's late-century writing moves the idea of southern Jewishness forward from Hellman's confusion or Rubin's image of two "camps." Much of his writing responds to the idea of separate southern and Jewish identities, and to assertions such as those of W. J. Cash in his *Mind of the South* (1941). Southern Jews, says Cash, "were usually thought of as aliens even when their fathers had fought in the Confederate armies."[16] Evans's *The Provincials* (1973) demonstrates that southern Jewishness is its own identity, not only a footnote to Jewishness or southernness at large. By both explaining and celebrating southern Jewishness from an insider's point of view, *The Provincials* stakes its claim as an American identity. To demonstrate how entrenched in and important to the South Jewish people actually are, Evans uses his own reflections and history. "I love the South and that's the hell of it," he writes. "It frightens me and inspires me, it excites me and threatens me. . . . But events have overcome the three-hundred year contest for the soul of the South. For me, a reconciliation goes to the nature of my being. It is as if the New South has released the Jewish instincts inside me, and drawn me closer to the roots of each in the process."[17] As Evans's South grows and matures, it becomes a more hospitable place for southern Jewishness. Even with the complexity of being both southern and Jewish, images of roots and earth evoke this entangled relationship.

Besides autobiographical writing like that of Evans, fiction provides another space for southern Jewish writers to explore their identities and place in society. Much of Rubin's fiction, for example, features a semiautobiographical Charleston boy named Omar Kahn. In his 1961 novel about coming of age in Charleston, *The Golden Weather*, Omar explains that "to be Orthodox . . . was to be 'Uptown' and to look Jewish and alien. . . . To be Reform . . . [was] to be, that is, not Jewish, but as it was customarily put, of the Fine Old Jewish Families of Charleston. There were very few of Us left, as compared with a great, swarming multitude of Them."[18] By emphasizing the difference between the German and eastern European Jews in the South, (a tension that Alfred Uhry's 1997 play *Last Night at Ballyhoo* also exposes), Omar shows the intricacy of southern Jewishness. Instead of simply existing in contrast to northernness or being Gentile, southern Jewishness has its own divisions and conflicts.

With Lancelot "Rosy" Rosenbaum, a professor in Charleston and the protagonist of Rubin's *The Heat of the Sun* (1995), the author ponders southern Jewishness further. Likening the landscape to a carpet, Rosy thinks "he was a third generation American Jew—bereft of his heritage by history, engaged in being woven into the fabric of the place, the land—raveled by the turning of the tide along its edges and throughout its network of creeks, transformed into something else again, he was not sure what."[19] With a focus, like Cohn's and Hellman's, on the land and his identity as both American and Jew, Rosy questions his role in the society around him.

The characters in Tony Kushner's musical, *Caroline, or Change* (2004), consider their southern Jewish background somewhat as Rosy does but take their comfortable situation for granted. Set in Lake Charles, Louisiana, during the beginnings of the civil rights movement, the chamber opera features Noah Gellman, a boy whose mother dies. He looks up to Caroline, the stoic African American maid who works for his family as he struggles with his new step-mother, Rose. Family members and Caroline attempt to find their way in a South that is being redefined around them. "Let's wish our Negro neighbors well!" sing the southern grandparents. "And may Bull Connor roast in hell," rejoins Rose's northern father.[20]

Also drawing on autobiography to create drama, Alfred Uhry wrote the play (and later, screenplay) that captures southern Jewishness: *Driving Miss Daisy* (1989). "That really was my grandmother and her driver," he has said.[21] Miss Daisy has become an icon over the years, partially owing to Jessica Tandy's rendition of the role on Broadway and in the film, in which Morgan Freeman played her dutiful driver, Hoke. Daisy simultaneously exists inside and outside southern culture. In the film, she is depicted as representative because of her status as a white southern matriarch. She is different, however, because of her Jewishness.[22]

Daisy and Hoke have a rough start, as Daisy insists she does not need Hoke's services. He tells her: "'A fine rich Jewish lady like yourself ain't got no business dragging herself up the steps of no trolley carrying no grocery store bags. How about I come along and carry them for you?' 'I don't need you. I don't want you. And I don't like you saying I'm rich.'" For Hoke, "Fine," "rich," and "Jewish" are one thing.[23] "Jewish" remains the unspoken modifier for Daisy, but her fear of being imagined as rich demonstrates an associated fear of being stereotyped as a wealthy and greedy Jew.

Any Jewish person in Atlanta would naturally worry about slurs after the Leo Frank case. In 1913, a young girl named Mary Phagan was found murdered in the pencil factory in which she worked. Frank, a Jewish man who ran the factory, was implicated in the crime and eventually kidnapped from his jail cell and lynched by a mob. He was exonerated years later. Daisy would have been in her late twenties during the Frank case, and Hoke some ten years younger. As native Atlantans, both would have understood the legacy of Frank's lynching and the implications of "rich Jews" under attack in a case where a poor white girl like Mary Phagan was seen as a victim of a nefarious rich Jew. Hoke's comment is not actually antisemitic, as so many surrounding the Frank case were, but Daisy's vehement reaction indicates that it stings nevertheless.

As weighty as many of the subjects tacked in *Driving Miss Daisy* are, Uhry is unafraid to poke some fun at the Jewish Atlantans, too. "If I had a nose like Florine's I would not go around wishing anyone a Merry Christmas," says Daisy. She is secure in her status as a southern Jewish lady, acting appropriately and capable of judging others for their missteps. Daisy is not entirely virtuous, however, as her bigotry affects her daily life. When she chastises her grown son Boolie for refusing to accompany her to a Martin Luther King speech, he reminds his mother that if she is as unprejudiced as she claims, she would invite Hoke. She thinks King is "wonderful," as she tells Hoke, but believes that Hoke could "hear [King] anytime he wants," implying that simply being African American somehow provides access to King. Hoke ends up listening to the speech on Daisy's car radio while she sits inside, an empty seat beside her.

Because Daisy and Hoke are both members of southern minorities, their pairing extends beyond the King situation to the temple bombing in Atlanta. The audience sees Daisy alone in the car, clearly stuck in traffic, as rain drums loudly. Hoke returns and tells Daisy why they are not moving: "'Somebody done bombed the temple.' 'I don't believe it.' 'Well, it's what the policeman just said up yonder. . . .' 'Who would do such a thing?' 'You know as good as me, Miss Daisy. It will always be the same ones.'" Hoke tries to establish common ground. He tells Daisy about a lynching he witnessed as a child, but all Daisy says is: "'Why did you tell me that story?' 'I don't know, Miss Daisy. Just seem like that there mess back there put me in mind of it.' 'That's ridiculous. The temple has nothing to do with that.' 'Yes'm. If you say so.' 'We don't even know what happened. How do you know that policeman was telling the truth?' 'Well, why would he go and lie about a thing like that?' 'You never get things right anyway.' 'Now, Miss Daisy, somebody done bomb that temple back yonder and you know it.'"

Hoke understands that he and Daisy have both been oppressed by bigots in their society, but she refuses to see the pairing. Daisy reels when a place in which she feels secure lies shattered. For it to fall to "the same ones," as Hoke calls the racist bombers, challenges her faith in her safety at home and as a southern Jew. In fact, Hoke may be more correct than even Daisy knows; activist Julian Bond called the bombing a "proxy attack," because he believed that white supremacists were trying to harm African Americans through the Jewish community.[24]

The thorny issues that mount in *Driving Miss Daisy* also appear onscreen in documentaries about Jews in the South. As it has in memoir, southern Jewishness has had a recent explosion on the documentary screen. Three films stand as the most vibrant examples of southern Jewish documentary, depicting the Jewish lives and influence of specific areas of the South. Brian Bain's *Shalom Y'all* (2002) combines his own grandfather's story with interviews of southern

Jews and scenes from modern southern Jewish culture, like a New Orleans Klezmer All-Stars concert and people catching the glittery bagels thrown by the campy Mardi Gras group Krewe de Jieux.[25] *Pushcarts and Plantations,* a 1998 film directed by Brian Cohen, discusses the history of Jewish life in Louisiana, while Mike DeWitt's *Delta Jews* (1998) explores Jewish worlds in the Mississippi Delta.

Cohen's film focuses on a narrowly defined place. He explains that "the voices in the film are those of Louisiana residents describing traditions, customs, and life experiences that make their communities unique." Various figures from Louisiana Jewish life appear in the documentary, including cooks who substitute gefilte fish to make a dish called Oysters Mockafeller and community members waging battle against David Duke's antisemitic rhetoric. These characters demonstrate how diverse southern Jewish identity is, even in a single state.[26]

DeWitt's film also tells the story of southern Jews in a specific place: the Mississippi Delta. His documentary is more complex and embraces a vision of a sometimes mystifying Jewish South. One of DeWitt's most quoted interviewees, farmer Ben Lamensdorf says in his strong Delta accent: "People are surprised that you're Jewish and a farmer. But we were farming a long time ago in Israel. We just went from sheepherders to raising cotton. . . . Cotton has been good to the Jewish people who came to the Mississippi Delta."[27] The film portrays the desire of Delta Jews to maintain their culture as their numbers dwindle. Efforts include events like a golf tournament called the Delta Jewish Open at which one golfer explains: "Other people say what town they're from. But when you're from the Delta you say you're from the Delta. . . . And everyone feels like they're all brothers and sisters and it's just a great feeling."

That "great feeling" dissipates somewhat when a female congregant, filmed sitting in a pew at synagogue, announces: "We were never really happy when young Jewish students would come through, as Freedom Riders. I mean, the congregation as a whole was not happy at all about that. They felt like it put the Jewish people in this community on the spot and they were not pleased. Occasionally some would come to temple on Friday night and people, I can't say, were really gracious." DeWitt unflinchingly reveals different sides of the Delta experience, from the golfer's heartfelt toast to the Miss Daisy–like prejudice the woman recalls. Even her use of the word *gracious* shows that she envisioned the tensions between northern and southern Jews in a context of manners, as the congregants were less than welcoming to the coreligionists they perceived as threatening their way of life.

Filmmakers such as Cohen and Bain, and writers such as Uhry and Rubin, use their insider status to create films about the southern Jewish experience. But the rest of the South weighs in on southern Jewishness as well, and non-Jewish

Southerners have much to contribute to the discussion. Jews are a consistent presence in southern literature authored by non-Jews, where they range from one-dimensional antisemitic sketches, to neighbors, to great symbolic figures. The chasm between Jews as symbols in a Christianized culture like the American South and Jews as shopkeepers down the street is a constant tension in the representation of Jews in southern literature. Southern Jewish characters provide clues to history, home, and its reverse—escape—all recurrent themes in southern writing.

The complexity of the southern Jewish character notwithstanding, traditional stereotypes of Jewish people as greedy and unprincipled do appear in southern literature. In Margaret Mitchell's novel *Gone with the Wind* (1936), Scarlett O'Hara frets that one of her employees is "a poor trader. . . . Anyone could Jew him down on prices."[28] Later, Rhett Butler says, "Ah, Scarlett, how the thought of a dollar does make your eyes sparkle! Are you sure you haven't some Scotch or perhaps Jewish blood in you as well as Irish?"[29] These hackneyed slurs circulate around commerce, using the oldest disparagements to denigrate Jewishness as synonymous with greed.

The idea of southern Jews as "foreign" brings out further stereotypes. In his autobiography, *A Childhood* (1978), Harry Crews remembers the Jewish peddler who came through his native section of south Georgia: "But he was different from the rest of us. . . . For that reason he was mysterious and used to scare the children with. People in the county would say to an unruly child, 'If you don't behave, youngun, I just might let you go off with the Jew.'"[30] For Crews, "the Jew" was basically the monster under the bed, an ogre to be feared. Thomas Wolfe's *Look Homeward, Angel* (1929) contains similar undertones, but the children in the novel torment the local Jewish families instead of an immigrant peddler. Eugene Gant and his boyhood friends "would wait on the Jews, follow them home shouting 'Goose Grease! Goose Grease!' which, they were convinced, was the chief staple of the Semitic diet."[31] Even though they are neighbors of their tormentors, these Jewish people represent a difference that is somehow threatening.

In Carson McCullers's first novel, *The Heart Is a Lonely Hunter* (1940), the young protagonist, Mick Kelly, befriends a Jewish boy named Harry Minowitz. "When they read about the Jew in *Ivanhoe* the other kids would look around at Harry and he would come home and cry."[32] Even though Harry's classmates are not as outwardly cruel as the children in Wolfe's novel, he is upset enough to drop out of school.

In contemporary culture, seeing Jewish neighbors as less than equal can appear uneducated. In Anne Tyler's novel *Saint Maybe* (1991), Ian Bedloe converts to an evangelical Christian denomination and embarrasses his mother by engaging Jewish neighbors in his beliefs. She accuses him of "scandaliz[ing] the whole neighborhood by trying to convert the Cahns." Ian replies: "'I wasn't trying to convert them! I was having a theoretical discussion.' 'A theoretical discussion, with people who've been Jewish longer than this country's been a nation!'"[33] For his mother, Ian's attempts are appalling not only because they are rude but because she views the Cahns' religion with respect, even if it differs from hers. She believes that Jewishness symbolizes history.

The same Jewishness that evokes tradition for Tyler can also symbolize escape in other texts. In Dorothy Allison's *Cavedweller* (1998), Cissy Byrd comes of age in the small, stifling town of Cayro, Georgia. She finds friendship with two women who share her love of spelunking, but her sister Amanda dislikes them. "Not Christian, exotic. Cissy knew what Amanda meant even as she resented her saying it. . . . They had dark hair, high cheekbones, clear skin, and long necks. . . . Mim was Jewish, though Jean was not."[34] The adjective "dark" mutates easily into "Jewish," and these appealing girls show Cissy that there is a way of life beyond what she knows of Cayro. The women enjoy caving, the novel's operative metaphor for escape, and want to see the world outside their small town.

The exoticism or difference of Jewishness in the South is often juxtaposed with African Americanness, as Hoke tries to explain to Miss Daisy. Many other works demonstrate this linkage. The persistent question of where southern African Americanness stands in relation to southern Jewishness is an important refrain in southern literature and history, and southern African American authors throw the question into relief. Many of the novels by African American writer Charles Chesnutt deal with African American characters who choose to pass for white. Chesnutt himself was very light skinned and experienced with passing. In a journal entry dated July 31, 1875, Chesnutt writes: "Twice today, or oftener, I have been taken for 'white.' At the pond this morning one fellow said 'he'd be damned' if there was any nigger blood in me. At Colemans I passed."[35] In his novels, Chesnutt uses Jewishness to explain a condition he himself had experienced: the sometimes navigable quality of being African American in the South.

Chesnutt's novel *The House behind the Cedars* (1900) shows the way in which Jewishness and blackness merge in the South through images of passing and ethnic otherness. The plot plays considerably off Sir Walter Scott's 1819 *Ivanhoe*. Chesnutt writes: "The South before the war was essentially feudal, and Scott's novels of chivalry appealed forcefully to the feudal heart."[36] In *The House behind the Cedars*, Chesnutt uses Scott's story of Rebecca, "the lovely Jewess," to tell his own story of Rena, John Warwick's "ivory"-skinned sister. "Rena" is named for

Scott's Saxon princess Rowena, whose "complexion was exquisitely fair" and who had a "clear blue eye."[37] Rena mimics her fairness, with her beauty and ivory skin. Chesnutt names her white rival "Blanche," proving that no matter how "fair" she may be, his Rowena is not the whitest woman.

James Weldon Johnson's *Autobiography of an Ex-Colored Man* (1912) also explores adopting Jewishness as a foil. The African American narrator of the novel, passing for white in a Jim Crow train car, discusses race with others on board, including "a fat Jewish-looking man": "He had the faculty of agreeing with everybody without losing his allegiance to any side," Johnson writes. "He knew that to sanction Negro oppression would be to sanction Jewish oppression and would expose him to a shot along that line."[38] Because he is passing, the narrator understands the Jewish passenger's position, trying to find his place in a dangerous South.

In *Cane*, a 1923 poetic novel by Johnson's Harlem Renaissance compatriot Jean Toomer, collusion between African Americanness and Jewishness suggests enigma and empathy. A black woman named Fernie May Rosen has an "aquiline, Semitic" nose, sings like a "Jewish cantor."[39] Fernie's combination of mystery and knowledge foreshadows a deaf-mute named Mr. Singer in McCullers's *The Heart Is a Lonely Hunter*. Dr. Copeland, an African American, becomes convinced that another character is Jewish because "he was not like other white men. . . . In his face there was something gentle and Jewish, the knowledge of one who belongs to a race that is oppressed."[40]

Alice Walker's novel *Meridian* (1976) presents a northern Jewish woman who comes to the South during the civil rights era and is treated as an infiltrator. Lynne Rabinowitz feels superior to southern Jews and ridicules their amazement at becoming targets: "They were shocked, the papers said. Aghast at the bombing! She laughed at their naïveté. Laughed at their precarious 'safety.' Laughed with such bitter contempt that she could not speak to a Southern Jew without wanting to hit him or her."[41] Lynne is the northerner to whom synagogue members were not "gracious," as reported in *Delta Jews*, and clearly the relationship is doubly marked by animosity. As Hoke would be the first to point out, southern African Americans and Jews form more of a community than southern and northern Jews, albeit one sometimes created by the classification of others.

Walker Percy has created some of the most poignant representations of Jews in southern literature. In his novels Jews function as a quasi-religious symbol. For the Catholic Percy, the idea of Jewishness is preoccupying. He writes: "It may take a Southern Jewish voice to articulate the fact, increasingly evident, that the modern world is in the grip of demonic powers." He maintains that he makes "no claim to prophetic powers," but Percy's fiction does confer these powers on Jewishness.[42] His characters tend to use Jewishness in general, and southern Jewishness in particular, as they search for their own spirituality.

Binx Bolling, the New Orleans stockbroker protagonist in Percy's *The Movie-goer* (1960), embarks on such a quest. He decides that Jews are his "first real clue": "I am Jewish by instinct. We share the same exile. The fact is, however, I am more Jewish than the Jews I know. They are more at home than I am. I accept my exile."[43] Binx says that his southern Jewish neighbors bear this exile in the same way that the "Jews" in his broader formulation do: "Sidney is a short fresh-faced crinkle-haired boy with the bright beamish look Southern Jews some-times have. There has always been a special cordiality between us."[44]

Binx is not the only Southerner paying attention to Jews. The same collision of Jewishness as portentous and quotidian takes place in Percy's novel *The Second Coming* (1980). Narrator Will Barrett cannot believe that Cheryl Lee is both a Jewish violinist and a star of the pornographic Foxy Frolics. "Are you sure [she's Jewish]?" he asks. The reply is, "Sure I'm sure. Her old man is Sol Goodman in dry-goods."[45] Sol Goodman's mercantile standing shows he is the stereotypical southern Jew, down to the quaint expression "dry goods." Barrett thinks, "Could it be that a native North Carolina girl was still here? that she had not only not re-turned to Israel, but was hanging around the Highlands making erotic movies and having parties with Gentiles, Jutes like Ewell? If so, what did that sig-nify?"[46] His questioning shows the gap between the kind of southern Jewish-ness that could somehow facilitate his spiritual search and the kind of southern Jewishness that Sarah Goodman represents. She is an all-too-human product of American society, both assimilated and dipping into the sordid world of Ameri-can pornography—a place Will sees as the provenance of "Gentiles and Jutes." His belief that Jews are somehow special creatures suffers at the reality of Sarah's baser activities.

In his novel *The Thanatos Syndrome* (1987), Percy introduces a Jewish figure who is closer to the narrator, the religiously named Thomas More, than Sarah Goodman is to Will. More has a friend named Max, who "is one of those South-ern Jews who are embarrassed by the word *Jew*."[47] Like Binx and Will, Thomas considers Jews somewhat holy and significant. He cannot reconcile the idea that Jewishness is nothing less than the presence of God with the idea that it is noth-ing more than ordinary people like Max, Sam, and Julius. Percy's brand of south-ern Jewishness connects mythology and day-to-day history, enfolding people queasy about the word *Jew* and adult film stars.

Like Percy, Robert Penn Warren assigns southern Jewishness special signifi-cance for non-Jewish characters. His novel *Flood*, he said in an interview, "be-gins to deal with the question 'What is home?' Ultimately home is not a place, it's a state of spirit, it's a state of feeling, a state of mind, a proper relationship to the world."[48] The quest for home resonates in a southern Jewish character named Izzie (whose real name is notably Israel), as well as in the novel's protagonist, Bradwell Tolliver. Izzie is long dead during the novel. His friend Brad returns to Fiddlersburg to move his grave, as government engineers prepare to flood the town and build a dam. Brad is "enough the true-born son of Fiddlersburg to carry the image of a Jew in his head as the archetypal image of all exoticism."[49] Yet as the novel progresses, images of home, region, and the South converge around Izzie, evoking a southern Jewishness that combines a quest for home with a search for spirituality. When the flood finally comes, and Brad realizes that "there is no country but the heart," he has Izzie to thank. A southern Jewish figure brings understanding and peace.

Jewish figures can represent the heritage, history, and tradition that are so often envisioned as southern literary themes. John Kennedy Toole's novel, A Confederacy of Dunces (1980), features a New Orleans Jewish merchant whose family business is at a crossroads. His wife speaks for Leon Levy, Gus's father and the founder of the Levy Pants factory. She tells her husband, "[Your father] started peddling pants in a wagon. Look what he built that into. With your start you could have made Levy Pants nationwide."[50] Leon Levy begins as a "rag man" in Atlanta, like Solomon Rosenbaum in Evelyn Scott's 1920 novel The Wave and the "little peddlers who went through the Delta selling needles and pins" in Ellen Gilchrist's 1995 short story "Music." Levy later attains an enviable social position and wealth, and because of this rise in status his son feels pressure to succeed as well. Eventually, Gus shoulders his responsibility and inverts the Wandering Jew prototype by founding a new factory in New Orleans, aptly named Levy Shorts. Southern Jewishness gains a future with Levy's decision to reformulate his father's historic establishment into something viable and current.

The span of representations of southern Jewishness in southern literature and film is both deep and wide. But even with the broad range of lives and experience that encompass both historical and fictional southern Jewishness, there is an anecdote that blends both and shows how much stories of southern Jewish life share with each other. It appears in many forms in stories of the Jewish South, both invented and real, both by Jewish and non-Jewish southerners. This repeated tale reveals common themes in narratives of southern Jewishness.

In the apocryphal story, the protagonist is somehow confronted with members of the Ku Klux Klan. He (or another sympathetic figure) recognizes one or more of the hooded and masked Klansmen, usually by their shoes or even bed sheets. Often this is because he, as the local merchant, sold them to the Klansman in the first place. This scene appears in various forms in To Kill a Mockingbird, *The Peddler's Grandson*, *The Jew Store*, and Dinah Shore's biography, *Dinah!*, where the lumbago of one Klansman gives him away. Perhaps it is the power that recognition grants the observer that makes the story so popular. No longer the putative victim of the Klan, the southern Jewish merchant holds the knowledge that defuses the mystery beneath the hoods. The story's reappearance demonstrates its appeal.

Like this anecdote, southern Jewishness represents the South in all its complexity. Southern Jews have woven their own stories about the South, and in doing so have depicted their own space. The narratives of southern Jewish characters act as explorations of myth and history and reveal the tension between the abstract and the concrete. Jewishness and southernness may inhabit their own spaces as identities, but their entanglement exposes the range of both southern and American literature. The plurality and diversity of representations of southern Jewishness sustain the concept of a truly heterogeneous culture, in which literature is expanding even as it looks inward.

NOTES

1. Leta Weiss Marks, *Time's Tapestry: Four Generations of a New Orleans Family* (Baton Rouge: Louisiana State University Press, 1997), 108.

2. Helen Jacobus Apte, *Heart of a Wife*, ed. Marcus D. Rosenbaum (New York: Scholarly Resources, 1998), 18.

3. Ibid., 21.

4. Stella Suberman, *The Jew Store* (Chapel Hill, N.C.: Algonquin Books, 1998).

5. Louis D. Rubin, *My Father's People* (Baton Rouge: Louisiana State University Press, 2002), 29.

6. Ibid., 4.

7. Edward Cohen, *The Peddler's Grandson* (Jackson: Mississippi University Press, 1999), xi.

8. David Lewis Cohn, *God Shakes Creation* (New York: Harper & Bros., 1935), 21.

9. David Lewis Cohn, "I've Kept My Name," *Atlantic Monthly*, April 1948, 43.

10. Ibid.

11. Lillian Hellman, *Three*, intro. Richard Poirier (Boston: Little, Brown, 1979), 396.

12. Ibid., 281.

13. Ibid., 366.

14. Louis D. Rubin, "The Experience of Difference: Southerners and Jews," in *The Curious Death of the Novel* (Baton Rouge: Louisiana State University Press, 1967), 262–81.

15. Ibid., 281.

16. Wilbur J. Cash, *The Mind of the South* (1941; rpt., New York: Vintage, 1991), 298.

17. Eli N. Evans, *The Provincials: A Personal History of Jews in the South* (New York: Atheneum, 1973), 273.

18. Louis D. Rubin, *The Golden Weather* (1961; rpt., Baton Rouge: Louisiana State University Press, 1995), 22.

19. Louis D. Rubin, *The Heat of the Sun* (Marietta, Ga.: Longstreet, 1995), 240.

20. Tony Kushner, *Caroline, or Change* (New York: Theatre Communications Group, 2004), 85.

21. Alfred Uhry, interview with Paul Rudd, *Bomb* (Summer 1997): 35–41.

22. *Driving Miss Daisy*, dir. Bruce Beresford, Warner Pictures, 1989.

23. All quotations from films are my transcriptions.

24. Quoted in Melissa Fay Greene, *The Temple Bombing* (Reading, Mass.: Addison-Wesley, 1996), 247.

25. *Shalom Y'all*, dir. Brian Bain, Shalom Y'all Productions, 2003.

26. *Pushcarts and Plantations*, dir. Brian Cohen, Apple West Productions, 1998. Quote from Brian Cohen, "Director's Statement," July 1999, San Francisco Jewish Film Festival, http://www.sfjff.org/sfjff19/filmmakers/08D.html.

27. *Delta Jews*, dir. Mike DeWitt, PBS, 1998.

28. Margaret Mitchell, *Gone with the Wind* (1936; rpt., New York: Avon, 1964), 734.

29. Ibid., 759.

30. Harry Crews, *A Childhood* (Athens: University of Georgia Press, 1995).

31. Thomas Wolfe, *Look Homeward, Angel* (1929; rpt., New York: Collier, 1957), 88.

32. Carson McCullers, *The Heart Is a Lonely Hunter* (1940; rpt., New York: Bantam, 1967), 212.

33. Anne Tyler, *Saint Maybe* (New York: Random House, 1991), 156–57.

34. Dorothy Allison, *Cavedweller* (New York: Dutton, 1998), 273.

35. Charles Chesnutt, *The Journals of Charles W. Chesnutt*, ed. Richard Brodhead (Durham, N.C.: Duke University Press, 1993), 78.

36. Charles Chesnutt, *The House behind the Cedars* (1900; rpt., Ridgewood, N.J.: Gregg Press, 1968), 46.

37. Walter Scott, *Ivanhoe* (1819; rpt., New York: Signet, 1962), 61.

38. James Weldon Johnson, *The Autobiography of an Ex-Colored Man* (1912), in *Three Negro Classics: Booker T. Washington, W. E. B. DuBois, James Weldon Johnson*, introduction by John Hope Franklin (New York: Avon Books, 1965), 391–511, 481.

39. Jean Toomer, *Cane* (1923; rpt., New York: Harper and Row, 1969), 24.

40. McCullers, *The Heart Is a Lonely Hunter*, 114.

41. Alice Walker, *Meridian* (New York: Pocket, 1976), 180.

42. Walker Percy, *Signposts in a Strange Land* (New York: Farrar, 1991), 179.

43. Walker Percy, *The Moviegoer* (1960; rpt., New York: Knopf, 1979), 88–89.

44. Ibid., 185.

45. Walker Percy, *The Second Coming* (New York: Ballantine, 1980), 161.

46. Ibid., 163.

47. Walker Percy, *The Thanatos Syndrome* (New York: Farrar, Straus, Giroux, 1987), 351.

48. Floyd Watkins, John T. Hiers, and Mary Louise Weaks, eds., *Talking with Robert Penn Warren* (Athens: University of Georgia Press, 1990), 111.

49. Robert Penn Warren, *Flood* (New York: Random House, 1963), 15.

50. John Kennedy Toole, *A Confederacy of Dunces* (Baton Rouge: Louisiana State University Press, 1980), 83.

MARCIE COHEN FERRIS

I am a southerner, born and raised in a small cotton-growing town in northeast Arkansas, where eating pork barbecue is evidence of one's regional upbringing and loyalty. Being southern, but also Jewish complicated this act of solidarity for my family, but not enough to keep any of us away from the Dixie Pig, the most popular barbecue institution in my hometown. The barbecue they serve in northeast Arkansas—hickory-smoked chopped pork shoulder covered with a spicy vinegar-based sauce—is one of the great dishes of the South. As I encountered "forbidden foods" like barbecue as a child, I discovered the cultural boundaries that defined my southern Jewish family. There were southern foods and there were Jewish foods, and eating both shaped who we were. Whether we ate chopped barbecue with sauce "on the side" at the Dixie Pig or barbecued beef brisket prepared by the sisterhood at Blytheville's Temple Israel, the occasion was memorable. Those moments reminded me that my family straddled two worlds—the American South and American Judaism. Throughout their history in the South, these worlds came together for Jews at the dinner table, at times effortlessly and at other times with a struggle.

Jews have encountered southern worlds of "sacred and profane" food for more than three centuries. Since the seventeenth century, Jews in the American South have been tempted by regional foods that are among the most delectable in the area but that are also forbidden by Jewish law. Members of each generation balanced their southern and Jewish identities as they considered the plate set before them. These encounters of region, religion, and food unveil a unique chapter in American Judaism. Dining with the Deep South diaspora, we discover both rural and urban worlds in the region, diverse Jewish populations who came to the South from central and eastern Europe, Greece, and Turkey, and Reform, Orthodox, and Conservative Jewish communities. Southern Jews adapted their culinary traditions within predominantly Christian worlds, where they were strongly influenced by the region's traditions of race, class, and gender.[1] "Southern Jewish" cooking is defined by the following: traditional Jewish recipes passed down from one generation to the next; the influence of regional ingredients, flavors, and cooking methods; a deeply ingrained sense of hospitality and sociability; the importance of family and regional Jewish connections; and the presence and influence of African American cooks and caterers.

Food is key to understanding southern Jews. For more than four centuries, they have both eaten and rejected foods that are indigenous to the places where they live. Food then becomes a barometer, a measuring device that determines how southern Jews acculturate, while also retaining their own heritage. As they introduced new food, recipes, and cooking methods, Jews quickly defined boundaries between older residents and newcomers. Southern Jews also adapted their eating habits to match those of their neighbors. Their cuisine revealed both how they merged with the cultures they encountered in the region and how they separated themselves from these cultures.

Southern Jews faced a familiar predicament. How can Jews be Jewish in a world where catfish is easier to find than kishka? (Kishka is a kosher version of sausage.) Jewish dietary laws known as *kashrut* specify which foods Jews cannot eat, how foods should be prepared, and the manner in which animals should be slaughtered.[2] "Keeping kosher" in the South is particularly challenging because so many regional dishes feature pork, shrimp, oysters, and crab, all of which are forbidden by kashrut.

Foodways traditions pass from generation to generation through stories. Although written records exist in the form of recipes, diaries, cookbooks, and prescriptive literature, the primary source of foodways knowledge is oral. Simply put, cooks teach others to cook in the kitchen. This communication is the heart of the subject. From a simple meal at home to an elaborate public celebration, food allows us to communicate and share.

Observant Jews believe that eating is an act of divine law that is dictated in the Bible and expanded in the Talmud. Blu Greenberg, an Orthodox *rebbetzin* (wife of a rabbi) and an authority on the precepts of traditional Jewish life explains, "kashrut is not simply a set of rules about permitted and forbidden foods; kashrut is a way of life."[3] This way of life determines which foods Jews cannot eat, how certain foods should be prepared, and how animals should be slaughtered. Observant Jews must only eat meat from animals that chew their cud and have cloven hooves. They may also eat fish that have both fins and scales, but they must never combine dairy and meat dishes.

Jewish response to kashrut in the South ranges from complete avoidance to strict adherence, a pattern that dates from the first Jewish settlers in the colo-

Shohet knife with sharpening stone and cloth used by Jake Kalinsky in Holly Hill,
South Carolina, ca. 1920. Metal, bone, stone, and cotton. Knife: 8 × 1 × ½ inches.
Stone: 1¾ × 7 × ¾ inches. Cloth: 15 × 21¼ inches. Kalinsky used these items to provide kosher
chickens for his family. In 1912, at age fourteen, he left Trestina, Poland, with his mother, Ida, and
his sisters Libby and Lena. His father, Meyer, had come ahead and opened a little store in Holly Hill.
Jake stayed long enough in Charleston to learn to slaughter chickens in the ritually prescribed
manner, then joined his family in the countryside. Private collection. Photo courtesy of Special
Collections, College of Charleston Libary.

nial South to the present. During the colonial era, the eating patterns of Jewish
settlers defined their religious identities—"they were what they ate."[4] Today,
many Orthodox and Conservative Jews in the South keep kosher, a difficult task
in rural areas where kosher food must be purchased by mail, telephone, or the
Internet. Some observant Jews in the region adjust dietary laws when they cannot follow the letter of the law and are "quietly kosher."

At the other end of the spectrum, some Reform Jews eat pork, barbecue,
shrimp, and crab. Others enjoy these dishes more discreetly, and they also
eat "kosher-style" foods when they find them in delicatessens, restaurants, and
supermarkets in the South. "Kosher-style" is an American term that allows Jews
to ignore the rigor of Jewish dietary laws by distinguishing between rules of
kashrut that they observe and others they choose to ignore.[5] Reform Jews in the
region enjoy a "southernized kashrut" that allows them to enjoy forbidden foods
with a minimal sense of guilt. They avoid eating pork barbecue or ham at home,
but they enjoy it at local restaurants. My mother never served a ham roast or a
Virginia ham at home. Instead, she served prepackaged sliced ham that could

pass for sliced turkey or chicken. One family in the Mississippi Delta had a special set of glass plates for forbidden foods like shrimp and barbecue, while another family never ate bacon on the Sabbath.

Southern Jewish jokes about keeping kosher reflect the dilemma of Jews as they approach the dining table.[6] A Jewish man with five sets of gold teeth is going through customs. The customs agent asks him why he needs so many. "Well," he explains, "I'm an Orthodox Jew. I've got one set for meat and one set for milk." "What about the other three?" the agent asks. "Well, I need one for milk and one for meat for Passover." "And the last set?" asks the agent. "Barbecue," he replies.[7]

While observant Jews in cities like Atlanta and Memphis strictly define their ethnicity at the table, their lifestyle is rarely possible for Jews in the rural South. Given the limited Jewish support services, its small Jewish population, and the strong influence of Protestant fundamentalism, expressions of Jewish life in the South are understandably diverse, and Jewish southerners respect this diversity. Food ledgers, cookbooks, recipes, synagogue banquet menus, sisterhood minutes, and Jewish social club invitations all reveal the fascinating mix of cultures within southern Jewish life. These documents reflect Old World memories, the blending of ethnic and regional identities, and the influence of race and class. When southern Jewish women write their recipes in diaries and publish them in cookbooks, they codify the food customs and social mores of their time. For centuries women described their housekeeping chores, wrote recipes for friends and family, and spoke of their domestic duties in their personal journals and diaries.[8] As cookbooks were published in the nineteenth century through both commercial and community-sponsored efforts, women's domestic culture became a permanent resource for women's history.[9]

Daisy Hutzler Heller's cookbook journal offers a glimpse into the Richmond, Virginia, Jewish community in the early 1900s. Heller was a member of the city's first Reform congregation, Beth Ahabah. She includes both Jewish foods and regional specialties, including treyf (nonkosher) dishes made with shrimp and ham. Recipes for lebkuchen, "mother's matza cake," matzoh ball soup, brod torte, and sponge cake coexist alongside southern favorites such as watermelon preserves, lemon ice box pie, angel food, ginger cakes, mayonnaise, caramel icing, Mrs. Bradley's Sally Lunn (a rich cakelike bread), and the forbidden boiled shrimp and ham.[10] By including "outside foods" like shrimp and ham in her family meals, Daisy Heller affirmed her southern allegiance.[11] After the Civil War, southern Jews faced growing antisemitism. By eating like their Gentile neighbors, they affirmed both their solidarity with white society and their loyalty to the segregated South.

During the twentieth century, women's clubs, benevolent organizations, and religious institutions in the Jewish South published hundreds of community cookbooks. These volumes are by women who shaped the daily Judaism of their families and the communal expression of religion in their synagogues and organizations. They describe everyday "lived religion" overseen by women in the home. Because many southern Jews lived in small communities where there were no synagogues and rabbis, their primary expression of religious observance was at the dinner table.[12] Community cookbooks describe the love of Jewish southerners for regional cooking, as well as their religious views, which ranged from Orthodoxy to liberal Reform.

Food prepared by sisterhood members came from Jewish and southern cookbooks, journals, newspapers, and mothers' and grandmothers' recipe boxes. It expressed both their Judaism and their women's community. When the Hebrew Ladies Benevolent Society in New Albany, Georgia, celebrated their Diamond Jubilee in 1953, their members presented a skit that joked about the large quantities of food consumed at Benevolent Society functions. In it, the secretary describes the rich mix of southern and German Jewish foods consumed at the last meeting: roast goose with apple dressing, fried chicken with corn fritters, sliced cold turkey with cranberry preserves, chicken salad, homegrown sliced tomatoes, homemade beaten biscuits, assorted jams and jellies, and for dessert an apple strudel and a "straissal [streusel] kuchyen." One member complains that she has gained thirty-four pounds since joining the Benevolent Society and that her husband claimes that she spends "more time preparing our luncheons that I do preparing his meals." After discussing the need to cut back on the food for their next meeting, a vote is taken, and the group agrees to eliminate sliced tomatoes.[13]

Lena Moritz and Adele Kahn belonged to the Montgomery, Alabama, German Jewish community and published The Twentieth Century Cook Book (1897) and Every Woman's Cookbook (1926). Their recipes for fried matzoh balls and "opossum with sweet potatoes" suggest that nonkosher wild game could appear on their tables as often as chicken or brisket. Moritz and Kahn presented southern versions of German Jewish matzoh balls, "filled fish" (gefilte fish), brisket, macaroon charlotte russe, and schaum torte, as well as quail, squab, rabbit, squirrel, and even opossum, which they described as a "real southern dish." Their recipe for fried matzoh balls blends Jewish tastes with southern cooking methods: "Make same as Matzos Balls, boiled. When ready to cook, heat one half cup [goose or other] fat in a hot skillet, put in balls carefully. Let brown on one side, turn on other side."[14]

Among the most poignant cookbooks are those never intended for public use. These books reflect private musings of Jewish mothers, aunts, or grand-

"*Aunt Jemima's Latkes, with the Beloved Old [Fashioned] Plantation Flavor.*" *Advertisement in the* Jewish American (Der Americaner), *September 7, 1934. Image courtesy of Rabbi Yaakov Horowitz, American Jewish Legacy, Jersey City, N.J., http://www.ajlegacy.org.*

mothers as they shaped their family's expression of Judaism.[15] Lillian Opotowsky of New Orleans has an early twentieth-century ledger book that her Grandmother Preis filled with handwritten recipes from friends and family, along with food columns clipped from newspapers and magazines. As a "foodways autobiography," this ledger reflects Mrs. Preis's ethnic heritage; her network of family, friends, and workers; her position in the society of Waterproof, Louisiana; and the culinary world that she created for her family.[16]

During the colonial era, a pivotal relationship emerged between Jewish and African American women in home and synagogue kitchens, where they shared recipes for collard greens and matzoh balls. They formed an unlikely alliance as outsiders—Jews because of their religion and blacks because of their race.[17] The kitchen became a "free zone" where African American and Jewish women bonded as they prepared meals.[18] Within this space, an important blend of southern and Jewish cuisine emerged.

Although Jewish women were in charge of the kitchen, black women affirmed their authority and creativity through the dishes they prepared for Jewish families. Eli Evans describes an "Atlanta Brisket" prepared by black cooks Zola Hargraves and Roady Adams, who worked for the Evans family in Durham, North Carolina.[19] Their secret ingredient was Coca-Cola. Jewish and African American women created similar blended dishes such as lox and grits, sweet potato kugel, collard greens with gribbenes ("cracklins" made from rendered chicken fat or "schmaltz"), sweet and sour shad, Sabbath fried chicken, Rosh Hashanah "hoppin' john" (the black-eyed peas and rice dish traditionally served in January on New Year's Day), and barbeque brisket.

Black cooks and caterers baked sweet potato pies and cornbread dressing for Jewish employers and went home after holiday meals and bar mitzvahs with leftover chopped liver and kugel. Recipes and food traveled between Jewish and African American homes. Mary Jordan, an African American caterer in Atlanta, began cooking for Jewish families in the 1940s. She learned to prepare Jewish specialties better than her Jewish employers. Her son Windsor explained, "The grandmamma's—they just died so fast. And the recipes went home with the maid and the bartender and the chauffeur."[20]

By the beginning of the twentieth century, a generational pattern of women's work emerged among southern Jewish women in which grandmothers were supervisors, African American women cooks and housekeepers, and married daughters club members. Between 1890 and 1920, the number of white female servants declined by one-third, and black female domestics increased by 43 percent. By 1920, 71 percent of all nonagricultural black women wage earners performed household labor.[21] This pattern supported the transition of Jewish women from their southern homes into the public world of volunteer work and paid employment. Black women managed Jewish households while Jewish women raised funds for their synagogues through benefit meals, temple bazaars, and the sale of community cookbooks.

Ironically, although African American women were central figures in synagogue and home kitchens throughout the Jewish South, they rarely are mentioned in synagogue and community cookbooks from the early twentieth century to the present. An occasional reference to a black cook in a recipe title or text is often the only testimony to her lifetime of work for a white family. The poignant absence of African American women in the cookbooks of southern white women, including those written by Jews, reflects attitudes in an era defined by racial segregation.

While segregation influenced synagogue and family cookbooks, it was most visible in the relationships between African American domestic workers and their female employers in the Jewish home. Like their white Gentile neighbors, Jewish women rarely addressed African American employees by their last names, whereas blacks spoke to their employers respectfully as "Mrs." This practice of using first names for black employees is telling of the ways that Jews conformed to white southern racial codes.

Southern Jews created regional cuisines shaped by local animals and plants in the area, as well as by access to seafood, kosher butchers, bakeries, and imported goods. In the colonial South, Jews interacted with enslaved African Americans, Native Americans, and newly arrived immigrants from France, England, and Germany. In the nineteenth and twentieth centuries, Jews encountered immigrants from Italy, Greece, Latin America, and Asia.

Jewish immigrants brought to the South food traditions from their countries of origin—the Ashkenazim from central and eastern Europe and the Sephardim from countries bordering the Mediterranean. From Germany came kuchens, strudels, breads, roasted goose, matzoh balls, and gefilte fish; from the Mediterranean, feta, olive oil, fish, rice dishes, and filo dough pastries; from eastern Europe, chopped liver, kishke, stuffed cabbage, roasted chicken, kreplach, tzimmes, and herring; from Alsace and Lorraine, tortes, pastries, breads, onions and garlic, cheeses, and baked and stewed fish dishes.

As southern Jewish identity evolved from the eighteenth to the twentieth centuries, some women kept southern and Jewish dishes separate, while others mixed the cuisines by adding pecans, fresh tomatoes, okra, butter beans, and sweet potatoes to holiday menus. They also substituted regional specialties such as fried chicken, gumbo, and beef ribs for the traditional roasted chicken served at Friday evening Sabbath suppers. Today Jewish women prepare southern and Jewish foods in ways that celebrate the distinctive foodways of both the region and their religious heritage. Dishes frequently prepared in the region include gefilte fish, chopped liver, matzoh ball soup, potato latkes, noodle kugel, kreplach, stuffed cabbage, borscht, brisket, strudel, and tzimmes. These traditional foods are infused with regional ingredients, and their cooking methods suggest the continuity of Jewish life in the South.

In the South Carolina and Georgia low country, Jewish settlers encountered a cuisine that featured treyf shellfish served at oyster roasts, at crab boils, and in home-cooked meals of shrimp and grits. Locally grown rice known as "Carolina Gold" was a staple of most meals. Rice was cultivated and harvested by African Americans whose ancestors grew rice in Senegal, the Congo, and Angola. In the creole world of New Orleans and the communities along the lower Mississippi River, Jewish merchants discovered redfish, red snapper, and pompano. Jambalaya, gumbo, and etouffee' were laden with shrimp, crab, oysters, crawfish, duck,

Jake Kalinsky and his mother and sisters, Trestina, Poland ca. 1912. Photo no. 6/97.6,
Jewish Heritage Collection, College of Charleston, courtesy of Special Collections,
College of Charleston Library.

and salty pork sausages like andouille and boudin. In Atlanta and throughout the interior South, Jews—depending on their religious practices—enjoyed fried chicken, pork barbecue, "meat n' three" plate lunches, vegetable casseroles, and sweet tea. In Memphis and the Mississippi and Arkansas Delta, pork barbecue was the local food of choice. Also popular in Memphis and the Delta were hot tamales; thick, garlic-infused steaks; and salads dressed with sweet Greek vinaigrette and "cumback" sauce (a version of Thousand Island dressing) served at local steakhouses operated by Greek restaurateurs.[22]

Spices, methods of cooking, and food names changed from region to region, but white and black, Jew and Gentile shared southern cuisine from the colonial era through the twentieth century. Southern cooks braised, stewed, and fried meats, and most meals included vegetables slow-cooked over a low simmer. Techniques like stewing and braising were also familiar to Jewish cooks.

The region's moderate climate provided a long growing season and bountiful crops of fresh vegetables and fruits that southern women preserved and pickled to eat through the winter and late spring. Home gardens and curb markets offered easy access to fresh foods that included a wide selection of field peas and seasonal greens not known outside the South. Because of their urban backgrounds and restrictions against owning land in the Old World, few Jews had a tradition of vegetable gardening. Mildred Covert, a descendent of eastern European Jews who moved to New Orleans in the early 1900s, recalls, "If my grandmother had a tomato bush, it was by accident."[23] Jewish women did, however, bring traditions of pickling and preserving from central and eastern Europe that easily blended with the summer canning traditions of Gentile southerners.

During the Civil War and the Depression, all southerners suffered from a lack of nutritious foods owing to the disruption of home life, farms, and small businesses. Both black and white women learned to stretch a "one-pot dish" to feed as many mouths as possible. Meals might feature a slow-cooked pot of greens flavored with fat-back and served with hoecakes made from cornmeal and water. Observant Jewish households took pains to extend food, while avoiding pork and other nonkosher dishes.

In better times an abundance of pork and corn defined daily meals, which also included freshwater and saltwater fish, venison, poultry, duck, and game birds like dove and quail. Observant Jewish families avoided pork and shellfish wherever possible. No meal was complete without cornbread or biscuits—yeast rolls on Sunday—and desserts such as custard pie, fruit cobbler, layer cake, pudding, and stewed seasonal fruits. Because many of these dishes used lard for frying and butter as shortening, observant Jews faced a special predicament. How could one avoid serving fried chicken, pies, and cakes and still be consid-

Nathan Bass (far right), with crates and bushels of "North Brand Select Tomatoes," packed by Culler & Bass, North, South Carolina, ca. 1932. After exploring the idea with New York wholesalers while on a buying trip for his dry goods store, Bass was trying to develop a market for local farm products. Photo courtesy of Lucille Bass Lipsitz. Special Collections, College of Charleston Library.

ered a loyal southerner? The introduction of Crisco in 1912 as a certified kosher vegetable shortening solved an age-old problem for both Jewish women and for African American women who cooked for observant Jewish families in the South. Crisco was considered *parve*, a neutral food by kashrut standards, and was eaten with both dairy and meat dishes. When the product first appeared, Procter and Gamble announced, "The Hebrew Race has been waiting 4,000 years for Crisco."[24] For observant southern Jews who lived in a culinary culture of cast iron frying pans, foods fried in lard, and shortening-enriched desserts and breads, it *felt* like four thousand years.

Because agriculture has dominated southern history, rhythms of farm life shaped southern cuisine. Home cooking was common among rural southerners until World War II. Following the war and the region's economic shift from agriculture to industry, thousands of rural southerners moved to southern cities. As they did, their eating patterns changed. Factory workers carried lunches in sacks and metal pails from home or bought a quick snack of sardines, pickles, crackers, and cheese from grocery stores, many of which were owned by east-

Party for Carolee Rosen's first birthday, Asheville, N.C., 1931. Collection of Carolee Rosen Fox. Photo courtesy of Special Collections, College of Charleston Library.

ern European and Sephardic Jewish merchants. Cafés and restaurants also served inexpensive plate lunches to city workers.

Jewish immigrants and their southern Gentile neighbors alike celebrated daily life, holidays, and important life passages with food. Old World Jewry used food to distinguish between "holy and mundane spheres" of Jewish life.[25] On the Sabbath they enjoyed a feast of roast chicken, rich soup, gefilte fish, puddings, challah, and cakes instead of the plain daily fare of vegetable soups and dark bread. When white and black Gentile southerners commemorated special occasions their tables were laden with favorite foods. Jews quickly adopted southern traditions that embraced festivity, bounty, and hospitality.[26]

Eating in the South is regarded as seriously as religion, and for most southerners eating is like a religion. "There is nothing we do here without food," says Rabbi Arnold Mark Belzer of Savannah's historic Congregation Mickve Israel, founded in 1735. Every week of the year their Saturday morning service is followed by a hot lunch prepared by the temple's catering staff. Until her recent retirement, Alberta Everett, an African American cook at Mickve Israel, was known for her delicious kugels and challahs. Congregation Mickve Israel also hosts monthly catered Sabbath dinners before the Friday evening services for congregants and guests. In the summertime "Exotic Resort Location Sabbaths" at con-

Bar mitzvah celebration of Charles Borochoff at the home of Tobias Borochoff, Atlanta, Georgia, 1934. Charles Borochoff is seated first on the left. Photo CAB 160.4 courtesy of the Ida Pearle and Joseph Cuba Archives of the William Breman Jewish Heritage Museum, Atlanta, Georgia.

gregants' beach homes feature "covered dishes" from fried chicken to kasha (buckwheat groats). According to Rabbi Belzer, these events are "the best places to eat in town."[27]

Food events among Jewish southerners include both social gatherings, where congregants share a meal at home or at a local restaurant, and religious gatherings such as Passover seders. In the nineteenth- and early-twentieth-century South, Jewish food celebrations included "Purim entertainments," temple fundraising fairs and bazaars, "Ballyhoo" luncheons, "Break-the-fast" dances, congregational picnics, "Simchat Torah Balls," nonkosher oyster roasts, strawberry festivals, wedding receptions, and candy pulls.[28] Similar events today include home-cooked meals for visiting rabbis, potluck suppers at the temple, community Passover seders at the synagogue, Sabbath fried chicken at Jewish summer camp, sisterhood-sponsored food bazaars, Jewish golf tournaments, and synagogue-sponsored "barbecue" competitions.

Throughout the South, sense of place, that unique blending of geography and culture, strongly shaped regional expressions of Jewish life. Jews in the

Thirty-fifth anniversary dinner in honor of Mr. and Mrs. Emil Dittler, Standard Club, Atlanta, February 14, 1935. Photo courtesy of the Ida Pearle and Joseph Cuba Archives of the William Breman Jewish Heritage Museum, Atlanta, Georgia.

Carolina and Georgia low country developed a culture that differed from that of other Jewish southerners. On the eastern seaboard, trade was central to low country Jewish life for generations, and buying and selling food was the heart of this trade. In Savannah and Charleston, Jews worked as dry goods merchants, innkeepers, fruit peddlers, bakers, butchers, caterers, and cooks. They were linked to other Jews throughout the Atlantic region by religion, business connections, family ties, marriage, memories of Europe, and most important, culinary traditions. A fundamental shared connection within this extended Jewish community was their commitment to kashrut, which supported a healthy coastal trade in kosher meat.[29]

The Minis family arrived with the first group of Jewish settlers who came to Savannah in 1733. Abraham Minis was a merchant-shipper, plantation owner, and rancher, and when he died in 1757 his wife Abigail was left with eight children to support. Like many women of her era, she opened a tavern to support her family.[30] Abigail Minis's tavern was the scene of "elegant entertainment," including a gala evening in 1764 for "His majesty's council," merchants, and other "gentlemen" of Savannah, and in 1772 she hosted a celebration of the king's birthday for seventy guests.[31] The elegance of her entertaining is suggested by the serving dishes and dining furniture listed in the inventory of personal property taken after her death in 1794. There were mahogany serving tables and card tables, almost two dozen mahogany chairs, three cases of knives and forks, a gold carpet, "a lot" of glass and crockery ware, a pair of plated candlesticks, a pair of silver mugs, a pair of butter boats and ladles, eight tablespoons, thirteen teaspoons, a pair of tea tongs, as well as her kitchen furniture.[32]

Like other colonial Americans of her era, Abigail Minis established her status in society through the display and use of personal property.[33] At her death, Abigail Minis left property to her five unmarried daughters, "who with great affection have always treated me as their fond Mother." Minis believed that her daughters' frugality and support enabled her to "keep together my Estate" after her husband's death.[34] The booming economy of the late eighteenth century allowed women like Abigail Minis and her daughters to purchase goods for their homes that reflected their desire for refinement.[35] Minis clearly understood the importance of "setting a good table" to establish her position in southern white society and to assure her Gentile neighbors that Jews had the same loyalties and ambitions as other middle- and upper-class white Americans.

The Ashkenazic Jews of Charleston pushed their "quest for gentility" beyond mere material goods. To raise their status within the community, they adopted the practices of Charleston's prestigious Sephardic Jewish families who were descended from the city's first Jewish settlers.[36] These practices extended to the dining table, where German-descended Jews preferred the tastes of Iberian-inspired cuisine. By preparing the recipes of their Sephardic friends, such as cold lemon-stew fish, Ashkenazic women in Charleston redefined their Jewish lineage.[37]

In 1825, twelve members of Charleston's Congregation Beth Elohim petitioned leaders of the synagogue to change the congregation's worship service. The reformers sought to adapt their religion to the southern world in which they lived. Their reforms led to a split within the congregation and the creation of the "Reformed Society of Israelites," also in 1825, which marked the beginning of Reform Judaism in America. The call for changes in the worship service influenced congregants' homes as well, as Charleston Jews increasingly challenged dietary laws. By adopting the eating habits of their neighbors, younger Jews affirmed their allegiance with white Gentile southerners. By abandoning kashrut, meals became a statement of their dual "ethnic" identities as progressive Jews and as white southerners.[38]

The creole world that midnineteenth-century German and French Jews encountered in New Orleans and rural Louisiana was as complex as the gumbo they ate. Like the rich seafood stew inspired by African, Indian, and Franco-Spanish cultures, their society was shaped by Caribbeans, French, Spanish,

New Grocery Store.

THE subscriber respectfully informs the citizens of Columbia, and its vicinity, that he has opened a handsome assortment of Groceries, in the store formerly occupied by R. A. Taylor, which he will dispose of on the most moderate terms. He has made such arrangements as will enable him to keep a constant supply of the following articles:

First rate French Brandy, Gin, Rum, Whiskey,
Tenoriffe and Malaga Wine,
Molasses, Brown, White and Loaf Sugar,
Coffee, Tea, Rice, Flour, Crackers,
Pepper, Spice, Mustard,
Soap, Starch, Sperm and Tallow Candles,
Powder and Shot.
And all other articles in the Grocery line.
                                    JACOB C. LYONS.
Nov. 9.   45 3

Advertisement for the Lyons family's "New Grocery Store," Columbia Telescope, November 9, 1827. Operated by Isaac Lyons and his son, Jacob C. Lyons, the business earned its reputation as an oyster saloon catering to students from South Carolina College. Photo courtesy of Special Collections, College of Charleston Library.

Choctaw and Natchez Indians, enslaved Africans, free "people of color," French Canadian exiles, Irish, Italians, and Greeks.[39] Sephardic, German, and French Jews added their own heritage to world. Apart from their religious practices, New Orleans Jews were virtually indistinguishable from their white Protestant and Catholic neighbors.

From the early 1800s until the present, Jews in New Orleans, in rural Louisiana, and in communities along the Lower Mississippi have been intimately linked with Caribbean, creole, and African American people who entered their home and synagogue kitchens as professional cooks. They brought exotic flavors of hot peppers, chilies, filé, and spices; yams and eggplants; grains such as rice, grits, and cornmeal; confections made with cane syrup, coconuts, pecans, sesame seeds, and peanuts; and even shellfish and pork, which were prohibited by Jewish dietary laws.[40] These foodstuffs entered Sephardic and Ashkenazic house-holds where they mixed with recipes from Jewish countries of origin—the West Indies, France, Germany, and eastern Europe.

The Civil War dramatically disrupted the Jewish middle class in New Orleans. "What true Southerner can ever fail to remember that on the 12th of April 1861, the first collision of the Confederate and Federal forces took place," Clara Solomon recorded in her diary, a year later on April 12, 1862. "It was at 4½ in the morning that the bombardment of Fort Sumter, Charleston harbor, com-menced." In her descriptions of daily life as the war approached New Orleans, she recalled foods that she loved—shrimp, blackberries, and "mush-melon"—and those that were increasingly denied—butter, flour, coffee, and meat—as wartime food shortages grew. During Passover in the spring of 1862, Solomon described the "motsoe" (matzoh) shortage in New Orleans. After services at Dis-persed of Judah Synagogue, congregants complained to each other and to Mr. Da Silva, the synagogue's sexton who procured matzohs for the congregation.[41]

Although it was difficult to find matzoh in cities like New Orleans, the chal-lenge of preparing for Passover in the battlefield was far greater. In April 1864, Private Isaac J. Levy of the 46th Virginia regiment wrote to his sister Leonora and described his Passover "celebration" at Adam's Run, South Carolina. Thanks to a letter from his mother, Isaac Levy knew the date of the first seder. Levy's brother Zeke purchased enough matzoh to last them a week, and in Charleston he bought the ingredients for a seder stew. Together the brothers prepared a meal in a "truly Orthodox style" with their soup of onions, parsley, carrots, turnips, a "young cauliflower," and a pound and a half of fresh beef.[42]

After the Civil War, Jewish peddlers and merchants returned to their trades. They filled an important niche in the cash-poor South during Reconstruction.[43] Jewish women shaped the religious lives of their families while their husbands managed their stores and landholdings. In rural Louisiana, grandmothers, moth-ers, and aunts focused on the spiritual needs of their families, and such matters were negotiated at the dinner table. In the town of Geismar, Louisiana, an un-likely trio of women—Evelyn Vessier Geismar, a convert from Catholicism to Judaism; Sara Geismar, Evelyn's Alsatian relative by marriage; and Rosa Smith, an African American cook—oversaw the family's religious and culinary needs. "I'm a Cajun Jewish Alsatian," writes Evelyn Geismar's daughter, Lee Stamler. "My Cajun cooking has a Jewish slant, and my Jewish cooking has a Cajun slant, with a few Alsatian influences." Lee recalls how her mother shared her love of Cajun cuisine with her children. Descended from the French Acadians of Nova Scotia and raised in a Catholic orphanage, Evelyn Vessier had no knowledge of Jewish beliefs. Stamler explained that her mother "read books to raise us Jewish."[44]

The women of the Geismar households defined their culinary worlds in ways that reflected their diverse racial, religious, class, and ethnic identities. As an affluent Jewish woman of French descent, Sara Geismar cooked Jewish foods and creole entrées, and also oversaw domestic labor, gardens, and livestock. As an African American woman, Rosa Smith prepared daily meals and fed the family. And as a Cajun, Catholic woman of means, Evelyn Geismar prepared desserts and dainty sweets. Together, these three women fed their family, as well as the house servants and field laborers. Like three points on a compass, Rosa Smith, Sara Geismar, and Evelyn Geismar embodied the African American, Alsatian-Creole, and Acadian cultures that shaped Jewish identity in rural Louisiana.

German Jewish immigrants like the Geismers were followed by eastern European Jewish immigrants, who arrived in the South after the Civil War and during the first decades of the twentieth century. Although their numbers were much smaller than those Jews who settled in the Northeast, their presence reinvigorated Orthodoxy and traditional observance in the South. They clung more tightly to kashrut than the German Jews who preceded them. As a result, eastern Europeans Jews who settled in the South opened Jewish butcher shops, bakeries, and delicatessens in the early decades of the twentieth century. Here landsman could find kosher matzoh and traditional foods that they had known in their countries of origin, foods such as bagels, borscht, chicken soup, stuffed cabbage, cholent, tzimmes, herring, kreplach, and tongue.

In New Orleans, Pressner's kosher delicatessen in the Dryades Street neighborhood at the corner of Baronne and Foucher Streets first opened as a small grocery in the 1930s. The Pressner family came from eastern Europe to New Orleans and lived in an apartment above their store.[45] Around the corner, their uncle Max Pressner owned a chicken business, and a shohet came each Friday to slaughter chickens for the Sabbath dinner table. African Americans, Italians, and Jews lived in this neighborhood, which became the heart of the New Orleans eastern European Jewish community from 1910 until after World War II.

During this period, German Jews defended themselves from stereotypes directed at recent Jewish immigrants by embracing New South boosterism and symbols of the Old South. Excluded from white Gentile clubs such as Atlanta's Piedmont Driving Club or New Orleans's exclusive Mardi Gras krewes, they founded Jewish social clubs that excluded eastern European and Sephardic Jews whom they considered "too Jewish." Fear of association with immigrants also influenced the dining tables of German Jews. African American cooks and caterers served German Jews foods enjoyed by white antebellum planters and their descendants, rather than the foods of their Jewish ancestors. They ate at restaurants that catered to the tastes and segregationist practices of their white Atlanta neighbors. An occasional matzoh ball or kuchen was the sole culinary acknowledgment of their German Jewish heritage.

Eastern European peddlers and merchants who settled in Atlanta refused to abandon the tastes of their homelands. Excluded from both white Gentile and German Jewish clubs in southern cities, they formed a tightly knit community grounded in the small grocery stores, delicatessens, and cafés of Atlanta's South Side. They served Jewish and African American customers and catered to the tastes of both cultures. With accents and religious practices that made it impossible to hide their Jewishness, eastern Europeans saw themselves as the sons and daughters of hard-working immigrants.

Eastern Europeans Jews formed Orthodox synagogues, such as Atlanta's Ahavath Achim and Shearith Israel. They hired African American cooks and caterers, to whom they taught the rules of kashrut and recipes from the old country. Barbecue meant beef brisket, and turnip greens were flavored with schmaltz. Delicatessens supplied basic Jewish items such as kishka, knish, salami, and corned beef, tastes savored on Sunday evenings and at shul gatherings.

No group within the South's diverse Jewish community preserves their Old World culture through food better than the Sephardic Jews who arrived in Georgia and Alabama from the Isle of Rhodes, Turkey, Asia Minor, and Greece during the first decade of the 1900s. Fear surrounding the Leo Frank case and his subsequent lynching colored the early years of the Sephardim in Georgia. Regina Rousso Tourial remembered her father-in-law warning her mother-in-law "not to dare go out of the house" during the Frank trial for fear of lynch mobs and the vulnerability of Atlanta's Jews. The desire to stay among "their own kind" strengthened the retention of Sephardic cooking methods and recipes. Regina Tourial, explains: "We weren't roast and brisket eaters. That came much later in our lives."[46]

As Atlanta's old South Side Jewish neighborhoods changed and the Sephardim followed earlier migrations of German and eastern European Jews to Atlanta's suburban neighborhoods, collaborative baking and cooking sessions created a sense of camaraderie that mothers passed on to their daughters. Today, their sense of community and intimacy is reaffirmed each year at their Chanukah-time Sephardic food bazaar, an important fundraising event for Congregation Or VeShalom that began in the 1950s. The success of their bazaar inspired the sisterhood to publish *The Sephardic Cooks*, a cookbook that has gone through several printings. "One day, we were at a sisterhood meeting," says Emily Amato. "I said, 'We have to have a cookbook because I can't remember, and I'm tired of calling my mother up every time I want a recipe.' Once I said it, we had to do it."[47] Second- and third-generation Sephardic women in Atlanta continue to cook as their grandmothers did on the Isle of Rhodes and in Turkey. "This food holds us together," says Jeanette Arogeti. "It's in our blood."[48]

In the early 1930s, Rabbi Tobias Geffen received inquiries from Orthodox rabbis across the nation about the kosher status of Atlanta-based Coca-Cola. Was this internationally popular soft drink kosher for Passover? There was much at stake for observant southern Jews. They enjoyed cold refreshing drinks as much as any southerner, and to refuse a Coke because it was not kosher denied them a southern ritual as sacred as fried chicken and watermelon. Rabbi Geffen approached Harold Hirsch, an attorney for the Coca-Cola Corporation, and told him he had to know what ingredients were in the "secret recipe" to certify the drink's kosher status. Sworn to secrecy about the recipe, in 1935 Geffen published a *teshuva*, or Jewish legal response, affirming Coca-Cola's kosher certification for Passover.[49]

The Mississippi and Arkansas Delta—a fertile alluvial plain formed by the Mississippi River and its tributaries—is far removed from the urban world of Atlanta. Jews have built businesses and organized synagogues in the Delta since the late nineteenth century. Obtaining Jewish food supplies there is a challenge. Jewish travelers who visited Jackson, Memphis, St. Louis, Birmingham, New Orleans, and especially New York returned with bagels, lox, corned beef, and dark loaves of pumpernickel for friends and family in the Delta. Delicatessens and kosher butcher shops like the Old Tyme Delicatessen in Jackson and Rosen's, Segal's, and Halpern's in Memphis were known throughout the Delta because of advertisements in the *Hebrew Watchman* and the *Jewish Spectator.* These advertisements guaranteed "prompt attention given out-of-town orders" and assured Delta Jews their foods that would be delivered by bus and train.[50]

The region's overall population dropped because of the arrival of the boll weevil in the early 1900s, the mechanization of cotton picking in the 1940s, and the "great migration" of black laborers out of the Delta to northern industrial cities like Chicago. The decline of downtown business districts and the growth of regional discount stores forced third- and fourth-generation Jews out of their small mercantile businesses in the Delta and into professions located in cities.[51] While congregations in the Delta have closed their doors in recent years, the "end of the story of small-town Jewish life in the Delta has not been written."[52]

By the first decade of the 1900s, downtown Memphis and "the Pinch" were home to Jewish grocery stores, delicatessens, butcher shops, a kosher bakery, and a kosher fish market. Customers could select a live chicken at a kosher butcher shop, like Aaron Dubrovner's or Makowsky's, and a shohet slaughtered the animal while they waited. Ridblatt's Bakery in the Pinch was popularized by the owner's son, a prizefighter nicknamed "Rye" in honor of the bakery's best-

David Hazan's Fruit Stand, Atlanta, ca. 1920. Photo courtesy of the Ida Pearle and Joseph Cuba Archives of the William Breman Jewish Heritage Museum, Atlanta, Georgia.

selling bread.[53] Shoppers on North Main Street frequented Rosen's kosher grocery delicatessen, "the largest delicatessen in the Entire South," and Albert Seessel and Son's grocery store, known for its smoked and pickled tongues and fresh meats. Goldstein's Delicatessen advertised itself as "not the largest, but the cleanest and best in the city."[54] Segal's Kosher Delicatessen on South Second Street used Memphis summers to attract customers: "Don't cook these hot days. Eat a delicious delicatessen meal."[55]

What happened to Jewish businesses like Halpern's that supported Jewish life in Memphis and the Delta? Their fate was sealed by supermarkets like Piggly Wiggly and Krogers, which opened impressive kosher sections that featured a kosher bakery, frozen meat, packaged goods, specialty frozen foods, wines, and housewares. Even Krispy Kreme donuts are now available to Jewish customers in a kosher version. Given the success of chain stores and the small size of the southern Jewish population, it is difficult for family-owned kosher food businesses to survive. The handful that continue to serve the region include Steve Gilmer's Quality Kosher market in Atlanta and Joel and Natalie Brown's Kosher Cajun Delicatessen in New Orleans.

No one speaks of food in Memphis without thinking of barbecue. As long as barbecue has been eaten in the city, the aroma and taste of this forbidden meat

The Economy Deli located on Auburn Avenue in Atlanta was a Jewish-owned business serving only black customers. Left to right: holding on to chair, owners, Nace Galanti, Ralph Galanti, Abraham Romano. Photo courtesy of the Ida Pearle and Joseph Cuba Archives of the William Breman Jewish Heritage Museum, Atlanta, Georgia.

has tempted Jewish Memphians. Memphis barbecue historically is pork, primarily the shoulder cut and the ribs, rather than beef. Today, Memphis Jews have made peace with barbecue and have embraced its distinctive regional taste. In the early 1990s, Orthodox congregation Anshei Sphard-Beth El Emeth launched the "world's only Kosher Barbecue Contest" in Memphis. The annual event celebrates barbecue varieties that a "higher power" could bless, including kosher beef ribs, brisket, and chicken. The involvement of Anshei Sphard-Beth El Emeth's congregants in the culture of barbecue reinforces their southernness. The event brings together all segments of the Jewish community of Memphis and strengthens both their Jewishness and their southern ties.

An equally significant development is under way at Jewish-owned Corky's, one of Memphis's most popular barbecue restaurants. Owners Barry and Don Pelts, longtime members of Memphis' Reform congregation Temple Israel, now sell a kosher version of their popular barbecue sauce, as well as kosher smoked turkeys and beef briskets, available in their restaurant and by mail-order. (To order the new products, you still must call their "treyf" number, 1-800-PIGSFLY.)

Are Jews becoming less Jewish because they live in the South and eat the same foods as other southerners? Is the South the "Sahara" of Jewish culture, to borrow a phrase from H. L. Mencken, who in 1920 described the region as a cultural and intellectual wasteland?[56] The answer is clearly no. Grits and barbecue did not lead southern Jews astray. Like Jews in other regions of the United States, Jews in the South developed an identity that enriches and expands our understanding of the American Jewish experience. Southern Jews embrace their ethnic and religious worlds through their food traditions—traditions that vary from one southern state to the next and from the low country to the Mississippi Delta.

Both kosher and nonkosher, both deeply southern and deeply Jewish, food traditions endure and are reinterpreted by each generation of southern Jewish cooks who mix regional flavors with Old World ingredients. The older generation of Jewish grandmothers and mothers preserve flavors that remind them of family, ancestral places, and historic memories. Contemporary Jewish southerners create spicier and healthy versions of old-style recipes. As the number of observant Jews grows in the urban South, the availability of kosher products is greater. Today, home cooks increasingly "kosherize" traditional southern recipes. They prepare kosher red beans and rice with kosher salami instead of pork sausage. There are new versions of traditional southern foods, such as Corky's Kosher Barbecue Sauce in Memphis. Another food "trend" to watch in the South is the emergence of young Jewish chefs, restaurateurs, and food professionals who are shaping the world of southern cuisine. These leaders include Karen Blockman Carrier at Another Roadside Attraction, a catering firm in Memphis; Laurence Gottlieb at Gottlieb's Restaurant and Dessert Bar in Savannah; and Dana Berlin Strange at Jestine's in Charleston.

Today's southern Jewish population is centered in cities such as Atlanta, New Orleans, and Memphis, but prior to the midtwentieth century, the southern Jewish experience was divided between rural communities and multiethnic ports such as Charleston and Savannah. Life in isolated rural worlds with a largely Christian white and black working-class population, as well as the rich ethnic melding of southern seaports strongly influenced southern Jewish cuisine. The heritage of Jewish southerners, their isolation, and their need to connect with each other made food especially important.

Food can be read like a book. When we open its pages in the Jewish South, we find stories set in rural and urban home kitchens, synagogues, social halls, grocery stores, and butcher shops that speak of the long and rich Jewish history of the region. We learn how food has connected southern and Jewish cultures, creating both bridges and divisions between Jews and their Gentile neighbors. Southern Jews, whether descendents of colonial families or twentieth-century urban transplants, appreciate their braided identity. Matzoh ball gumbo, peach kugel, and barbecued brisket evoke the multilayered, richly flavored worlds of the Jewish South.

NOTES

1. Jonathan D. Sarna, "American Judaism in Historical Perspective," David W. Belin Lecture in American Jewish Affairs (Ann Arbor, Mich.: The Jean and Samuel Frankel Center for Judaic Studies, 2003), 10. Sarna argues that what is distinctive in American Judaism has been largely shaped by Judaism's adaptation to a religious environment shaped by American Protestantism. He also identifies other pivotal factors, including "the canons of free market competition, the ideals of freedom, and the reality of diversity."

2. The origins of kashrut are found in the Bible, and further elucidated in the Talmud, the massive collection of oral traditions that interpret the Torah. The Torah usually refers to the first five books of the Bible: Genesis, Exodus, Leviticus, Numbers, and Deuteronomy.

3. Blu Greenberg, How to Run a Traditional Jewish Household (New York: Simon and Shuster, 1983), 95.

4. The range of Jewish views toward kashrut in the South affirms ethnographer Fredrik Barth's theory of ethnic boundaries. Barth argues that ethnic boundary maintenance and negotiation, rather than the survival of cultural traits, are central to the definition of ethnic groups. He believes that ethnic boundaries, rather than the "cultural stuff that it encloses" are the primary indicators of ethnicity and that maintenance of these boundaries is central to its persistence. Barth claims that ethnicity is about the "social organization of cultural difference." Foodways are perhaps the clearest measure of the ethnic boundaries of a group because the enjoyment and dislike of particular foods defines both in-group membership and outsider status. See Fredrik Barth, Ethnic Group and Boundaries: The Social Organization of Culture Difference (Prospect Heights, Ill.: Waveland Press, 1969), 6, 14–15.

5. Jenna Weissman Joselit, The Wonders of America: Reinventing Jewish Culture, 1880–1950 (New York: Hill and Wang, 1994), 173–74. Joselit defines kosher-style or selectively kosher as the "gastronomic equivalent of ethnicity." She explains that kosher-style allowed Jews to separate "food from the traditional restrictions governing its use."

6. Dale Rosengarten, telephone conversation with author, October 2003.

7. Christine Arpe Gang, e-mail to author, October 23, 2002.

8. Ann Romines, The Home Plot: Women Writers and Domestic Ritual (Amherst: University of Massachusetts Press, 1992), 12–15, 17. Romines examines the descriptions of housekeeping and cooking, what she describes as the "home plot," in the literature of women writers such as Eudora Welty, Sarah Orne Jewett, and Mary Wilkins Freeman and argues that this tradition of "writing domestic ritual" reveals the "essential rhythms of women's lives" and honors their obscured domestic history.

9. Ann Romines, "Reading the Cakes: Delta Wedding and the Texts of Southern Women's Culture," *Mississippi Quarterly* (Fall 1997): 7, 10. Community cookbooks published as fundraisers for women's organizations date back to the Christian Ladies Aid Societies and Sanitary Fairs of the Civil War.

10. Daisy Heller cookbook journal, Heller/Hutzler collection, Beth Ahabah Museum and Archives, Richmond, Va.

11. Ruth Abusch-Magder, "Eating 'Out': Food and the Boundaries of Jewish Community and Home in Germany and the United States," *Nashim* 5 (2002): 54–55. Abusch-Magder argues that once German Jews came to the United States, food "was used both to establish and to break connections."

12. David Hall uses the phrase *lived religion* to distinguish the study of actual daily practices from more traditional religious studies of formal religion that focus on the history of theology, the church, and the state. See David D. Hall, ed., *Lived Religion in America: Toward a History of Practice* (Princeton, N.J.: Princeton University Press, 1997), vi.

13. The Hebrew Ladies Benevolent Society, Diamond Jubilee, February 10, 1953, New Albany Hotel, New Albany, Ga., MSS 87, 1875–1985, William Breman Jewish Heritage Museum, Atlanta.

14. Mrs. Charles Moritz and Adele Kahn, *Every Woman's Cookbook* (New York: Cupples and Leon, 1926), 151 and 238.

15. Janet S. Theophano, *Eat My Words: Reading Women's Lives through the Cookbooks They Wrote* (New York: Palgrave, 2002), 182–88. Theophano examines these "home-produced" cookbooks and how these texts were expressions of women's literary imaginations. She explains that after the midnineteenth and into the twentieth century, the accessibility of inexpensive newspapers, magazines, and pamphlets gave women a wide breadth of material to add to their compiled cookbooks. These texts most resembled a "collage or scrapbook in which print and script were placed side by side." Readers and compilers of these books wrote marginalia near recipes, expressing their thoughts about a particular recipe or an opinion about a related issue.

16. Lynne Ireland, "The Compiled Cookbook as Foodways Autobiography," in *The Taste of American Place: A Reader on Regional and Ethnic Foods*, ed. Barbara G. Shortridge and James R. Shortridge (Lanham, Md.: Rowman and Littlefield Publishers, 1998), 112. Ireland argues that the compiled cookbook can be viewed as "foodways autobiography" that reveals information about the author(s), food preferences, "taboo foods," holidays and special occasions, ethnicity, and assimilation.

See also Charles Camp, *American Foodways: What, When, Why, and How We Eat in America*, The American Folklore Series, W. K. McNeil, ed. (Little Rock, Ark.: August House, 1989), 99. Camp emphasizes the importance and poignancy of these sources: "A cook's records are the records of how regularly social worlds—special occasions, friends, family—and the world of food—recipes, instructions, mementoes—converge, and how much the records of one world stand for the other." He notes the "wholeness" of these collections, the overlap of holiday recipes and souvenirs, recipes from friends and the local newspaper, and their juxtaposition of private and public worlds.

17. George Tindall, *Natives and Newcomers: Ethnic Southerners and Southern Ethnics* (Athens: University of Georgia Press, 1995), 23.

18. Dale Rosengarten, telephone conversation with author, October 2003.

19. Eli N. Evans, *The Provincials: A Personal History of Jews in the South* (New York: Free Press, 1997), 304.

20. Interview with Windsor Jordan by Marcie C. Ferris, August 22, 2001, in the Southern Oral History Program Collection (#4007), Southern Historical Collection, Wilson Library, University of North Carolina at Chapel Hill.

21. David M. Katzman, *Seven Days a Week: Women and Domestic Service in Industrializing America* (New York: Oxford University Press, 1978), 72, 74.

22. John T. Edge, *Southern Belly: The Ultimate Food Lover's Companion to the South* (Athens, Ga.: Hill Street Press, 2000), 151. Edge explains that "cumback sauce" originated in Jackson, Mississippi, in the 1930s at a local Greek seafood restaurant and then was copied by other Greek restaurants and cafés in the city.

23. "At Mildred's Table," Commemorative Program, Newcomb College Center for Research on Women, New Orleans, April 1, 2004.

24. Quoted in Susan Strasser, *Satisfaction Guaranteed: The Making of the American Mass Market* (Washington, D.C.: Smithsonian Institution Press, 1989), 14. Crisco was pronounced kosher by Rabbi Lifsitz of Cincinnati and Rabbi Margolies of New York. It was Margolies, according to "The Story of Crisco," who coined the phrase about the Hebrew race.

25. Andrew R. Heinze, *Adapting to Abundance: Jewish Immigrants, Mass Consumption, and the Search for American Identity* (New York: Columbia University Press, 1990), 54–55.

26. John Egerton, *Southern Food: At Home, on the Road, in History* (New York: Alfred A. Knopf, 1987), 38. According to Egerton, "serving large quantities of good things to eat to large numbers of hungry people, of sharing food and drink with family and friends and strangers, proved to be a durable tradition in the South, outliving war and depression and hunger."

27. Interview with Rabbi Arnold Belzer by Marcie C. Ferris, October 13, 2001, in the Southern Oral History Program Collection (#4007), Southern Historical Collection, Wilson Library, University of North Carolina at Chapel Hill.

28. Ballyhoo was a weekend of socializing for southern Jewish youth (primarily families of German Jewish origin) that took place in Atlanta from the 1930s through the 1950s. See Alfred Uhry's play that examines a Jewish family in 1939 Atlanta, in which the impending Ballyhoo weekend reveals social tensions in the Jewish South. Alfred Uhry, *The Last Night of Ballyhoo* (New York: Theatre Communication Group, 1997).

29. Eli Faber, *A Time for Planting: The First Migration, 1654–1820* (Baltimore: Johns Hop-

kins University Press, 1992), 50. Faber explains that the colonial congregations depended on one another both for the financial resources needed to build new synagogues, as well as for salaried Jewish professionals, such as mohels, hazzans, and shohet, who were frequently shared by Jewish communities. Charleston's ties to Jewish communities around the Atlantic were so strong that when Congregation Beth Elohim created a board of trustees for their new cemetery in 1765, they appointed men from congregations in New York, Newport, Savannah, and Jamaica.

30. Kaye Kole, *The Minis Family of Georgia, 1733–1992* (Savannah: Georgia Historical Society, 1992), 8–9.

31. Ibid., 9. See also Saul Jacob Rubin, *Third to None: The Saga of Savannah Jewry, 1733–1983* (Savannah: S. J. Rubin, 1983), 82; and Holly Snyder, "A Sense of Place: Jews, Identity and Social Status in Colonial British America, 1654–1831" (Ph.D. diss., Brandeis University, 2000), 334–37, for additional discussion of Abigail Minis.

32. Kole, *The Minis Family*, 15.

33. See Edward A. Chappell, "Housing a Nation: The Transformation of Living Standards in Early America," in *Of Consuming Interest*, ed. Cary Carson (Charlottesville: University Press of Virginia, 1994), 167, for a discussion of the consumer revolution in eighteenth-century America.

34. Quoted in Holly Snyder, "Queens of the Household: The Jewish Women of British America, 1700–1800," in *Women and American Judaism: Historical Perspectives*, ed. Pamela S. Nadell and Jonathan D. Sarna (Hanover, N.H.: University Press of New England, 2001) 30.

35. Chappell, "Housing a Nation," 168.

36. Theodore Rosengarten and Dale Rosengarten, eds., *A Portion of the People: Three Hundred Years of Southern Jewish Life* (Columbia: University of South Carolina Press, 2002), 88.

37. Joan Nathan, *An American Folklife Cookbook* (New York: Schocken Books, 1984) 271. Nathan identifies cold lemon-stew fish as one of the oldest recipes among Charleston's Jewish community, coming from its Sephardic Jewish settlers.

38. The concept of "southern" as an ethnic designation was developed by John Shelton Reed, who described a persistent "southern-ness" and labeled the South a "quasi-ethnic" regional group. See John Shelton Reed, *One South: An Ethnic Approach to Regional Culture* (Baton Rouge: Louisiana State University Press, 1982), 5.

39. Egerton, *Southern Food*, 110–11, 278. Egerton says that the word *gumbo* is derived from an African term for okra, the base of such stews made in New Orleans from the early nineteenth century to the present. Bill Neal explains that while seafood gumbos are most typical, there are many versions of gumbo in the South to which are added chicken, turkey, duck, ham, sausage, and venison. The staple ingredients are the "holy trinity of Cajun cooking: onions, peppers, and celery," and a butter-and-flour-enriched roux that thickens the mix. See Bill Neal, *Southern Cooking* (Chapel Hill: University of North Carolina Press, 1985), 15–16. According to Gwendolyn Midlo Hall, the word *gumbo* means

okra in Bambara and in many other African languages. See Gwendolyn Midlo Hall, *Africans in Colonial Louisiana: The Development of Afro-Creole Culture in the Eighteenth Century* (Baton Rouge: Louisiana State University Press, 1992), 188.

40. Jessica B. Harris, *Beyond Gumbo: Creole Fusion Food from the Atlantic Rim* (New York: Simon and Schuster, 2003), 8.

41. Solomon quoted in ibid., 29, 46, 67, 233, 295, 325, 326, 328, 353, 363, 383.

42. Isaac J. Levy letter to Leonora E. Levy, Adams Run, S.C., April 24, 1864, Amy Hart Stewart papers, SC-12013, 1864–1916, American Jewish Archives, Cincinnati, Ohio.

43. Michael Wayne, *The Reshaping of Plantation Society: The Natchez District, 1860–80.* (Urbana: University of Illinois Press, 1983), 151.

44. Lee Stamler, *From Gumbo to Matzo Balls: A Cookbook and an Autobiography* (Traveler's Rest, S.C.: privately printed, 1997), 2–3. Evelyn Vessier was converted to Judaism by Rabbi Eli Leipziger of Touro Synagogue in New Orleans. He oversaw her conversion on March 19, 1922, and conducted the marriage ceremony for Evelyn and Leon Geismar the next day. See interview with Florette Geismar Margolis Neuwirth by Marcie C. Ferris, October 24, 2001, in the Southern Oral History Program Collection (#4007), Southern Historical Collection, Wilson Library, University of North Carolina at Chapel Hill.

45. Jackie Pressner Gothard, interview with Mildred L. Covert, May 8, 2001, Newcomb College Center for Research on Women, New Orleans.

46. Regina Rousso Tourial, interviews with Patty Maziar, May–July 1989, Jewish Oral History Project of Atlanta, William Breman Jewish Heritage Museum, Atlanta.

47. Emily Benbenisty Amato and Regina Rousso Tourial interviews, May–July 1989, Jewish Oral History Project of Atlanta, William Breman Jewish Heritage Museum, Atlanta.

48. Interview with Jeanette Arogeti by Marcie Cohen Ferris, August 21, 2001, in the Southern Oral History Program Collection (#4007), Southern Historical Collection, University of North Carolina at Chapel Hill.

49. Rabbi David Geffen, telephone interview with author, Scranton, Pa. January 9, 2002. See also Joel Ziff, *Lev Tuviah: On the Life and Work of Rabbi Tobias Geffen* (Newton, Mass.: Rabbi Tobias Geffen Memorial Fund, 1988), 117, 121.

50. Segal's Kosher Delicatessen advertisement, the *Hebrew Watchman*, Memphis, March 30, 1928; Halpern's Kosher Snack Shop advertisement, *Hebrew Watchman*, Memphis, December 12, 1946; Rosen's Kosher Delicatessen, advertisements for Dalsheimer's Brothers and Albert Seessel and Son, in *Jewish Spectator*, Memphis, 1885–1908, 23rd anniversary ed.

51. As a response to these changing demographics and the decline of small-town congregations in the region, the Museum of the Southern Jewish Experience was founded in Utica, Mississippi, in 1986. The museum preserves, interprets, and documents southern Jewish life through exhibits, public programs, publications, historic preservation, and community outreach. Today the museum is operated under the aus-

pices of the Goldring/Woldenberg Institute of Southern Jewish Life. The institute includes twelve southern states: Alabama, Arkansas, Georgia, Kentucky, Louisiana, Mississippi, North Carolina, Oklahoma, South Carolina, Tennessee, Texas, and Virginia. See http://www.msje.org.

52. Jennifer Stollman, "We're Still Here: Delta Jewish Women in the Twentieth Century," lecture, Southern Jewish Historical Society Annual Conference, Memphis, November 1, 2003.

53. Selma S. Lewis, A Biblical People in the Bible Belt: The Jewish Community of Memphis, Tennessee, 1840s–1960s (Macon, Ga.: Mercer University Press, 1998), 73.

54. Ibid., 75. Rosen's Kosher Delicatessen advertisement, 291 N. Main Street, Memphis, Hebrew Watchman, August 10, 1939. Rosen's was founded in 1905 by Frieda and Herman Rosen. Their daughter, Fannie, and her husband, Sam Goldstein, operated the deli in later years. See Marcia Levy and Lynnie Mirvis, "Kosher and Kosher-Style Restaurants and Delis in Memphis," Plough Towers Golden Cookbook, vol. 1; Albert Seessel and Son advertisement, 248 N. Main Street, Memphis, in Jewish Spectator, 23rd anniversary ed., 1885–1908; Goldstein's Delicatessen advertisement, 311 N. Main Street, Memphis, Hebrew Watchman, March 14, 1929; Miner's Kosher Delicatessen, 320 N. Main Street, Memphis, Hebrew Watchman, February 14, 1929.

55. Segal's Kosher Delicatessen advertisement, 171 S. Second Street, Memphis, Hebrew Watchman, May 31, 1929.

56. In his 1920 essay, "The Sahara of the Bozart," published in his work, Prejudices, Second Series, H. L. Mencken claimed the South, once the "American seat of civilization," had become a cultural and intellectual desert. Mencken believed that "poor white trash" had replaced the Anglo-Saxon elites of the antebellum South, and with this change, artistic and intellectual cultures in the South disappeared. See Fred Hobson, Serpent in Eden: H. L. Mencken and the South (Baton Rouge: Louisiana State University Press, 1995), 14–15; James T. Farrell, introduction to Prejudices: A Selection, by H. L. Mencken (Baltimore: Johns Hopkins University Press, 1996), xvii, 70.

11

JEWISH ANTIQUES ROADSHOW
RELIGION AND DOMESTIC CULTURE
IN THE AMERICAN SOUTH

DALE ROSENGARTEN

There was no room for a sukkah in the backyard of the Sholk family's apartment in Charleston, South Carolina, in 1925, so Harry Sholk erected a miniature one for his daughter, Mary, in the dining room.[1] A perfect example of the creole traditions that characterize the American Jewish South, the tiny sukkah had Gothic windows and rough wooden rafters hung with fake fruit, and the family outfitted the structure with dollhouse furniture, porcelain figurines, and a tiny tea set complete with candlesticks. After Mary Sholk married Irvin "Dunny" Zalkin, a son of Charleston's kosher butcher, they and their three daughters continued to decorate the sukkah each autumn. In place of the palm branches Charlestonians traditionally lay on their sukkahs, the Sholks and Zalkins topped theirs with green pine needles and Christmas three lights, the only lights available.

The dollhouse sukkah, along with its layers of meaning, arrived at the doorstep of the Jewish Heritage Collection at the College of Charleston just in time to be included in the 2002–2003 exhibition, "A Portion of the People: Three Hundred Years of Southern Jewish Life," which had been launched by the College of Charleston, McKissick Museum at the University of South Carolina, and a new grassroots organization, the Jewish Historical Society of South Carolina, to collect, preserve, and exhibit artifacts and archival material illustrating Jewish life in the American South.

Early in the project we circulated a brochure entitled "A Call for Candlesticks," asking people to search their attics, drawers, albums, and memories for items representing their families' experiences as southern Jews. The photograph on the cover of the brochure shows a pair of candlesticks from Knyszyn, Poland, belonging to Sophie and Allan Sindler of Camden, South Carolina, with partly burned candles still in their holders. Exhibition curators are always on the lookout for icons—objects whose worth lies not in their market value, but in their associations and in the stories people tell about them. Shabbat candlesticks are just such emblems. Universal symbols of women's role in Jewish custom and ceremony, they conjure up the image of a beloved mother, hands shielding her eyes, welcoming the Sabbath into the home. This is tenderly expressed in a passage written by my great-uncle Szaie Katzovitch, from Kryvitsh, Poland, sole survivor of a large family murdered by the Nazis.

> Sabbath eve, my mother, may she rest in peace, would bless the candles in five brass candlesticks. Before this, of course, would be the regimen of cleaning and polishing, in order to get the brass to gleam. She would rub two bricks together to obtain a kind of brick powder, which was a wonderful polishing agent. When I got back home [from the candle maker] . . . , my mother was ready: Dressed in her long Sabbath gown with a new cloth on her head, her face clean and shining with a joyous light in her eyes—all finished with her hard day's work. The floors had been swept and covered with clean yellow sand, everything in the house was immaculate. Her hands shielding her eyes, she recited the blessing over the candles. For all of us children, it became Sabbath at that moment.[2]

For observant Jews, candles signify joy, spirituality, life, and its passing. A yahrzeit candle burns for twenty-four hours on the anniversary of a death; a broken candle represents a life cut short. Because they were commonly carried to America by Jewish immigrants and are so durable, candlesticks have come to symbolize the travails of the Old World, arduous journeys to new lands, and the tenacity of family ties. Tracing their origins tells us where people came from—England, Germany, Poland, Lithuania, Russia, the Ukraine—and helps piece together a map of the Diaspora.

Consider two small candlesticks that came to rest in Helen Silver's cupboard in Charleston. Their story begins in Lithuania, where they belonged to Helen's great-aunt Lena Berke, who fled her homeland before World War I. Instead of traveling west across Europe to attempt an Atlantic passage to America, Lena went east, crossed Siberia, and boarded a ship in Japan bound for California. On arrival she weighed eighty pounds—her sister fainted when she saw her. Lena had tucked the brass candlesticks, a mere three inches tall, in her knapsack. A hundred years later, the tale of their travels still stirs strong emotions.

In the first half of the twentieth century, Jewish museums framed their mission narrowly. Judaism was interpreted as a religion, comparable to Protestantism or Catholicism, and exhibitions typically featured ritual objects or fine art. Jewish museums increased in number in the 1970s and 1980s, alongside scores of institutions such as the Afro-American Historical and Cultural Museum in Philadelphia, the Swedish-American Museum in Chicago, and the Museum of Chinese American History in Los Angeles. The new "ethnic museums," founded in the wake of the civil rights movement, helped a generation of hyphenated-Americans discover and reclaim their identities.[3] In the forefront of this trend, curators at Jewish museums began to redefine their objectives. They saw their role less as keepers of Judaica and more as social historians exploring the lives of ordinary people. High culture made way for material culture, which offered a more democratic approach to the past.

Material culture, formerly the domain of anthropologists, has in the past forty years dramatically affected other scholarly disciplines, including history, art, folklore, and women's studies. Objects found in daily life reveal a great deal about how people construct their identities. A generation of historians sympathetic to women, the working poor, and people of color found in the study of material culture, as in oral history, an effective way to give voice to the unwritten and poorly documented stories of the underrepresented majority.

Meanwhile, a renaissance of regionalism enriched the new wave of ethnic studies. Eli N. Evans's *The Provincials: A Personal History of Jews in the South* (1973) signaled a shift from the discussion of Jews as Americans to Jews who were southerners, midwesterners, Californians, and down-easters. In the case of those ubiquitous candlesticks, do any tell a *southern* story? Photographer Bill Aron captured a striking still life in Cary, Mississippi: a pair of Shabbat candles sits to the right of a kiddush cup and two loaves of challah on a cloth-draped table. Behind the table a window looks out onto a field of cotton that stretches to the horizon.[4] The juxtaposition seems at once startling and plausible, its power derived from the viewers' recognition of candlesticks and cotton as iconic symbols, emblematic of two cultures—Jewish and southern—that are seldom linked in the mind's eye.

Some candlesticks come with a more complex and specific story, rooted in a particular time and place. In the colonial era, the port of Charleston was an attractive destination for Jewish tradesmen. A number of merchant families grew wealthy enough to pass into the landowning gentry. Isaiah Moses, born in Bremerhaven in the Kingdom of Hanover, came to America before 1800 and for the next dozen years was listed in the Charleston directory as a "grocer" or "shopkeeper." In 1813, he purchased The Oaks at Goose Creek, a 794-acre rice plantation. That same year, his wife of six years, Rebecca Phillips, received a pair of candlesticks inscribed with her married initials, RJM. Silversmith John Settle designed the English Sheffield candlesticks in the neoclassical or federal style

Rebecca Isaiah Moses, née Phillips (1792–1872), painted by C. W. Uhl, Charleston, South Carolina, 1843. Oil on canvas, 38½ × 34 inches. Private collection. Photo courtesy of Special Collections, College of Charleston Library.

characterized by decorative elements such as parallel ridges, swags, and beads. Made in 1792, the year of Rebecca's birth, the objects bear much of their history in their inscriptions. The initials of subsequent owners with their dates of acquisition are also engraved on the candlesticks.[5]

Rebecca Isaiah Moses must have lit candles in these candlesticks every Shabbat. Religious traditionalists, she and Isaiah were among those who seceded from Kahal Kadosh Beth Elohim in 1840 when the congregation voted forty-six to forty to install an organ in the new synagogue building.[6] The Moses' son-in-law, Jacob Rosenfeld, became first hazzan (religious leader) of the breakaway congregation, Shearit Israel, a bastion of Old World values in what Orthodox Jews perceived as a dangerous reform environment. Apart from their religious meaning, Rebecca's candlesticks were tokens of wealth and gracious living that could have adorned the table of any member of Carolina's landed elite. The Moses family's genealogy is literally writ on the square bases of these treasured objects.

"A Call for Candlesticks" was a metaphor for a much broader search. We hoped to find a range of objects that immigrants carried from the old country, and indeed, samovars, musical instruments, a carpenter's plane, a shoemaker's certificate, a cigarette case engraved with a Russian village scene, and (most unexpected) a set of *bankas*, or medicinal cups, did turn up. Everyday objects associated with the newcomers' struggle to make a living—a kosher butcher's knife,

Candlesticks belonging to Rebecca Isaiah Moses, made by John Settle, England, 1792.
Silver, 12½ × 5 × 5 inches. Private collection. Photo courtesy of Special Collections,
College of Charleston Library.

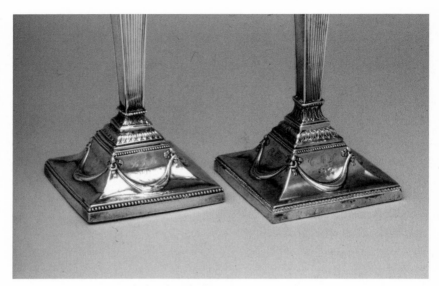

Detail of candlesticks showing inscriptions of owners.
Note "R.I.M. 1813" in the base of the candlestick on the left.

a sign for a dry goods store, a cash register, a hat maker's mannequin—were relatively easy to come by. But a peddler's pack, at the top of our priority list, eluded us entirely.

The artifacts that most strongly evoke the South were heirlooms passed down in Jewish families who had lived in South Carolina for generations. Portraits, inscribed silver, colonial charters, surveyors' plats, prenuptial agreements on parchment, manuscript prayer books, ritual objects, textiles—a wealth of fine and decorative art represents the affluence and remarkable degree of inclusion Jews enjoyed in southern society. Southerners and Jews alike take genealogy seriously. For both, the record of descent from the ancestors provides evidence of belonging to the tribe and establishes a pedigree. For Jews, genealogy has an additional appeal. The concept of an afterlife, so vivid to Christians, is only vaguely delineated in Jewish theology. You live on by living in memory. The Old Testament list of begats is not merely a device for recording lineage but a way of remembering the dead.

Apart from her inscribed candlesticks, Rebecca Moses was involved in creating an extraordinary piece of domestic art—an album quilt made for Eleanor Israel Solomons, née Joseph (1794–1856), the mother of one of Rebecca's sons-in-law. Composed of sixty-three blocks, the quilt front is pieced and appliquéd chintz and calico on muslin. Sewn between the years 1851 and 1854, the handiwork was organized by Eleanor's sister Charlotte Joseph, as Eleanor prepared to

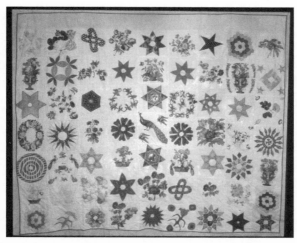

Album quilt made for Eleanor Israel Solomons, née Joseph (1794–1856), various contributors, blocks fabricated 1851–54. Pieced and appliquéd chintz and calico on muslin, 102 × 113 inches. Private collection. Photo courtesy of Special Collections, College of Charleston Library.

move from South Carolina to Savannah, Georgia. Women and girls, family members and friends, each sewed a block, inscribed (perhaps by Eleanor herself) with the maker's name, date, and sometimes her place of residence.[7] The youngest contributor to Eleanor's quilt was Cecilia Solomons, the six-year-old granddaughter of both Eleanor and Rebecca.

The majority of contributors were Jewish, but besides their names nothing in the quilt design or motifs suggests religious affiliation. Even the eight six-pointed stars sewn onto the muslin were not specifically symbolic of Judaism in this era. Making album or friendship quilts was a genteel pastime for middle- and upper-class white women in America in the first half of the nineteenth century. Baltimore emerged as the epicenter of the album quilt craze. As its popularity spread, regional variations developed. Eleanor Solomons's quilt combines the red-and-green geometric and floral appliqué fashionable in the mid-Atlantic and southeastern states in the 1840s and 1850s, mixed with an earlier style of bouquets, wreaths, vases, and birds cut from printed English chintz and stitched onto the fabric.[8]

Like Rebecca Moses's candlesticks, Eleanor's quilt can be "read" quite literally. The inscriptions written or stitched onto each block function as autographs in an album, reminding the recipient of loved ones near and far. Taken as a whole, the quilt constitutes a map of Eleanor Solomons's social circle (women only), centered in Georgetown and Charleston, South Carolina, and extending

Detail of album quilt showing block inscribed "My Servant Rinah."
Rinah was a slave of the Solomons family.

north to Poughkeepsie, New York, and south to Savannah. One block on the quilt marks it as unmistakably southern. Penned beneath a seven-pointed sea-green star are the words "My servant Rinah." The piece was appliquéd by an enslaved mulatto woman who had nursed the Solomons children. While documents in the family archives list Rinah and her children as property pledged for Eleanor's bridal trust and as collateral on loans Israel struggled to repay, Rinah's block in the album quilt suggests that a bond of affection and familial feeling might have coexisted with the bond of servitude between mistress and slave.

Eleanor's quilt is a southern artifact not because album quilts were a southern convention but because this one alludes to the South's "peculiar institution" of slavery. Similarly, a silver rice spoon engraved with the Lazarus family monogram symbolizes the owners' place in a society built on the cultivation of rice. Adapted from oversize English stuffing spoons, rice spoons served the grain that produced great wealth for low country planters and merchants and fed Carolinians of all ranks. As slave owners, as furnishers of supplies to planters who made their money from "Carolina Gold"—the popular name for the variety of rice grown in the low country—and as citizens eager to assimilate, the Lazaruses took part in the general culture to the fullest extent possible.

With their Sephardic roots and Revolutionary ancestor (duly noted in Malcolm Stern's compendium of American Jewish first families), the Lazaruses be-

Kiddush cup of Aaron Lazarus, Tiffany, ca. 1850. Silver, 8 × 3¼ × 3¼ inches. Lazarus family rice spoon, ca. 1830. Silver, 2¼ × 12 inches. Lazarus family cake knife, attributed to Wood and Hughes, New York, ca. 1850. Silver, 1¾ × 12½ inches. Private collection. Photo courtesy of Special Collections, College of Charleston Library.

longed to Charleston society.[9] Like their Christian counterparts, they were prominent in "church" affairs. The first Michael Lazarus was secretary of Beth Elohim in 1749, when the congregation first organized. His son, Marks, fought in the American Revolution with Lushington's militia, an outfit known as the "Jews' Company" because of the number of Jewish men in the troop. In 1820, Marks Lazarus was elected to Beth Elohim's conservative governing body. Marks's son, Michael, introduced steam navigation on the Savannah River, and—in opposition to his father—joined the leadership of the Reformed Society of Israelites. A younger son, Joshua, brought gas lighting to the city of Charleston and supported reform at Beth Elohim. He served as congregation president from 1850 to 1861.[10] As late as 1987, a Lazarus family descendant occupied this prestigious post.[11]

Writing in the *Occident and American Jewish Advocate* in July 1843, Rabbi Isaac Leeser of Philadelphia called his readers' attention to an address that Nathaniel Levin had delivered a year before to the "Society for the Instruction of Jewish Youth in Charleston, S.C.," in which he expressed appreciation for the creative power of women. Although women's roles may be confined to the home, Leeser observed, their influence extended through their husbands and sons, fathers and brothers, to the wider world.

"Not by the force of eloquence and strength," wrote Leeser, but by their "sway over the domestic hearth," women made their authority felt. "As mothers they can instruct from early childhood till the son or daughter leaves the paternal roof . . . as sisters they can chide and reprove, praise and encourage . . . as daughters they can perhaps open the heart of an obdurate parent to his sinfulness . . . and lastly, as wives, they can urge and entreat the object of their dearest affection to ponder over a course of sin."[12]

In assessing the role of women chiefly in relation to men, Leeser was engaged in wishful thinking. Certainly women served as helpmates to the men in their lives, but they also wielded power in their own right as intellectuals, educators, writers, and religious innovators. Caroline de Litchfield Harby, sister of Charleston journalist and teacher Isaac Harby, assumed the role of "Little Mother" to his six children on the untimely death of his wife, Rachael. "She was a very small and beautiful young woman of great intelligence," one memoirist recalled, and "refused several fine offers of marriage in order to continue the charge of her brother's orphaned children."[13] Yet her contribution to Isaac Harby's cause—the Reformed Society of Israelites—went well beyond her domestic duties. Caroline composed a prayer for the Sabbath that Harby included in his manuscript prayer book, which the reformers adopted in 1830.

Southern Jewish women put a high premium on education and were well represented among writers and diarists. Penina Moïse (1797–1880), sister of Isaac Harby's protégé Abraham Moïse Jr., published regularly in newspapers and journals in Charleston, Boston, and New Orleans, sometimes signing her poems "M. P." A volume of her poetry entitled *Fancy's Sketch Book* appeared in 1833. In 1842, dozens of her hymns were printed in Beth Elohim's hymnal, the first published by a Jewish congregation in America.[14] Like many women writers, she did not make a living from her craft but supported herself by sewing lace and embroidery. Apart from Moïse's published work, at least two manuscript poems survive, as well as two sets of cards she used as didactic tools in the classroom.[15] A portrait of Moïse, circa 1840, survives today, and her looking glass hangs on the wall of a family descendant.

Moïse dedicated *Fancy's Sketch Book* to "The Misses Pinckney," Maria Henrietta and Harriott, daughters of Charles Cotesworth Pinckney, her friends and possibly her patrons. The commingling of upper-class Protestants and Jews struck astute observers such as Mary Boykin Chesnut as characteristic of the South, and yet peculiar. "Elsewhere Jews may be tolerated," Chesnut remarks in her famous Civil War journals. "Here they are haute volée" (from *être de la première*

Penina Moïse (1797–1880), attributed to Theodore Sidney Moïse, ca. 1840. Oil on canvas,
30 × 26 inches. Private collection. Photo courtesy of Special Collections,
College of Charleston Library.

volée [to be of the first water, of high rank]). In her diary entries she reports hobnobbing with members of the elite Cohen, DeLeon, and Lyons families. "Everybody has their own Jew exceptions," she explains. "I have two—Mem Cohen, Agnes DeLeon. Mary Preston has her Rachel Lyons."[16] Miriam DeLeon (Mem) Cohen and Mary Chesnut were closest friends, and both were aware that their relationship was exceptional. "You despise a Jew in your heart," Chesnut quotes Cohen. "Don't answer—I know you do. You like me," Mem declares, "but that is in spite of my being one."[17]

Like Chesnut's commentary, which was not confined to so-called women's interests but crossed into the male-dominated political world of her husband, Senator James Chesnut, Penina Moïse's sympathies knew no boundaries. Champion of many causes, she wrote fervently on the plight of the Irish during the famine of the 1840s, on religious intolerance in England, and on the persecution of Jews in Damascus, Syria. After the Civil War, she and her sister Rachel Levy and Rachel's daughter Jacqueline returned to Charleston from refuge in Sumter, South Carolina, and opened a secular school for girls on Queen Street. Moïse's teaching methods were based on a pedagogy known as "Magnall's Questions." Every Friday afternoon her students played the game "Facts for You and Me," drawn from geography, history, antiquities, and biblical events. To keep physically and mentally fit, Moïse, who suffered from neuralgia, exercised daily by walking around her bed. She would choose a letter from the alphabet and call out the cities, mountains, rivers, historical figures, and literary characters whose names began with the letter. The next day she would select another letter and again walked a mile around her bed until she had exhausted her subject.[18]

Educating the rising generation was a task that traditionalists like Levin and Leeser situated squarely in the sphere of the "Jewish female." Levin praised Sally Lopez, who in 1838 founded Beth Elohim's Sabbath school along the model of Rebecca Gratz and shared lessons with her Philadelphia colleague.[19] He failed to acknowledge, however, the influence of Reform leaders such as Caroline Harby and Penina Moïse, whose "force of eloquence" did indeed influence Jewish religious life.[20] Both women in their own ways discovered avenues for spiritual expression and created places for themselves in the synagogue. They were part of a vanguard that, inspired by their Protestant peers, started benevolent societies, Sunday schools, and later, sisterhoods, seizing the reins of religious education and establishing organizations that operated in the public realm.[21]

Neither Caroline Harby nor Penina Moïse ever married. Isabel Rebecca Lyons Mordecai (1804–95), on the other hand, fulfilled the conventional roles of wife and mother expected of a white woman. Her portrait, painted around 1835 by Penina Moïse's nephew, Theodore Sidney Moïse, shows a dark-eyed beauty,

Isabel Rebecca Lyons Mordecai (Mrs. Moses Cohen Mordecai) (1804–95), painted by Theodore Sidney Moïse (1808–85), United States, ca. 1835. Oil on canvas, 38 × 33 inches. Private collection. Photo courtesy of Special Collections, College of Charleston Library.

head resting on hand, elegantly dressed in a soft grey gown and lace blouse, her collar tied snugly around her neck with a yellow bow. At age twenty-four, she married Moses Cohen Mordecai, a state senator and shipping tycoon, and bore eight children. In an 1848 portrait of her husband's flagship, by Edward McGregor, the name Isabel waves on a banner at the top of the mainmast.[22]

At every turn, Isabel Mordecai's biography reveals far-reaching integration into elite society. In cities, towns, and the countryside, southern Jews felt in harmony with the pursuits and pastimes of their white Gentile neighbors. Isabel's legacy also demonstrates a basic truth about material culture. A portrait, a journal, a prayer book, a volume of poetry, or a painting of a ship may be valuable for its artistry and for the information it conveys about when and where it was created. As an heirloom, however, its worth derives from the *relationships* it signifies. An object embodies attachments to people and loyalties to family, place, time, and cause. A single sheet of paper, a bound volume filled with spidery script, a collection of poems published posthumously by children or grandchildren— such "literary" objects often are the first things people reach for when they have to leave a place in a hurry, and the last thing they hold on to at the end of their days.

Isabel Mordecai, the only daughter among Isaac and Rachel Cohen Lyons's six children, watched in grief as three of her brothers died of consumption within two years. Some twenty years later, her son, David Henry Mordecai, also succumbed to tuberculosis. Between 1849 and 1859, David filled several volumes with observations of his travels abroad and commentary on politics, Judaism, and the institution of slavery. Isabel kept a travel diary of her own, fragments of which remain. She wrote poems and, in an exquisite hand, copied poetry she admired into a journal.[23] But what she will be remembered for best are the volumes she salvaged from the Civil War—her son's journals and the diary of her brother Joseph.[24]

A text that survives the vicissitudes of life ultimately tells two stories: one read on the page and another pieced together from myriad sources, the tale of its migrations to the present day. The survival of Joseph Lyons's diary was by no means assured. It saw "action" in the Civil War and for a time fell into Union hands, seized as booty or perhaps merely perused by a Yankee soldier one night in a house in Columbia, South Carolina, occupied by federal troops. Immediately below Joseph's last entry, under the dateline "Camp Columbia South Carolina United States forces," are drawings and words written in a different hand. Private Commodore Perry Malone of the 70th Ohio Veterans Volunteer Infantry signed his name, recorded General W. T. Sherman's chain of command, and noted his birthdate "in the year of our Lord, 1839," coincidentally the same year that Joseph Lyons died. Somehow the diary was returned to his sister, and the volume descended in the family to Isabel's grandson, historian and genealogist Thomas Jefferson Tobias.[25]

Southern Jews shared the prevailing commitment to the cause of southern independence. Even reluctant secessionists such as M. C. Mordecai, who preferred to save the Union than to form a separate country, embraced the war once the battle began. The South had been good to Jews, and their sympathies were not surprising. The Reverend Max J. Michelbacher, rabbi of Beth Ahabah Congregation (House of Love), in Richmond, Virginia, appealed to the Almighty to be a protector to "the Army of the Confederacy, as thou were of old, unto us."[26] After the war, white southerners, both Jew and Gentile, continued to express their political allegiance with religious fervor. Jews articulated a variation on the "Religion of the Lost Cause." In the words of Jonathan Sarna, they "employed biblical metaphors of catastrophe, sanctified regional values and cultural symbols rooted in the old Confederacy, and imagined themselves to be divinely chosen as southerners *and* as Jews."[27] Consider the testimony of four Jewish women from South Carolina who produced graphic accounts of their experiences during the Civil War—three avid Confederates, Phoebe Yates Pember, Eleanor Cohen, and Octavia Harby Moses, and one, Septima Levy Collis, who watched from behind enemy lines.

Phoebe Pember grew up Phoebe Levy on East Bay Street in Charleston. Born in 1823, she was the fourth of seven children of Jacob Clavius Levy and Fanny Yates Levy. The family was well-to-do. Her grandfather had been president of Beth Elohim and a founder of Scottish Rite Masonry in Charleston, and her father treasurer of the congregation and a member of the Reformed Society of Israelites. Widowed in 1861 when her husband Thomas Pember died of tuberculosis, Phoebe stayed for a time with her parents, who were then refugees in Marietta, Georgia. With encouragement from Mary Elizabeth Adams Randolph, wife of Confederate Secretary of War George Randolph, Phoebe Pember sought a way to serve the cause.[28]

During the war, Pember was as close to the battle as any woman could be. The first female administrator of Chimborazo hospital outside Richmond, Pember endured the resentment of male army doctors and stewards, who were unused to a woman in a position of authority. In the three years she worked at the hospital, seventy-six thousand sick and wounded soldiers passed through. When Richmond was evacuated in 1865, she stayed at her post even after the male nurses fled and the slave cooks defected. She followed her patients as they were removed to another hospital and remained until "the sick were either convalescent or dead, and at last my vocation was gone."[29]

Although Pember's war diary is preserved only in its published form, about 150 items of her correspondence can be found in the Southern Historical Collection at the University of North Carolina. In a letter to her sister Eugenia, dated September 13, 1863, she rejoiced that as a Jew she was not required to turn the other cheek. "At last I lifted my voice," Pember wrote, "and congratulated myself at being born of a nation, and religion that did not enjoin forgiveness on its enemies, that enjoyed the blessed privilege of praying for an eye for an eye, and a life for a life, and was not one of those for whom Christ died in vain, considering the present state of feeling." The extent to which she practiced Judaism is not known, but she proposed to her Christian friends "that till the war was over they should all join the Jewish Church, let forgiveness and peace and good will alone and put their trust in the sword of the Lord and Gideon."[30]

No less a fire-eater was Eleanor H. Cohen, daughter of Charleston pharmacist Philip Melvin Cohen and Cordelia Moïse Cohen. When the port city came under siege, the family fled to Columbia, where they witnessed Sherman's arrival on February 16, 1865. As fire engulfed the capital and the inferno approached their neighborhood, the Cohens ran for their lives, leaving behind their dearest possessions—"letters of loved, absent ones, pictures of our precious relations, [and] tokens and souvenirs of childhood." Among the treasures consumed in the flames were the journals Cohen had kept for ten years. She wasted no time beginning again. "All the labors of years, all the records of my girlish triumphs, of my 'first love,' all have been destroyed," bemoaned the twenty-six-year-old, "and yet I am determined to recommence the labors, to rebuild from the ashes of dispair [sic], a new record, and enthrone 'blue eyed hope' as the presiding deity."[31]

In the diaries she lost, Cohen had rendered an "accurate account" of "the fearful war that is now ravaging our land." She reported "how determined the enemy were to possess dear old Charleston, how they shelled the city and we were hurried away, how my brave city, and [its] forts held out." Though "this precious record" was destroyed, "thank God, it lives in my heart and in the heart of every true Southern man, woman, and child." She addressed her new diary as "Dear journal," and five months later as "this dear old book."[32] The volume became her best friend and confidant, to whom she confessed love and misgivings about her faraway beau, fear for his safety and for her becoming an old maid, and horror and indignation about the occupation of Columbia.

"Oh, God, can I ever forget that day?" It made Cohen's "southern blood boil to see them [Yanks] in the streets!" She wondered if "time with Lethean draughts [could] ever efface from my memory the deep sorrow, the humiliation, the agony of knowing we were to be under the Yankees, that our beloved flag was to be pulled down and the U.S.A. flag wave over the city." "Slavery is done away

Eleanor H. Cohen (Mrs. Benjamin Seixas) (1841–74), by Lawrence Cohen (b. 1836), Columbia, South Carolina, ca. 1865. Pencil on paper, 12 × 10 inches. Eleanor's brother, Lawrence Cohen, had traveled to Dusseldorf, Germany, as a youth to study painting. By 1859, he was back in Charleston, earning his living as a clerk. The sketch of Eleanor, reproduced here, likely is the one that she sent to her beau, Benjamin Mendes Seixas, in anticipation of his birthday. On June 23, 1865, she informed her diary: "Next week is Mr. S.'s birthday, and I have written him and sent him a small picture of myself done by Lawrence. I hope it will please him." Private collection. Photo courtesy of Special Collections, College of Charleston Library.

with," she wrote. "I, who believe in the institution of slavery, regret deeply its being abolished. I am accustomed to have them wait on me, and I dislike white servants very much." She felt betrayed by the servants who left but pleased that Rose and Helen "were true," and that Lavinia "gave us cotton homespun and behaved like a friend." Cohen's vitriol toward the Yankees spilled further over when she learned that Abraham Lincoln had been shot. "So our worst enemy is laid low and [Secretary of State William H.] Seward, the arch fiend, was also stabbed." She rejoiced over "the glorious tidings that the Yankee Congress had a row, and [Vice President] Andy Jo[h]nson was killed"—a false rumor, it turns out. "God grant so may our foes perish!"[33]

Compare the reaction of Charleston-born Septima Maria Levy Collis, who was in Baltimore on her way to Philadelphia when she first heard, "The President has been murdered." Married to Philadelphian Charles H. T. Collis, a captain rising rapidly in the Union ranks, Septima had met "Mr. Lincoln" and had learned to love him. "I had seen him weep, heard him laugh, had been gladdened by his wit and saddened by his pathos." She considered Lincoln "inspired," "the best of the very best," and was grateful only that "his untimely death was the act of a mad fanatic, and that my people who had fought a desperate but unreasonable war had no hand in it." Collis never ceased calling southerners "my people," and when questioned about her "conversion" to the northern cause, answered with the quip: "I had only followed the example of many other Southrons—I had 'gone with my State,' mine being the state of matrimony."[34]

The original manuscript of Eleanor Cohen Seixas's diary remains in the family, along with a sketch of herself drawn by her brother, likely the same one she sent to her beau, Benjamin Seixas, in honor of his birthday. Cohen's anxiety surfaces when she learns that Seixas is suspected of "intimacy with the Yankees," perhaps even being "in their *pay*." After their marriage on August 2, 1865, she is apprehensive about traveling to meet his family in New York. Her feelings are yet "*too* bitter," and besides, though she now has "a neat, comfortable trusseau [*sic*], very nice for Charleston," she fears it is "not fit to go North . . . where fashion and dress rule the day."[35]

Within hours of Robert E. Lee's surrender to Ulysses S. Grant at Appomattox, Octavia Harby Moses' eldest son Joshua—whom Eleanor Cohen called "the flower of our circle"—was killed in action at Fort Blakely near Mobile, Alabama.[36] His brother Horace had been captured and his brother Perry wounded the day before. Moses expressed her rage and grief in poetry. In a poem dated 1868, "To My Dead Son, J. L. Moses, Killed at the Battle of Blakely, Ala.," she says that it was just as well he had not lived to see his homeland "ruled by traitor and by slave."

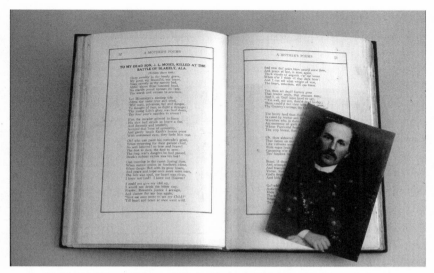

"To My Dead Son, J. L. Moses, Killed at the Battle of Blakely, Ala.," in A Mother's Poems by Octavia Harby Moses, "published by her children and grandchildren," South Carolina, 1915. Paper and ink, with gilded cloth over. Private collection. Photo courtesy of Special Collections, College of Charleston Library.

Yes, thou art dead! forever gone
That tender smile, that pleasant tone;
And I, oh God! have lived to say,
"'Tis well, my son, thou'rt dead to-day;
Thou could'st not view with spirit tame,
Thy Country's wrongs, thy Country's shame!

The lovely land thou died'st to save,
Is ruled by traitor and by slave;
Wretches who in their thirst for gain,
An eminence of guilt attain;
Whose Parricidal fingers tear
The very breast, that did them bear!"[37]

The year after Moses composed these lines, she called a meeting to raise funds for a monument to the Confederate dead of Sumter County, in the midlands of South Carolina. She was elected president of the "Ladies Monumental Association"—all the other officers were men—which purchased land on Washington Street between Liberty and Hampton Streets. A cornerstone was laid in 1874. Moses was succeeded in this crusade by her daughter Rebecca

Moïse, whose daughter Dulce declared that she too had been "raised for the good of the Monument."[38]

Octavia Harby was born in Charleston in 1823, the eighth child of Isaac Harby and Rachael Mordecai Harby. Orphaned at age six, she was raised by her aunt, Caroline de Litchfield Harby. At age twelve, Octavia took up her father's métier and began to write. In 1839, she married Andrew Jackson Moses, seven years her senior, settled in Sumter, and bore seventeen children, fourteen of whom lived to maturity. After the eleventh child, her husband wrote in the family Bible, "Heaven spare her and make her the last one." But six more would follow, the last in 1866. Moses confessed that it was her servants—the Moseses owned sixteen slaves in 1860—who made it possible for her to raise such a large family. Her son Perry recalled that a nurse slept in his room and would wake him with a warm baked sweet potato.[39]

When the Civil War broke out, Moses' husband joined the home guard, and one by one their five eldest sons went off to battle. She threw herself into war work, organizing a sewing society to make uniforms for the soldiers, sending off boxes of clothes and provisions, meeting every train with food and blankets, promoting entertainments for the troops, and assisting the Ladies Aid Association, whose members knitted socks, rolled bandages for dressing wounds, and solicited hospital supplies.[40]

Once the carnage ceased, women on both sides of the Potomac devoted themselves to memorializing their dead. The bloodiest war in American history had cost the lives of 630,000 soldiers, Blue and Grey. The Confederates' shattered dream for independence and ruined way of life compounded and prolonged their grief. "While northern Jews put the war behind them and moved on," writes Jonathan Sarna, "southern Jews . . . made the Lost Cause the centerpiece of their faith. Focusing on the martyrdom of lost sons, they insisted that the cause for which so many had fought and died was right."[41]

In 1915, Isaac Harby Moses, the son Octavia named for her father, collected her work for publication under the title A Mother's Poems. The title is well chosen, as so many verses are grounded in Moses' maternal feelings. The poem "Exhortation," written in "the dark days 'After the War,'" is suffused with the pain of losing Joshua, Isaac's older brother, an emotion magnified by the humiliation she feels at the occupation of her beloved land:

Oh, Land of the South, be thy soil ever sacred!
    Enriched as it is by the blood of the brave,
To thee our love, to thy foes our hatred,
    Thou birth-place of Heroes! Of Martyrs, the grave![42]

Dollhouse sukkah made by Harry Sholk, Charleston, 1925. Wood and mixed media, 31 × 18 × 18 inches. Gift of Susan Z. Hitt, Jane Zalkin, and Sally Z. Hare, in honor of Ida and Harry Sholk and in memory of Mary Sholk Zalkin. Special Collections, College of Charleston Library. Photo courtesy of Darcie Fohrman.

Mary Sholk Zalkin's three daughters donated the dollhouse sukkah their grandfather built to the College of Charleston's Jewish Heritage Collection in honor of their grandparents and in memory of their mother. According to Susan Zalkin Hitt, the middle of the three girls, the sukkah had come to represent their mother's childhood home at 438 King Street, where they visited their grandparents. Indeed, the address loomed so large in family lore that when Mary Zalkin died in the year 2000, she was buried, by request, at 4:38 in the afternoon.

"Please find Mama's sukkah a good home," the daughters implored. They had married out of Judaism. Until her children were grown, Susan Hitt and her family decked out the sukkah every fall. In the off-season it doubled as a soldiers' fort, a Barbie house, and a stuffed animal hospital. Then, like many childhood treasures, it was relegated to the attic. Though clearly the repository of powerful family feelings and an almost palpable connection to place, the sukkah had become "orphaned," belonging to a class of artifacts that, "due to any number of historical events, some painful to consider, were separated from their owners and their communities."[43]

Orphaned objects frequently are found in pawnshops and junk stores. Macy Hart, founder of the Museum of the Southern Jewish Experience in Utica, Mississippi, has made it his mission to rescue ritual objects from this fate by collecting arks, eternal lights, and Torahs from small-town synagogues forced to close their doors because of shrinking memberships. The disappearance of Jewish households and communities from small towns and rural areas—a demographic trend the South shares with other regions—motivates cultural reclamation and preservation projects across the country.

Attempts to memorialize sites and objects from the past entangle the current generation in a paradox, for memory does not emanate from a place or thing, but is projected onto it by acts of remembrance. The created memory is not a memory of the past, but a new way of thinking. Objects are reanimated by endowing them with stories and enhanced by what can be learned from research. Thus the artist or curator becomes, in critic James E. Young's phrase, an "agent of metamorphosis."[44] An object remains inert until someone consciously recounts its history or imbues it with new meanings.[45]

The crusade to adopt and repatriate Jewish objects is most intense for things stolen or damaged by the Nazis. Even in Mississippi, efforts to fortify Jewish memory reflect a collective attempt to deal with the communal losses of the Holocaust. A proliferation of Holocaust memorials, museums, movies, courses, and degree-granting programs focuses public attention on the past. Together these endeavors express anxiety about Jewish survival in the future.

Perhaps the most dramatic discovery in the search for artifacts for "A Portion of the People: Three Hundred Years of Southern Jewish Life" were four miniature paintings of the Levy family of Camden, South Carolina. These delicate portraits, averaging two by three inches and painted in watercolor on ivory, were taken to Mississippi in 1838 when Chapman Levy and his law partner William McWillie moved there to litigate Indian land claims.[46] For generations the miniatures were handed down in the family, long after the descendants had married out of Judaism and the identity of the ancestors had grown hazy. One of the four paintings was a leather-cased likeness of Chapman Levy as a grown man. The other three—one dubbed by the family, "Grandma Moses," and two nameless individuals—were missing.

Barbara Karesh Stender, associate curator for "A Portion of the People," spent three years tracking down the lost objects. As it turns out, they had been wrapped in socks for safekeeping and tucked in the back of a drawer in a nursing home in Jackson, Mississippi. When their last owner, a distant descendant of the Levys of Camden, passed away, the miniatures were discovered by a social worker. Today, the Levy heirs proudly acknowledge their Jewish ancestry,

Chapman Levy as a youth, artist unknown, ca. 1798. Watercolor on ivory, 3 × 2¼ inches. Gift of Lane Dinkins. Photo courtesy of Special Collections, College of Charleston Library.

Sarah Moses Levy (d. 1839), artist unknown, ca. 1798. Watercolor on ivory,
2½ × 1¾ inches. Sarah Moses Levy, wife of Samuel Levy, poses in an elegant lace cap and collar
and wears a miniature of her young son Chapman. The intriguing pair of portraits had stayed
together for more than two hundred years, a testament to the strength of the bond between mother
and son. Gift of Lane Dinkins. Photo courtesy of Special Collections,
College of Charleston Library.

though they are no longer Jewish. They graciously agreed to donate the four paintings to the Jewish Heritage Collection and send them back "home" to South Carolina.

When the "orphans" arrived at the College of Charleston Library, Barbara Stender carefully unwrapped each tiny painting. There sat a portrait later identified as Chapman's mother, Sarah Moses Levy, and a miniature of her son, the young Chapman, both painted in the late 1790s. On close examination, we could see that Sarah Moses Levy wore the very same miniature of her son that now gazed up at us with wistful eyes. The feelings of this mother for her child were immortalized in the delicate brushstrokes of the image that hung at the end of a chain just below the lace frill of her collar.

An exhibition creates a kind of alchemy. Dormant objects acquire the power to make the viewer think, feel, and remember. However, the questions that shape narratives today are not the questions asked a generation ago, nor are they the questions that will be posed twenty years from now. In 1950, the portrait of an antebellum southern Jew dressed in fine clothes may have prompted the question, what public offices did he hold? Today, the same object provokes us to ask, how many slaves did he own? (In Chapman Levy's case, the answer is, more than any other Jew of his day.) What will Levy's portrait mean in the South of 2025 as the region grows in ethnic diversity and the old paradigm of white and black gives way to a new American reality?

In the popular television series, *Antiques Roadshow*, the owners of attic treasures tell where the objects came from while experts reveal facts about their manufacture and estimate their current market value. The climactic question always gets answered in American dollars or British pounds. Objects borrowed for museum exhibitions also are appraised, if only for insurance purposes, but the dollar value never appears in the label copy. Their ultimate worth lies in their capacity to trigger the imagination and to carry museum visitors to other worlds.

NOTES

1. A sukkah is a temporary shelter constructed for the festival of Sukkot to celebrate the fall harvest and to recall the tabernacles of the Exodus.

2. Yehoshua Katzovitch, "Old Kryvitsh Lights Up in My Memory," *Kryvitsh: A Yzkor Book*, 1976. Transcript of translation (p. 22) on file in Special Collections, College of Charleston Library, Charleston, S.C.

3. Margo Bloom, foreword to *A Worthy Use of Summer: Jewish Summer Camping in America*, ed. Jenna Weissman Joselit with Karen S. Mittelman (Philadelphia: National Museum of American Jewish History, 1933), 1.

4. Bill Aron and Vicki Reikes Fox, *Shalom Y'all: Images of Jewish Life in the American South* (Chapel Hill, N.C.: Algonquin Books, 2002), n.p. [vi].

5. For additional information on Isaiah and Rebecca Moses, see Theodore Rosengarten and Dale Rosengarten, eds. *A Portion of the People: Three Hundred Years of Southern Jewish Life* (Columbia: University of South Carolina Press, 2002), 100–111.

6. For an account of the controversy over the organ, see James William Hagy, *This Happy Land: The Jews of Colonial and Antebellum Charleston* (Tuscaloosa: University of Alabama Press, 1993), 240–43. Note Isaiah Moses' signature on the petition to incorporate Shearit Israel, ibid., 258. For Moses' involvement as "a leading opponent of innovations and reforms in the Sephardic Service," see Henry A. Alexander, *Notes on the Alexander Family of South Carolina and Georgia, and Connections: 1651–1954* (Atlanta: Henry A. Alexander, 1954), 51.

7. The inscriptions were first noted in 1941 by Rae Neely and published by family historian Henry A. Alexander, *Notes on the Alexander Family*, 124–25. Judith W. Shanks, a descendant of Rebecca and Isaiah Moses and an associate curator of "A Portion of the People: Three Hundred Years of Southern Jewish Life," brought the quilt to our attention and researched and annotated the list of contributors. For a detailed analysis of the quilt, see Judith W. Shanks, "'For My Dear Mrs. Solomons': Kinship and Friendship Stitched into a Quilt," unpublished paper (2003), appendix A, 12–14, copy on file in Special Collections, College of Charleston Library.

8. Merikay Waldvogel, "The Evolution of the American Quilt," in *American Quilt Classics, 1800–1980: The Bresler Collection* ed. Kristen S. Watts (Charlotte, N.C.: Mint Museum of Craft and Design, 2003), 18–21.

9. For the Lazarus family tree, see Malcolm H. Stern, *Americans of Jewish Descent: A Compendium of Genealogy* (1960; reprint, New York: Ktav, 1971), 151.

10. Information on the Lazarus family is drawn from Charles Reznikoff and Uriah Z. Engelman, *The Jews of Charleston: A History of an American Jewish Community* (Philadelphia: Jewish Publication Society of America, 1950), 18, 91, 134, 181; and Hagy, *This Happy Land*, 58, 113, 134, 137, 139, 145, 153, 266. In Hagy's biographical appendix, the Lazarus family occupies three and a half pages, 342–45.

11. Dr. Aaron Solomon Raisin, son of Rabbi Jacob S. Raisin and Jane Levy Lazarus Raisin, served as president of Beth Elohim between 1985 and 1987. [Sol Breibart], *Kahal Kadosh Beth Elohim Synagogue, 250th Anniversary: 1749–1999* (Charleston, S.C.: Kahal Kadosh Beth Elohim, 1999), 42.

12. "Literary Notices," *Occident and American Jewish Advocate*, 1:4 (July 1843). Accessed online, March 15, 2004, at http://www.jewish-history.com/Occident/volume1/july1843/literary.html, 1–2.

13. See "Memoir" by I. H. Moses, dated November 1914, which serves as an introduction to Octavia Harby Moses, *A Mother's Poem: A Collection of Verses* (Sumter, S.C.: "Published by Her Children and Grandchildren," 1915), n.p. [i–ii].

14. *Fancy's Sketch Book* (1833; reprint, Charleston, S.C.: J. S. Burges, 1883); *Hymns Written for the Service of Hebrew Congregation Beth Elohim of Charleston, S.C.* (Charleston, S.C.: Levin and Tavel, 1842).

15. The manuscript poems, ca. 1840, are entitled "On Parting with My Press" and "To the Consecration." Special Collections (Mss. #1034–49), College of Charleston Library. Moïse's card sets are in the collection of Kahal Kadosh Beth Elohim, Charleston, S.C.

16. C. Vann Woodward, ed., *Mary Chesnut's Civil War* (New Haven, Conn.: Yale University Press, 1981), 547.

17. Ibid., 317.

18. Harold Moïse, *The Moïse Family of Sumter, S.C. and Their Descendants* (Columbia, S.C.: R. L. Bryan, 1961), 66. For more on the life and work of Penina Moïse, see ibid., 61–69; *Secular and Religious Works of Penina Moïse, with Brief Sketch of Her Life*, complied and published by Charleston Section, Council of Jewish Women (Charleston, S.C.: Nicolas G. Duffy, 1911); and Solomon Breibart, "Penina Moise, Southern Jewish Poetess," in *Jews of the South: Selected Essays from the Southern Jewish Historical Society*, ed. Samuel Proctor and Louis Schmier, with Malcolm Stern (Macon, Ga.: Mercer University Press, 1984), 31–43.

19. N. L. [Nathaniel Levin], "Address Delivered before the Society for the Instruction of Jewish Youth, in Charleston, S.C., on the Anniversary of the Society, February, 1842," *Occident and American Jewish Advocate* 1:4 (July 1843). Accessed online, March 15, 2004, at http://www.jewish-history.com/Occident/volume1/july1843/address.html, 11–12.

20. For more on Isaac Harby and Abraham Moïse's "talented and educated sisters," see Deborah Dash Moore, "Freedom's Fruits: The Americanization of an Old-time Religion," in Rosengarten and Rosengarten, *A Portion of the People*, 14–19.

21. Karla Goldman, *Beyond the Synagogue Gallery: Finding a Place for Women in American Judaism* (Cambridge, Mass.: Harvard University Press, 2000), 60–68. Reform Rabbi Isaac Mayer Wise went so far as to declare: "American women . . . are more religious, and in many instances more intelligent that their 'lords of creation.' They are the religious teachers of their children, the priestesses of the house, and we are morally obligated to attach them closer to the synagogue." *The Israelite*, November 27, 1863, 172, quoted in Stanley R. Brav, "The Jewish Woman, 1861–1865," *American Jewish Archives* 17:1 (April 1965): 46.

22. For more on Isabel Lyons and M. C. Mordecai, see Rosengarten and Rosengarten, *A Portion of the People*, 127–30; Belinda Gergel and Richard Gergel, *In Pursuit of the Tree of Life: A History of Columbia, South Carolina, and the Tree of Life Congregation* (Columbia, S.C.: Tree of Life Congregation, 1996), 42–44; and Hagy, *This Happy Land*, 24, 43, 50, 91, 93–95, 112, 159, 194, 243, 272, 369, 370.

23. Isabel Lyons Mordecai's commonplace book and miscellaneous manuscript pages can be found in the Thomas J. Tobias Papers (Mss. #1029 5/9), Special Collections, College of Charleston Library.

24. Joseph Lyons's diary and David Henry Mordecai's journals are in the Thomas J. Tobias Papers (Mss. #1029 8/5, 5A/11–14, 6/1–2), Special Collections, College of Charleston Library. A new and unabridged transcript of Joseph Lyons's diary is available in Marie Ferrara, Harlan Greene, Dale Rosengarten, and Susan Wyssen, "The Diary of Joseph Lyons (1813–1839)," *American Jewish History* 91:3 and 4 (September and December 2003): 493–606.

25. "The Diary of Joseph Lyons," 522–25.

26. From "The Prayer of the C. S. Soldiers," by the Reverend Max J. Michelbacher, rabbi of Beth Ahabah Congregation (House of Love), Richmond, Virginia, quoted in Robert N. Rosen, *The Jewish Confederates* (Columbia: University of South Carolina Press, 2000), 211, 212.

27. Jonathan D. Sarna, *American Judaism: A History* (New Haven, Conn.: Yale University Press, 2004), 123.

28. George C. Rable, introduction to Phoebe Yates Pember, *A Southern Woman's Story* (1879; reprint, Columbia: University of South Carolina Press, 2002), ix.

29. Pember, *A Southern Woman's Story*, 88.

30. Letter from Phebe [*sic*] Pember to her sister Eugenia Levy Phillips, September 13, 1863, Richmond [Virginia], in Phoebe Yates Pember, *A Southern Woman's Story: Life in Confederate Richmond*, ed. Bell Irvin Wiley (Jackson, Tenn.: McCowat-Mercer Press, 1959), 168. For a recent analysis of this passage, see Dianne Ashton, "Shifting Veils: Religion, Politics, and Womanhood in the Civil War Writings of American Jewish Women," in *Women and American Judaism: Historical Perspectives*, ed. Pamela S. Nadell and Jonathan D. Sarna (Waltham, Mass.: Brandeis University Press, 2001), 91.

31. "Eleanor H. Cohen, Champion of the Lost Cause," in *Memoirs of American Jews, 1775–1865*, ed. Jacob R. Marcus (Philadelphia: Jewish Publication Society of America, 1955) 3:362, 359. Marcus's transcription of Cohen's journal was based on a copy found in the American Jewish Archives. The diary was published again, in 1986, this time from a typescript in the collection of the American Jewish Historical Society. See "The Diary of Eleanor Cohen Seixas: Columbia, South Carolina, 1865–1866," in *Private Pages: Diaries of American Women, 1830s–1870s*, ed. Penelope Franklin (New York: Ballantine Books, 1986), 303–23. An online version is also available at http://www.jewish-history.com/eleanor.html, accessed March 21, 2005.

32. "Eleanor H. Cohen, Champion of the Lost Cause," in *Memoirs of American Jews*, 3:360, 369.

33. Ibid., 361, 367, 368, 364, 366. A lethean draught, in classical mythology, refers to the Lethe, a river of Hades, whose waters when imbibed cause oblivion or forgetfulness of the past.

34. Septima M. Collis, *A Woman's War Record: 1861–1865* (New York: G. P. Putnam's Sons, Knickerbocker Press, 1889), 313, 315, 314. Accessed online, March 27, 2005, http://docsouth.inc.edu/collis/collis.html.

35. "Eleanor H. Cohen, Champion of the Lost Cause," in *Memoirs of American Jews*, 3:368, 366, 369.

36. Ibid., 367.

37. Moses, *A Mother's Poems*, 52–54.

38. Ruth J. Edens, *"It Takes a Heap o' Livin'": The Families of the Sumter County Museum Home* (Sumter, S.C.: Sumter County Museum, 1996), 13.

39. Ibid., 3–4.

40. "Recollections A. D.—1903, Narrative by Mrs. Octavia Harby Moses (aged 80 years) of Sumter, South Carolina," typescript (p. 1) on file in Special Collections, College of Charleston Library.

41. Sarna, *American Judaism*, 124.

42. Moses, *A Mother's Poems*, 61.

43. Erica T. Lehrer, "The Collector as Portrait Artist," in *Portrait of a People: The Jewish Heritage Collection Dedicated to Mark and Dave Harris* (Ann Arbor: University of Michigan Library, 2005), 13. Thanks to Susan Zalkin Hitt, Ann Livingstain Mandel, and Betty Sholk Quait for providing information and insights on their family history and the background of the sukkah.

44. James E. Young, *At Memory's Edge: After-Images of the Holocaust in Contemporary Art and Architecture* (New Haven, Conn.: Yale University Press, 2000), 62.

45. Curator Erica Lehrer argues, "I'd go so far as to say that objects are *never* just being reframed with their original histories, but that the preserver/handler/viewer is always projecting 'new' histories onto it from the present standpoint." Personal communication with the author, April 5, 2005.

46. Rosengarten and Rosengarten, *A Portion of the People*, 118–19.

12

THE FALL AND RISE OF
THE JEWISH SOUTH

STUART ROCKOFF

Carla Levingston is a proud southerner. Her great-grandparents settled in the region at the turn of the twentieth century, and her family has lived there ever since. Her paternal grandfather owned a store in the small Mississippi Delta town of Ruleville. Carla was born in Cleveland, Mississippi, in 1980, where the Levingstons were one of the few Jewish families in town. Her congregation, Adath Israel, had only three or four families with children, who gathered in one room on Sunday mornings to receive instruction from Rabbi Moses Landau. Carla had no Jewish friends in her secular school. Her only Jewish friendships came from a Jewish summer camp and through her involvement in the regional Reform Temple Youth program. Carla's experience is typical of Jewish life in the small-town South after World War II.

When she graduated from high school, Carla's parents urged her to leave Mississippi for college. They wanted her to go somewhere with a large Jewish population, which no school in Mississippi had. At the University of Texas, Carla joined a Jewish sorority, and for the first time in her life, she had a Jewish social life. After graduate school in New Orleans, Carla never considered moving back to Cleveland, where her parents still lived. There were no career opportunities in the town of fourteen thousand people, and as a single Jewish woman, little prospect of meeting a Jewish husband there. Like many other Jews from the rural South, Carla moved to Atlanta, now a mecca for young Jewish singles. Meanwhile, the Mississippi Delta has fallen deeper into economic decline and many of its Jewish congregations have closed.

In many ways, Carla's journey from the small town of Cleveland, Mississippi, to the metropolis of Atlanta encapsulates the story of southern Jewish life since 1945. Large southern cities like Houston and Atlanta have attracted a growing number of Jews from around the country while small towns have witnessed an exodus of their Jewish population. It is the story of both boom and bust, not as a cycle, but as concurrent and interrelated developments. In a seeming contradiction, the Jewish South has grown tremendously, while experiencing serious decline. The Jewish South has become less distinctive and yet has exhibited a growing interest in the nostalgic memory of plantations and peddler's carts and the ubiquitous "Jew store." Though it has been transformed by the economic, demographic, and religious changes brought on in the decades since 1945, the Jewish South continues to flourish. This chapter traces these trends while outlining the changes in the economic, social, and religious character of the Jewish South.

Much attention has been rightly focused on the far-reaching social changes brought about by the civil rights movement, but perhaps less noticed though just as revolutionary was the economic transformation of the South during the latter half of the twentieth century. Although the economic dislocations brought on by the Great Depression and the federal government's Agricultural Adjustment Act began the process, World War II was the watershed event that revolutionized the South's economy. Its most dramatic effect was to drain the region's farm population. Between 1940 and 1945, four million people, or 25 percent of the South's total farm population, left the land, joining the armed forces or moving to the city to work in the booming war industries. Those leaving the farm were laborers, tenants, and sharecroppers drawn by the greater economic opportunities that the war created. In the old industrial cities of the North and Midwest, and the growing industrial cities of the South, these migrants found work and a healthier economy. The migration of labor accelerated the decline in tenant farming that began in the 1930s. The southern farm population continued to shrink after the war. In 1940, sixteen million southerners, 42 percent of the region's population, lived on farms. By 1960, only 15 percent of the region's population remained on farms.[1]

Federal spending during the war greatly benefited the South. Sleepy southern ports became bustling centers of trade and manufacturing. The population of Pascagoula, Mississippi, a small town on the Gulf Coast, exploded after the opening of the Ingalls Shipyard, growing from six thousand residents in 1940 to thirty thousand in 1944. Small cities like Mobile, Alabama, and Norfolk, Virginia, also experienced similar growth during the war. In addition, because the South's warm climate enabled the quick training and deployment of troops, new military training bases were built throughout the region. Many northern soldiers received their first taste of southern life when they were stationed south of the Mason-Dixon line during the war. Government wartime spending transformed the South as the region saw higher incomes and improved lifestyles. According to one study, government payrolls accounted for 25 percent of all the wages earned in the South in 1944.[2]

The emptying of the southern countryside during the war produced significant labor shortages within the cotton industry, prompting companies like International Harvester to develop a viable mechanical cotton picker. Prototypes of such a machine existed, but because cotton production was embedded in the established system of sharecropping and tenant farming, there was not enough demand to inspire large companies to spend money refining the technology. This changed during World War II. The years following the war marked the beginning of a revolution in southern agriculture as mechanized farm production replaced the Old South's paternalistic system of sharecropping. In 1950, only 5 percent of the U.S. cotton crop, heavily centered in the South, was harvested by machine. By 1960, 50 percent of the crop was mechanically reaped; by 1970, the figure had grown to 98 percent. Tractors and mechanical cotton pickers enabled farm owners to do the work of many sharecroppers. These changes led to a sharp decline in the South's farming population, and the drop was steepest amongst African Americans, most of whom had been sharecroppers. In 1940, 882,000 African Americans farmed in the South; by 1969, only 90,000 did so. Plantations that had previously supported many sharecroppers became industrialized farms with little need for human labor.[3]

The area's agricultural economy also became more diversified after World War II. Cotton, which had been dominant throughout much of the South, was no longer king after the war. Growing demand for new synthetic fibers like rayon and increased cotton production in Asia, Africa, and South America weakened the market for southern cotton farmers. In fact, southern cotton production largely died out, with the exception of the Mississippi Delta. By 1949, more than half of U.S. cotton production came from western states. By 1959, cotton was the leading crop in only eleven southern counties, as other crops such as soybeans became more profitable. By 1975, the South produced 3 million bales of cotton and 523 million bushels of soybeans.[4]

These changes in Southern agriculture corresponded with the rise in the South's urban population. In 1940, 25.7 percent of the South's population lived in metropolitan urban areas. By 1960, this figure rose to 48 percent. Urbanization continued throughout the remainder of the century. By 2000, more than 75 percent of the South's population lived in urban metropolitan areas.[5] Several southern towns became large cities during the postwar years. In 1940, the South had five of the twenty-five largest cities in the United States. By 1990, it had ten.[6]

These growing cities became the epicenter of the South's economic transformation away from agriculture to industry and commerce. After the war, southern states actively courted industry, offering tax rebates and low-wage, nonunionized labor. The result was the development of a modern economy, with increasing wages and standard of living. The South was no longer the poor relation of the rest of the United States.[7] By the 1970s, the national media recognized the economic rise of the South, proclaiming the region a thriving "sunbelt" that it contrasted with the declining "rust belt" of the Midwest and Northeast.[8] In the 1960s, the South reversed a long trend of outward migration, as more people moved to the region than left it during the decade. By 1980, 20 percent of people living there were not native southerners.[9]

Not every area of the South took part in the boom. Historian David Goldfield has observed that the so-called Sunbelt South "was a crazy quilt of patches of prosperity zigzagging between traditional areas of poverty." The South's economic success story was largely restricted to its growing cities and suburbs.[10] Other parts of the South were left behind by this economic upturn. For example, the Mississippi Delta, labeled by historian James Cobb as "the most Southern place on earth," has steadily lost population, declining from 394,000 people in 1940 to 258,454 in 2000, with no sign of a reverse in sight, aside from casino-rich Tunica County.[11] The story of the Jewish South mirrors these twin trends of growth and decline.

These changing economics of the South transformed the region's Jewish population. Previously, Jewish merchants were scattered throughout the region, and their businesses dominated southern downtowns. Jews first arrived in the rural South in significant numbers in the mid- to late-nineteenth century, just as formerly isolated regions were brought into the national economy by the expansion of the railroad. Jewish peddlers, and later merchants, became the economic link between rural southerners and the national market. Although relatively few Jews engaged in farming, the southern Jewish economy was closely linked to agriculture. In the Mississippi Delta, Jews settled throughout this fertile cotton-growing region, opening retail stores that catered to the local farmers and sharecroppers. With the structural changes to the Delta's cotton economy described above, Jewish merchants lost much of their customer base. It was no longer economically feasible to operate retail stores in many Delta towns.

While much attention has been paid to the phenomenon of the declining Jewish communities in the South, a look at Jewish population data for its individual states shows a more complex picture (see table 1). Jewish population has fallen in five states, but it has increased in six, and in most of them significantly. On the whole, the population of southern Jews has doubled since 1937. Yet this growth has not been steady. From 1937 to 1968, it grew 6.6 percent. Since then, the southern Jewish population has rapidly expanded, growing 20.6 percent in the 1970s, 39 percent in the 1980s, and slowing to 11.7 percent in the 1990s. Dur-

Goldie Fleischer closed her family's dry goods store in Shaw, Mississippi, after her husband's death.
Theirs was the last Jewish-owned store in this small Delta town. Photo by Bill Aron,
in the collection of the Goldring/Woldenberg Institute of Southern Jewish Life,
Jackson, Mississippi.

ing the same period, the American Jewish population stagnated, and according to some studies, declined, which makes this significant growth in the South even more striking.[12]

This growth is largely due to the migration of Jews to the South from other regions of the United States. As table 1 indicates, the Jewish population of North Carolina more than doubled during the 1980s. Barbara Shapiro Thiede grew up just outside Chicago, but moved to Charlotte, North Carolina, after her husband accepted a teaching position at the local university. The Thiedes settled in Concord, thirty miles outside suburban Charlotte. In 2003, the Thiedes and the other Jews of Cabarrus County, formed a new congregation, Havurat Olam. Of the twenty dues-paying families, only two are native southerners.[13] As the Charlotte metropolitan area continues to expand, Cabarrus County has become one

In many small southern towns, little remains of the once-prominent Jewish merchant class.
Photo by Bill Aron, in the collection of the Goldring/Woldenberg Institute of Southern Jewish Life,
Jackson, Mississippi.

of the fastest-growing counties in the state. Most of the congregation's members are professionals, including several professors at the University of North Carolina–Charlotte. These northern migrants came South seeking employment in the burgeoning Sunbelt, warmer climates, and a lower cost of living.

One major destination of this Sunbelt growth has been Florida, which has seen its Jewish population grow from 21,000 in 1937 to 620,000 in 2001. In fact, far more Jews currently live in Florida than in all of the other southern states combined. This growth has been especially pronounced in the southern part of the state, as many Jews from the North have been drawn by the area's quality of life and tropical climate. Yet the rise of Jewish Florida seems distinct from the story of southern Jews and is not treated in this chapter. Indeed, few Florida Jews would consider themselves "southern," and the Jewish culture of the state has much more in common with New York City and its suburbs than the rest of the former Confederacy.[14]

No place typifies the growth in the Jewish South better than Atlanta, Georgia. The city that emerged from the ashes of the Civil War to become the economic capital of the New South also led the way during the Sunbelt era. The Atlanta

TABLE 1. SOUTHERN JEWISH POPULATION, BY STATE

	1937	1960	1968	1980	1990	2001
Alabama	12,148	10,000	9,465	8,835	8,350	9,000
Arkansas	6,510	3,400	3,065	3,395	2,389	1,700
Georgia	23,781	24,800	26,310	34,610	72,747	93,500
Kentucky	17,894	11,000	11,200	11,583	14,810	11,500
Louisiana	15,000	16,100	15,639	16,340	15,625	16,000
Mississippi	4,603	4,000	4,015	3,200	2,466	1,500
North Carolina	7,333	10,300	9,450	13,240	28,870	26,500
South Carolina	5,905	7,100	7,285	8,660	8,558	11,500
Tennessee	25,811	16,800	16,710	16,765	17,474	18,000
Texas	49,196	60,900	65,520	72,545	107,980	131,000
Virginia	25,066	31,200	37,350	59,360	66,564	66,000
Total	193,247	195,600	206,009	248,533	345,833	386,200

Source: American Jewish Yearbook population estimates.

metropolitan area grew from 726,789 people in 1950 to 4,247,981 in 2000. Atlanta remains one of the fastest-growing cities in the United States, with its metro area growing 38.4 percent between 1990 and 2000.[15] The Jewish community of Atlanta has grown at an even faster pace than the city itself. According to estimates in the *American Jewish Yearbook*, Atlanta had just over 10,000 Jews in 1946, and 14,500 in 1960. By 1980, 27,500 Jews lived in Atlanta. Since then, the Jewish population has increased by more than 300 percent, to 86,000 in 2000. Estimates in 2005 put the total population well over 100,000.[16]

Jews come to Atlanta for the same reason their forebears went anywhere—economic opportunity. According to a 1947 study of the city's Jewish population, "Atlanta is the commercial, financial and industrial center of the southeast." It was a railroad nexus that became a major air travel hub. By 1946, the Atlanta airport was already the third-busiest in the nation. By 2003, it was the world's busiest airport, with 79 million passengers passing through its terminals each year.[17] Atlanta's position as a vital transportation hub, combined with its temperate climate, has prompted many corporations to locate their headquarters in the city. Atlanta has grown from a regional to an international business center. This status is reflected in the rise of CNN as an international news organization and by the city's hosting of the 1996 Summer Olympics. By the end of 2004, seven hundred of the Fortune 1000 firms had offices in Atlanta.[18] The city is also the headquarters of Delta Airlines, Coca-Cola, BellSouth, Georgia Pacific, Home Depot, and United Parcel Service.

Atlanta's rise as a corporate center occurred as southern Jews entered the corporate world in larger numbers. From their first arrival in the South, Jews were self-employed, concentrating in retail and wholesale commerce. Jewish storeowners sent their children to college, with hopes that they would become professionals. Hiring restrictions faded as Jews were increasingly welcomed into leading law firms and corporations, and the South saw a tremendous increase in its number of Jewish professionals. According to a 1984 study of Atlanta's Jewish community by the city's Jewish Federation, 57 percent of primary wage earners were professionals, while 25 percent held managerial occupations.[19] The growth of Atlanta's Jewish community since World War II reflects the movement of southern Jews away from retail business ownership and toward corporate and professional occupations, most of which are based in large cities.

Jay Tanenbaum's life reflects these trends. Born and raised in the small town of Dumas, Arkansas, which had only eighteen Jews in 1937, Jay grew up steeped in the culture of small-town Jewish life. His father started a regional chain of discount stores, which were in decline when Tanenbaum finished college in 1978 because of increased competition from Wal-Mart. He decided not to join the family business in Arkansas and enrolled in Harvard Business School. After graduating, he gave no thought to returning to his boyhood home of Dumas, which offered no economic opportunity. Wanting to remain in the South, Jay moved to Atlanta where he worked for the local office of a national investment firm.[20]

Tanenbaum settled in Atlanta in 1994, a time when the city's Jewish population was experiencing incredible growth. This Jewish population explosion is clearly reflected in the increasing number of Jewish congregations in the city. A 1947 survey identified six; by 2004, there were thirty-eight congregations in metropolitan Atlanta, with more being founded every year. Of these thirty-eight, thirty-three were founded after 1968. These new congregations are concentrated in suburbs like Marietta, Dunwoody, and Alpharetta, where Jews are seeking places to worship close to home, a process no doubt influenced by Atlanta's notorious traffic problems.

This movement to the suburbs began as far back as 1946, when the local Jewish Welfare Board found that "the trend of [general] population is from the central area of the city towards the outskirts and the suburbs." Jews had primarily lived in south Atlanta and gradually moved to northeastern Atlanta and its northern suburbs. The Jewish Welfare Board studied the Jewish population in 1946 to determine a location for a new Jewish Community Center, which was eventually built in northeastern Atlanta.[21] By 1984, 70 percent of the city's Jewish population lived outside of the city limits. In the late 1990s, the Jewish Community Center followed the city's Jewish population, moving to the northern suburb of Dunwoody. As of 2005, there was no JCC located within Atlanta's city limits.

The northern suburbs of Atlanta are the cutting edge of the South's Jewish population in the early twenty-first century. In 2004, the Atlanta Jewish Federation commissioned a demographic study of this suburban Jewish community. The area experienced rapid growth during the previous decade. In 1996, when the federation analyzed the metro area's Jewish population, the northern suburbs were not even included in "Jewish Atlanta." By 2004, they found that 16,100 Jews lived in northern suburbs like Alpharetta and Roswell. More Jews lived in these few suburbs than in Alabama, Arkansas, and Mississippi combined. Most of these suburban Jews were young: 78 percent were under the age of fifty, and 36 percent were under eighteen, making this group much younger than the overall American Jewish population.[22]

But is this a southern community? According to a 1996 study of Atlanta's Jewish population, only 26 percent of Atlanta Jews were born in the metro area. Thirty percent were born in the Northeast. The Atlanta Jewish Federation found that 27 percent of Jewish households had lived in the area for fewer than five years. A 1998 update of the study found that the Jewish population had grown by 11 percent in a three-year period. This increase stands in stark contrast with other Jewish communities. Table 2 shows that Jews in Atlanta are more likely to be non-natives than Jews elsewhere in the United States.[23] This trend is even more pronounced in the new northern suburbs. The 2004 survey found that only a tiny fraction of the northern suburbs' Jewish population, 7 percent, were native Atlantans. Six percent were born in the former Soviet Union, 32 percent were born in New York State, while 49 percent came from elsewhere in the United States. More than one-third of the Jewish population had been in the Atlanta area for fewer than ten years.

This demographic growth has occurred for several decades. Since the 1970s, the Atlanta suburb of Marietta has grown from a small town of twenty-seven thousand people to a thriving suburb of sixty-three thousand residents in 2004.[24] Jews were part of this growth. In 1975, a group of young Jewish families founded the city's first congregation, Etz Chaim. Most were recent transplants from Florida or the East Coast who saw themselves as "landsmen" in the strange new world of the South. The Conservative congregation grew quickly from a handful of founders to hundreds of families. A second congregation, the Reform Temple Kol Emeth, was founded in 1982.

TABLE 2. NON-NATIVE JEWISH POPULATION OF SELECTED CITIES

	Est. no. of Jews 2001	Percentage locally born
Atlanta	86,000	26
Baltimore	106,000	50
Cleveland	86,000	59
New Orleans	13,000	50
St. Louis	54,500	51

Source: Atlanta Jewish Federation, "The 1996 Jewish Population Study of Atlanta Summary Report," pp. 14–15.

For students of southern Jewish history, this thriving Marietta Jewish community seems somewhat ironic. After all, Marietta was the site of the 1915 lynching of Leo Frank, the Atlanta Jew accused of murdering Mary Phagan, a fourteen year-old girl who worked in the pencil factory Frank managed. It was the home of the antisemitic mob that forcibly removed Frank from his jail cell and hung him from a tree in Mary Phagan's hometown. The Frank lynching had a chilling effect on Atlanta's Jews. According to Steven Hertzberg, "for several decades the Frank case hung like a threatening cloud over the Jewish community." Local Jewish leaders kept a low profile. When Hollywood produced a film rendition of the Frank case in 1937, Jewish leaders convinced distributors not to show it in Atlanta.[25]

Despite Marietta's infamous history, Rabbi Shalom Lewis of Etz Chaim says his congregants feel very much at home there in 2005. The town's library has an extensive Jewish section, and local schools are careful not to schedule major events on Jewish holidays. Marietta Jews have even been elected to public office, including Sam Olens, a New Jersey–born member of Etz Chaim whose was elected chairman of the Cobb County Board of Commissioners in 2002. Rabbi Lewis suggests that northern Jewish transplants are more outspoken and less affected by vestiges of the Frank case or the fear of antisemitism.[26]

Etz Chaim and other new Atlanta-area congregations reflect the changing face of southern Jewry, which is becoming at once religiously more traditional and nontraditional. Historically, southern Jewish congregations were more likely to be Reform. Yet many of the Jews moving to Atlanta from the North are more observant. Indeed, new congregations in Atlanta are much more likely to be Orthodox. Since 1984, twenty-three congregations have been founded in the metropolitan area, thirteen of which are Orthodox or traditional. Only four of the new congregations are Reform or Conservative. Grocery stores have opened kosher sections to appeal to this growing observant population. There is even an *eruv* in the northern suburbs of the city, an unbroken string around the perimeter of an area that symbolically extends the borders of one's home, allowing Orthodox Jews to carry items on the Sabbath.[27] Yet another religious trend in Atlanta is nontraditional Jewish congregations. Since 1985, two Reconstructionist congregations, three multidenominational, one humanist, and one gay and lesbian congregation have been founded. The religious diversity of Atlanta's Jewish community now matches that of any city in the United States.

Since 1980, Atlanta has emerged as a center of American Jewish life. By 2005, it was among the ten largest Jewish population centers in the United States.[28] Its tremendous growth is partially the result of the influx of people like Jay Tanenbaum and Carla Levingston who came from small towns across the South seeking greater economic and social opportunities. But perhaps more significant, Atlanta has attracted thousands of Jews from northern and midwestern cities. People who once would never consider moving to the South have embraced the northern suburbs of the quintessential city of the "New South." Atlanta is only the most dramatic example of the Jewish Sunbelt boom, as Houston, Dallas, Austin, and Charlotte have also experienced tremendous growth in their Jewish populations in the 1980s and 1990s.

While these growing Sunbelt cities reflect a remarkable increase in the number of Jews living in the South, other areas of the region have seen a significant reduction in their Jewish population. Perhaps the most telling symbol of this decline is the growing number of disbanded congregations. During the 1980s and 1990s, Jewish congregations in Wharton, Texas; Ardmore, Oklahoma; Blytheville, Arkansas; Clarksdale, Mississippi; Demopolis, Alabama; and Weldon, North Carolina, among others, were forced to close their doors owing to dwindling memberships.

In fact, small Jewish communities in the South have been shrinking for decades. Woodville, Mississippi, a small town just north of the Louisiana border, flourished in the late nineteenth century, when it was known as "Little Jerusalem" because of the high percentage of Jews living there. By 1910, few if any Jews remained, and the synagogue was being used as a school. Today, all that remains of this once-vibrant community is a Jewish cemetery.[29] In the early twentieth century, many of Woodville's Jews moved to towns where economic opportunity was burgeoning.

Small Jewish communities throughout the South continued this cycle of rise and decline during the late nineteenth and early twentieth centuries. As Jewish communities in St. Francisville, Louisiana, and Port Gibson, Mississippi, disappeared, new ones formed in North Carolina and the Mississippi Delta. But in the twenty-first century, this cycle of death and renewal has been broken, as few new southern Jewish communities have been founded outside of major metropolitan areas. Southern Jewish life, once based largely in small towns, now mirrors the urban and suburban Jewish life of the North.

There are exceptions to this trend. Increasing numbers of Jewish professors are working at southern universities, leading to the growth of Jewish communities and new congregations in college towns. In Durham and Chapel Hill, North Carolina, home to Duke University and the University of North Carolina, the Jewish population has grown by almost 800 percent since 1970. Knoxville, home of the state university of Tennessee, has experienced steady growth—from 800 Jews in 1960 to 1,800 in 2001. In other cases, southern college towns maintained their Jewish populations, as Jewish merchants were replaced by Jewish academics. Tuscaloosa, Alabama, site of the state university, has maintained its size of approximately three hundred Jews since 1960.[30]

In Arkansas, the newest and fastest-growing Jewish community is in Bentonville, where thirty local Jewish families founded the town's first synagogue in July 2004. The founders of Congregation Etz Chaim are not following in the footsteps of the roving peddlers who first settled in the small towns of Arkansas. Rather, they are drawn to Bentonville because it is the home of Wal-Mart, the world's largest employer. Ironically, this same retail juggernaut put many small-town Jewish merchants out of business. Most all of the members of Etz Chaim either work for Wal-Mart or for Wal-Mart suppliers who relocated to northwestern Arkansas to be near their biggest customer. In fact, according to one of the founders, the congregation was created in part because "it would be an asset to the [Wal-Mart] vendor community to have a Jewish congregation for recruitment."[31] The great majority of the congregation is made up of recent transplants from other parts of the country. Unlike older, small southern congregations, Etz Chaim's membership is young. In 2005, there were thirty children in their religious school, while many comparably sized congregations in the region have few or no children. Etz Chaim's exception to the trend of small-town Jewish decline is further evidence of the replacement of the old Jewish merchant class by a new generation of Jewish professionals.

The story of Bentonville stands out when compared with the fate of small-town Jewish communities in the Mississippi Delta. Jews flocked to the Delta when it emerged as the leading cotton-producing region of the country in the late nineteenth century. Jewish merchants and their families opened stores in most every Delta market town. In 1937, the Mississippi Delta was home to forty-six different Jewish communities, ranging from 450 Jews in Greenville to single families living in places that were little more than wide places in the road. All told, about 2,300 Jews lived in the Mississippi Delta in 1937.[32] Delta Jews formed cohesive social and religious networks that brought this dispersed population together. Families drove many miles to one of the seven synagogues in the Delta, which served as regional congregations. It was not unusual for Jewish teenagers to travel hours through the Delta's flat farmlands to attend balls and social mixers designed to introduce young Jews to potential spouses.

As portrayed in countless newspaper articles and the documentary film *Delta Jews*, this region has seen a dramatic reduction in its Jewish population. In 2005, no more than three hundred Jews lived in the Delta, scattered in eight different communities, each of which was contracting. Several congregations have closed, and the remainder are struggling to remain open. Few Jewish children raised in the Delta have stayed there. In many cases, as with Carla Levingston, parents have discouraged their sons and daughters from returning to the region. A central concern of most Jewish parents is that their children marry other Jews. This became increasingly difficult in a place like the Mississippi Delta. In addition, the Delta no longer offers economic opportunity for enterprising businesspeople. Jewish retail businesses have been undermined by the general economic decline of the region and the rise of chain discount stores.

Clarksdale, Mississippi, is located in the physical and spiritual heart of the Delta. It is the birthplace of the blues and the site of the legendary "crossroads" where Robert Johnson supposedly sold his soul to the devil in exchange for his musical talent. It also was once home to one of the largest Jewish communities in the state. According to a 1937 study, Clarksdale's 412 Jews ranked just behind Greenville's Jewish population. As one of the mercantile centers of the most fertile cotton-growing region in the country, Clarksdale thrived in the early twentieth century; but with changes in the cotton economy, and the general malaise of the Delta, the town is now a shell of its former self. Empty storefronts line its main business streets. Jewish-sounding names are visible in sidewalk tiles in front of old buildings or on faded signs, testament to Jewish retailers' former prominence in the community.

Mirroring the decline of Clarksdale itself, the local Jewish community has withered to the point where the town's only congregation voted to disband and sell its synagogue building. The last president of the congregation, Arnold Himelstein, plans to leave town after he retires. His children did not return to the Delta after college. As he notes in an interview with the *Forward* newspaper, "the young people didn't come back. They went places with more opportunities— can't fault them for that."[33] With their congregation closed, the main goal of the few Jews that remain in Clarksdale is to raise money for their cemetery fund, to ensure that it is cared for long after the last Jew has left. They realize that in the

Stores like Aaron Kline's Whale Store in Alligator, Mississippi, and Okun's Shoes in Clarksdale, Mississippi, are now largely a thing of the past in the small towns of the South. Photos by Bill Aron, in the collection of the Goldring/Woldenberg Institute of Southern Jewish Life, Jackson, Mississippi.

future, the cemetery will be the only visible vestige of what was once a flourishing Jewish community.

A few hundred miles south of Clarksdale, Congregation B'nai Israel in Natchez, Mississippi, is facing a similar situation. B'nai Israel was the first Jewish congregation founded in the state as Jewish immigrants from the German states and Alsace settled in this important antebellum trading center, situated north of New Orleans on the Mississippi River. The Natchez Jewish community thrived in the nineteenth century. By 1900, about 450 Jews lived in Natchez, and their affluence is clearly reflected in the grandiose synagogue the congregation built in 1906. Soon after the building was dedicated, the area's cotton crop, which fueled the city's economy, suffered from boll weevils and low market prices, leading to a long, slow dwindling of Natchez's Jewish population. By 1937, only 125 Jews were left. By 2005, 10 remained. In 1992, the remaining members realized that they could not continue indefinitely and made arrangements with the Museum of the Southern Jewish Experience to preserve their building as a museum of Natchez Jewish history.

Clarksdale and Natchez are just two of many examples of the retreat of small-town Jewish life in the South. All across the former Confederacy, small Jewish communities have faced the demographic reality that their numbers will likely never increase. Many have made arrangements for the end of their congregations. Much press attention has been devoted to lamenting these dying Jewish communities. Yet, ironically in 2005, Jewish life in the South has never been stronger as more Jews live there than ever before. The easiest way to understand Jewish demographics in the South is to look at which areas are thriving economically and which are languishing. Jews in America have always been drawn to economic opportunity, wherever it might be. As small-town economies have suffered, Jews have left for the booming Sunbelt metropolises of the South and beyond.

If Jewish life in the South is flourishing, can the same be said for southern Jewish identity? That is to say, are the Jewish communities in the former Confederacy still southern? Does the adjective *southern* merely denote geographic location, or does it signify a set of cultural differences that mark the southern Jew as distinct from Jews in the rest of the country? Scholars have long debated the issue of southern Jewish distinctiveness. To some, southern Jews have more in common with their coreligionists in New York than with their Gentile neighbors, and what passes as the "unique southern Jewish experience" is more a result of small-town life than southern culture.[34] While a provocative argument, it overlooks the important role of culture and identity.

For many southern Jews, their identity is based more on being a southerner than a Jew. Hattie Heiman of McGehee, Arkansas, described herself as "southern first, and then I'm Jewish." Interviewed for the documentary film *Shalom Y'all*, Jay Lehmann of Natchez, Mississippi, expressed the same sentiment. When I. A. Rosenbaum left Meridian, Mississippi, for college at Vanderbilt in the late 1930s, he joined a Jewish fraternity but did not get along very well with his primarily northern brothers. Rosenbaum was unfamiliar with the Yiddish phrases they often used. He eventually moved out of the fraternity house to live with a Gentile friend from Meridian, with whom he felt he had more in common.[35] In 2004, a *Moment* magazine reporter spent time in the small Jewish community in McGehee and concluded, "listening to these women speak, it's apparent that they have less in common with Jews living in New York than they do with Christians living next door. They eat, dress, speak, and even worship very much like the Southerners they are."[36]

This cultural difference between southern and northern Jews, while difficult to quantify, is reflected in the historical predominance of Reform Judaism in the South. In 1907, 40 percent of the congregations affiliated with the Reform Union of American Congregations were located in the South, at a time when only 5 percent of American Jews lived in the region.[37] In 1917, 72 percent of southern congregations used English in their worship services, with 19 percent using English exclusively. In the rest of the country, 81 percent of congregations used Hebrew exclusively.[38] Jews who came south were less interested in maintaining traditional Jewish observance and thus did not mind moving to an area where kosher meat was difficult to find. As a small minority of the population, southern Jews were anxious to fit into their surroundings. Throughout the South, this meant adapting their religious practice to prevailing Protestant norms. Thus, Reform Judaism, with its English prayers and Christian-based elements such as choirs, organs, and Confirmation rituals, became popular in the South. Also, Reform Judaism's deemphasis on rigorous daily observance of rabbinic law made it especially suitable in the South, where merchants had to keep their shops open on Saturday to survive economically. This prominence of Reform Judaism set southern Jews apart from the rest of the country's Jewish population.

While the degree of southern Jewish distinctiveness may be debated by historians, what is undeniable is that the region and its Jews have become less distinct since the midtwentieth century. One of the cultural effects of the rise of the Sunbelt has been the homogenization of the South. Travelers can drive through these southern metropolises on the interstate with little sense that they are in the South. The same chain restaurants, stores, and motels are everywhere. A similar process has transformed southern Jewish life. Jews from the North have moved to southern cities, bringing their own religious and cultural traditions. Few Jewish children raised in Houston or Atlanta today speak in a southern accent, once a universal signifier of southern identity.

In past decades, an important characteristic of southern Jewish life was the prevalence of the small-town experience. Instead of congregating in major cities like New York, Philadelphia, or Chicago, southern Jews settled in hundreds of little places. Jews found homes wherever farmers brought their goods to market. Although cities like Houston, New Orleans, and Atlanta attracted significant Jewish populations before 1945, they were far smaller than the industrial cities of the North. In 1920, 45 percent of all Jews in the United States lived in New York City. The northern Jewish experience was overwhelmingly urban, whereas the southern Jewish experience was centered in small towns. With the demographic changes in the South since 1945, this is no longer the case. The small-town Jew has by and large become a museum piece, featured in numerous journalistic profiles as a dying breed. The northern-born suburban Jew living outside of Atlanta or Dallas is more characteristic of contemporary southern Jewish life. Jewish families living in the suburbs of Atlanta are little different from those living in the suburbs of Chicago.[39]

The mythic image of the southern Jew as assimilated small-town merchant is no longer salient in a region where Houston-born Michael Dell, raised as a Conservative Jew, opened a small computer business in Austin, Texas, transforming the Lone Star State's capital into a southern version of Silicon Valley. Dell built a fortune by selling computers "direct" to customers and cutting out the middleman retailer. Ironically, southern Jews long thrived as economic middlemen, selling their customers decidedly low-tech merchandise. How should we understand the story of Dell Computer? Is it an iconic southern Jewish success story, like SteinMart, the discount retail chain that began in Greenville, Mississippi, or simply a Jewish story that is located in the South?

Though the face of southern Jewry has changed since 1945, there have never been more Jews living south of the Mason-Dixon Line, and population trends show little sign of this growth ending. And yet, in other ways the Jewish South is dying, just as surely as its small-town communities are dying. Historians should avoid predicting the future, but it seems likely that at the turn of the twenty-second century, there will no longer be a distinct southern Jewish identity. Houston, Dallas, Charlotte, and Atlanta will simply be some of the Jewish population centers in the country, with little or no cultural difference from cities in other regions of the United States. Aside from a handful of college towns, small southern towns will no longer have Jewish communities. The era of the small-town Jewish merchant class will be long passed. And yet, one fact will remain unchanged. Jews will continue to follow economic opportunity wherever it may take them, be it the South or anywhere else.

NOTES

1. Gavin Wright, *Old South, New South: Revolution in the Southern Economy since the Civil War* (New York: Basic Books, 1986; reprint, Baton Rouge: Louisiana State University Press, 1996), 241; Numan Bartley, *The New South, 1945–1980* (Baton Rouge: Louisiana State University Press, 1995), 8–11, 123.

2. Bartley, *The New South*, 9–11; David R. Goldfield, *Promised Land: The South since 1945* (Arlington Heights, Ill.: Harlan Davidson, 1987), 5–6.

3. Wright, *Old South, New South*, 244–46; Goldfield, *Promised Land*, 26.

4. Wright, *Old South, New South*, 248; Bartley, *The New South*, 127; Goldfield, *Promised Land*, 24. Bartley classifies Texas and Oklahoma as western states in his statistic about more than half of American cotton being grown in the West.

5. Frank Hobbs and Nicole Stoops, U.S. Census Bureau, Census 2000 Special Reports, *Demographic Trends in the 20th Century* (Washington, D.C.: Government Printing Office, 2002), A-5.

6. Campbell Gibson, Population Division, U.S. Census Bureau, *Population of the 100 Largest Cities and Other Urban Places in the United States, 1790 to 1990* (Washington, D.C.: Government Printing Office, 1998), table 25.

7. Wright, *Old South, New South*, 257, 270; Bartley, *The New South*, 146.

8. *New York Times*, February 8, 1976, 1. This was the first of a weeklong series on the Sunbelt phenomenon.

9. Bartley, *The New South*, 277, 429–30.

10. Goldfield, *Promised Land*, 138; Bartley, *The New South*, 287–88.

11. *Mississippi Statistical Summary of Population, 1800–1980; Mississippi Statistical Abstract 2003* (Jackson, Miss.: The Company, 1983), passim.

12. According to the *National Jewish Population Survey of 2000–2001* (New York: United Jewish Communities, 2003), the Jewish population of America was 5.2 million people, down from 5.5 million in the 1990 survey.

13. Author interview with Barbara Thiede, December 21, 2004.

14. See Deborah Dash Moore, *To the Golden Cities: Pursuing the American Jewish Dream in Miami and L.A.* (New York: Free Press, 1994).

15. The 1950 figures come from http://www.demographia.com; and U.S. Census Bureau, Census 2000, table 3a, "Population in Metropolitan and Micropolitan Statistical Areas Ranked by 2000 Population for the United States and Puerto Rico: 1900 and 2000," at http://www.census.gov.

16. Jacob Rader Marcus, *To Count a People: America Jewish Population Data, 1585–1984* (Lanham, Md.: University Press of America, 1990), 50; *American Jewish Yearbook 2002* (New

York: American Jewish Committee), 257. The 2005 estimates come from the Atlanta Jewish Federation.

17. Airports ranked by Airports Council International. Atlanta is the world's busiest airport, handling more than 79 million passengers in 2003. The next closest is Chicago's O'Hare Airport, with 69.5 million passengers.

18. The Fortune 1000 refers to a list of the largest public companies in the United States, based on revenue, published annually by *Forbes* magazine.

19. "Metropolitan Atlanta Jewish Population Study: Summary of Major Findings, February 1985" (Atlanta: Atlanta Jewish Federation), 4.

20. Marcus, *To Count a People*, 17; author interview with Jay Tanenbaum, December 15, 2004.

21. "A Study of the Jewish Population, Atlanta, Georgia, 1947," prepared by the National Jewish Welfare Board. William Breman Jewish Heritage Museum, Atlanta, Ga.

22. "The Jewish Community Study of North Metro Atlanta: 2004" (Atlanta: Jewish Federation of Greater Atlanta).

23. "The 1996 Jewish Population Study of Atlanta Summary Report," 14–15; and "1998 Update of the 1996 Jewish Population Study of Atlanta" (Atlanta: Atlanta Jewish Federation).

24. Figures are from the Cobb County Chamber of Commerce Web site: http://www.cobbchamber.org.

25. Steven Hertzberg, *Strangers within the Gated City: The Jews of Atlanta, 1845–1915* (Philadelphia: Jewish Publication Society of America, 1978), 215.

26. Author interview with Rabbi Shalom Lewis, January 18, 2005.

27. On the Sabbath, Jews are proscribed from carrying things outside of the home. The *eruv* symbolically extends the home, enabling observant Jews to carry necessary items to synagogue.

28. Atlanta's Jewish population was growing much faster than that of Baltimore, Detroit, or Cleveland, which were all still ranked ahead of Atlanta in 2000. By 2005, it had passed each of them to become the tenth-largest Jewish population center in the country.

29. Leo E. Turitz and Evelyn Turitz, *Jews in Early Mississippi* (Jackson: University Press of Mississippi, 1983), 3.

30. Marcus, *To Count a People*, 13, 165–66, 209; *American Jewish Yearbook*, 2002, 259, 266–67.

31. Quoted in *Arkansas Democrat Gazette*, October 16, 2004.

32. Linfield, "Jewish Communities of the United States," *American Jewish Yearbook*, 1938–1939, 250.

33. *Forward*, September 12, 2003, 23.

34. See, for example, Mark K. Bauman, *The Southerner as American: Jewish Style* (Cincinnati: American Jewish Archives, 1996).

35. Interview with I. A. Rosenbaum, September 9, 1999, Institute of Southern Jewish Life Oral History Collection, Jackson, Mississippi.

36. Jennie Rothenberg, "Cotton, Catfish & Challah: Tales of a Traveling Rabbi," *Moment*, February 2005, 57.

37. These figures were calculated from data in the *American Jewish Yearbook*, 1907–8, 115–18.

38. *American Jewish Yearbook*, 1919–20, 330–32.

39. Marcus, *To Count a People*, 151, 241.

13

JEWISH FATES, ALTERED STATES

STEPHEN J. WHITFIELD

The southern Jewish experience has characteristically been recounted in terms of its incongruities. Those scholars and other commentators who have tried to do justice to southern Jewish history have usually taken the South to be distinctive. They have presupposed the peculiarity of the Jewish people as well, and a blending of this region with this minority was not really expected to occur. During the span of the history of the region, it was usually assumed to be too rural, too bigoted, too backward, too oppressively conformist to serve as a congenial home for Jewish immigrants and their descendants. Recent feature stories in the press continue to express surprise at the existence of a durable Jewish life in the region, which is depicted as exotic rather than commonplace.

Most of the ancestors of today's American Jews came from the *shtetlach* of eastern and central Europe barely more than 120 years ago; and the new world to which they so eagerly adapted was mostly urban, mostly industrializing and mostly above the Mason-Dixon Line. Yekl, the eponymous protagonist of Abraham Cahan's 1896 novella, changes his name to Jake and proclaims: "I am an *American feller*, a *Yankee*." He stays in New York, where there was little risk that Yekl would become a yokel. The typical *bubbie* did not want to raise a Bubba. The Jewish character ideal (primarily male) was to be a mensch, not a good old boy—as profiled by journalist Tom Wolfe. This type is endowed with "a good sense of humor. . . . [He] enjoys ironic jokes, is tolerant and easygoing . . . and has a reasonable amount of physical courage." The Jews tended to associate the male character ideal with scholarship, in contrast to the indelible generalization of Henry Adams that "the Southerner had no mind; he had temperament. He was not a scholar: he had no intellectual training, he could not analyze an idea, and he could not even conceive of admitting two."[1]

No wonder then that the Jews who came to the region were alien, at least at first. In an overwhelmingly agrarian order, they had little yearning for forty acres and a mule and therefore created an occupational structure that was undeniably different from their neighbors'. Southern Jewry constituted what Napoleon said with a sneer of the British: "a nation of shopkeepers." Retailing is such a risky business that the list of those who have failed at it include two presidents: Ulysses S. Grant and Harry S. Truman. Jews had to prevail among neighbors who displayed much ambivalence toward capitalism and entrepreneurship, because such phenomena were often perceived as instruments of Yankee ingenuity and hegemony. Jewish merchants were not always given credit for helping to modernize the South and making it more prosperous. Even from Wilhelmine Germany, Max Weber took notice; the sociologist claimed that Reform Jews "were able to pursue the very profitable business of usuriously exploiting the rural Negro." Ditto the 1903 edition of *The Souls of Black Folk*, in which W.E.B. Du Bois referred to the "shrewd and unscrupulous Jews" who took advantage of a helpless peasantry—white and black—after Reconstruction.[2]

Merchants who sunk roots in hamlets that cartographers could barely find had no effective shield against such criticism. But these businessmen constituted the heart of southern Jewry, and their destiny got entwined with the history of the region. In the early nineteenth century, Thomas Jefferson bought supplies for Monticello from David Isaacs's dry goods store on Main Street in Charlottesville, Virginia. His coreligionists included the Lesem family, which owned a dry goods store in antebellum Hannibal, Missouri, where Samuel Clemens—the future Mark Twain—grew up. Early in the twentieth century, Pancho Villa was not only a temporary lodger above the El Paso, Texas, store of the family of Haymon Krupp; the rebel *bandido* also crossed the border to purchase troop supplies and uniforms from other Jewish merchants in the city. Even though the notorious lynching of Leo Frank in 1915 helped inspire the rebirth of the Reconstructionist-era Ku Klux Klan, its members did not bother to boycott the Jewish retailers on Main Street. Who else would have sold Klansmen their denims, their shoes, and even their sheets? When Elvis Presley decided to outfit himself in an *outré* black style, the couturier to the king was Bernie Lansky on Beale Street in Memphis, Tennessee, where the rocker had grown up so destitute that his parents could neither afford a telephone nor always pay their water bill. Both services were kindly provided by their neighbors, the rabbi of Beth El Emeth Congregation, Alfred Fruchter, and his wife Jeanette. In Americus, Georgia a, once and future president, Jimmy Carter, bought his suits from A. Cohen & Sons.[3]

The mercantile enterprise at which many of their compatriots excelled meant that the South mostly skipped the working-class phase of the economic and social history of the Jews. Not that there was no poverty, nor terrible struggle to transcend the limits of a marginal existence. But businesses were built in the re-

Kessler Dry Goods, Macon, Georgia, ca. 1911. Photo courtesy of the Ida Pearle and Joseph Cuba Archives of the William Breman Jewish Heritage Museum, Atlanta, Georgia.

gion well before an industrialized labor force was needed or wanted. Substituting for the International Ladies' Garment Workers Union or the Amalgamated Clothing Workers of America was the prototypical "Jew store," whether it was Cohen Brothers in Jacksonville, Florida, or E. J. "Mutt" Evans' United Dollar Department Store in Durham, North Carolina, or an emporium-like Nieman-Marcus in Dallas. Minding the store was ever on the mind of southern Jewry. The historian Daniel J. Boorstin was born in Atlanta in 1914 because his grandfather, Benjamin Boorstin, had fled the Pale of Settlement in the late 1880s and had abruptly halted his quest for refuge in Monroe, Georgia. (No reason for that destination was ever given.) Benjamin Boorstin's brother arrived about the same time and opened a store directly across the street.[4]

These backwoods boutiques contributed to whatever well-being might be eked out in such towns, though friction was not thereby avoided. When William Faulkner's Jason Compson encounters a salesman, he assumes that the stranger is Jewish and tries to put him at ease: "'I'm not talking about men of the jewish religion,' I says. 'I've known some jews that were fine citizens. You might be one yourself,' I says. 'No,' he says, 'I'm an American.'" Reassured, Compson then explains the source of his concern: ". . . It's just the race. You'll admit that they produce nothing. They follow the pioneers into a new country and sell them clothes." Even while disclaiming prejudice ("I don't hold a man's religion against

Prystowsky & Sons ("Mike, Sam & Jake's"), 521 King Street, Charleston, South Carolina, ca. 1930. Photo courtesy of Arnold and Shirley Prystowsky. Special Collections, College of Charleston Library.

him"), Compson proposes that he and the drummer agree that they are both Americans, which leads to the glum conclusion: "Not many of us left."[5]

The villages and small towns where such Americans met newcomers and shopkeepers represent the most evocative sites in the shaping of southern Jewish history. Cities were too few and too small to harbor significant Jewish communities. At the dawn of the nineteenth century, Jewish communities were so precarious that they hugged the coastline. Charleston, South Carolina, was home to the largest, but its population numbered only about five hundred. In 1820, 191 Jews lived in Richmond, Virginia, and another 94 in Savannah, Georgia. When the Civil War broke out, the roughly two thousand Jews living in New Orleans formed the largest such community in the Confederacy. Two itinerant peddlers were the first Jews to arrive in Atlanta in 1845. When the 1910 census was taken, four thousand Jews were living there—at a time when half a million Jews were vacuum-packed into New York's Lower East Side, making it also the most dense Jewish neighborhood in America. Today, Atlanta's population of 86,000 Jews puts it in a dead heat with Cleveland-Akron, Ohio, Jewry as the twelfth-biggest among the nation's metropolitan statistical areas.[6]

Eli Evans (right), student body president, class of 1957, University of North Carolina at Chapel Hill, greeting former presidential candidate Adlai Stevenson arriving at the Raleigh-Durham Airport for a speech on campus. Collection of Eli N. Evans.

But impressive as the growth of Atlanta has been, consider that in 1923 there were almost twice as many Jews already living in a New York neighborhood like Harlem. No wonder then that Eli Evans entitled the book that established the paradigm of southern Jewish history *The Provincials*. They seemed to be bystanders, operating on the periphery. Jewish sensibility was so fully formed in New York City that Lorenz Hart's idea of a romantic song was to have a love-smitten Broadway singer vow: "I'll go to hell for ya, / Or Philadelphia."[7] If a metropolis only a short distance away thus operated below the cultural radar, even towns that were named after pioneer peddlers—like Kaplan, Louisiana; Felsenthal, Arkansas; and Marks, Mississippi—could hardly expect to be pivotal to the Jewish saga in America.

Why did it matter that southern Jewish life was defined by the villages in which it was conducted? Even a cosmopolitan statesman like Thomas Jefferson had not even *entered* a town until he was almost eighteen, which did not prevent him from virtuoso advocacy of the Enlightenment. Others were not scarred by the experience of origins even in the Delta, like Faulkner, who managed to win a Nobel Prize in Literature. Craig Claiborne was born in Sunflower (population fewer than five hundred) and was raised in Indianola, Mississippi. He has recalled having "numerous friends . . . who were Jews," thanks to a mother who thought that such families were classier than Gentiles and that Jews took greater "pleasure in conversation and tale-telling." The food editor of the *New York Times* was "initiated into the joys of matzoh balls, gefilte fish, matzoh brie, and so on" in the Delta, rather than in New York City.[8] For Jews who were fully ensconced in the South, however, the consequence of speaking in a village voice was conformism to sectional mores, and the dilution of distinctiveness.

Emily Bingham's monograph on three generations of the Mordecai family measures the pressures of assimilation in a region not famous for cherishing pluralism. Isolated in Warrenton, North Carolina, the Mordecais faced long odds against remaining Jewish. There were considerable inconveniences to the practice of tradition, such as keeping the dietary laws when there were no kosher butchers in the vicinity, nor any *mohel* around to circumcise the newborn sons; and keeping the Jewish Sabbath was difficult as well. To be sure, other Jews in small southern towns, in the nineteenth century and thereafter, managed to meet such challenges. But if the Mordecai family mostly abandoned Judaism, that was presumably because it was seen neither as a source of spiritual inspiration, nor as a fount of ethical wisdom, neither as a stimulus to *tikkun olam*, nor as the adhesive of solidarity with Jews elsewhere in the South or elsewhere on the planet. The Mordecais who reflected somewhat favorably on Judaism apparently considered it a faith to be honored out of a sense of duty. But in a republic that had so recently justified its rebellion against an empire because the right to pursue happiness had been alienated, duty could not easily compete with convenience. Nor could a set of onerous obligations vie with satisfactions stemming from material comfort and enhanced social status. Judaism simply could not invoke any positive claims on the Mordecais. The bonds of ancestral loyalty were too thin to stop the grandchildren (with one exception) from marrying outside of a faith that seemed to offer nothing to affirm.

The process of secularization is not truly illustrated in Bingham's account of the Mordecai family, which had made itself southern well before Reform Judaism might have effectively cushioned the dissipation of piety. Five of Jacob and Judy Mordecai's children (out of thirteen) married Christians, and a sixth— a daughter—was engaged to a Christian when she died. Five of their offspring— and not only those who married Gentiles—converted to Christianity, and only one of his twenty-eight grandchildren opted for endogamy. Therefore secularization does not seem *le mot juste*. The progeny of Jacob and Judy Mordecai evidently interpreted Christianity as superior to Judaism rather than worse than no

E. J. "Mutt" Evans being sworn in as mayor of Durham, North Carolina, 1953, for the second of his six terms. Photo by Harold Moore, Durham Morning Herald. Collection of Eli N. Evans.

real faith at all—which is what secularization would have entailed. Such local settings made the power of Christianity appear formidable, while Jewish particularism looked narrow and ungenerous. Jacob and Judy Mordecai adhered to the universalism of the Enlightenment and professed to honor "virtue in whatever garb it appeared." One daughter was grateful to live in a "happy country where religious distinctions are unknown."[9]

That, of course, was a delusion. Even in the following century, in the slice of the western hemisphere that was most saturated with Protestantism, the superiority of the majority faith continued to be asserted. In 1935, when Shelby Foote arrived at the University of North Carolina as an undergraduate, his fraternity brothers quizzed the future historian about his "feelings about Jesus Christ." Such a test was mandated because Foote's maternal grandfather had been an Austrian Jew. In 1978, Democrat Max Heller was favored to win a race for a U. S. Congressional seat in South Carolina. An immigrant from Austria (class of 1938), Heller had twice served as mayor of Greenville. But when the word got out that he did not accept Jesus as savior, the tide turned, and a Republican was elected.[10] Small-town Jewry experienced Sunday as the loneliest day of the week. But the six successful mayoralty campaigns of Eli Evans's father in Durham did not conceal credentials like the presidency of Beth-El Synagogue. On the contrary, the practice of Judaism was a political advantage, as hizzonner explained: "People down here respect church work."[11]

Other Jews were more vulnerable to the combination of Christian triumphalism and majoritarian pressure. The psychic damage done to Charleston's Ludwig Lewisohn was transmuted into literary art, and into a poignant memoir of how the conventional wisdom of the region got internalized. By the age of fifteen, the precocious, Berlin-born devotee of Methodism had become "an American, a Southerner, and a Christian . . . believing that the South was right in the War between the States, that Christianity was the true religion . . . [and] that the Democratic party was the only means, under Providence, of saving the White Race. . . ." A quick study, Lewisohn picked up these ideological foundations of the southern way of life easily enough to contribute an early story to Joel Chandler Harris's *Uncle Remus' Magazine*.[12] Lewisohn's return to Judaism as well as the commitment to Zionism that would redefine his life were achieved long after he had left Charleston.

A northern rabbi, Abraham Ruderman, served the Hebrew Union Temple of Greenville, Mississippi, from 1966 until 1970. The brevity of his service was a result not only of his identification with the plight of local blacks but with his resistance to performing mixed marriages. The Christian partners refused to consider conversion, and the Jewish parents, he speculated in his diary, may have harbored "a secret desire . . . to let their children escape from Judaism and merge into the majority religion." The Massachusetts-born Ruderman added: "To stand by supinely and watch one's children reared in a strange faith requires an indifference to one's faith that is hard to fathom."[13] Such Jews were not the children of pride. Adolph Ochs once counseled the congregants of Chattanooga, Tennessee's Mizpah synagogue against strutting around as though they were the chosen people. "We should live quietly, happily, unostentatiously," the future publisher of the *New York Times* advised. "Don't be too smart. Don't know too much."[14] Pick a low profile.

The subjugation to public opinion was hardly restricted to small towns. In New Orleans, for example, the Civil War marked an extreme version of this effort at blending into conformist sentiment. One rabbi, Bernard Illowy, could bizarrely proclaim that "liberty, fraternity and equality" constituted "the fundamental principles of our glorious Confederacy." Because his fellow southerners were taking up arms against the United States, a proclivity for "treason" was as plausible a credo as the slogan of the French Revolution. But neither Illowy nor the other Jews who ardently championed and even died for the cause of the Confederacy seemed to have detected any contradiction between their own "freedom" and the human bondage upon which their society was founded. Clara Solomon did not connect the dots between the refusal of her fellow Rebels to accept Abraham Lincoln as their president and the consequences of military resistance. Food shortages meant that neither flour nor butter was available for baking matzo, and worse was to come with Union troops: "N. O. [New Orleans] soon will be in the hands of the cussed Yankees." Solomon found the prospect of occupation "by Yankee devils . . . too terrible to contemplate," she complained.[15]

Those who went South went native. They became amazingly acculturated, as though sheer will could overcome the incongruities. In South Carolina, nineteenth-century Jews bore names like George Washington Harby, Thomas Jefferson Tobias, Andrew Jackson Moses. To defend their honor, they even fought duels; after all, they were eligible as "gentlemen." Such adaptation achieved a sense of security that enabled the nineteenth-century South to produce, as the historian Frederic Jaher has noted, "the first governor, the first U. S. senators, and the first American cabinet officer of Jewish stock." But the price remained an ardent conformism, well into the twentieth century as well—as Randy Newman, born in New Orleans in 1943, and a professional songwriter only seventeen years later, has noticed. On the track called "Dixie Flyer," on his album *Land of Dreams* (1996), southern Jews like his mother's family are depicted as "Tryin' to do like the Gentiles do / Christ, they wanted to be Gentiles, too. / Who wouldn't down there, wouldn't you?" Indeed, by the second half of the twentieth century, according to Natchez, Mississippi, locals, the Gentiles with Jewish ancestors outnumbered the Jews who still lived there.[16]

Yet the archetypal Jews of the South belong to a bygone era. They live in hamlets where almost nobody ever stops on purpose, and the tiny communities that Professor Lee Shai Weissbach in particular has studied are kept alive only by artificial respiration. Once the most populous *shul* in Mississippi was Congregation Beth Israel in Clarksdale, located in the Delta. But the last Sabbath service held there was conducted in May 2003. Once there had been had a full-time rabbi. Now a Memphis rabbi comes to Beth Israel four times a year, and too few Jews exist to form a *minyan*. No Jewish children remain in Clarksdale, which is why the average age of the congregants hovers around sixty. Perhaps the average age should be pegged at "deceased," because Arnold Himelstein, the unofficial president of this Reform synagogue, has called the cemetery just outside of Clarksdale "the only part of the Jewish community that's still growing." His own children live in Florida and California. If the synagogue building can be sold, the proceeds will be used for the upkeep of the cemetery. Were the small town to remain the essential site of southern Jewry, its sociology would be a mortuary science. The Mississippi Delta sustains perhaps only about three hundred Jews—barely enough to pack a typical suburban synagogue elsewhere. There is thus a nostalgic, elegiac quality to the Jewish historical scholarship on the Delta.[17] Sweet home Alabama is currently home to a mere nine thousand Jews—more than half of whom live in Birmingham. The agrarian class that once depended on trade with village merchants is disappearing along with them. There is still a Department of Agriculture, because farmers remain politically influential. But statistically they have become insignificant.

Decline and oblivion are not the inevitable markers of Jewish history, however; it can be supple and surprising too. Take one of the most remarkable of all the tales of the ba'alei teshuvah, a status that Julius Lester was highly unlikely to occupy. In Look Out, Whitey! Black Power's Gon' Get Your Mama (1968), he transcribed centuries of accumulated anger into the fierce idiom of black nationalist ideology. Lester served as a field secretary of the Student Nonviolent Coordinating Committee (SNCC), the sole civil rights organization to amplify the attack on Jim Crow into a systematic opposition to American society. He later served as host of his self-titled show on New York's WBAI-FM, a program that became notorious for Judeophobia. During the Ocean Hill–Brownsville school melee in New York in 1969, he permitted the reading of an antisemitic poem, from which neither Lester (nor the young poet's teacher) distanced himself. He also became a professor of Black Studies at the University of Massachusetts, though Lester's roots were southern. His father had been a Methodist minister who served congregations in Tennessee and Kansas, and as a child in the 1940s, Julius Lester visited his grandmother in Arkansas. He once noticed that the name on the mailbox was Altschul. That was the surname of his great-grandfather, a Jewish immigrant from Germany who came as a peddler to Pine Bluff, served in the Confederate Army, and then married a former slave named Maggie Carson. He is buried in the Jewish cemetery in Pine Bluff. Growing up, Lester had heard about his white, Jewish relatives; but after becoming a Jew himself, at the age of forty-two, he decided to contact the other descendants of Adolph Altschul, informing them that he shared not only their genes but their faith as well. He wrote to all the Altschuls in the Pine Bluff phone book, only to discover that all had become Gentiles. Their newly introduced black cousin was the sole descendant who was Jewish.[18]

Families like the Altschuls, who succumbed to the mores of the majority, typified small-town Jewry. The doom of its way of life is acknowledged even in an affectionate tribute to it like Brian Bain's documentary, Shalom Y'all (2002), which depicts southern Jews in a spirit of celebration rather than critical detachment. They show an aptitude to sustain Judaism that is tenacious, and

Shalom Y'all praises their endurance. But on the soundtrack, the death rattle can be heard too.

The small-town Jewry that Eli Evans demystified is dying, and no one has memorialized it more evocatively. More than anyone else, he deprovincialized American Jewish historiography by elucidating the experience of his coreligionists in the region and in three impressive books inspired others to pursue the subject. Evans did justice to the charm as well as the ordeal of southern Jewish history and merits the gratitude of all aficionados of the subject. But the case for a new paradigm must be advanced.

That is because the South to whose literary legacy he has contributed has proved to be something other than timeless and unchanging. It did not remain xenophobic, a closed society. The songwriter and singer Janis Ian ("Society's Child"), lesbian and liberal as well as Jewish, moved to Nashville, Tennessee, in 1986, when she "walked off the plane . . . and thought, I'm home."[19] A new South that is something other than the fantasy of boosters seeking outside investment must be reckoned with, with implications for the fate of the Jews of the region.

A few years ago a female cousin of mine was about to move to Mississippi to join her partner, and I asked him how congenial that part of the state would be for her. "Oh, don't worry," I was reassured, "the [Ku Klux] Klan down there is pretty liberal." So peculiar and indulgent a standard imparts something of the flavor of the region. The Klan was once important enough either to join (as did Dr. Simon Baruch) or to fight (as did Louis Isaac Jaffé, who won a Pulitzer Prize for his editorials in the Norfolk *Virginian-Pilot* in 1929). The second Klan was in fact more influential and dangerous in the Midwest and Southwest than it was in the Deep South and was at least as hostile to immigrants and to Roman Catholics as it was to Jews or blacks in particular. Indeed, the Imperial Wizard, Hiram Wesley Evans, found German Jews acceptable, because of their capacity to "amalgamate. . . . Quite different are the Eastern Jews of recent immigration, the Jews known as the Ashkenasim [sic]." The third Klan of the 1950s and 1960s committed terrible atrocities, but its fecklessness in defending the hegemony and orthodoxy of racism is obvious. Indeed the Klan in Natchez, for example, abandoned a culture war against Jews, when the grand dragon promised to oppose only blacks and outside agitators.[20]

Apocalypse was postponed, in no small measure because of the communitarian and religious resources that could be tapped within southern culture. Its values not only enabled black activists to find a remedy for the toxins of bigotry but also sanctioned the reconciliation that both races accomplished after the legal victories over Jim Crow. The sense of a common heritage and terrain eased the shock of this tectonic shift from what H. L. Mencken had called the Bible Belt to the looser designation of Sunbelt. A beleaguered region that cultivated a bring-it-on defiance became modernized and urbanized, divided as much by class as by race. The historian might conclude that by 1985 the primal racism that had scarred the Old South was gone. That is when Governor George C. Wallace and the Reverend Jesse Jackson met for a moment of reconciliation and sipped tea together in Montgomery, Alabama. Two years earlier Wallace had attracted as much as a third of the black vote.[21]

So dramatic a change suggests that the ancien régime had already been cracking for decades. Even if the fissures in the system of Jim Crow were not always exposed, something to shatter it had already been gathering momentum in the transition from the 1950s to the 1960s. One religious minority was not irrelevant to that transformation, though the best-known Jew then living in the region was there not by birth but by choice. As editor of the *Carolina Israelite* from 1941 until 1968, and as the best-selling author of books consisting of pieces that first appeared in his one-man monthly, Charlotte's Harry Golden made a homespun, humorous, pickle-barrel case against the sickness of white supremacy. The transplanted New Yorker noticed the distinction between the threat that southern Negroes posed when sitting down (in a restaurant or a diner, in a library or on a bus) and the tranquillity that coincided with an upright position. Golden then proposed a Vertical Negro Plan, by which public schools would eliminate seats for pupils, and thus resolve the racial crisis: "It is only when the Negro 'sets' that the fur begins to fly." In championing desegregation, Golden generated no public anxiety among his coreligionists in the South; nor did it hurt that subscribers to the *Carolina Israelite* included Harry Truman and William Faulkner. Indeed, Golden seemed to exemplify sanity and common sense in an atmosphere of sectional fanaticism. A satiric talent helped. Not that the author of *Only in America* ignored Judeophobia. But the cure that he proposed was culinary: "If we gave each anti-Semite an onion roll with lox and cream cheese; some chopped chicken liver with a nice radish, and a good piece of brisket of beef with a few potato pancakes, he'd soon give up all this nonsense. It is worth a try."[22] The Department of Defense has run with the idea; the cuisine served to radical Islamicists captured in Afghanistan and held at Camp Delta on Guantánamo Bay has included lox and bagels.

There were other signs of racial progressivism even as Jim Crow remained legal and obligatory virtually everywhere in the former Confederacy. Only a year after the Temple in Atlanta was bombed because of the eloquent desegregationist sermons that Rabbi Jacob Rothschild had delivered from the pulpit, the Reform Temple of Nashville installed a wall mosaic. The artist was Ben Shahn, whose oeuvre as a painter, photographer, and calligrapher was noteworthy for its devotion to social justice as well as for its aesthetic elegance. The mosaic depicts five faces—all male, to be sure, but also of different racial characteristics. The prophet Malachi is quoted, both in Hebrew and in English: "Do we not have one father, has not one God created us? Why then do we act faithlessly with each other, so as to profane the covenant of our brothers?" So pointed a message of racial brotherhood was hardly consistent with the conventional understanding of the public culture of the South in 1959. But the Nashville synagogue's endorsement of such art was a harbinger.[23]

One year later, history cracked wide open, when four black college students ignited the sit-in movement in Greensboro, North Carolina, and SNCC was founded in Nashville. Also in 1960, two deaths were recorded: those of the expatriate novelist Richard Wright and the lawyer and businessman David Cohn. The Yale-educated Cohn had made himself into perhaps the most articulate defender of the social system of the Mississippi Delta—the contours of which he had famously defined in 1935 as "begin[ning] in the lobby of the Peabody Hotel in Memphis and end[ing] on Catfish Row in Vicksburg." Five years later, when Wright published Native Son, Cohn reviewed it vehemently, as "a blinding and corrosive study in hate," a highly exaggerated and inflammatory depiction of the dilemma of race relations that only demonstrated that it was "insoluble." Cohn contrasted the animus of Native Son with the suffering of his own people, which had responded to two millennia of oppression with "an intense family and communal life and [which had] constructed inexhaustible wells of spiritual resource." The novelist rebutted by wondering whether Cohn was seriously "recommending his 'two thousand years of oppression' to the Negroes of America," who would—Wright safely predicted—"perish in the attempt to avoid it." He could see nothing wrong in demanding that the rights guaranteed to whites be fully extended to black Americans as well, and therefore found the problem of white supremacy quite remediable; see under: U.S. Constitution.[24] This exchange, conducted in 1940 in the Atlantic Monthly, was memorable, if only because the future belonged to Wright rather than to Cohn. Even when one state legislator from the Mississippi Delta justified the formation of the new Citizens' Councils by arguing that "a few killings" would prevent "a lot of bloodshed later on," the old ultraviolence could not be perpetuated; that particular legacy of the Old South could not be sustained.[25] Mechanical cotton pickers eliminated the need for cheap labor, and a revolution of rising expectations was sweeping through the entire region. There even the most patient blacks were getting tired of spending a lifetime in dead-end jobs like driving Miss Daisy.

Nor could passionately liberal and radical Jews be blocked from crossing the

Mason-Dixon Line to make trouble; no Checkpoint Charlie had warned them that they were leaving the American Sector. Barriers could not be erected against civil rights activists, many of them Jews. Their impact on the movement for racial equality was noted as early as 1961 by the most unsparing black opponent of the civil rights movement. In a weird meeting that occurred in Atlanta, Malcolm X of the Nation of Islam warned Ku Klux Klansmen (in remarks recorded by the FBI) "that the Jew is behind the integration movement, using the Negro as a tool." (Malcolm X later expressed remorse over his participation in this meeting.) In 1956, Howard Zinn went from New York to chair the history and social sciences department at Atlanta's Spelman College. When the civil rights movement erupted, he became an adviser to SNCC in its early and heroic phase, which Zinn later recounted in a stirring book. By 1967, he had concluded from his encounters with white southerners that their prejudices could be blunted, that the region was more open to change and vulnerable to correction—if pushed—than many observers had realized.[26] Zinn was right. Because the civil rights movement proved to be the winning side, scholars remain intrigued by the role of Jews in helping to transform the region.[27] Some came as activists, to promote voter registration or community organization. Some came as lawyers, some as teachers, some as rabbis. Other Jews stayed behind, but gave decisive financial support. Their impact helped achieve the historic change that led one native Alabamian to realize, in 1974: "We've been saying farewell to the South as a singular region long enough. . . . But . . . I have the distinct impression that this is it."[28]

In a sense the most important attorney battling in behalf of racial equality had been Nathan Margold, a protégé of Felix Frankfurter at Harvard Law School. Early in the 1930s, Margold proposed to the NAACP the strategy that proved to be successful. To smash the structure of Jim Crow, its laws should not be challenged head-on. What should be demanded instead is that, if southern states wished to maintain segregation, then separate facilities must be made fully equal. Thurgood Marshall recalled reading Margold's 218-page proposal carefully: "It stayed with me. The South would go broke paying for truly equal, dual systems." At the age of twenty-five, the recent graduate of Howard Law School devoted the first part of his career to applying Margold's idea. The rest—spanning the remaining decades of the century—is history.[29] In 1995, a thirty-year anniversary was held in Mississippi among the attorneys who had answered the appeal from the southern outpost of the American Civil Liberties Union (ACLU), the Lawyers Constitutional Defense Committee. The Jackson *Clarion Ledger* ran a story on the anniversary below the headline "Civil Rights Lawyers Revisit Their 1960s Battleground; All-White, Mostly Jewish, Group of Attorneys Fought for

Freedom in Repressive Mississippi." The daily had in fact undercounted. "About the only place where one might encounter a higher percentage of Jews," one of the veterans conjectured, "would have been at a rabbinical conclave."[30]

The attorneys who personified the old paradigm of southern Jewish historiography generally ignored racial injustice because it seemed so intractable, so difficult to remedy. Such lawyers sought to achieve their own social inclusion, rather than engage in political dissent. Daniel Boorstin's father "always spoke with a warm and soft Georgia accent," the historian recalled. Samuel Boorstin attended and graduated from the University of Georgia at Athens and was only twenty-one years old when he received his law degree. He "became the youngest member of the Georgia bar. In Atlanta he . . . spent his spare time joining every fraternal organization that would let him in. These included the Elks, the Odd Fellows, the Red Men, and the Masons." Despite his Jewishness, Samuel Boorstin "might have had a career in Georgia politics," his son speculated. But then the Leo Frank case erupted. The young attorney helped in Leo Frank's defense and advised some of the outside attorneys, including Louis Marshall. When the jurors—contaminated by a combination of prejudice and fear—convicted the defendant, it was Sam Boorstin's task to tell the horrible news to Leo Frank's wife, Lucille. After the lynching, further revenge was taken against Atlanta's Jewish merchants, whose store windows were smashed. The future historian's uncles fled the city after their clothing store was vandalized, and joined his parents, who relocated in Tulsa, Oklahoma.[31] The paradigm that put bigotry at the center of the "southern way of life" would fragment after the 1960s.

Southern Jewish attorneys like Morris Abram deserve some of the credit. In the new paradigm that emerged, race lost its salience and is no longer what the historian Ulrich B. Phillips had claimed in 1928: the central feature of southern history. A personification of the new paradigm might be Mickey Cantor, born in 1939 in Nashville, where his family ran a furniture store. He played varsity baseball at Vanderbilt, and after law school at Georgetown, represented a variety of clients, including migrant farm workers. Cantor also lobbied on behalf of giant oil and aerospace companies, even as he supported liberal Democratic candidates in a number of states. The most important of these politicians was Bill Clinton, who selected Cantor to be the U.S. trade representative as the nation faced tougher economic competition and the novel challenges of globalization.[32] In 1996–97, Cantor served in Clinton's cabinet as secretary of commerce. Were race integral to the southern experience, a black Jew like Reuben Morris Greenberg would be inconceivable as the police chief of Charleston, South Carolina.

The old paradigm was primarily about how Jews became southerners. The new paradigm is about how some of them remained or became Jews. The Jewish population of South Carolina, for example, remains minuscule—less than half of 1 percent. But the self-definition is changing, and Jews there are now less likely than in the past to think of themselves as "southerners who happen to be Jewish," according to a recent commemorative volume. Instead they are apt to consider themselves as "southern Jews, Jews who happen to live in the South." Even Hebrew day schools have established beachheads in Columbia and in Myrtle Beach, a phenomenon that would have baffled Hobcaw's Bernard M. Baruch (1870–1965), the self-important financier who was reputed to attend services on the High Holy Days only to hear his surname frequently invoked. Nor was classical Reform able to sustain itself, even in the city where this version of Judaism took its first baby steps. In 1825, Isaac Harby of the Reformed Society of Israelites helped ignite an appreciation of "the necessity of adapting many of the institutions of the great legislator [Moses], to the circumstances of the times in which we live." By the end of the twentieth century, a different equilibrium was discernible. The urge to "divest [Judaism] of rubbish" was receding; a yearning to restore tradition had become evident. In recent decades a less reductive version of Jewish religion had emerged even at Kahal Kadosh Beth Elohim, so that one longtime member, a droll attorney named Morris Rosen, was astonished to realize that "*Jews* are taking over the temple."[33]

The archetypal artist of the old paradigm was sculptor Moses Ezekiel of Richmond (though he lived most of his adult life in Rome). Ezekiel did not eschew formally Jewish art. For example, he designed the seal for the Jewish Publication Society of America, with the inscription: "Israel's mission is peace." For the centennial of American independence in 1876, Ezekiel accepted a commission from the B'nai B'rith and the result was *Religious Liberty*. It depicts a woman with an outstretched arm, as though she is bestowing the gift of freedom of worship to Americans. There is no reference to Jews, and their fate does not seem to have interested him, much less inspired him. Ezekiel is best known for his memorial to the Confederate dead, located in Arlington National Cemetery, and dedicated in 1913 by President Woodrow Wilson himself. The Lost Cause remained so much the sculptor's that he is even buried at the base of the Confederate monument. The inscription makes no allusion to his artistic achievements but instead places him within the tradition of military honor to which so many southerners have belonged. Moses J. Ezekiel himself wished to be identified only as "Sergeant of Company C, Battalion of Cadets of the Virginia Military Institute."[34]

The new paradigm is marked by a growing number of museums and exhibitions that highlight and celebrate how entwined Jews have been in southern history. Dedicated in 1989, the Museum of the Southern Jewish Experience has an associated unit in the Goldring/Woldenberg Institute of Southern Jewish Life.

The William Breman Jewish Heritage Museum was established in Atlanta in 1994, and the Jewish Heritage Foundation of North Carolina was formed in Chapel Hill eight years later. When an exhibition on "Commonwealth and Community: The Jewish Experience in Virginia" was mounted in Richmond in 1997, historian Melvin Urofsky underscored how integral the Jews have been to the Old Dominion, "sharing the ups and downs of Virginia for nearly four centuries. They have done so not as a despised minority cravenly seeking tolerance but as proud citizens of the state." In another characteristic note in the historiography of southern Jewry, Urofsky observed that "religious beliefs" were virtually what alone "distinguish[ed] Virginia Jews from their Christian neighbors."[35] In 2002, the McKissick Museum of the University of South Carolina devoted a major exhibition to the history of Jews in the state. Curator Dale Rosengarten needed eight years of planning and implementation, during which she collected Sabbath candlesticks and other Judaica, paintings, photographs, documents, and tchotchkes. The exhibit traveled to the Center for Jewish History in New York City and spun off an elegant companion volume, A Portion of the People. The director of the Jewish Museum of Florida, Miami's Marcia Zerivitz, was speaking not only for herself when she explained: "If you have Jewish memories, you'll always be Jewish; so what we're doing is creating, renewing or bringing to the front the Jewish memories," and thus a heritage can be bequeathed.[36]

The representative playwright of the old paradigm was Lillian Hellman; her counterpart in the new paradigm might be Tony Kushner. Both of them grew up in Louisiana, and both moved to New York. The politics of both dramatists could incontestably be characterized as leftist—a stance that southern Jews have rarely adopted. Hellman displayed no interest in Jewish life and subtly erased the Jewishness of the characters whom she presented on stage (drawn from her own family). But while sharing Hellman's liberalism and universalism, Kushner put Jews directly before the audience in part 1 of his most famous play, Angels in America: Millennium Approaches (1992), in which Roy Cohn and Ethel Rosenberg recite the mourners' Kaddish. Most recently, Kushner's musical, Caroline, or Change (2003), explores the dynamics of a Jewish family that has employed a black maid in Lake Charles, Louisiana. (The "change" in the title is, at the most literal level, Chanukah gelt.) Kushner has stepped onto turf already occupied by Alfred Uhry, who had won his Pulitzer Prize for Drama five years earlier. Uhry is unmatched as a guide to the assimilatory proclivities of southern Jewry. But he is a transitional figure between the two paradigms—exposing the desire of Atlanta's allrightniks to join respectable society, and criticizing them for their delusions, both in Driving Miss Daisy (1987) and in The Last Night of Ballyhoo (1997).

Above all, the new paradigm acknowledges the extent to which the condition of southern Jewry has become urbanized. Whether you're going to heaven or hell, according to one adage, you've still got to change planes in Atlanta—a city to be reckoned with when considering the trajectory of southern Jewry. When Evans began researching *The Provincials*, Atlanta had no more than half a dozen synagogues. The number is now above thirty, which suggests that the city is poised to become pivotal to American Jewry. Demography will nevertheless impose limits, and optimism about the growth of Atlanta should be held in check. In 1948, there were more than six times as many Jews living in the Bronx as there are Jews now living in Atlanta—and there were more Jews living in that particular borough (650,000) than in the newly established state of Israel. In the 1930s and 1940s, the Bronx was about 44 percent Jewish, and some neighborhoods in it were 70 percent Jewish.[37] Such residential patterns neither Atlanta nor any other city is likely to reproduce.

The concentration of southern Jews in metropolises also comes with a cost. The hamlet could be *heimish*, giving its Jewish residents a sense of intimacy and turning the entire region into an intricate kinship network. Yet the city at its worst has offered alienation, such that Binx Bollings, the New Orleans loner who narrates Walker Percy's sad first novel, declares his Jewishness not by birth but "by instinct. We share the same exile." (Indeed he thinks that his own estrangement makes him "more Jewish than the Jews I know. They are more at home than I am.")[38] Urbanization tends to coincide with the decline of courtly manners once seen as indigenous to the South, a reverence for good breeding so profound that the humorist Lewis Grizzard once explained why the young ladies of the Junior League were reluctant to participate in orgies—"all those thank-you notes." Nevertheless the increasing size of the Jewish community in a city like Atlanta is certainly better than the historic alternative of demographic declension throughout the region. Urban growth compensates for the decay of small-town Jewry, as does the emergence of communities that are attached to academic and scientific centers, like the Research Triangle in North Carolina. They have given a jolt of energy to southern Jewry, ensuring that it would be free at last, free at last of the old paradigm.

The new paradigm does have a *problèmatique*, however. It can be summed up in one word: Florida (or perhaps in two words: south Florida). Does the most tropical state in the union (with the exception of Hawaii) belong in the story at all? Is the most southern state in the union part of the South? (The Bureau of the Census certainly thinks so.) Or should historians consider attitudes more than latitudes? A test posted not long ago on the Internet offers a clue to the difficulty that Florida poses. (The source happens to be anonymous—which presents another problem. *Pirkei Avot* 5.21 stipulates that those who cite their sources hasten the redemption.)

Five ways you know you live in the Deep South:

1. You can rent a movie and buy bait in the same store.
2. "Y'all" is singular and "all y'all" is plural.
3. After five years, you still hear "You ain't from around here, are ya?"
4. "He needed killin'" is a valid defense.
5. Everyone has two first names: Billy Bob, Jimmy Bob, Mary Sue, Betty Jean, etc.

Five ways you know you live in Florida:

1. You eat dinner at 3:15 in the afternoon.
2. All purchases include a coupon of some kind—even houses and cars.
3. Everyone can recommend an excellent dermatologist.
4. Road construction never ends anywhere in the state.
5. Cars in front of you are often driven by headless people.

Are Floridians truly part of the South? They themselves barely think so. When pollsters asked residents of the former Confederacy if they considered themselves southerners (the poll was conducted over the span of a decade, 1991–2001), just over half—only 51 percent—of Floridians defined themselves as such. That proportion is the lowest of any southern state.[39] No wonder then that, when Harry Golden conducted the research for his 1974 book on *Our Southern Landsman*, he did not bother to venture below Jacksonville. Photographer Bill Aron's *Shalom Y'all: Images of Jewish Life in the American South*, published as recently as 2002, displays no portraits of Floridians.

That they are out of mind of the South is not self-evident. The region was long associated with poverty—so why not include Florida, since the poorest city in the nation is now Miami? The South has been historically associated with violence—so why not include Florida, since in 1980–81 Miami had smashed all previous records in its murder rate? The sheer velocity and pace of life in Florida, which engenders so wacky an atmosphere that it is morally vertiginous, have produced a prison population of about six hundred Jews. The bad news is that one of them, Alan Cotton, is currently serving a life sentence for homicide at Everglades Correctional Institute. The good news is that, as a result of a lawsuit he launched against the Florida Department of Corrections, he can now eat kosher food. At first, penitentiary officials were reported to be reluctant to settle the lawsuit because of the fear that "any inmate could convert to Judaism and demand the special meals, which are considered healthier than the standard jailhouse grub."[40]

A backwoods bastille that is required to honor the dietary laws—at least for Alan Cotton—is a rather solid indication of the deepening respect for religious difference that now marks the South. Located at the bottom of a section histori- cally associated with cultural homogeneity, Florida was slow to embrace the ideal of diversity. Only half a century ago a black customer was forbidden to sit down for a cup of coffee in a department store or a five-and-ten in downtown Miami. South Florida was still the South, in impugning the basic dignity and rights of black citizens. On the other hand, Miami was not the Delta, and the vi- tality of tourism served as a catalyst for making racial attitudes more enlight- ened than elsewhere in the South. Signs in Miami bus stations like "Reservados Para Hombres Blancos" meant that an incipient cultural pluralism was already complicating Jim Crow and making it anachronistic, and waitresses at Wool- worth's even in the 1950s were willing to serve that cup of coffee to dark-skinned customers—as long as they spoke Spanish. Jewish activists who wanted the pace of pluralism to be accelerated could nevertheless be accused of oversensitivity to injustice. In Dade County in the postwar era, Christmas pageants and other Yuletide celebrations in the public school system provoked protest by Jewish and Unitarian parents. They lost. But in 1960, when they appealed all the way to the Florida Supreme Court, its judges huffed that the parental grievance consti- tuted "just another case in which the tender sensibilities of certain minorities are sought to be protected against the allegedly harsh laws and customs enacted and established by the more rugged pioneers of this nation."[41]

Those pioneers came late to Florida. Not long before the West was won, which Geronimo acknowledged when he surrendered (and was sent to Florida for incarceration), south Florida was still untamed. The U.S. Census of 1880 could count only 257 whites residing in Dade County, which was then so huge that it ran from present-day Stuart all the way down to the upper Keys. Were Dade County to have maintained the same borders, cities like West Palm Beach and Fort Lauderdale, as well as the Miami metropolitan area, would have been in- cluded; and the census would now have listed more than five million people. What Ross Perot would have called a "giant sucking sound" has drawn so many visitors to Florida that the annual number of tourists is estimated to be 37 mil- lion, this in addition to the more than 16 million permanent residents.[42] They live in what is now the largest state east of the Mississippi River (as the result of a recalculation in the 1990 census of the length of the Florida littoral). Bigger than the Empire State, Florida is the eight-hundred-pound gorilla in the room that adjoins the archives where historians of southern Jewry toil.

Paradox is embedded in the framework within which Florida Jewry is obliged to operate. The political discourse of the Old South was pocked with distrust of the central government. The regional exaltation of states' rights remains so deeply entrenched in public memory that, when President George W. Bush's secretary of the interior, Gale Norton, visited a Confederate cemetery, she lamented: "We lost too much. We lost the idea that the states were to stand against the federal government gaining too much power over their lives." Such lingering regret for the Rebel surrender at Appomattox nevertheless did not hamper the state of Florida from taking $8 billion from Washington to try to restore the ecosystem of the Everglades. This environmental project, though less consequential than, say, the parting of the Red Sea, will nevertheless be the most expensive in all of history.[43]

"Spring ahead, fall back, winter in Miami" is how many Jews mark time; and the permanent Jewish population in Florida has grown from 21,000 in 1940 to today's estimate of 620,000, which is larger than figures for French Jewry (496,000) and even larger than the combined Jewish populations of the United Kingdom (299,000) and Russia (244,000). As of 2001, the Miami–Fort Lauderdale metropolitan statistical area had the third-largest Jewish population in the United States, trailing only New York and Los Angeles. West Palm Beach and Boca Raton are eighth.[44] And yet not until the publication in 2005 of *Jews of South Florida*, edited by Andrea Greenbaum, did scholars show any cognizance of this Jewry. Put it another way. Recall the map that has become more famous than anything distributed by Rand-McNally: Saul Steinberg's *New Yorker* cover, "View of the World from 9th Avenue" (1976). If such a map were superimposed on the discourse that historians of southern Jewry have conducted, Florida would be barely discernible, vaguely off in the distance, somewhere below Valdosta. Hardly visible is Jacksonville, which has an estimated Jewish population of 7,300. But because the city limits are coextensive with Duval Country, Jacksonville itself boasts of the largest population of any southern city east of Texas. The city of Jacksonville is more populous than Miami or Atlanta. Yet not even a scholarly article— much less an entire book—is extant on to the experience of Jacksonville's Jewry.

The northern part of Florida—say, above Orlando—may well be deemed authentically or at least recognizably southern. John Shelton Reed, the premier sociologist of the contemporary South, is a bit more precise. He would place the regional dividing line at Daytona Beach. And while acknowledging the claim that the Mississippi Delta constitutes "the most Southern place on earth," Reed has also made an on-site inspection of "the Florabama Lounge on Perdido Key in the Florida panhandle, and it's a contender." That only begs the question of how to categorize what lies below Daytona Beach or Orlando. A book Reed coauthored with his wife Dale Volberg Reed admitted that they were tempted to peel Florida away from the South, "if there were anywhere else to put it."[45]

A slightly more elegant way to resolve the problem is to suggest that a reasonable definition of the region must allow for historical evolution. The South should be permitted to transform itself from the plantation legend, and to escape from a dreamy time-warp of homogeneous Protestants (black and white) into full appreciation of the increasingly diverse region that it has become. It is entitled to operate under the sense of the inevitability of change to which the rest of America is subject. The South too consists of altered states. (Even the power of one inflammatory symbol should not be exaggerated. Only a tenth of southerners own a Confederate flag, and even fewer display it.)[46] The village can be the baseline against which change can be measured, but should not be the time line that is synchronous with the southern Jewish experience itself. If Florida is entitled to share in the destiny of the other states that had tried to detach themselves from the Union, if the idea of a changing and more inclusive South is legitimated, then the history of southern Jewry becomes richer, fuller, and longer.

If the new paradigm is accepted, then the inference follows that the region becomes less distinctive and its Jews less exotic. Historian Mark Bauman has argued that the case for southern Jewish uniqueness is much overstated anyway, that none of the special traits ascribed to the region's Jews are absent elsewhere in the United States. Bauman has a point. But he does not reckon sufficiently with the *consciousness* of difference, the subjective sense that the region feels unlike other parts of the nation. Perhaps that helps explain why a standard reference work like *The Harvard Encyclopedia of American Ethnic Groups* (1980) includes southerners among its 106 minorities. Bauman has anticipated, however, how much southern Jews are increasingly coming to resemble other Jews.

Evans's own sense of the future of the erstwhile provincials must be classified as ambiguous too. On the one hand, he has predicted that all newcomers will be working within the same groove as previous generations, struggling to reconcile differing allegiances. They are direct descendants of the exemplars of the old paradigm. The latest wave of southern Jews will adapt, "will find their American, Jewish and Southern identities becoming intertwined like a challah." On the other hand, Evans suspects, an acute awareness of distinctiveness is bound to weaken (if not evaporate): "Southerners in the 21st century will be more like other Americans, and Jews in the South will be more like other Jews,"[47] rather than like, say, NASCAR dads. The temptation to play off the incongruities of an allegiance to both the South and Jewry will recede. The old paradigm has not entirely lost its authority and has not been completely superseded. All traces of the past that has shaped Dixie so decisively are not so easily obliterated. Old times there are not entirely forgotten—however much memories dim and however much only slivers of the past ever get salvaged. No historian of southern Jewry should echo the phrase heard in junior high schools these days: it's so *over*. But evidence continues to mount that, while the particularity of a mercantile and village way of life is dying, southern Jewry itself is not. And while eternity is not one of the options either, this durable community may be around till the Messiah comes, or (in the regional idiom) till the last dog dies.

NOTES

1. Abraham Cahan, *Yekl and The Imported Bridegroom and Other Stories of the New York Ghetto* (New York: Dover, 1970), 70; Tom Wolfe, *The Kandy-Kolored Tangerine-Flake Streamline Baby* (New York: Farrar, Straus and Giroux, 1965), 129; Ernest Samuels, ed., *The Education of Henry Adams* (Boston: Houghton Mifflin, 1973), 57–58.

2. Max Weber, *Ancient Judaism*, tr. Hans H. Gerth and Don Martindale (Glencoe, Ill.: Free Press, 1952), 353; W.E.B. Du Bois, *The Souls of Black Folk* (New York: Alfred A. Knopf, 1993), 135; Leonard Dinnerstein, *Antisemitism in America* (New York: Oxford University Press, 1994), 200.

3. Melvin I. Urofsky, *Commonwealth and Community: The Jewish Experience in Virginia* (Richmond: Virginia Historical Society and Jewish Community Federation of Richmond, 1997), 30; Hollace Ava Weiner, *Jewish Stars in Texas: Rabbis and Their Work* (College Station: Texas A&M University Press, 1999), 111; Daniel S. Mariaschin, "Hometown Boy: Elvis and the Jews of Memphis," *B'nai B'rith International Jewish Monthly* 116 (Winter 2002): 9; Hugh Sidey, "Impressions of Power and Poetry," *Time* 109 (June 20, 1977): 31.

4. Ruth F. Boorstin, ed., *The Daniel J. Boorstin Reader* (New York: Modern Library, 1995), 893.

5. William Faulkner, *The Sound and the Fury: The Corrected Text* (New York: Vintage, 1984), 191.

6. Eli Faber, *A Time for Planting: The First Migration, 1654–1820* (Baltimore: Johns Hopkins University Press, 1992), 110, 111; Hasia R. Diner, *Lower East Side Memories: A Jewish Place in America* (Princeton, N.J.: Princeton University Press, 2000), 131–32; "Jewish Population in the United States, 2003," in *American Jewish Year Book 2004*, ed. David Singer and Lawrence Grossman (New York: American Jewish Committee, 2004), 125.

7. Lorenz Hart, "Any Old Place with You" (1919), in *The Complete Lyrics of Lorenz Hart*, ed. Dorothy Hart and Robert Kimball (New York: Alfred A. Knopf, 1986), 12.

8. Richard Hofstadter, *The American Political Tradition and the Men Who Made It* (New York: Alfred A. Knopf, 1948), 27; Craig Claiborne, *A Feast Made for Laughter: A Memoir with Recipes* (New York: Holt, Rinehart and Winston, 1982), 46–47.

9. Quoted in Emily Bingham, *Mordecai: An Early American Family* (New York: Hill and Wang, 2003), 4.

10. Leonard Rogoff, *Homelands: Southern Jewish Identity in Durham and Chapel Hill, North*

Carolina (Tuscaloosa: University of Alabama Press, 2001), 161; Jack Bass, "Just Like 'One of Us,'" in A Portion of the People: Three Hundred Years of Southern Jewish Life, ed. Theodore Rosengarten and Dale Rosengarten (Columbia: University of South Carolina Press, 2002), 39.

11. Quoted in Eli N. Evans, The Provincials: A Personal History of Jews in the South (New York: Atheneum, 1973), 8.

12. Ludwig Lewisohn, Up Stream: An American Chronicle (New York: Boni and Liveright, 1922), 74; Ralph Melnick, The Life and Work of Ludwig Lewisohn (Detroit: Wayne State University Press, 1998), 1:39–49, 115.

13. Quoted in David B. Ruderman, "Greenville Diary: A Northern Rabbi Confronts the Deep South, 1966–70," Jewish Quarterly Review 94 (Fall 2004): 646, 656, 659.

14. Quoted in Susan E. Tifft and Alex S. Jones, The Trust: The Private and Powerful Family behind The New York Times (Boston: Little, Brown, 1999), 25.

15. Quoted in Robert N. Rosen, The Confederate Jews (Columbia: University of South Carolina Press, 2000), 244, 247–48.

16. Frederic Cople Jaher, A Scapegoat in the New Wilderness: The Origins and Rise of Anti-Semitism in America (Cambridge, Mass.: Harvard University Press, 1994), 189; Jack E. Davis, Race against Time: Culture and Separation in Natchez since 1930 (Baton Rouge: Louisiana State University Press, 2001), 113.

17. Lisa Keys, "A Congregation Sings the Blues as Synagogue Goes on Market," Forward, September 12, 2003, sec. 1, p. 23; Marcie Cohen Ferris, "Feeding the Jewish Soul in the Delta Diaspora," Southern Cultures 10 (Fall 2004): 52–85.

18. Julius Lester, Lovesong: Becoming a Jew (New York: Henry Holt, 1988), 5–12, 219–25.

19. Quoted in Peter Applebome, Dixie Rising: How the South Is Shaping American Values, Politics, and Culture (New York: Random House, 1996), 255–56, and in John Shelton Reed, Minding the South (Columbia: University of Missouri Press, 2003), 34.

20. Hiram Wesley Evans, "The Klan's Fight for Americanism" (1926), in The Culture of the Twenties, ed. Loren Baritz (Indianapolis: Bobbs-Merrill, 1970), 106–7; Davis, Race against Time, 112.

21. David R. Goldfield, Black, White and Southern: Race Relations and Southern Culture, 1940 to the Present (Baton Rouge: Louisiana State University Press, 1990), 231–32.

22. Harry Golden, Only in America (Cleveland: World, 1958), 122, 149; Eli N. Evans, The Lonely Days Were Sundays: Reflections of a Jewish Southerner (Jackson: University Press of Mississippi, 1993), 51–54.

23. Ezra Mendelsohn, "Jewish Universalism: Some Visual Texts and Subtexts," in Key Texts in American Jewish Culture, ed. Jack Kugelmass (New Brunswick, N.J.: Rutgers University Press, 2003), 174–75.

24. David L. Cohn, Where I Was Born and Raised (South Bend, Ind.: University of Notre Dame Press, 1967), 12; "Letters: Richard Wright/David L. Cohn," in Richard Wright Reader, ed. Ellen Wright and Michel Fabre (New York: Harper and Row, 1978), 57–67.

25. Quoted in James C. Cobb, *The Most Southern Place on Earth: The Mississippi Delta and the Roots of Regional Identity* (New York: Oxford University Press, 1992), 214.

26. Clayborne Carson, *Malcolm X: The FBI File*, ed. David Gallen (New York: Carroll and Graf, 1991), 29, 203–4; Howard Zinn, *The Southern Mystique* (New York: Touchstone, 1972), 8–9.

27. Mark K. Bauman and Berkley Kalin, eds., *The Quiet Voices: Southern Rabbis and Black Civil Rights, 1880s to 1990s* (Tuscaloosa: University of Alabama Press, 1997); Marc Dollinger, *Quest for Inclusion: Jews and Liberalism in Modern America* (Princeton, N.J.: Princeton University Press, 2000); Debra L. Schultz, *Going South: Jewish Women in the Civil Rights Movement* (New York: New York University Press, 2001); Clive Webb, *Fight against Fear: Southern Jews and Black Civil Rights* (Athens: University of Georgia Press, 2001); Howard Ball, *Murder in Mississippi: U.S. v. Price and the Struggle for Civil Rights* (Lawrence: University Press of Kansas, 2004).

28. Marion Barry in Howell Raines, *My Soul Is Rested: Movement Days in the Deep South Remembered* (New York: Bantam Books, 1978), 311; Paul Hemphill, *The Good Old Boys* (Garden City, N.Y.: Anchor Press/Doubleday, 1975), 12, 13.

29. Mark V. Tushnet, *The NAACP's Legal Strategy against Segregated Education, 1925–1950* (Chapel Hill: University of North Carolina Press, 1987), 27–28; Jerold S. Auerbach, *Unequal Justice: Lawyers and Social Change in Modern America* (New York: Oxford University Press, 1976), 213–14; Juan Williams, *Thurgood Marshall: American Revolutionary* (New York: Times Books, 1998), 75–76.

30. Harold Ticktin, "'Mostly Jewish': Reunion in Mississippi," *Congress Monthly* 63 (March–April 1996): 15.

31. Boorstin, *Daniel J. Boorstin Reader*, 894–96.

32. Dan Goodgame, "Trade Warrior," *Time* 141 (March 15, 1993): 51, 52.

33. Quoted in Gary Phillip Zola, *Isaac Harby of Charleston, 1788–1828: Jewish Reformer and Intellectual* (Tuscaloosa: University of Alabama Press, 1994), 126, 127, and in Rosengarten and Rosengarten, *Portion of the People*, 191.

34. Mendelsohn, "Jewish Universalism," in *Key Texts*, 172–73, 174; Rosen, *Jewish Confederates*, 368.

35. Urofsky, *Commonwealth and Community*, viii.

36. Quoted in Maya Bell, "Historical 'Mosaic,'" *Chicago Tribune*, March 13, 1994, sec. 12, p. 6.

37. Evans, *Provincials*, rev. ed. (New York: Free Press, 1997), xvi; and Eli Evans, "A New Jewish South," *Jewish South* (October 2003): 32; Jonathan Marks, "For the Bronx, It's Desolation Row," *Jewish Week* 216 (July 7–11, 2003): 1.

38. Walker Percy, *The Moviegoer* (New York: Noonday Press, 1967), 89.

39. John Shelton Reed, "Where Is the South?" *Southern Cultures* 5 (Summer 1999): 116–17.

40. Edna Buchanan, *The Corpse Had a Familiar Face: Covering Miami, America's Toughest Crime Beat* (London: Bodley Head, 1988), 4–5; Julie Kay, "Florida Prisoner to Receive Kosher Food," *Forward*, December 5, 2003, 11.

41. Quoted in Howard M. Sachar, *A History of the Jews in America* (New York: Alfred A. Knopf, 1992), 796–97; Raymond A. Mohl, with Matilda "Bobbi" Graff and Shirley M. Zoloth, *South of the South: Jewish Activists and the Civil Rights Movement in Miami, 1945–1960* (Gainesville: University Press of Florida, 2004), 26–27, 140, 168.

42. Eliot Kleinberg, *Black Cloud: The Great Florida Hurricane of 1928* (New York: Carroll and Graf, 2003), 23–24; Michael Grunwald, "Water World," *New Republic* 230 (March 1, 2004): 23.

43. Quoted in Ira Berlin, "American Slavery in History and Memory," *Journal of American History* 90 (March 2004): 1,252, 1,253n; Grunwald, "Water World," 23.

44. Sergio DellaPergola, "World Jewish Population, 2004," in *American Jewish Year Book 2004*, 508, 509; "Jewish Population in the United States, 2003," in *American Jewish Year Book 2004*, 125.

45. John Shelton Reed, "South but not Southern," *Forum* (Florida Humanities Council) 27 (Fall 2003): 10; John Shelton Reed and Dale Volberg Reed, *1001 Things Everyone Should Know about the South* (New York: Doubleday, 1996), 7.

46. Jason Zengerle, "Flag Poll," *New Republic* 229 (November 24, 2003): 14.

47. Evans, "New Jewish South," 38.

SELECTED BIBLIOGRAPHY

ERIC L. GOLDSTEIN & MARNI DAVIS

The following is by no means meant to be a comprehensive bibliography of the southern Jewish experience but is instead intended to provide a snapshot of the directions the field has been taking over the last two decades. The organization is thematic, and although many titles could fit under multiple headings, we have avoided duplication by choosing what we feel is the most relevant category for each work.

In selecting titles, we have been guided by four main principles. First, we have listed mainly recent works, although we have also included a few classic titles that remain authoritative. Second, we have emphasized works by professional scholars. For a fuller catalogue of synagogue histories, community studies, and other works by amateur historians, see our more comprehensive bibliography, *Southern Jewish History: A Research Guide to Archival Resources in the Atlanta Area and a Bibliography of Published Sources* (Atlanta: Emory University, 2001). Third, we have concentrated on books instead of articles, as Mark K. Bauman has already published an exhaustive bibliography of articles on southern Jewish history that have appeared in the journals *American Jewish History, American Jewish Archives Journal,* and *Southern Jewish History* (see *Southern Jewish History* 3 [2003]: 163–85). The few articles that are found here are from other periodicals and therefore are not included in Bauman's bibliography. Finally, in order to reflect the state of recent research on southern Jews, we have included several unpublished doctoral dissertations.

GENERAL WORKS

Bauman, Mark K. *The Southerner as American: Jewish Style.* Cincinnati: American Jewish Archives, 1996. (On the question of southern Jewish distinctiveness).

Bauman, Mark K., ed. *Dixie Diaspora: An Anthology of Southern Jewish History.* Tuscaloosa: University of Alabama Press, 2006. (A collection of important, previously published articles in the field of southern Jewish history.)

Dinnerstein, Leonard. *Jews in the South.* Baton Rouge: Louisiana State University Press, 1973. (An anthology of important early articles on southern Jewish history.)

Evans, Eli N. *The Lonely Days Were Sundays: Reflections of a Jewish Southerner.* Jackson: University Press of Mississippi, 1993.

————. *The Provincials: A Personal History of Jews in the South.* Rev. ed. Chapel Hill: University of North Carolina Press, 2005. (Evans's classic history, originally published in 1973, brought up to date with several new chapters, a new introduction, and photographs.)

Hagedorn, Leah Elizabeth. "Jews and the American South, 1858–1905." Ph.D. diss., University of North Carolina at Chapel Hill, 1999.

Kaganoff, Nathan M., and Melvin I. Urofsky, eds. *"Turn to the South": Essays on Southern Jewry.* Charlottesville: University Press of Virginia, 1979.

Peck, Abraham J. "That Other 'Peculiar Institution': Jews and Judaism in the Nineteenth-Century South." *Modern Judaism* 7 (February 1987): 99–114.

Proctor, Samuel, and Louis Schmier, eds. *Jews of the South: Selected Essays from the Southern Jewish Historical Society.* Macon, Ga.: Mercer University Press, 1984.

Whitfield, Stephen J. *Voices of Jacob, Hands of Esau: Jews in American Life and Thought.* Hamden, Conn: Archon Books, 1984. (Part 4 deals with "The Jew as Southerner".)

ANTISEMITISM AND JEWISH-CHRISTIAN RELATIONS

Dinnerstein, Leonard. *The Leo Frank Case.* New York: Columbia University Press, 1968.

————. *Uneasy at Home: Antisemitism and the American Jewish Experience.* New York: Columbia University Press, 1987. (Includes several chapters on the southern Jewish experience.)

Golden, Harry. "Jew and Gentile in the New South: Segregation at Sundown." *Commentary* 20 (November 1955): 403–12.

MacLean, Nancy. "The Leo Frank Case Reconsidered: Gender and Sexual Politics in the Making of Reactionary Populism." *Journal of American History* 78 (1991): 917–48.

Oney, Steve. *And the Dead Shall Rise: The Murder of Mary Phagan and the Lynching of Leo Frank.* New York: Pantheon Books, 2003.

Powell, Lawrence N. *Troubled Memory: Anne Levy, the Holocaust and David Duke's Louisiana.* Chapel Hill: University of North Carolina Press, 2000.

Schmier, Louis. "No Jew Can Murder: Memories of Tom Watson and the Lichtenstein Murder Case of 1901." *Georgia Historical Quarterly* 70 (Fall 1986): 433–55.

Shapiro, Edward S. "Anti-Semitism Mississippi Style." In *Anti-Semitism in American History,* edited by David A. Gerber, 129–51. Urbana: University of Illinois Press, 1986. (On the anti-Semitism of Mississippi Senator Theodore G. Bilbo and Congressman John E. Rankin.)

BIOGRAPHY

Armbrester, Margaret. *Samuel Ullman and "Youth": The Life, the Legacy.*
Tuscaloosa: University of Alabama Press, 1993. (On an Alabama civic leader
and social reformer of the late nineteenth century.)

Bingham, Emily. *Mordecai: An Early American Family.* New York: Hill and Wang,
2003. (On a prominent North Carolina family of the antebellum period.)

Kraut, Allen M. *Goldberger's War: The Life and Work of a Public Health Crusader.* New
York: Hill and Wang, 2003.

Leidholdt, Alexander S. *Editor for Justice: The Life of Louis I. Jaffé.* Baton Rouge:
Louisiana State University Press, 2002. (Jaffé was an editor and
antilynching advocate in Norfolk, Va.)

Monaco, C. S. *Moses Levy of Florida: Jewish Utopian and Antebellum Reformer.* Baton
Rouge: Louisiana State University Press, 2005.

Urofsky, Melvin I. *The Levy Family and Monticello, 1834–1923: Saving Thomas
Jefferson's House.* Charlottesville, Va.: Thomas Jefferson Foundation, 2001.

BLACK-JEWISH RELATIONS AND JEWISH RACIAL IDENTITY

Bauman, Mark K., and Berkley Kalin, eds. *The Quiet Voices: Southern Rabbis and
Black Civil Rights, 1880 to 1990s.* Tuscaloosa: University of Alabama Press, 1997.

Dollinger, Marc. *Quest for Inclusion: Jews and Liberalism in Modern America.*
Princeton, N.J.: Princeton University Press, 2000. (A national study that
compares the Jewish approach to African Americans in the North and
South after 1945.)

Goldfield, David. "A Sense of Place: Jews, Blacks, and White Gentiles in the
American South." *Southern Cultures* 3 (Spring 1997): 58–79.

Goldstein, Eric L. *The Price of Whiteness: Jews, Race, and American Identity.*
Princeton, N.J.: Princeton University Press, 2006. (A national study that
compares the Jewish approach to African Americans in the North and
South in the early twentieth century.)

Light, Caroline Elizabeth. "Uplifting 'the Unfortunate of Our Race': Southern
Jewish Benevolence and the Struggle Towards Whiteness." Ph.D. diss.,
University of Kentucky, 2000.

Melnick, Jeffrey. *Black-Jewish Relations on Trial: Leo Frank and Jim Conley in the New
South.* Jackson: University Press of Mississippi, 2000.

Mohl, Raymond A., with Matilda "Bobbi" Graff and Shirley M. Zoloth. *South of
the South: Jewish Activists and the Civil Rights Movement in Miami, 1945–1960.*
Gainsville: University Press of Florida, 2004.

Rockoff, Stuart. "Jewish Racial Identity in Pittsburgh and Atlanta." Ph.D.
diss., University of Texas at Austin, 2000.

Rogoff, Leonard. "Is the Jew White?: The Racial Place of the Southern Jew."
American Jewish History 85, 3 (September 1997): 195–230.

Webb, Clive. *Fight against Fear: Southern Jews and Black Civil Rights.* Athens:
University of Georgia Press, 2001.

BUSINESS HISTORY

Ashkenazi, Elliott. *The Business of Jews in Louisiana, 1840–1875.* Tuscaloosa:
University of Alabama Press, 1988.

[Decter, Avi Y., ed.] *Enterprising Emporiums: The Jewish Department Stores of
Downtown Baltimore.* Baltimore: Jewish Museum of Maryland, 2001.

Schmier, Louis. "Helloo! Peddler Man! Helloo!" In *Ethnic Minorities in Gulf Coast
Society,* edited by Jerrell Shofner, 75–88. Pensacola, Fla.: Historic Pensacola
Preservation Board, 1979.

CIVIL WAR

Ashkenazi, Elliott. *The Civil War Diary of Clara Solomon: Growing Up in New Orleans.*
Baton Rouge: Louisiana State University Press, 1995.

Evans, Eli N. *Judah P. Benjamin: The Jewish Confederate.* New York: Free Press, 1988.

Korn, Bertram Wallace. *American Jewry and the Civil War.* New York: Atheneum, 1970.

Rosen, Robert N. *The Jewish Confederates.* Columbia: University of South
Carolina Press, 2000.

COMMUNITY STUDIES

Decter, Avi Y., and Karen Falk, eds. *We Call This Place Home: Jewish Life in
Maryland's Small Towns.* Baltimore: Jewish Museum of Maryland, 2003.

Goldstein, Eric L. *Traders and Transports: The Jews of Colonial Maryland.* Baltimore:
Jewish Historical Society of Maryland, 1993.

Greenberg, Mark I. "Creating Ethnic, Class, and Southern Identity in
Nineteenth-Century America: The Jews of Savannah 1830–1880." Ph.D.
diss., University of Florida, 1997.

Hagy, James W. *This Happy Land: The Jews of Colonial and Antebellum Charleston.*
Tuscaloosa: University of Alabama Press, 2003.

Hertzberg, Steven. *Strangers within the Gate City: The Jews of Atlanta, 1845–1915.*
Philadelphia: Jewish Publication Society of America, 1978.

Moore, Deborah Dash. *To the Golden Cities: Pursuing the American Jewish Dream in
L.A. and Miami.* New York: Free Press, 1994.

Rogoff, Leonard. *Homelands: Southern Jewish Identity in Durham and Chapel Hill,
North Carolina.* Tuscaloosa: University of Alabama Press, 2001.

Rosengarten, Theodore, and Dale Rosengarten, eds. *A Portion of the People: Three
Hundred Years of Southern Jewish Life.* Columbia: University of South Carolina

Press, 2002. (An exhibition companion volume focusing on Jewish life in South Carolina.)

Weiner, Deborah R. *Coalfield Jews: An Appalachian History.* Urbana: University of Illinois Press, 2006.

Weissbach, Lee Shai. *Jewish Life in Small-Town America: A History.* New Haven, Conn.: Yale University Press, 2005. (A national study that includes information on small southern Jewish communities.)

———. "Kentucky's Jewish History in National Perspective: The Era of Mass Migration." *Filson Club Historical Quarterly* 69 (1995): 255–74.

JEWISH WOMEN

Apte, Helen Jacobus. *Heart of a Wife: The Diary of a Southern Jewish Woman.* Edited by Marcus D. Rosenbaum. Wilmington, Del.: Scholarly Resources, 1998. (Apte records her experiences in Miami, Tampa, and Atlanta during the early twentieth century.)

Greenberg, Mark. "Savannah's Jewish Women and the Shaping of Ethnic and Gender Identity, 1830–1900." *Georgia Historical Quarterly* 82 (Winter 1998): 751–74.

Machlovitz, Wendy. *Clara Lowenberg Moses: Memoir of a Southern Jewish Woman.* Jackson, Miss.: Museum of the Southern Jewish Experience, 2000. (Moses [1865–1951] lived in Natchez, Miss.).

Stollman, Jennifer. "'Building Up a House of Israel in a Land of Christ': Jewish Women in the Antebellum and Civil War South." Ph.D. diss., Michigan State University, 2001.

MATERIAL AND POPULAR CULTURE

Ferris, Marcie Cohen. *Matzoh Ball Gumbo: Culinary Tales of the Jewish South.* Chapel Hill: University of North Carolina Press, 2005.

McGraw, Eliza R. L. *Two Covenants: Representations of Southern Jewishness.* Baton Rouge: Louisiana State University Press, 2005. (A survey of popular and literary representations.)

Weissbach, Lee Shai. *The Synagogues of Kentucky: Architecture and History.* Lexington: University Press of Kentucky, 1995.

Whitfield, Stephen J. "Is It True What They Sing about Dixie?" *Southern Cultures* 8 (Summer 2002): 9–37. (On Jewish popular songwriters' frequent use of southern themes.)

MEMOIRS

Cohen, Edward. *The Peddler's Grandson: Growing Up Jewish in Mississippi.* Jackson: University Press of Mississippi, 1999.

Ellenson, David. "A Separate Life." In *Jewish Spiritual Journeys: 20 Essays Written to Honor the Occasion of the 70th Birthday of Eurgene B. Borowitz*, edited by Lawrence A. Hoffman and Arnold Jacob Wolf, 93–101. New York: Behrman House, 1997. (Includes reflections on Ellenson's boyhood in Newport News, Va.)

Marks, Leta Weiss. *Time's Tapestry: Four Generations of a New Orleans Family*. Baton Rouge: Louisiana State University Press, 1997.

Rubin, Louis D., Jr. *My Father's People: A Family of Southern Jews*. Baton Rouge: Louisiana State University Press, 2002. (Memoir of a Jewish family from Charleston, S.C.)

Silverstein, Clara. *White Girl: A Story of School Desegregation*. Athens: University of Georgia Press, 2004. (On Silverstein's experiences during integration in Richmond, Va., public schools.)

Suberman, Stella. *The Jew Store: A Family Memoir*. Chapel Hill, N.C.: Algonquin Books, 1998. (On growing up in a family business in small-town Tennessee.)

RELIGIOUS LIFE AND LEADERSHIP

Bauman, Mark. *Rabbi Harry Epstein and the Rabbinate as Conduit for Change*. Rutherford, N.J.: Fairleigh Dickinson University Press, 1994. (On a Conservative rabbi from Atlanta.)

Corley, Robert. *Paying "Civic Rent": The Jews of Emanu-El and the Birmingham Community*. Birmingham, Ala.: A. H. Cather, 1982.

Cowett, Mark. *Birmingham's Rabbi: Morris Newfield and Alabama, 1895–1940*. Tuscaloosa: University of Alabama Press, 1986.

Greene, Melissa Fay. *The Temple Bombing*. Reading, Mass.: Addison-Wesley, 1996. (Primarily a biography of Jacob M. Rothschild, a rabbi and civil rights activist in Atlanta.)

Gurock, Jeffrey S. *Orthodoxy in Charleston: Brith Sholom Beth Israel and American Jewish History*. Charleston, S.C.: College of Charleston Library, 2004.

Malone, Bobbie. *Rabbi Max Heller: Reformer, Zionist, Southerner*. Tuscaloosa: University of Alabama Press, 1997. (Heller was a rabbi in New Orleans.)

Umansky, Ellen M. *From Christian Science to Jewish Science: Spiritual Healing and American Jews*. New York: Oxford University Press, 2004. (A national study that includes a discussion of southern Jews active in the Jewish Science movement.)

Weiner, Hollace Ava. *Jewish Stars in Texas: Rabbis and Their Work*. College Station: Texas A&M University Press, 1999.

Zola, Gary. *Isaac Harby of Charleston, 1788–1828: Jewish Reformer and Intellectual*. Tuscaloosa: University of Alabama Press, 1994.

ABOUT THE CONTRIBUTORS

EMILY BINGHAM received her Ph.D. in history from the University of North Carolina at Chapel Hill and is an independent scholar living in Louisville, Kentucky. She is the author of *Mordecai: An Early American Family* (Hill and Wang, 2003) and the coeditor, with Thomas A. Underwood, of *The Southern Agrarians and the New Deal* (University Press of Virginia, 2001).

MARNI DAVIS is a doctoral candidate and teaching fellow in the history department at Emory University. Her dissertation examines the role of, and anxieties surrounding, Jews in the American liquor industry in the late nineteenth and early twentieth centuries. In 2004, she received a doctoral dissertation fellowship from the National Foundation for Jewish Culture.

HASIA DINER is the Paul and Sylvia Steinberg Professor of American Jewish History at New York University and director of the Goren-Goldstein Center for American Jewish History. She is the author of numerous books, most recently, *The Jews of the United States, 1654–2000*, published in 2004 by the University of California Press.

ELI N. EVANS was born and raised in Durham, North Carolina, and is a graduate of the University of North Carolina at Chapel Hill and the Yale Law School. He is author of *The Provincials: A Personal History of Jews in the South; Judah P. Benjamin: The Jewish Confederate;* and *The Lonely Days Were Sundays: Reflections of a Jewish Southerner.* He is president emeritus of the Charles H. Revson Foundation and chairman of the advisory board of the Carolina Center for Jewish Studies at the University of North Carolina at Chapel Hill.

MARCIE COHEN FERRIS is an assistant professor in the Curriculum in American Studies at the University of North Carolina at Chapel Hill and associate director of the Carolina Center for Jewish Studies. Ferris is the author of *Matzoh Ball Gumbo: Culinary Tales of the Jewish South* (University of North Carolina Press, 2005).

ERIC L. GOLDSTEIN is assistant professor of history and Jewish studies at Emory University in Atlanta. He is the author of *The Price of Whiteness: Jews, Race, and American Identity* (Princeton University Press, 2006). He serves as the book review editor of the journal *Southern Jewish History.*

MARK I. GREENBERG received his Ph.D. in history from the University of Florida under the direction of Samuel Proctor. He is author of several articles on Savannah Jewish history and a history of the University of South Florida.

Currently he is director of the Special Collections Department and Florida Studies Center in the University of South Florida Tampa Library.

ELIZA R. L. MCGRAW is the author of *Two Covenants: Representations of Southern Jewishness* (Louisiana State University Press, 2005). Her work has appeared in *Southern Cultures*, *The Mississippi Quarterly*, and the *South Atlantic Quarterly*. She lives in Washington, D.C.

STUART ROCKOFF completed his Ph.D. in U.S. history from University of Texas in 2000 with a special emphasis on immigration and American Jewish history. In June 2002, he became director of the history department at the Goldring/Woldenberg Institute of Southern Jewish Life and the Museum of the Southern Jewish Experience, where he is working to preserve and document the history of southern Jews.

ROBERT N. ROSEN is an attorney in Charleston, South Carolina. He received his M.A. degree in history from Harvard University in 1970 and his J.D. degree from the University of South Carolina School of Law in 1973. He is the author of *A Short History of Charleston; Confederate Charleston: An Illustrated History of the City and the People during the Civil War;* and *The Jewish Confederates,* all published by the University of South Carolina Press. He is a past-president of the Jewish Historical Society of South Carolina.

DALE ROSENGARTEN is curator of the Jewish Heritage Collection at the College of Charleston and coordinated research for a major museum exhibition, "A Portion of the People: Three Hundred Years of Southern Jewish Life," which opened at McKissick Museum at the University of South Carolina in 2002. She coedited a book by the same title, published by University of South Carolina Press. The Jewish Historical Society of South Carolina awarded her its second Annual Arts and Cultural Achievement Award for her work in fostering and preserving Jewish arts and culture, and, in March 2003, she received the first Governor's Archives Award for developing the Jewish Heritage Collection.

JENNIFER A. STOLLMAN is an assistant professor in the Department of History and Political Science at Salem College in Winston-Salem, North Carolina. She specializes in American intellectual and social history.

CLIVE WEBB is reader in American history at the University of Sussex in Brighton, England. He is the author of *Fight against Fear: Southern Jews and Black Civil Rights* (University of Georgia Press, 2001) and editor of *Massive Resistance: Southern Opposition to the Second Reconstruction* (Oxford University Press, 2005).

STEPHEN J. WHITFIELD holds the Max Richter Chair in American Civilization at Brandeis University. He is the author of eight books, most recently *In Search of American Jewish Culture* (Brandeis University Press, 1999), and the editor of *A Companion to 20th-Century America* (Blackwell Publishing, 2004). He served as Fulbright visiting professor of American Studies at the Hebrew University of Jerusalem and at the Catholic University of Leuven, Belgium, and has taught two semesters as visiting professor of American Studies at the Sorbonne. Professor Whitfield most recently taught American Jewish history and culture in the spring of 2004 at the University of Munich.

GARY PHILLIP ZOLA is associate professor of the American Jewish Experience at Hebrew Union College–Jewish Institute of Religion and the executive director of the Jacob Rader Marcus Center of the American Jewish Archives. He is editor of *The American Jewish Archives Journal* and has written extensively on the history of American Reform Judaism. His publications include *Isaac Harby of Charleston, 1788–1828: Jewish Intellectual and Reformer* (University of Alabama Press, 2004), *The Dynamics of American Jewish History: Jacob Rader Marcus's Essays on American Jewry* (UPNE/Brandeis University Press, 2004), *Women Rabbis: Exploration & Celebration* (HUC-JIR Rabbinic Alumni Association Press, 1996), and a forthcoming volume titled *A Place of Our Own: The Beginnings of Reform Jewish Camping in America*, coedited with Michael M. Lorge.

Page numbers in *italics* represent illustrations.

antisemitism (*continued*)

Civil War, 178, 196; desegregation crisis and rise of, 196–99, 204; of David Duke, 217; Leo Frank case, 13, 135, 150, 244, 293, 305, 318; in Germany, 32; Golden on food for eliminating, 315; Jewish women writers questioning, 75–80; Jews eating like Gentiles for coping with, 229; Jews excluded from elite Gentile society, 14; Jews seen as disloyal and cowardly, 115; in late-nineteenth-century South, 12; of Lester, 313; in New England, 128n.11; social clubs excluding Jews, 139; the South associated with, 2; "Wandering Jew" stereotype, 115, 222; of "white cap" vigilantes, 138

Apte, Helen Jacobus, 210, 211

Ardmore (Oklahoma), 294

Arkansas: Bentonville, 295; Blytheville, 226, 294; cuisine of, 226, 235; Dumas, 291; Felsenthal, 308; Jewish Confederate soldiers from, 119; Jewish food supplies in, 245; Jewish politicians support black disenfranchisement, 142; Jewish population growth in, 290; Little Rock school crisis, 197, 203–4; McGehee, 299; Memphis as distribution center for, 7; Pine Bluff, 138, 144, 145, 313

Arogeti, Jeanette, 245

Aron, Bill, 257, 322

artillery, 119

Ashkenazi, Elliott, 23n.37, 106n.6

Ashkenazic Jews: in Charleston, 240; cultural differences with Sephardic Jews, 27, 33–40; in eighteenth-century South, 4; food traditions of, 233; intermarriage with Sephardic Jews, 39; in Savannah, 31; settling in South in nineteenth century, 6

assimilation: in antebellum Louisiana, 109; German Jews promoting, 12; Jewish

versus African American, 134; as litmus test for American Jews, 47; Mordecai family and, 47; pressures for, 309–10; southern Jews "going native," 312

Atlanta (Georgia): Ahavath Achim Congregation, 10, 244; airport, 290, 321; antisemitism during desegregation crisis, 197; "Ballyhoo," 14, 238, 251n.28, 320; blackface minstrel shows staged by Jews, 143, 154n.67; Charles Borochoff bar mitzvah, 238; as business center, 290–91; as center of American Jewish life, 294, 321; Concordia Association, 10; cuisine of, 235; current Jewish population of, 17, 307; eastern European Jews settling in, 10–11, 243–45; Economy Deli, 247; first Jewish settlers in, 307; Leo Frank case, 13, 135, 150, 193–94, 215, 244, 293, 305, 318; Gentleman's Driving Club, 139; German Jews settling in, 9–10; Gilmer's Quality Kosher market, 246; Caroline Haas said to be first white woman in, 143; David Hazan's fruit stand, 246; Hebrew Benevolent Congregation, 10, 13, 16, 143, 146; Jewish community in antebellum, 109; Jewish food traditions in, 243–45; Jewish immigrants living in black community, 147–48; Jewish politicians falling into disfavor in, 139; Jewish population growth in, 290–93; Jewish population in 1910, 307; Jews from country attracted to, 284; keeping kosher in, 229; as mecca for young Jewish singles, 284; as New South's capital, 13, 289, 294; non-native Jewish population in, 293; number of Jewish congregations in, 291, 321; Orthodox congregations in, 10, 293–94; Or VeShalom Congregation, 244; population growth of, 289–90; prewar as relatively small, 300; race riot of 1906, 146, 148; Reform syn-

agogue bombing of 1958, 199, 315;
Rich brothers in, 104; Sephardic Jews
settling in, 12; Shearith Israel Congre-
gation, 10, 244; South Side, 244; Stan-
dard Club, 14, 239; suburbs of, 244,
291–93; in Uhry's *Driving Miss Daisy*,
215–16, 320; William Breman Jewish
Heritage Museum, 19–20, 320
Atlanta Constitution (newspaper), 13
Atlanta Jewish Federation, 292
Atlas, Seymour, 205
Aunt Jemima's Latkes, 231
Austin (Texas), 294, 300
Autobiography of an Ex-Colored Man (John-
son), 220
Avodat Ha-Kodesh: Service of the Sanctuary
(Levy), 167, 188n.32
Ayers, Edward L., 14
AZA (Aleph Zadik Aleph), 25n.79

bacon, 229
Baer, Max, 113, 121
bagels, 243, 245
Bain, Brian, 216–17, 313–14
"Ballyhoo" (Atlanta courtship weekend),
14, 238, 251n.28, 320
Baltimore (Maryland), 139, 261, 293
barbecue: brisket, 232, 244, 247; in Mem-
phis, 246–47; pork, 226, 228, 235, 247;
special plates for, 229; synagogue-
sponsored competitions, 238, 247
Baron Hirsch Congregation (Memphis),
10
Barth, Fredrik, 249n.4
Baruch, Bernard M., 114, 319
Baruch, Herman, 114
Baruch, Simon, 112, 114, 314
Bass, Nathan, 236
Baton Rouge (Louisiana), 8
Bauman, Mark, 2–3, 325
Belmont, August, 112
Belzer, Arnold Mark, 237, 238
benevolent societies, 7, 266

Benjamin, I. J., 111
Benjamin, Judah P.: Confederate service
of, 116–18; father in Reform movement, 5; "as Israelite with Egyptian
principles," 112; leaves country after
Civil War, 126; moves to New Orleans,
7; as U.S. senator, 109, 111
Benjamin, Philip, 5
Bentonville (Arkansas), 295
Berith (B'rith) Shalom Congregation
(Charleston), 10, 187n.28
Berke, Lena, 256
Beth Ahabah Congregation (Richmond):
archive of, 20; Beth Shalome reunites
with, 170–71; choir of, 169; family pews
and organ of, 169; Harris as rabbi, 170,
176; Daisy Hutzler Heller's recipes,
229; identifies itself as Reform, 170;
Michelbacher as rabbi, 125, 169, 269;
organization of, 169, 188n.37; rabbis
of, 170, 188n.39
Beth-El Congregation (Birmingham), 199
Beth-El Congregation (Durham), 311
Beth El Congregation (Miami), 198
Beth El Emeth Congregation (Memphis),
305
Beth Elohim Congregation (Charleston):
amalgamates with Shearith Israel,
165–66; Chumaceiro as rabbi, 166;
classical design of synagogue, 6; as
cradle of Reform Judaism, 5–6, 56,
157–67, 240; decline in 1850s and
1860s, 164–65; dietary laws challenged
by, 240; Eckman as rabbi, 164, 187n.21;
Elzas as rabbi, 167; founded in 1749, 3,
4, 156; Lazarus family and, 263; David
Levy as rabbi, 166–67; Levy family and,
269; Marcuson as rabbi, 167; Mayer as
rabbi, 165; Penina Moise hymns used
by, 264; organ installed at, 163, 165,
166, 173, 187n.24, 258; petition for
reform at, 159–60, 184n.10, 185n.11;
Poznanski as rabbi, 163–64; Reformed

Freedom Riders, 204, 217
fried chicken, 230, 232, 235, 238
Friedman, Lee M., 106n.5
friendship quilts, 261
Frisch, Ephraim, 145
Fruchter, Alfred and Jeanette, 305
Fundamental Constitution of Carolina, 111
fundamentalism, xii, 73, 179, 229
Future of the American Negro, The (Washington), 141

Gaba, Morton, 197
Gadsden (Alabama), 202
Galante, Nace and Ralph, 247
Gall, Jacob, 121
Gallagher, Gary, 114
Galveston (Texas), 109
Garrison, William Lloyd, 113
Gastonia (North Carolina), 198, 199
Geffen, Tobias, 245
gefilte fish, 230, 233, 237
Geismar (Louisiana), 242–43
Geismar, Evelyn Vessier, 242–43, 253n.44
Geismar, Sara, 242, 243
genealogy, 260
Gentleman's Driving Club (Atlanta), 139
Georgia: Alpharetta, 291, 292; Americus, 305; Columbus, 14, 109; cuisine of, 233, 239; Dunwoody, 291; Jewish peddlers in, 98, 99; Jewish population growth in, 290; Macon, 99, 109, 202, 306; Monroe, 306; New Albany, 230; opposition to Jews immigration in colonial, 28–29; religious tolerance in colonial, 38; Roswell, 292; Sephardic Jews in, 244; Talbotton, 101; Thomasville, 101. *See also* Atlanta; Marietta; Savannah
German Jews: assimilation advocated by, 12; conditions in eighteenth-century Germany, 31–33; cultural differences with Portuguese Jews, 27, 33–40; economic success of, 12; elite social organ-

izations created by, 14; food traditions of, 230, 233, 240, 243–44; Leo Frank case, 13; intermarriage with Portuguese Jews, 39; Ku Klux Klan on, 314; New South promoted by, 13, 243; as peddlers, 98; in Rubin's *The Golden Weather*, 214; settling in Atlanta, 9–10; settling in Memphis, 6–7; settling in New Orleans, 7; settling in South in nineteenth century, 6; social distance from eastern European Jews, 11
Gilchrist, Ellen, 222
Gilman, Samuel F., 159, 184n.8
Gilmer, Steve, 246
Glanz, Rudolf, 106n.5
God Shakes Creation (Cohn), 212
Goldback, Abraham, 118
Golden, Harry, 315, 322
Golden Weather, The (Rubin), 214
Goldfield, David, 24n.58, 287
Goldstein, Eric, x, 13–14
Goldstein-Lowell, Benjamin, 194
Goldstein's Delicatessen (Memphis), 246
Gone with the Wind (Mitchell), 218
Goodman, Andrew, 2, 192, 201
Goodman, Isadore, 204
Gottlieb, Laurence, 248
Gottlieb's Restaurant and Dessert Bar (Savannah), 248
Grady, Henry, 13
Grant, U. S., 101
Gratz, Rebecca, 60, 61, 110, 113, 266
Green, Nancy, 90
Greenbaum, Andrea, 324
Greenberg, Blu, 227
Greenberg, Mark I., x, 4
Greenberg, Reuben Morris, 318
Greensboro (South Carolina), 316
Greenville (Mississippi), 212, 213, 295, 296, 300, 311
Greenville (South Carolina), 310
Greenwood (Mississippi), 2, 16, 20
Grimes, William, 59